TWO THOUSAND YEARS OF
TEXTILES

1. Wool Tapestry. A Woman's Head

SYRIA OR EGYPT, 3RD–4TH CENTURY, POSSIBLY EARLIER

The Detroit Institute of Arts

TWO THOUSAND YEARS
OF TEXTILES

THE FIGURED TEXTILES OF EUROPE
AND THE NEAR EAST

Adèle Coulin Weibel

PUBLISHED FOR

THE DETROIT INSTITUTE OF ARTS

PANTHEON BOOKS

NEW YORK

1952

The publication of this book has been made possible by grants of

THE KRESGE FOUNDATION

DETROIT

LIBRARY OF CONGRESS CATALOGUE CARD NO: 52-7395

MANUFACTURED IN THE U.S.A. FOR
PANTHEON BOOKS, INC. 333 SIXTH AVENUE, NEW YORK 14, N. Y.
BY KINGSPORT PRESS, INC., KINGSPORT, TENNESSEE
COLOR WORK BY FREDRICK PHOTOGELATINE PRESS, INC., NEW YORK
COLLOTYPES BY THE MERIDEN GRAVURE CO., MERIDEN, CONN.
DESIGNED BY ANDOR BRAUN

For Liselotte Moser

BEST OF DAUGHTERS,
BEST OF FRIENDS

FOREWORD

THE past thirty years have brought from their hiding places many wonderful textiles which now enrich the museum collections in this country. The study of documents has been increased, and the importance of technical research has been recognized. Yet much essential work remains to be done and many questions are still controversial. This book gives mere glimpses of the treasures waiting to bring joy to the beholder.

The publication of this work is due to many happy circumstances. I am deeply grateful to my friends and colleagues everywhere, to the staff and trustees of my own beloved museum, and to the directors of the Kresge Foundation for their advocacy of liberal grants. I take my leave with the words with which, a thousand years ago, the venerable nun Hroswitha of Gandersheim prefaced her comedies on legends of the saints: *Si enim alicui placet mea devotio, gaudebo; si autem nulli placet, memet ipsam tamen juvat quod feci* —"If my work pleases you, I shall be glad; but if it pleases nobody, I have myself enjoyed what I have done."

ADÈLE COULIN WEIBEL
Curator Emeritus of Textiles and Islamic Art,
The Detroit Institute of Arts

CONTENTS

TWO THOUSAND YEARS OF
TEXTILES

INTRODUCTION

W EAVING, "the most magnificent art which truly distinguishes mankind from the animal" (Goethe), is the oldest of the great crafts. It appears at the very dawn of history, and all progress of civilization is exemplified by it.

Man, born without a weapon but with the finest tool, the hand, soon learned to make baskets and fences by plaiting flexible rods of canes, and mats by crossing reeds and grasses. Clever individuals must have found that by twisting these together they obtained a longer and more resilient fiber. This is the origin of spinning and weaving.

I. MATERIAL

1. *THE*
FIBERS

Cotton

Nature provides four main fibers: cotton and flax, wool and silk.

Cotton, from the Arabic *qutun*, is the most important vegetable fiber of civilization. It has been cultivated from time immemorial and many varieties have been developed from the original wild-growing plant. Cotton is mentioned in an Egyptian papyrus belonging to the University of Michigan; and it was raised by the Assyrians, who may have used it for their padded armor. For thousands of years the bolls were handled carefully, to detach the hairs from the seeds, until Eli Whitney invented the "gin" in 1793. The *charkha*, a more primitive machine used in India for hundreds of years, was never adopted by Western countries. The seeds, long rejected as a positive nuisance, are now milled for oil and the residue is used as a food for cattle and for making of plastic appliances.

The worst enemy of cotton is the boll weevil, whose pernicious activity has become the subject of a great ballad. It is still alive and growing, and in one verse

> Boll weevil say to de farmer:
> "You can ride in dat Fohd machine.
> But w'en I get through wid yo cotton,
> Can't buy no gasoline,
> Won't have no home, won't have no home."

In India threads of the cotton fiber had been used for two thousand years when Herodotus recorded that the Indians clothed themselves exclusively in cotton fabrics of wide variety. This indigenous cotton possibly was *Gossypium herbaceum*, from which many types have been cultivated and acclimatized in many countries of the Old and New World. In the Andean area of South America several varieties of cotton are indigenous. The most important of these is *Gossypium peruvianum*, a perennial shrub that loses its property of roughness, caused by hook-shaped projections along the fibers, when transplanted into other countries. This cotton is either white or tinted; the pigmentation may be caused through the action of some insect pest or from a chemical reaction in the soil. Yet about 1550 one of the Spanish chroniclers, Don Pedro Gutiérrez de Santa Clara, wrote: "There is in this country much cotton which of itself is blue, brown, tawny, yellow, and the color is so fine that it is something to be noted, as though it had been in dye for a long time, for the painter of the world gave to it those vivid colors."

Among the earliest cultivated plants, traceable to the Neolithic Age, is flax. In Pharaonic Egypt it was so important that as one of the ten plagues of Moses "the flax and the barley were smitten" (Exodus 9:31). The Egyptian flax, *Silene cretica*, sacred

Flax　to Isis, is a different plant from the northern flax, *Silene linicola*, sacred to Freya.

The outstanding quality of flax is resiliency and toughness; this, together with lustrous smoothness, made it the preferred fiber of many parts of the world. Its resiliency is illustrated by the often-repeated tales of linen fabrics so fine that they could be pulled through a finger ring, and of netted fabrics weighing so little that a man's load could be spread to cover an entire forest. Toughness is the quality required for the cuirasses of quilted linen worn by Homer's Greek and Phrygian heroes; for the propellers of windmills and the sails of all times. These were often woven with the fibers obtained from another plant stalk, hemp, *Cannabis sativa*, which was first known for its narcotic quality, hashish, and only later as a textile fiber. Even then the odium attached to the pernicious plant remained; the "hempen shirt" of the medieval penitent is just one instance.

The preparation of both flax and hemp requires much painstaking work. The textile fiber is the bast between the woody core and the bark. This is loosened by retting, breaking, swingling and hackling, all of them difficult procedures.

Other related plants, jute, sisal, alfa grass and nettles, all share with flax the lack of affinity to dyes and are at their best in a natural or a bleached state.

Wool, the most beautiful of textile fibers, has one great drawback: its at-

Wool　traction for destructive animal pests. For this reason it is difficult to delineate the evolution of woolen textiles. Its adiathermic qualities and low specific weight made it a preferred medium from earliest times in warm climates such as the Near East. Wool is the most important fiber of the Asiatic nomads, who work it not only into garments but also into bags, rugs, and tents. Because of its scaly structure and waviness, wool lends itself to matting or felting to a greater degree than other textile fibers. No other textile can be draped so beautifully as the woolen; no other has such affinity to dyes, even the darkest color being vibrant and clear. "Dyed in the wool" has become the equivalent for thoroughness.

Pliny devotes an entire chapter to sheep raising and wool culture (*Historia naturalis*, VIII, 48). He tells that in early times the sheep were plucked or combed, later shorn. The

4

wool was washed in hot water with soap. In Pliny's day soap was made of saponaria root and potash, and during the Roman Empire it was an important article of export of the Gallic and Teutonic tribes (Pliny, Martial, Suetonius). Pliny mentions two types of soaps, soft and hard, and believed that the blond hair of the Germans was due to bleaching action. After washing and drying, the wool was a matted lump and had to be loosened before it could be spun. This was probably done with a wooden bow strung with a sinew. Carding, the pulling of the loosened wool over a board fitted with thorns or nails, also was of early origin. According to Pliny, use was made of the natural colors; the best black wool came from Spain, a rusty-red from Greece. By carding together different colors, a variety of shades was obtained not unlike those of the modern tweed. Woolen cloth of excellent quality was imported from Gaul, the Teutonic countries, and Britain. Here deer or cattle hair was often blended into sheep wool. Rabbit and hare wool was used also, probably for its softness and silky gloss; sometimes the hair of wild animals is found, not spun lengthwise but folded into the wool, so that the ends protrude.

In Asia, camel wool was used from early times. In Peru, the wool of the llama, alpaca, and vicuña is found in the earliest known culture level, that of the Paracas cemeteries, and often spun to an almost incomprehensible fineness.

Silk   A Chinese legend tells us that on an auspicious day more than four thousand years ago, Hsi-ling Shi, the wife of Emperor Huang-ti, walked in the palace garden with her ladies. On the boughs of mulberry trees hung silvery balls. The great lady examined one of these, and her clever fingers soon found the beginning of a thread. Thus Hsi-ling Shi discovered silk, the most marvelous of nature's fibers. Later generations gave her a place among the benevolent genii and worshiped her as the "spirit of the mulberry tree and silkworm." The earliest preserved Chinese texts mention silk. When about 530 B.C. the wise Confucius spoke of its beauty and of the economic value of the silk industry, it had been established, according to tradition, for two thousand years. No other medium has played a role comparable to silk in the commercial history of two great cultural spheres widely separated not only in space but also in mentality: China and the Roman Empire.

Only two insects have been domesticated, the honeybee and the silkworm. To the breeder the intelligent, lively bee must be vastly more endearing than the silkworm, which, although a voracious eater, is so lazy that during the month of its growth it must daily be lifted onto its new supply of chopped mulberry leaves. But on the thirty-second day *Bombyx mori* starts working and for sixty hours ceaselessly spins one long fine thread, round and round, with pendulous motion of the head and figure-of-eight movements of the fore part of the body. The spinning glands exhausted, he rests in his cocoon, and after two or three weeks the chrysalis breaks the wall of the cocoon and emerges as a moth, psyche, imago. But only a few selected cocoons are permitted the fulfillment of their natural function. Most of the pupae are treated by steam or dry heat; the cocoon is then immersed in a hot bath, to loosen the gelatinous binder. Then four or five of the four-hundred- to a thousand-yard-long threads from as many cocoons are reeled off simultaneously and twisted into one strong thread. Eventually the breeders discovered that artificially dyed food changed the color of the silk substance. Thus, if the mulberry leaves are dyed with madder, the cocoon is yellow instead of white. Indigo produces a greenish yellow, madder and indigo together a bright green, and cochineal an orange shade.

Silk is mentioned by the prophet Ezekiel when he speaks of the young woman, the emblem of Jerusalem, as clad in *schesch* and *meschi* (16:10 and 13). Thus silk was known in Syria-Palestine during the early sixth century B.C. This, however, was probably not real silk but "bombycine," wild silk, garnered from one of several cocoon-producing insects, possibly the Coan moth, *Pachypasa otus Drury*. These insects, after the moth has broken through the chrysalis, leave the empty shell on the bark of a tree, whence it can be scratched off, hackled, and spun. Wild silk was produced also in India and China. Nearchos, one of Alexander the Great's officers, told on his return from India that "serika [silk] is a kind of linen, scratched from the bark of trees." Aristotle, the first Greek who mentioned the silkworm, gave a remarkably accurate description of its culture.

The ruling dynasties of China successfully kept the process of silk culture a secret for a long time. During the second century B.C. a Chinese princess, betrothed to a prince of Khotan, in eastern Turkestan, is said to have smuggled silkworm eggs in her coiffure to her new home. This she could do easily, for one ounce of eggs or "seed" produces about 36,000 worms. How sericulture came to the Eastern Roman Empire is reported by Procopius. Two Persian monks, probably Syrian Nestorians who were welcome in China at all times, brought to the Emperor Justinian, about the year 552, silkworm eggs hidden in their hollow canes. Syria became the center of the new industry, which spread to the plains south of the Balkans, the Peloponnesus, and the Greek islands. Through the conquests of the Arabs sericulture came to Spain and Sicily, thence to Italy. But for many centuries Western silk production was unable to cope with the demand, and silk in hanks continued to be an important article of exportation from China.

In Europe the silkworm always remained a stranger; folklore and literature talk of the mysterious creature, sometimes in Gargantuan mood, again in spiritual exaltation. Here are two quotations:

> . . . *les bonnes femmes de mesnaige, recognoissant que rien n'estoit*
> *plus prouffictable que la vertu, taschèrent d'élever et nourrir toutes*
> *leurs filles pucelles; mais le mestier feut aussy chanceulx que celluy*
> *d'educquer les vers à soye, si subjects a crever . . . .*
> —BALZAC, *La Pucelle de Thilhouse*

> *La mia letizia mi ti tien celato,*
> *Che mi raggia d'intorno, e mi nasconde*
> *Quasi animal di sua seta fasciato.*

6

(My joy holds me concealed from thee,
Raying around me, and hides me
Like to a creature swathed in its own silk.)

—DANTE, *Paradiso*, c. 8, v. 52–54

Curiosa

Besides these staple fibers there are others, curiosities rather than mercantile articles. Such are spiders' webs, spun into thread and used for knitting very costly gloves and stockings; piña cloth, made from the fibers of the leaves of the pineapple plant; byssus, threads formed by the glandular secretion of a salt-water mussel, the woven fabric looking like fine linen, and known in Greece and in Egypt as late as the Mamluk period. Human hair also was used, possibly in many places. The Peruvians sometimes used a weft line of lustrous black hair to set off the beauty of the dull wool. The hair of Charles I of England, obtained from his valet, was treasured by royalist ladies and used in their embroidered portraits of the martyred king. Minerals have been converted into woven fabrics, such as asbestos, spun from the fibrous rock. Many anecdotes are told of great men from Alexander to Charlemagne who shocked their guileless guests by throwing a fine napkin into the blazing fire, whence it emerged clean and unharmed. The same story is found also in the Han annals, where asbestos cloth is mentioned among the goods imported to China from Syria. It was used there for table napkins and for lamp wicks "that would never come to an end."

Metal Thread

Gold and silver thread has always been a great luxury. Literary sources as early as the Old Testament tell of gold thread embroidered or woven into fabrics. Thus Exodus 39:2–3 describes how Moses made the ephod for Aaron: "And they did beat the gold into thin plates, and cut it into wires, to work it in the blue, and in the purple, and in the scarlet, and in the fine linen, with cunning work." Darius the Achaemenid wore a mantle on which two golden hawks were pictured as if pecking at one another. These were probably embroidered, possibly as a development from the Achaemenid custom of sewing thin gold plaques on costumes. But textile fragments with inwoven gold, wire beaten into flat strips, have been discovered in Crimea. They can be dated to the third century B.C. The early Roman Empire deemed such luxury vainglorious and likely to incite jealousy. Verrius, the tutor of the princes Gaius and Lucius, grandsons of Augustus, told his charges how Tarquinius Priscus, fifth legendary king of Rome, first to celebrate a triumph after the Etruscan fashion, appeared there clad in a golden tunic, and Josephus has a similar tale about Herod Agrippa, who wore a mantle woven of silver, wonderful to behold in the rays of the evening sun. Both men were eventually assassinated.

Old inventories, particularly the *Liber pontificalis*, a list of gifts to churches and monasteries by the popes of the eighth and ninth centuries, mention repeatedly fabrics interwoven with gold, yet very few actual specimens have been preserved. Probably such fabrics, when threadbare, were unraveled or burned in order to recover the gold. A hank of matted gold thread without any trace of a fiber core, "probably the remains of an embroidered garment which had been burnt . . ." (Louisa Bellinger), was found at Dura-Europos. And it is said that forty pounds of pure gold were realized from the ashes of the mantle in which Maria, wife of the Emperor Honorius, had been buried in 408, in Old St. Peter's. The mantle was found when her tomb was opened more than a thousand years later, when the old basilica was torn down to make room for the Renaissance sanctuary that exists today.

About the beginning of the eleventh century, real gold thread made of flattened wire wrapped around a linen core was replaced by a new thread of small metal value, animal membrane covered on the outside with very thin leaf gold, *aurum battutum*. This less expensive thread had another advantage: it was soft and pliable and lighter. But it lacked the magnificent luster of the pure gold, *aurum tractitium*, and the thin gold layer rubbed off easily. This skin or membrane gold was probably an adaptation of the Chinese gilt-leather strips, introduced to the Near East in brocaded silk fabrics, where the old technique of twisting the flattened gold wire around a linen core was continued simultaneously with the new membrane, sometimes called "false gold thread." In China and Japan the flat gilt-leather strip was eventually superseded by gilt paper.

During the Middle Ages the inventories record *aurum filatum cyprense*, and the troubadours refer to *or de Chypre*. Cyprian gold thread was of the finest quality and naturally the most expensive. Less costly was the gold thread of Bologna and Cologne. The waning of the Middle Ages marks the disappearance of membrane gold; the weavers of the Renaissance used again the true metal wound around a thread core. Tinsel, very thin sheet metal cut into narrow strips, was used in later centuries for the production of fabrics of little weight and reduced cost.

2. THE
DYES

One of man's fundamental urges is for color, and at an early period in his evolution he painted the walls of his sanctuaries, colored his body, placed pigmented stuffs in the tombs of his ancestors. Dyeing, the craft of imparting to a medium a color different from its natural state, is even older than weaving. But with the use of the great natural fibers came the improvement of dyes. Man demanded that cloth, produced by much labor, should be not only beautiful but also enduring. The dyes should withstand destructive agents, the rays of the sun, the body's effluvia, and resist repeated washing. This resulted in the invention of mordants, colorless liquid preparations with which materials are saturated before dyeing to hold the dyestuff. The earliest mordant seems to have been alum, which is still used. Other mordants were gallnuts, soapwort, salt of tartar, and the oxides of iron and other metals. The dye bath was either cold or boiling hot; lighter or darker shades were obtained by repeating the immersion. The material was then thoroughly rinsed to remove surplus dye and the unpleasant smell owing to the use of urine as a binder, that of camels being the most effective. One of the earliest known works on chemistry, the *Papyrus Anastasi* of the third century A.D. (Upsala University), states that "the hands of the dyer reek like rotting fish." Pliny did not consider dyeing a free man's occupation. He talks of sea dyes, *colores marinae*, and earth dyes, *colores terrenae;* the first include algae and shellfish, the second plants and insects.

Woad

The principal dyestuff of the ancient and medieval world was woad, *Isatis tinctoria*, which was among the earliest cultivated plants. Its leaves, crushed and fermented, give an excellent and versatile dye. The fresh solution dyed black; then as it grew weaker, blue and finally green were obtained. Used as a base with madder, a purple tint was produced. Woad was cultivated wherever soil contained sufficient chalk. The Celtic and Teutonic peoples introduced it to northern Europe; woad was their most important dye plant during prehistoric times. Blue garments have been found in tumuli and bog burials. The sagas tell that Odin wore a mantle of this color.

Woad is mentioned by Theophrastus (*c*. 371–287 B.C.), a pupil of Aristotle, and by Dioscorides, a famous Greek physician of the first century A.D. A recipe for obtaining a fast blue dye from woad by adding soapwort to the boiling bath is contained in the *Papyrus Anastasi*. In the Middle Ages the substitution of indigo as a stronger and more reliable dye caused many rebellions, especially in France, where the best woad was then cultivated.

Indigo

The regulations of the Saffron Guild (Safran Zunft) of Basel throw interesting light on the trade in dyestuffs. This powerful guild was the intermediary between Venice, whence the costly Eastern dyes were imported, and the merchants of northern Europe. When the first big shipment of indigo arrived, the guild members had qualms; they feared that the new dye might be harmful to the fabrics. Yet, notwithstanding such alarming rumors, indigo soon ousted woad in the dye trade.

Many varieties of indigo grow in tropical and subtropical countries. The most important of these, *Indigofera tinctoria*, has been cultivated from early times in India, whence the dyestuff was exported to Babylon and Judaea, then to Egypt, Greece, and Rome, and later to Venice. Another variety was known to the Indians of ancient Peru and Mexico. Marco Polo refers to indigo as something familiar to his readers, when he describes its manufacture "in the kingdom of Kulam on the west coast of India, where it is produced in great quantities and in excellent quality. It is extracted from a species of herb which is plucked out by the roots, put into tubs of water, and left to rot. Then the juice is pressed out, dried to a paste by exposure to the sun, and then cut up into small pieces of the shape also familiar to us."

Orseille

Orseille, *Lichen roccella*, a plant growing on marine rocks, was sometimes used as a substitute for indigo in ancient times. *Papyrus Anastasi* mentions that sometimes it was added to a vat of woad dye. Orseille gave its name to a great merchant family of Florence, the Rucellai, just as the even better known della Robbia derived theirs from the madder plant.

Madder Madder, *Rubia tinctorum*, is a herbaceous plant of hardy growth, native in tropical and temperate zones of the Old and New World. The pigment is obtained from the root, and in the time of Pliny and Dioscorides it was cultivated to promote larger root growth. In the seventh century madder was grown near Saint-Denis in the vicinity of Paris, and a hundred years later on Charlemagne's estates at Aachen. During the Middle Ages fields within the system of crop rotation were often planted with madder. Besides the dye root, the top of the plant was good cattle feed, although the cows' milk had a reddish hue. During the sixteenth and seventeenth centuries Holland held practically a monopoly on madder cultivation. One of the innumerable benefits Colbert, the Comptroller General of Finances under Louis XIV, introduced into France was the madder industry. By the middle of the nineteenth century the madder root was cultivated all over the world; the Spanish conquerors of Mexico and Peru had found a species already growing there.

In 1869 Graebe and Liebermann produced a synthetic red dye that they called alizarin, from the Arab term, alizari, for madder. This discovery spelt disaster for all the madder-growing countries. Today the madder root is used only for artists' pigments.

Scarlet Scarlet, from the Persian *sakirlāt*, is the brilliant red color halfway between the cold yellowish carmine and the warm bluish vermilion. All three hues were obtained from the dried bodies of insects belonging to the species of the shield louse, coccidae. The Old World used kermes, the Indians of Mexico and Peru cochineal.

The word kermes means worm; the Sanskrit root *krmi* is preserved in *crimson* (English), *cramoisi* (French), *Karmin* (German), and *al-qirmiz* (Arab). As were many other dyestuffs it was also long used as a medicine. Kermes was cultivated in Languedoc and Provence and sent to Montpellier, a center of scarlet dyeing in the Middle Ages. For a long time kermes was considered a grain, the dyeing process being called *teinture en graine*. Chaucer tells of Sire Topas that "His rudde is like scarlet in grain." The privy-purse expenses of King Henry VIII for November, 1530, mention the purchase of "taffata crymysin in greyn."

In the ancient world kermes dye was expensive, but less so than true purple, for which it was sometimes a substitute. In 1467 Pope Paul II introduced scarlet as the color of the cardinals' robes because purple dyeing had been cut off with the fall of Constantinople to the Turks. In Venice the robes of the senators were of deep crimson velvet. And, more than a thousand years earlier, the Roman officers had worn scarlet cloaks.

As kermes was used by the Romans, so cochineal was used as an article of tribute by the Aztecs. The Spanish conquerors quickly recognized its superiority over their own native scarlet dye, and its export to Europe began. In Mexico the cultivation of the nopal plant on which *nocheztli* throve was henceforth encouraged by the Dominican Order. The Spanish government kept the monopoly of the cochineal trade until the eighteenth century. Attempts to transplant the insect to other countries proved generally unsuccessful; yet by the middle of the nineteenth century cochineal had been acclimatized in Guatemala, the Canary Islands, and Java.

The invention of aniline red caused an acute economic crisis in these countries; the dire distress of the population was only gradually eased by the substitution of coffee and tobacco culture. Today a little cochineal is used for the preparation of food dyes, and the oldest pharmacy in Florence is still famed for its Alkermes liqueur.

Saffron Yellow dyes were important because, besides being intrinsically beautiful, they could be used for the production of green over a foundation dye of woad or indigo, and orange over one of madder.

The "king of dyes" was saffron, obtained from the dried stigmas of *Crocus sativus*, a purple-flowered crocus that blooms late in autumn. Saffron was used as a spice, a medicine, a cosmetic, and a dye, and was vitally important in the trade of the ancient and the medieval world. It is mentioned in the earliest medical treatises of India, and in *Papyrus Ebers*, an Egyptian medical work of the eighteenth dynasty. In the Song of Songs *karkom*, crocus, is praised for its scent. Both Homer and Sappho sing of the golden-yellow dresses dyed with saffron, favored by ladies who probably used it also as a cosmetic. The streets of Rome were sprinkled with saffron when Nero made his entry into the city; Dio Cassius mentions the wasteful use of saffron among the many excesses of Elagabalus. Medieval Europe became acquainted with the many virtues of *zafarán* through the Arabs, who, in the tenth century, introduced the cultivation of *Crocus sativus* in Spain, and by the returning crusaders. It is mentioned in an English leech-book of the tenth century, and was cultivated at Saffron Walden, in Essex, from the fourteenth to the eighteenth century. But the best saffron was long imported directly from the Near East.

Other yellow dyes were obtained from the blossoms of safflower, *Carthamus tinctorius*, which from antiquity has been used for the adulteration of the more expensive saffron; from wau, *reseda luteola*, and even from pomegranate skin. Turmeric, *Curcuma*, whose powdered roots were formerly used as a dye, is still widely cultivated in southern Asia as the basis of curry powder.

Black Most difficult and least satisfactory of dyes was black. The best dye was lamp soot; solutions of sulphate of iron tended to fade and even rot fabric.

Purple The most coveted color in the ancient world was purple. It was extracted from the glands of certain shellfish, *Purpuridae*, chiefly from *Murex trunculus*. The production of purple was laborious and expensive; huge numbers of shells had to be crushed to obtain an infinitesimal quantity of the pure dye.

That Phoenicia is the original home of purple dyeing is proved by legend, history, and archeology. Legend tells of Melkarth's dog, which once crushed a shellfish and stained

11

his muzzle bright red. The Romans called this old Phoenician god Hercules Tyrius, which points to the city of Tyre, where the dye was made in the eighth century B.C., according to the prophet Ezekiel. Archeologically, the great age of the industry is proved by the discovery of a bank of murex shells one hundred and twenty yards long and eight yards high. These shells were broken uniformly in the same place, close to the purple gland, with little stone hammers, some of which were still preserved among the shells. Wherever the Phoenicians traveled, from the Sea of Marmara to the Atlantic coast of Morocco, they searched for purple-yielding shellfish, and where they found such they established dye works and trading stations. Near Tarentum, in southern Italy, there is a hill, Monte Testaccio, which consists of murex shells. The coins of Tarentum, like those of Tyre, were marked with the shellfish.

The different species of *Purpuridae* gave different colors. Purple was known by various names: hyazintha, amethystina, violacea, also blatta and oxyblatta, "color of congealed blood." And Homer tells how "the nymphs weave garments purple as the sea."

For thousands of years the wearing of purple was the prerogative of kings. The rulers of Babylonia and Assyria wore purple robes. Alexander the Great adopted the Achaemenid fashion and even shrouded the funeral pyre of his friend Hephaestion in purple curtains. The Israelites, neighbors of the Phoenicians, used purple at an early date. Moses decreed that the Holy of Holies be separated from the rest of the Temple by a curtain of purple, and the high priest wore a purple robe. The Hellenistic age brought a craving for such elegancies even to a provincial town like Athens. Yet it is surprising to find there, as the outstanding and wealthiest merchant of purple dyes, the founder of the Stoic philosophy, Zeno (*c.* 342–267 B.C.). A native of Citium, the principal Phoenician settlement on Cyprus, Zeno had inherited both his commercial instincts and his interest in philosophical speculation from his father Mnaseas (Diogenes Laertius, 7, 1).

In Egypt purple is not mentioned before the Ptolemaic period, when Cleopatra had purple sails on her flagship. Her friend Caesar arrogated to himself, as dictator, the right to wear purple robes while the senators were limited to *vestae clavatae*, robes with purple bands. An amusing literary reference to Tyrian purple is in Petronius' *Trimalchio's Feast*. It is concerned with the asking for intercession by a slave in the matter of the loss of the Intendant's clothes at the bath. "He has lost my dinner robes . . . genuine Tyrian purple . . . though only once dipped." The "only once dipped" is interesting; there may have been trading in a "black market" for objects of this kind. During the reign of Alexander Severus (222–235) the manufacture of purple became a monopoly of the state. The wearing of purple robes remained the exclusive privilege of the emperor, but the purple trimmings ceased to denote high rank and became purely decorative. The great industry survived the political decline of Phoenicia, but came to an end with the fall of Constantinople in 1453.

Today the charming hues that once were compared to the colors of precious stones can be produced synthetically whenever fashion asks for them.

From ancient times onward the waters of certain brooks and rivers have been endowed with mysterious virtues for dyeing. Thus the Greeks considered the stuffs dyed at Hierapolis, in Phrygia, as of superior quality, just as two thousand years later all Europe preferred the *toiles de Jouy* to printed cottons produced elsewhere. Possibly these excellent dyes should be credited to the high standards stressed by the Ionian dyers' guild and later by Oberkampf rather than to the Lycus and Bièvre, the rivers flowing by Hierapolis and Jouy.

II. TECHNIQUE

1. *SPIN-NING*   The prerequisite of textile art is the thread. Many stories have grown up concerning its production. Kind goddesses, Neith in Egypt, Athena in Greece, Freya in the Norse lands, taught their human daughters the craft of spinning, which eventually became the symbol of life: the Parcae and Norns spin the thread, tangle it up, and cut it short. Mary the Virgin still spins the fine threads that float in the air during the Indian summer. As a young girl she was visited by the Archangel Gabriel while spinning wool for the Temple curtain, which was rent asunder when her Son died on the cross.

Spinning consists of drawing out from a bundle of cotton, flax, or wool several fibers, called the roving, and twisting them into one strand of continuous length. Thousands of years ago, although probably not by Eve ousted from Paradise, two implements were evolved: the *distaff*, or rock, to which the bundle was tied, and the *spindle*, onto which the thread was wound. The distaff, a stick about twelve to thirty-six inches long, could be tucked under the arm, leaving both hands free for twisting the thread. The spindle, a shorter stick of six to ten inches in length, was weighted with the *whorl*, a bead generally of stone or clay. This helped to rotate the spindle in the direction opposite to the twisting and kept the thread wound around the spindle from slipping off.

From early times spinning became pre-eminently the occupation of women, the distaff the symbol of woman's work. Even today the female branch of a family is called the "distaff side," an unmarried woman a "spinster." Distaffs were occasionally made of costly materials; Homer mentions one of gold given to Helen of Troy by Alexandra of Egypt, and Theocritus tells how he presented one carved of ivory to the wife of his friend Nikias of Milesia. Whorls of clay and stone, often charmingly decorated, have been found in dwelling places of the new Stone Age in surprising numbers; as women used to spin while going about other business, many whorls were lost. Sometimes, like the distaffs, they were made of choicer materials, of bone, rock crystal, and bronze; at Troy Schliemann found an amber whorl.

Thread thus spun was ready for use in weaving. For sewing and knitting it could be strengthened by twisting the threads of two or more spindles into *yarn*. "Spinning a yarn" is telling a long story.

Spinning with the distaff was practiced for thousands of years; even today it has survived in remote places. Yet in time the spinners were irked by the limitations of the spindle. The stationary spinning wheel, which made possible the creation of an, at least theoretically, endless thread was invented, probably in India, some time between A.D. 500 and 1000. The use of this early spinning wheel, the *gharka*, was revived by Mahatma Gandhi as a symbol of Indian independence. From India the spinning wheel traveled to China and Japan, possibly in the train of Buddhist missionaries. In time the Chinese replaced the hand motion of the wheel by a treadle. In Europe the spinning wheel became known as one of the many benefits introduced by the Arab conquest of Sicily and Spain. North of the Alps the earliest records are of the late thirteenth century, the period of assimilation of Arab learning and craftsmanship. The Arabs also brought with them to Spain and Sicily their knowledge of silk culture and the use of a wheel for twisting the threads of several cocoons into one strong thread. The Norman conquest of Sicily introduced the art of silk manufacture to the Italian mainland, where the methods of producing silk thread were steadily improved; this gave to Italy a monopoly in silk for several centuries.

Mechanical spinning, one of Leonardo da Vinci's prophetic suggestions, came into use in the eighteenth century, but did not supersede the spinning wheel until the nineteenth century. Various countries have evolved different types of wheels, combining technical improvements with ornamental details that clearly reflect the art of their period. The "drawing-room" spinning wheels of the eighteenth century, of mahogany inlaid with mother-of-pearl, ivory, or precious woods, or lacquered in the *chinoiserie* taste, became a toy in the hands of great ladies, an affectation of domestic virtue in the best style of Jean-Jacques Rousseau.

The poetry of spinning is reflected in pictorial art from the wall paintings of Egyptian tombs and the vase paintings of Greece, through medieval book illumination, to the paintings and graphic representations of innumerable artists. Its finest expression it has found in the *Hilanderas* of Velázquez. Spinning is the most sociable of the great crafts; many folk songs have survived through spinning "bees." Omphale inveigled her strong friend Herakles to learn spinning by telling him that "there is no occupation in the world half so soothing as to sit and spin. The twisting whorl, the turning spindle, the white wool teased by one's fingers into a firm and even thread—these are inexpressibly pleasant toys. And as one spins, one sings softly to oneself, or chats with friends, or lets the mind wander at will. . . ." (Robert Graves, *Hercules My Shipmate*.)

2. *WEAV-ING*   There are different ways of building up a weave. Netting, knitting, and crochet work require only one thread, while for certain laces several threads are plaited together. But by far the largest group of fabrics is based on a system of intercrossing vertical and horizontal threads on the loom, man's greatest contribution to civilization. The loom is not a single invention but the result of a long series of improvements. The weaver of mats placed his reeds side by side on the ground, but the

spun thread required some form of support to prevent it from becoming entangled. The indispensable part of the loom is a beam to which a number of threads are fastened, side by side; these form the warp (Old Norse *varp*, a towline). To keep the warp threads stretched taut, two systems were devised, probably at the same stage of evolution, in different parts of the world.

One system, which ultimately resulted in the creation of the vertical loom, consisted in attaching a weight of stone, clay, or metal to the hanging end of each warp thread or to groups of them, the beam being supported between the forks of tree branches or of two upright sticks. Such weights have been found in great numbers all over Europe, in pits below the foundation of prehistoric dwelling places. This primitive loom is depicted on an urn of the Bronze Age found at Ódenburg, in Hungary (Robert Forrer, *Urgeschichte des Europäers*, Stuttgart, 1908, pl. 152). It is a ritual scene, showing the sanctity of weaving. Four richly dressed women stand in a row; one spins the thread, another weaves on an upright loom. The weighted warp threads disappear in a pit; the weave, with a big spindle carrying the weft thread, is clearly indicated. A third woman is seen singing to the accompaniment of a harp played by the fourth woman. Similar looms are found painted on Greek vases of the classical period, in illustrations of scenes of the Heroic Age; Circe and Penelope are the weavers. The loom with weighted warp threads has survived to this day on the Faeroe Islands.

The other system kept the warp in a more or less horizontal position. The beam was fastened to a peg driven into the soil, or to a tree. The ends of the warp threads were tied to a second beam and this to a belt worn around the weaver's body. By leaning backward he kept the warp taut; bending forward slackened it. This girdle-back loom is still used by the aborigines in several parts of the world. It was used by the weavers of ancient Peru down to the Spanish conquest.

In other parts of the world the two-beamed loom was further improved by connecting it with two supporting poles. Thus it formed a frame that could be used vertically or horizontally. The beams were movable and thus made possible the winding up of the weave at one end, of extra-long warps at the other.

In the most primitive form of weaving the spindle with the weft thread is passed under and over the warp threads, separating these one by one with the fingers of the other hand; on the return the operation is reversed. Thus the warp consists of two systems, the sheds, one of which comprises the odd- and one the even-numbered threads. Soon the weaver learned to "open the shed" by a single movement. A flat implement, the sword, inserted between the odd and even warp threads, lifted the odd threads when it was turned edgewise and made possible the easy passage of the shuttle. In order to lift the even warp threads, these were tied with strings to a stick, the "heddle rod." By pulling the heddle rod, the weaver opened the second shed. These sheds are sometimes called "natural" and "artificial"; by alternating the two movements, a plain cloth will be produced. In time the sword was replaced by a second heddle rod, and these could be multiplied at will. Twill weaves could be produced by lifting only every third or fourth warp thread in echelon, thus forming diagonal lines. With a system of four or more heddles, many small patterns could be woven by "floating," allowing warp or weft threads to run free for a short distance.

A further improvement, the first step in the mechanization of the loom, connected the heddles by pulleys with levers or treadles; thus both hands were kept free for passing the shuttle to and fro. A flat implement was found to be preferable to the round spindle. The result was the shuttle (French *navette*, German *Schiffchen*, thus recalling its likeness to a boat dividing the waves). After each passing of the shuttle, the wefts were pressed down with the batten in order to obtain an even weave.

These are briefly the principles of the loom, as evolved by practically all primitive civilizations. As time went on, the treadle loom with horizontal warp ousted the vertical loom, which for the last five hundred years has been used almost exclusively for tapestry and rug weaving.

A fundamental change in the method of pattern weaving took place in the early centuries of the Christian era. Until then all elaborate patterns had been produced by the technique of tapestry weaving. Now the desire to weave such patterns in mechanical repetition led to the most important improvement of the loom, the invention of the drawloom. Only one other invention equals that of the drawloom in revolutionary economic importance: the invention of the printing press a thousand years later.

The working principle of the drawloom is briefly as follows. To make possible the weaving of elaborate patterns, the weaver must be able to raise the warp threads in an absolutely free and irregular way, so that the same combination of warps raised at one time comes back only with the repeat of the pattern. A system is needed by which each warp thread can be raised independently. So each warp thread is fastened to a string; the strings pass through a drilled board, the comber board, which is fixed on the top of the loom. If the warp consists of six hundred threads, the comber board must have six hundred holes. But if the pattern is repeated six times in the width of the weave, it is evident that the raising of the warp threads will be the same in each repeat, that warps 1, 101, 201, 301, 401, 501 will be raised together, as well as warps 2, 102, 202, 302, 402, 502. All the corresponding warps will therefore be brought together to a single string, so that now the number of commanding strings and holes in the comber board is reduced to one hundred. If the pattern is symmetrical, warps 1 and 100, 2 and 99, 3 and 98, and so on will have identical movements; the symmetrically corresponding warps can consequently be tied to the same string, and thus the number of commanding strings will again be reduced by half: fifty strings will now command all the six hundred warp threads. This shows the enormous importance of symmetrical patterns for the drawloom. The commanding cords are attached to another system of vertical strings called the simple, and then passed horizontally to a bar fixed near the ceiling of the weaving room, whence they depend and are attached to another bar placed near the floor. Thus a cord of the simple commands a sympathetic group of warp threads. During the weaving operation, as many different groups of cords of the simple have to be pulled as there are different openings of the shed, until the pattern repeats itself. The weaver attends to the batten and shuttle while his helper, the drawboy, pulls the strings in succession.

The new technique made it possible, even desirable, to turn out weaves of the same pattern in great quantities. The mounting of the drawloom was an exacting operation, and the initial expense had to be balanced by mass production.

The drawloom may have been invented in China. When Pliny tells how the Chinese silk fabrics that reached the Roman Empire were unraveled, he believes this to have been done in order to save the precious raw material by using it again more sparingly. It is possible, however, that the weavers of Syria unraveled the fabrics in order to discover the secret of their weaving. But it is plausible that the drawloom was invented in Syria, and thence found its way to Sassanian Persia and ultimately, in the T'ang period (618–907), reached China.

The one discreditable sequel to the invention of the drawloom was the use of child labor. The strings of the simple could be pulled by an untrained person, and so children were pressed into service. Medieval illustrations of weaving sometimes show children winding thread on a spool or a spindle, but that looks like playing, as a modern little girl plays with a toy vacuum cleaner. The work of the drawboy required constant attention and dulled both body and mind. It is not impossible that sympathy for these children induced Leonardo da Vinci (1452–1519) to spend much thought on the invention of a mechanical loom. Several drawings prove how deeply he was interested, but his plans did not materialize. In 1661 Anton Möller of Danzig invented and built a mechanical ribbon loom; it was destroyed and the inventor drowned in the Vistula by the infuriated weavers, who were afraid of losing their jobs. Again, in 1678, M. de Gennes, a naval officer, published a design for a mechanical loom, worked by water power without human assistance. Neither this automatic loom nor the one invented by John Kay in 1745 was ever used. John Kay is better remembered for his invention of the fly shuttle in 1733, which nearly cost him his life. It is needless to say that the introduction of every improvement of the loom caused bitter struggles between the adherents of the new and the old systems. The archives of all weaving centers contain relevant documents. Yet the invention of improvements continued implacably, heedless of the weavers who lost their livelihood.

In 1785 Edmund Cartwright, a doctor of divinity and a poet, secured patent rights for a mechanical loom working on power supplied by an ox harnessed to a capstan. He improved his loom and protected it by patents taken out in 1786 and 1792; as part of the improvements the ox was replaced by a steam engine.

The Jacquard loom, the final improvement of the drawloom, is not the work of one man but the accumulation of a series of inventions extending over the entire eighteenth century. Every effort made tended toward replacing the drawboy by some mechanical device. In 1745 Jacques de Vaucanson constructed a loom in which he incorporated the previous inventions of Dangon (1600), Bouchon (1725), Falcon (1728), and others. A

17

series of perforated cards was substituted for the bunches of looped strings. Vaucanson, whom Voltaire called "the rival of Prometheus" for having invented an automatic flute player, now constructed an automatic weaver in the shape of an ass. Thus he took vengeance on the weavers of Lyons, who had pelted him with stones and narrowly missed killing him.

Joseph Marie Jacquard (1752–1834) deserves full credit for his construction of a practical automatic selective shedding machine, by simplifying and improving Falcon's and Vaucanson's inventions. With this new apparatus the weaver could work the entire loom by means of two treadles. Jacquard first demonstrated his invention at the Paris Industrial Exhibition in 1801. By 1812 it had been fitted to eighteen thousand looms at Lyons. In time it was adapted to fast-running power looms.

> The whirr of the spinning wheels has ceased in our parlors, and we hear no more the treadles of the loom, the swift, silken noise of the flung shuttle, the intermittent thud of the batten. But the imagination hears them, and theirs is the melody of romance.
>
> —Mary Webb, *Precious Bane*

3. *THE WEAVES* In any description of woven fabrics there occur four terms: *warp* and *weft; selvage*, the firmly woven border at the edges of the fabric; and *float*, a warp or weft thread that for a short distance is not interwoven with the other threads and therefore lies loose on the front or back of the fabric.

Simple Weave All hand-woven fabrics can be reduced to three fundamental types: cloth, twill, and satin. Of these, *cloth* is by far the oldest. The simple crossing of weft and warp, over and under, must have been used for a very long period, indeed, for "cloth" to have become practically the synonym of all woven fabrics. With the introduction of multiple heddles came *twill*. Here the first weft is passed over one warp, then beneath a group of warps, generally from three to five, then over one, and so repeated. On the return and in all succeeding throws of the shuttle, the one covered warp is moved in echelon to left or right, thus producing diagonal lines: \\ or /, sometimes called S and Z twill. This is warp twill; for weft twill the operations are reversed: the weft passes under one and over several warps in echelon. *Satin* is an irregular warp twill in which the weft threads disappear completely beneath the finer and more numerous warp threads. Its smooth, glossy surface makes satin the ideal weave for silk. Weft satin, also called *sateen*, is rarely used in silk weaving.

Cloth is universal. Twill may have been invented in central Asia and brought from there to the eastern Mediterranean and the north of Europe by migrating peoples. Twill-woven fabrics have been found in lake dwellings and bog burials of the Bronze Age. Satin was probably first invented in China, the silk land par excellence, and thence it may have

18

reached Persia and Europe. Yet it seems possible, even probable, that both twill and satin were evolved independently in several parts of the world.

These three fundamental or simple weaves have one set each of warp and weft threads. The weaver has found many ways to enhance their beauty. In simple cloth, by using warps and wefts of alternating different colors, he produces vertical stripes or horizontal bands, or checkers. The spacing, the width of the stripe, the combination of different colors, must have presented exciting problems and may at an early time have led to the adoption of certain combinations by families or clans. This has survived in the Scottish tartans. *Changeant* cloth is the result of contrasting colors in warps and wefts. Ribbed or corded cloth is produced by covering a heavy weft with finer, more numerous warps; fancy cloth by floats of warps or wefts, as in huckaback towels. The simple twill can be changed to herringbone by reversing the action of the loom, to fancy twill by irregular ribbing, which gives zigzags, lozenges, and similar small geometric patterns. Simple satin can be elaborated with pattern areas of a contrasting weave, cloth, twill, or sateen; if reversible, it is called *damask*.

Tapestry   Most important of all the elaborations of simple weaves is tapestry. It differs from the other weaves in which the shuttle is thrown across the whole width of the warp, from selvage to selvage, and is the least mechanical of all forms of weaving, really an intrinsic form of embroidery directly onto the warp. The weaver uses a number of bobbins, one for each of the different colors he needs. Each bobbin is taken only as far as its color is required and then turned back. If two color areas meet in a vertical line, a slit occurs. These slits can be avoided by the designer of the pattern; or by the weaver, by dovetailing the adjoining colors or by interlocking the weft threads of two colors at the meeting points. Sometimes, as in the Asiatic *kelims*, the slits are left open as part of the pattern, producing a play of light and shadow. In the European pictorial tapestries the slits are simply sewed together on the back after the weaving is finished. The weft threads are only very slightly twisted and much heavier than the warps, which they cover completely. A careful weaver will wrap loose ends around empty warps and thus produce a fabric that is alike on obverse and reverse.

Tapestry weaving is universal and can be traced far back in the history of mankind. When Homer tells of Helen

> weaving a web full ample,
> Twofold, purple; and into it many a battle she'd woven
> Battles of Troy's steed-tamers and bronze-mailed sons
> of Achaeans
> (*The Iliad of Homer* translated by William Benjamin Swift and Walter Miller.
> New York, 1944, book III, lines 125–27)

he probably refers to tapestry weaving. For until the invention of the drawloom, this was the only technique for the weaving of elaborate, polychrome patterns.

The Kashmir shawls of India are woven in twill tapestry. The wefts pass under one and over two or three warps and are interlocked with the wefts of the adjoining area. These beautiful fabrics are reversible.

Compound Weaves   Each of the three basic weaves becomes *compound* when its production requires additional warps or wefts or both.

Plain compound cloth has a main warp and weft and extra warps or wefts or both for the pattern. Warp-patterned plain compound cloths are relatively rare; obviously the weavers found it simpler to work with extra pattern wefts. Simple floated designs can be woven on a two-harness loom, one for the ground weave, one for the design. The pattern weft, when not required for the design, lies loose on the back, or is interwoven at intervals; it then appears as spots on the ground, between the design. This type of weaving occurs in Egypt during the Coptic period; it is even possible that Helen at Troy wove her battle scenes with floated pattern wefts rather than in tapestry technique. *Double cloth* has two main warps and two main wefts, generally of sharply contrasting color. The two cloths are woven simultaneously yet separately. Whenever the pattern demands a change in color, the back warps and wefts are brought to the front and the two cloths are interlocked, while elsewhere the two layers can be pulled apart. These cloths are reversible, the pattern and ground appearing in one color combination on the front, in reverse on the back. Another type of double cloth is closely interwoven all through, but the two warps and wefts are easily recognizable.

Compound twills have generally one or more additional wefts, which are used for independent designs and are bound by a second warp. These designs may be woven as twill or in another technique.

Compound satin includes all fabrics that have a foundation of satin weave and additional warps or wefts. Plain compound satins have the design in one or several extra wefts, which may require a second warp for binding. A type of fancy compound satin, which looks like a two-color damask but is not reversible, was called *lampas* in the eighteenth century. Compound satins with the silk surface backed and strengthened by a linen weave have long been called *brocatelle*.

Velvet   All simple or compound weaves can be elaborated into velvet by running an extra warp over a series of small rods, thus raising this thread over the basic fabric. When the rods are pulled out, small loops remain; this is *uncut velvet*. If a knife is run along a groove in the rod, or the loops are cut by hand, it is *cut velvet*. The combination of cut and uncut loops in one pattern is called a *ciselé velvet*, from its somewhat imaginary likeness to chiseled or chased metal.

There are two types of velvet. It is *solid* when the pile covers the entire surface of the fabric. It is *voided* when the pile is limited to part of the surface, either the pattern or the background, with the remaining part showing the basic weave. The heraldic term "voided," meaning "pierced through so as to show the field," is now generally accepted. Formerly such velvets were sometimes mistakenly called "cut velvet," from the idea that the parts without pile were the result of its having been cut away. As a matter of fact, the velvet warps are hidden in the foundation and lie flat in these areas.

Pile-on-pile velvet (Italian: *velluto contratagliato*). The design is carved from the solid velvet on a stretcher with specially constructed scissors. Soft contours and almost imperceptible graduations are thus obtained. Another method consists of weaving a velvet with loops of two different lengths. Here the pattern is raised over the ground in monotonous uniformity. *Polychrome* and *jardinière velvets* have multiple pile warps, one for each color. *Stamped velvet* has the pattern pressed into the pile with a hot iron, but this is really an extrinsic mode of decoration, not a matter of weaving.

Brocading
All simple, compound, or velvet fabrics may be further enriched by a kind of embroidery executed directly onto the warps in the process of weaving.

Like tapestry weaving, *brocading* is fundamentally a simple way of embellishing a fabric at a minimum expense of material; and, like tapestry weaving, it lends itself to sheer extravaganza.

While building up his fundamental fabric on the loom, the weaver at intervals introduces additional wefts, which are used only where needed for a desired effect; they do not run from selvage to selvage and are not a constituent part of the fabric. The French word for brocading is *brocher*, from *broche*, a spit; thus they compare this type of weaving to larding a roast. We prefer thinking of it as gilding the lily.

The brocading thread may be of cotton, linen, or wool. But as the chief reason for brocading is the economy of thread, it is especially suited for metal thread, chenille, or silk.

Twisted Weaving
In certain fabrics the warp threads intertwist among themselves, to give intermediate effects between ordinary weaving and lace, as in *gauzes*. In plain gauze the twisting of two warp threads together leaves open spaces between warp and weft. One warp thread from each pair is made to cross over the other, to the right and the left alternately, at every passing of the weft. *Leno* is fancy gauze weaving, with more than two warps engaged simultaneously, or with patches of regular weaving alternating with the open work. Voile, which is often confounded with gauze, does not belong to this group; it is merely a loosely woven plain cloth fabric, without the element of twisting.

Tablet Weaving
Narrow ribbons for straps and belts are sometimes produced by tablet weaving. For this technique the warp is set up in a multiple of four; each group of four warp threads passes through holes cut in the corners of one small square tablet. These tablets may be of thin wood, bone, ivory, parchment, or cardboard and are held firmly in one hand. After each passing of the weft, all the tablets are

turned simultaneously, so that the next warp lies now on the surface. Since the tablets must be twisted four times before coming back to the first warp, a large variety of small patterns can be achieved by stringing diverse colored threads through their holes. The patterns are variations of diamonds and zigzags, obtained by changing the direction of the twist, sometimes to the right, then to the left. Tablet weaving is practically universal as a simple elaboration of plaiting.

The *ceinture flèchée* of the Canadian habitants is not woven but braided, although it looks very much like tablet weaving.

Intricate mechanisms are not essentially required for the production of even the most complex textures. Many of the most beautiful specimens of the weaver's art have been accomplished upon very simple looms. The value of weaving analyses toward historic classification of fabrics is still unsettled. In tracing the historic evolution we shall find that it is impossible to set exact time limits for any specific weave. The more primitive will be continued for a more general market, while new types are introduced for the satisfaction of a limited clientele. The sometimes slow, sometimes almost abrupt changes in taste and their ramifications from a central focus can often be traced through the study of technical methods. But the designer must not be forgotten, for "he knows textiles not, who only weaving knows."

4. *THE WEAVERS*   Weaving is pre-eminently a home craft. Yet it became industrialized at an early time as a full-time profession rather than merely a part-time occupation for the needs of the household. The reason for this is simple: the capital required for the purchase of the raw material, and the marketing of the finished stuffs, were beyond the means of the weaver, so that the merchant took charge of all this. Henceforth the economic history of textile art is one continuous struggle between the two factions.

Certain clay tablets of about 2200 B.C., discovered at Ur, are the Chaldean equivalent of the modern account books. They show lists of weavers' names, with the amount of thread allotted to each by the priests of the great temple, and the measurements of the cloth returned. These cloths were then distributed to merchants, who at that early time were already organized into guilds not unlike the Hanseatic League of medieval Europe.

For Egypt, wall paintings and tomb models prove that the weavers worked under most unfavorable conditions. A model workshop, now in the Metropolitan Museum, shows ten girls spinning, reeling the thread, setting up a warp, and weaving, all in one small room where the air must have been thick with the dust of the fibers. And *Papyrus Anastasi* tells that "the weaver never tastes fresh air. If he does not produce his full day's allotment, he is beaten. He gives his bread to the doorkeepers so that he may get a glimpse of daylight." The author of the papyrus may have been prejudiced; he aims at persuading young men to enter the civil service rather than learn a trade or a craft, but many other signs, in succeeding centuries, prove that the weavers were not only overworked and underpaid but also held in contempt. Thus, a contemporary of Harun al-Rashid, Abu-al-Atahiyah, says with obvious condescension that "when a pious man fears God in the right way, it does not matter even if he should be a weaver." The merchants who traded the weavers' products were as highly esteemed as these were despised. In Fatimid Egypt the wealthiest man was a merchant in textiles, whose family paid in A.D. 912 an inheritance tax of 100,000 dinars. According to Ibn Mushahid, "a man of distinction is he who reads the Koran in the edition of Abu 'Amr, recites the poems of Ibn-al-Mutazz, and trades in fine linen."

Classical and medieval literature has casual references to the sad condition of the weavers. Thus Virgil says (*Aeneid*, VIII, 408–410): "When she who is forced to make a living by the distaff and the ill-paid loom . . ."; and he also comments on the hardship of the long hours of work for spinners and weavers. In the twelfth-century *Roman de Perceval* a man brags of how he forces his captives to do "the vilest job," weaving:

> *Li chevalier que je conquier*
> *Sont assis au plus vil mestier,*
> *Certes, qui soit en tout le mont,*
> *Car je l'vous di que teisser sont.*

As late as the end of the fifteenth century the admiral of the Catholic kings, Christopher Columbus, was often disparagingly called a *lanero*, a wool weaver. For as a boy he had worked in his father's workshop and had later made several voyages as a wool merchant.

Medieval Guilds   The origin of the medieval guilds is still the subject of numerous theories. It is known that about the year A.D. 1000 there came into being in many communities all over Europe brotherhoods for mutual assistance in times of material and spiritual distress. These may have crystallized into guilds of merchants and guilds of craftsmen.

In England guilds of merchants appear soon after the Norman conquest. They regulated the ever-increasing trade and guarded jealously their monopolies, mainly by warding off the competition of foreigners. Yet in 1259, the Company of the Merchants of the Steelyard, the London trading post of the Hanseatic League, was granted far-reaching privileges by Henry III. For a long time the League's outpost held practically a monopoly on the wool trade. Thus in 1551 it exported 44,000 bales of wool as against 1100 bales exported by all the other merchants together. During the reign of Edward VI, on the complaint of the Merchant Adventurers, the Merchants of the Steelyard were deprived of their privileges; they were formally expelled by Queen Elizabeth in 1597.

The merchant guilds may have forced the craftsmen to band together for their own protection. The crafts guilds supervised the quality of the wares produced by their members, the hours of labor, and the terms of apprenticeship. Among the earliest recorded crafts guilds was that of the weavers. It can be traced to the eleventh century at Cologne and Mainz on the Rhine, to the twelfth in London and Oxford, with charters granted by Henry I.

One aspect of guild activity was participation in the mystery and miracle plays that were performed annually on the days of the great religious feasts. Without the guilds the regular cycle of these plays could never have been elaborated. The guilds provided the actors and the money for the pageants, the scenery, and the costumes. Each guild was allotted one play; the actors were amateurs, guild members, who sometimes received a small remuneration for their services. Thus "two worms of conscience" were paid eight pence each. They must have been clowns who with their antics contributed much to the general enjoyment. In the Easter plays of the York cycle the Wefflers (weavers) performed *The Appearance of Our Lady to St. Thomas*, the Mercers (cloth merchants), *The Day of Judgment*. That the weavers produced good amateur actors may be inferred from the fact that Shakespeare allotted the part of the hero of "The most lamentable comedy of Pyramus and Thisbe" in *A Midsummer Night's Dream* to Nick Bottom, the weaver, wise and witty and beloved by the queen of the fairies.

Florence In Florence the weaving of stout woolen cloth for domestic use goes back to the early Middle Ages. In the weaving shop of the nuns of Or San Michele young women received instruction under supervision. This system was continued when cloth weaving had become an important industry; the most beautiful of the reliefs on Giotto's Tower illustrates such a scene: the "Maestra Petronilla" giving advice to the weaver, seen through the warps on her loom. From the thirteenth century onward two important guilds took charge of and represented the interests of their members: Arte di Calimala, the guild of the wool merchants, and Arte della Lana, the clothmakers' guild, which included, besides the weavers, the dyers, fullers, and shearers, all of whom had a share in cloth refining. The most modern methods of division of labor were used in Florence; the *trattato della lana*, preserved in a fifteenth-century manuscript (Codex Riccardianus 2580), proves that the processing of wool required about two dozen different workmen.

The silk industry seems to be documented by a decree of the Emperor Henry VI, of 1187; in return for privileges granted, the city of Florence must supply annually a bolt of "good velvet." By the mid-thirteenth century the two silk guilds were founded: Arte di Por Santa Maria, that of the merchants, and Arte della Seta, the weavers' guild; by the fifteenth century the Florentine silk industry had practically a monopoly on the markets of northern Europe.

The history of the Florentine textile trade reads like a fantastic account of the rise and fall of great families such as the Frescobaldi, Bardi, and Peruzzi. Toward the end of the fifteenth century the wool industry began to decline. This was blamed largely on the autocratic rule of the Medici, which undermined the power of the guilds; but the real cause must be sought in the general change from the medieval to the modern world. To some extent the decay of the guilds was owing to internal maladjustment. This led repeatedly to insurrection and riot of the weavers and their assistants. Best known is the *tumulto dei ciompi* in 1378, in which the wool carders, the *ciompi*, were joined not only by the thousands of other badly underpaid workers but also by some of the wealthier members of the guilds of cloth and silk weavers. This rebellion, like so many others, proved abortive; but it left the workers in a state of insecurity and restlessness. Their sullen brooding contributed its share to the astonishing success of Savonarola.

The wealth of the great guilds was used largely for the embellishment of the city. They built churches, hospices, palaces, and fine bridges across the Arno. Thus the Spedale degli Innocenti, the Foundlings' Hospital, was built at the order of the silk weavers' guild, of which Brunelleschi, the architect, was a member because he was also a goldsmith. The patronage of the wealthy merchants extended to many sculptors and painters. One of these, Piero di Cosimo, adorned the marriage chests and the study walls of members of Calimala and Arte della Lana with illustrations from the Voyage of the Argonauts. To the learned wool merchants of Florence this old tale of the Quest of the Golden Fleece must have been vastly entertaining.

Netherlands The merchants of Florence kept agencies in several cities of northern Europe. In the fifteenth century the best customers for their silks and velvets were the members of the splendidly arrogant court of Burgundy. There was, however, little demand there for imported woolen fabrics because the best cloth was produced in the cities of Flanders. Tradition tells that already Charlemagne included a mantle of Flemish cloth among his presents for Harun al-Rashid. In the tenth century weavers and fullers were established at Ghent by Count Baldwin III, who also initiated annual fairs at Ypres and Bruges. Baldwin, the grandson of Aelfthryth, a daughter of Alfred the Great, may even have started trade connections with wool-producing England.

In the succeeding centuries the cloth merchants—the self-styled patricians—became enormously wealthy through their exploitation of the weavers, the *horribles tisserands* of Froissart's chronicles. Theoretically, one and the other enjoyed equal civic rights, were free citizens. All the more, therefore, the intolerable injustice meted out to the workmen by the patricians caused intensive bitterness, which now and then found an outlet in open rebellion. Thus, in 1302, led by their guild master, Peter de Conync, the weavers of Bruges massacred the patricians. But such revolts were quickly suppressed, sometimes with the help of French armies, and the bitter lot of the weavers remained unchanged.

The last duke of Burgundy, Charles the Bold, died in 1477. Through his daughter Mary's descendants the Netherlands came under Spanish rule. The persecution of the Protestants by Charles V and Philip II ended with the secession of the Northern Provinces. A considerable number of Flemish weavers had embraced the fatalistic teaching of Calvin and many of these fled to Dutch territory. Here, especially in the city of Leyden, they found new scope for their craft. In the seventeenth century, in order to reduce the cost of production, the merchants resorted to the inhuman practice of child labor. The orphanages provided "apprentices," sometimes only six-year-old children. Whenever their supply ran short—the death rate appears to have been rather high—more little children were sent to the Leyden orphanages from similar institutions in other cities.

The finished fabrics were closely examined by the *Staalmeesters*, inspectors appointed by the magistrates of the different cities. In 1662 Rembrandt painted a marvelous portrait of the five regents for the Staalhof of Amsterdam.

Lyons

The constant struggle of the weavers, at all times and in all countries, becomes monotonous. Yet a few words must be said about the mode of life that prevailed in the eighteenth century at Lyons, the center of silk weaving in France. Here the industry had a precarious hold, largely dependent upon royal caprice, since the middle of the fifteenth century. Sericulture was among the economic problems besetting the reign of Henry IV (1589–1610). At the instigation of Olivier de Serres thousands of mulberry trees were planted around Lyons and all over Touraine. The peasants were instructed in the care of the silkworms, and thus the constant difficulty of securing the raw material was somewhat mitigated. At the same time a silk weaver, Claude Dangon, invented a drawloom for the weaving of elaborate, polychrome patterns; two hundred years of constant improvement of Dangon's loom resulted in the perfection of the Jacquard loom. These two hundred years are characterized by the contrast between artistic creation and economic instability. Even the system of centralization introduced by Colbert (1619–1683), minister of finance of Louis XIV, could not overcome the inherent weaknesses of this luxury trade.

At Lyons, as everywhere else, the weavers depended on the merchants, who reduced wages whenever possible. Court mourning was especially calamitous; a long period without *bals* and other festivities brought misery to the silk weavers. They could not even emigrate, for they were closely controlled, lest they take the secrets of their craft to foreign countries. When Marie Antoinette sponsored the fashion of wearing batiste and printed cottons, more than ten thousand looms stood idle at Lyons. The despairing weavers took their part in the Revolution, but even this only brought new misery to them, since their former customers were now its victims. Fortunately for them, Napoleon recognized the economic importance of the silk industry. Thus, under his patronage Lyons regained her leading position and held on to it all through the nineteenth century.

HISTORY

A perfect rag-bag of odds and ends . . . the whole assortment shall be lightly stitched together by a single thread. Memory is the seamstress.

—Virginia Woolf, *Orlando*

I. PRECURSORS OF WOVEN FABRICS

IN THE long period before the invention of the loom man used fur pelts and felted blankets. These must be considered as the forerunners of textile art, for it was during that period that all the principles of extrinsic decoration of textiles were evolved.

Genesis (3:7) tells how Adam and Eve "sewed fig leaves together, and made themselves aprons"; but it is more probable that they pinned the leaves together with thorns. Later generations tied a piece of gut or some grass fiber to one end of the thorn and wound it around the other end in order to keep it firmly secured: the safety pin, the ancestor of all brooches, was invented. The construction of bronze fibulae often shows an adaptation of this simple expedient as late as the Migration Period.

Genesis (3:21) continues: "unto Adam also and to his wife did the Lord God make coats of skins, and clothed them." The fur hides of large animals may have fully satisfied the needs of the earliest people, protecting them from wind, rain, and snow. But succeeding generations discovered the greater convenience of the soft, pliable pelts of small creatures, and learned to "baste" these together with bast fibers or with gut, sinews or strips of leather. In clever hands such seams became an ornament, and as such the source of one widely spread type of embroidery. No fur garment of the Stone Age has yet been discovered, but a fur robe about two thousand years old from a tomb at Oirotia, in Siberia, shows clearly a trend toward decorative overelaboration, the result of a long tradition. It is pieced together of hundreds of pelts of ermine, squirrel, and reindeer, all cut into narrow strips and arranged to form a pattern within a network of seams of brightly dyed reindeer gut. All over the surface are sewn thousands of small wooden buttons, some still showing traces of the gold leaf that once covered them.

This introduces another, a universal, type of extrinsic decoration, which may have been suggested by the wearing around the neck and arms of strings of berries, seed pods, shells, or the teeth and claws of wild animals. Such objects could also be tied or sewn to a basic fabric. In later stages plaques of gold, silver, or bronze, often worked with incised or hammered designs, were used widely. This type of decoration has survived in the modern sequin embroideries. It reached its finest expression in the *chaquira* of ancient Peru, garments of fine cotton cloth, scintillatingly splendid with spangles of precious metal.

Sometimes *chaquira* was combined with featherwork, another special glory of ancient Peru. The tiny feathers of hummingbirds were arranged to form elaborate patterns, not unlike a mosaic of precious stones, completely covering the basic cloth. Featherwork belongs to the earliest forms of extrinsic decoration. It is found in many primitive civilizations in many parts of the world, although nowhere else it even approaches the perfection of the work achieved by the Peruvian artists of the Early Nazca period.

When early man removed the shaggy hair from the pelts in order to prepare these for leather, he must soon have realized that by pounding the damp matted mass of hair this could itself be made into very practical warm blankets. Thus *felt* was invented. In warm parts of the globe, where the bark of trees was used for tents and many other purposes, the glutinous inner bark, bast fiber, was similarly subjected to pounding. The *tapa cloth* of the South Seas, paper thin yet tough, is a late survival of this old craft.

The simplest way of decorating such felted blankets and objects made of leather was by daubing onto them splashes of color. This is the origin and basic form of all painted and printed fabrics.

II. THE EARLIEST TEXTILES

Fragments of woven textiles have been preserved in the Neolithic lake dwellings of Switzerland and in the bog burials of northern Germany and Denmark, both dating from about 3000 to 2000 B.C. Both linen and wool were then in use. But in the lake dwellings only linen has been found because the alkaline acid of the chalk at the lake bottom dissolved all horny substance, not merely the horns of cattle and sheep—although cups and spoons made of such horns have been found in moors close by the lake dwellings— but also the thread spun from the hair of these animals. On the other hand, plant fibers are destroyed by the ammonia that results from the humic acid present in peat bogs and moors, while horny substances are preserved. Sometimes coffins of hollowed oak trees, securely fastened with pitch, are found, containing naturally mummified bodies fully dressed in woolen clothes. The linen thread of the seams has disappeared, but its use and presence have been ascertained by microscopical and chemical tests.

The Neolithic thread is generally spun with a right twist, but left twist also occurs and even fabrics with differently twisted threads for the warps and wefts, probably in order to obtain a more elastic weave. This proves the fallacy of theories based on the twist in spinning.

Even twill-woven fabrics have been found in the lake dwellings of Robenhausen, Switzerland, and Dömestorp, Sweden. Astonishing is the size of some of the preserved fabrics. Thus a mantle found at Torsberg, Denmark, measured eighty inches in length by ninety inches in width, with a strong selvage bordering all four sides. That weaver was truly a great craftsman.

These fabrics, as well as the mummy wrappings of ancient Egypt and the traces of disintegrated fabrics preserved on pottery and metalwork in many early sites, are simple weaves with no attempt at patterning. The earliest textiles with intrinsic designs, woven into the body of the fabric, belong to an altogether much later period.

Simple weaves, plain or patterned with small designs of a type that could be produced on a two- or four-heddle loom, have at all times been made in great quantities, for both home use and the open market. The reason so few of these have been preserved, while so many textiles of outstanding merit both technically and aesthetically have survived, is owing to the original cost and therefore rarity of the latter. Many noble textiles still exist because they served as wrappings for precious relics of saints, others as part of burial furnishings.

In a few instances there has been preserved a record of the general textile production at one center, of one or several generations. Thus are the scraps of plain and patterned stuffs preserved in the rubble of Dura-Europos, Roman frontier station on the Euphrates, [2] which was abandoned by its garrison and inhabitants in A.D. 256 and lay undisturbed beneath the desert sand until a few decades ago. These fabrics hardly add anything new to the textile repertory; yet their value as a general record is unique.

III. TAPESTRY WEAVING IN EGYPT AND SYRIA

The earliest preserved pattern-woven textiles are three linen cloths discovered in the tomb of Thutmose IV (reigned *c.* 1420–1412 B.C.) at Thebes. The largest and most important of these shows the cartouche of Amenhotep II (*c.* 1447–1420 B.C.) among rows of papyrus and lotus blossoms, another the cartouche of Thutmose III (*c.* 1479–1447 B.C.). The patterns are woven in tapestry technique of colored, mostly red and blue, linen thread; quite rightly, for Egypt was the country where the finest flax was grown.

About a thousand years later a change in taste infiltrated into Egypt through foreign traders and settlers and the temporary Persian occupation of the country. Pharaonic art was dead even before the Ptolemaic period (323–30 B.C.). The Romans found in their new province of Egypt an art congenial to them, one of many variants of the eclectic Hellenistic-Oriental art.

The use of wool for ornamental wefts was a Hellenistic innovation in Egypt, where, since predynastic times, sheep had been bred only for meat and for trampling seed into the mud after the annual inundation of the Nile. The new wool fiber made possible a far-wider range of colors and, once the weaver had overcome the difficulty of using the same warp with wefts of different tension, linen wefts for the body of the fabric, wool wefts for the decorated parts, it actually made his work easier. The heavier woolen wefts, inserted more slackly and beaten tightly, covered the linen warps and presented a practically unbroken surface. This type of weaving came to Egypt from Syria. A Greek tomb of the third century B.C. at Kerch, in Crimea, has yielded some fragmentary textiles, the earliest specimens of wool tapestry. One of these shows rows of ducks swimming on "the purple sea"; an almost three-dimensional effect is obtained by subtle graduation of color. Such shading is a specialty of the Syrian weavers. It is found again in a large cloth (preserved in the Musée des Tissus, Lyons, France), possibly of the Ptolemaic period, tapestry woven throughout, covered with fishes of diverse kinds, swimming to and fro and even casting their shadows on the greenish water. That the Syrian weavers even attempted the rendering of large, pictorial compositions is proved by the survival of one fragment that shows an about half-life-size head of a woman. Fabrics of such surpassing quality are always exceptional; but the tradition of shading from one color to another survived changes of fashion in Syria. Simple bands of shaded colors have been found at Palmyra and Dura-Europos.

The discovery at Palmyra of linen tunics with clavi and medallions woven in tapestry technique of wool dyed with true murex purple can be quoted as another instance of the excellence of Syrian textile art. In the many similar garments from Egyptian burial sites the ornaments are of imitation purple, with the wool dyed first with indigo and then with madder.

The preservation of so many tapestry-patterned textiles in Egyptian tombs of the centuries of Roman occupation is owing to the fact that, as in Pharaonic Egypt, the fertile soil of the Nile Valley was too precious to be used for burial grounds. The cemeteries were now placed at the foot of the hills, and the dry soil of this barren ground preserved the bodies and the textiles wrapped around them. Many burial sites, from the top of the Delta cataracts of the Nile, have been explored scientifically since the early eighties of the nineteenth century. But the shallow graves had long been the happy hunting grounds of the local population, and many of the finest specimens are today without benefit of pedigree.

The evidence of Hellenistic, Roman, and Early Christian mosaics and wall paintings proves that one fashion of dress, with scanty local differentiations, prevailed all over the Roman Empire. The main garment was the tunic (Greek: chiton), worn by both sexes. The Romans distinguished three types. The *tunica palmata*, worn at triumphs and in-augurations, was designed individually; the type is known mainly from the representations on the consular diptych. The *tunica laticlavia*, reserved for men of senatorial rank, was adorned with one broad purple stripe descending vertically from the neckline. The type in general use, *tunica angusticlavia*, showed two narrow stripes, one from each shoulder. Originally it had been the prerogative of men of equestrian rank, but had lost this sig-nificance by the end of the first century A.D. As time went on, more and more detached ornaments were added. One or two bands outlined the neck opening and finished the sleeves. The vertical stripes, the clavi, which at first had reached to the hemline, were shortened and finished at the waist with pendants hanging from narrow stringlike ribbons. These pendants, as well as the round or square motives woven onto the shoulders and below the clavi, near the hemline, are a transformation into weaving of the metal plaques, the *bracteates*, which even then were still favored by the Scythians of southern Russia,

30

barbarian neighbors of the Empire. Sometimes the woven medallions were further accentuated by framing them with angular motives, *gammadiae*, or the hemline itself was decorated with a border, *paragauda*. When a tunic became threadbare, the ornaments were often cut out and sewn to a new garment. This scheme of decorating the tunic remained in force, with little modification, for several centuries.

With the tunic was worn a mantle, the *pallium*, derived from the Greek *himation*. This was a large rectangular shawl and was thrown over both shoulders. In Early Christian art it is always worn by Christ and the apostles and, from the fourth century onward, it was reserved for the costume of saints. More practical than the pallium was the *sagum* or *paludamentum*, a less heavy and slightly smaller shawl, which was worn tied or pinned at the right shoulder. For traveling or bad weather the Romans used the *paenula*, a heavy semicircular cape with a hood, *cucullus tegillum*. This became the prototype of the most important vestment of the Christian Church, the *cappa* or *pluviale*.

With the Hellenization of Egypt the elaborate rites of embalming became obsolete. In Roman times the dead body, strewn with granular natron and dressed in the garments worn in daily life, was tied to a narrow board of sycamore wood and wrapped in shrouds. For these the dead person's mantle was used, or a curtain or hanging, or even special *pallia mortuorum*, which often were enriched with tapestry medallions in the corners. Lastly, the custom of stuffing old rags beneath and around the head, in order to produce a tidy bundle for burial, has helped to preserve several fine textile specimens.

The history of Egypt for the first thousand years of the Christian era is mirrored in her textile output. The ornaments of the earliest preserved fabrics are distinguished by their purely linear composition; they are woven in monochrome purplish brown, with the interior details of white linen thread, brocaded with the "flying shuttle." A wide repertory of designs, including the human figure, animals, plants, and abstract ornaments, is proof of the existence of pattern books. These must have originated in centers of fashion such as Alexandria, and thence thumbed their way through the provincial workshops, while the designs became coarser and more static. It was lucky that the dying Hellenism was infused with new strength by the rise of Christianity.

According to tradition, Christianity was brought to Egypt by St. Mark the Evangelist, who preached the Gospel in Alexandria about A.D. 59. The new creed spread rapidly; its doctrine of life after death was naturally congenial to the Egyptians, and appealed especially to the oppressed lower orders. One result of Christianity was the institution of a severe form of monachism. Best known among the founders of monastic institutions are St. Anthony, whose fame attracted thousands to a life of austere meditation; St. Pachomius, who demanded of his disciples manual labor joined to spiritual contemplation; and St. Shenute, the fiery organizer of the national Church. The Coptic Church uses for its dating the "era of the martyrs," which begins with A.D. 284, the year of the accession of the Emperor Diocletian, who cruelly repressed and persecuted the Christians in Egypt. In the fourth century, under Constantine, Christianity was officially recognized; it was declared the religion of the empire by Theodosius. From early times the word "Copts" was used to designate the Egyptian Christians. It was coined in medieval Europe in adaptation of the Arab term *qubt*, which in turn is an abbreviation of the Greek word *aigyptioi*, Egyptians. For their translations of the Holy Scriptures into the Coptic dialects, and for their own writings, the monks used the Greek alphabet, to which they added certain letters from the Egyptian demotic. Sometimes inscriptions are found also on Coptic textiles.

The best Coptic textiles were woven during the fourth and fifth centuries, when Christianity had become the favored creed of the Roman Empire and the peace of the Church was not yet disturbed by the ecclesiastical quarrels between the Melkites, the royalist, and the Jacobites, the nationalist, parties. These quarrels were to some extent instrumental in the conquest of Egypt by the Arabs in 641.

As in Graeco-Roman times, the garments worn by the Copts were still adorned with bands and separate motifs of wool tapestry on linen ground, but now the decoration often lacked the subtle moderation of the earlier period. Figured fabrics were also used for shrouds; both St. Basil (*c.* 330–379) and St. Ambrose (*c.* 340–397) frown upon such wastefulness. Other dignitaries of the Church, such as Asterius, bishop of Amaseia in Pontus (*c.* 330–410), censure the frivolous people "who bear the gospels on their mantles instead of in their hearts" and "look like painted walls." Biblical scenes now occur in tapestry weavings, though apparently not as often as might be expected from such vehement literary denunciations. In one case such a scene, *The Sacrifice of Isaac*, is set between two "international" designs, an all-over trellis pattern framing birds and floral motives, and a narrow border of detached rose petals. These petals are found again, now closely set to form a wreath around a saddled but riderless horse, one of the most delightful of God's creatures pictured in a Coptic fabric. Not quite Biblical, yet an offspring of the Coptic faith, is the cavalier-saint. It is plausible to assume that the Copts, who for the most part were quite poor people, liked to think that their saints in paradise enjoyed all the luxuries they had missed in life on earth; and riding a spirited horse instead of trudging afoot in heat and dust must have been especially appealing. The Western Church adopted several of these Coptic riders, the best known being St. George.

In the sixth century the polychromy becomes more and more unbridled; but there is also a return to monochrome tapestry. There the ornament now often consists of two superimposed squares, forming an octagonal star. The twisted ribbon, the guilloche, appears, not only in tapestries but in related crafts such as mosaics and illumination. As in the Hellenistic monochrome tapestries, so in these first truly Byzantine designs much of the interior pattern is done with the flying shuttle, with white linen thread.

An innovation of the fifth century, obviously the result of influence from near-by Asia, was the use of wool for the body of the tunic. Even in Egypt there are cold days. The Hellenistic population had been satisfied with linen fabrics woven with long loops, the wefts pulled up at intervals much as in the modern bath towels. The Copts now liked the comfort of woolen tunics, shawls, and scarves. Often these are dyed a bright yellow, green, red, or purple; generally they are tapestry woven throughout, on linen warps.

Curtains and hangings were sometimes executed in a variant of tapestry weaving, with wefts inserted so slackly that they could be pulled up into small loops; they are really uncut pile fabrics. Sometimes a shaggy cut pile forms the design on the plain linen ground. In these cases the pile wefts are brocaded in between the selvage-to-selvage ground wefts. For another form of very simple brocading of small patterns the term "inlaid" is often used.

Besides the great mass of tapestry weaves, there have been found some shuttle-woven fabrics, compound cloth weaves. Most of these show small all-over patterns, sometimes with animals. Yet more elaborate designs were not beyond the weavers' ken, complicated 37, 38 hunting scenes of truly late antique style. These must be quite early, before silk had become available. They were probably used for upholstery. A fabric of this type is shown covering the mattress on the so-called sarcophagus of Alexander Severus in the Capitoline Museum at Rome (Riegl, *Spätrömische Kunstindustrie*, 1947, fig. 23).

IV. THE EARLY SILK TRADE

Nothing in history surpasses in importance the early silk trade. Silk brought together two great cultural spheres that were widely separated not only in space but even more in their mentality: China and the Roman Empire.

In Western literature silk is mentioned by both Herodotus (*c.* 484–425 B.C.) and Xenophon (*c.* 430–after 355 B.C.), when they write of the luxurious "Medic" dress worn in Persia; a much later author, Procopius (sixth century A.D.), tells explicitly that "the garments called Medic of old are now called Seric." Strabo uses both terms when speaking of the wardrobe of Alexander the Great and his generals. The Seleucids and the Ptolemies introduced silk to Syria and Egypt, and thence it came to Rome in late republican or early imperial times. But in conservative Rome it did not meet with undivided approval. Thus Pliny was shocked into writing of "vestments which, while they cover a woman, at the same time reveal her naked charms . . . nor have the men felt ashamed to use garments made of this material on account of their exceeding lightness in summer; for so greatly have manners degenerated in our days." In the reign of Tiberius the senate decreed that "men should not defile themselves by wearing garments of silk." Similar interdicts appear henceforth with steady regularity, at least once in every generation. They prove that the use of these luxurious silk garments must have been considerable, arousing the bête noire of the national economists, the fear of a flow of good money abroad.

Silk was expensive. To the initial cost of production came the additional expense of sending a caravan overland, across China and Serindia, over the Pamir passes, through Parthia to Syria. Added to the hazards of sickness of men and beasts and the ever-present danger of highway robbery was the certainty of exorbitant taxes payable at each of the many frontier stations and bribes to many officials along the road. And to all this overhead cost the Roman merchant added his profit.

Of the manifold dangers of this long journey the passage of the salt swamp of Lop Nor, between the Gobi and Takla Makan deserts, seems to have been feared above all. From Tun-huang, the last military post on the Great Wall, the road led along a waterless track where saline dust raised by hot whirlwinds produced mirages of ghosts and demons. No caravan could have survived this two weeks' torture if there had not been depots of water and fresh provisions, which were arranged from Lou-lan, frontier city of Serindia. During the Han period (206 B.C.–A.D. 220) Lou-lan was a Chinese garrison and one of the most important stopping places for the caravans. For the student of textile art Lou-lan is hallowed ground, for here Sir Aurel Stein found the first fragments of two-thousand-year-old Chinese silk textiles.

From the ancient Chinese texts it becomes evident that the country in the Far West, the country that was so eager to buy the silks of the Far East, was not the Roman Empire with Rome as its capital. The country that the annalists call *Ta-tsin* was merely its eastern part, Syria, for *An-du*, Antioch, is mentioned as the capital. (And as late as A.D. 781 Nestorian missionaries at Si-ngan-fu declared themselves natives of Ta-tsin, "the country where our Lord Christ was born.")

What did the West trade in return for silk? According to the Chinese annals, articles made of colored glass—beads, cups, and bottles—were most highly valued; next in importance were woolen cloth, fine linen, dyestuffs, and storax, a medicinal balm.

The last incident concerning the Western empire mentioned in the annals is the siege of Antioch by the Arabs, in 636. With the fall of An-du the Chinese relations with Ta-tsin came to an end. The overland routes were useless; trade was impossible during the centuries of constant warfare that followed. By the time of the Mongol conquest of Asia the oasis-states of eastern Turkestan had practically disappeared, owing to desiccation of the Tarim basin and lack of irrigation.

Within the last twenty-five years silks of the Han period have been discovered at both ends of the three-thousand-mile trek of the caravan road. Besides the epoch-making discovery at Lou-lan by Sir Aurel Stein in 1913, a Russian expedition found, in 1924–25, a number of silk fragments in burial mounds at Noin-Ula, in Siberia. And in 1934 appeared the first publication of a group of figured Chinese silks found in tombs at Palmyra. The fragments discovered at Lou-lan and Palmyra are preserved in the museums of Delhi and Damascus. But specimens of silk fabrics from Noin-Ula have found their way to the 39–43 textile collections of America. The importance of these little gems, obviously gifts of a Han emperor to a chieftain of the Hsiung-nu, the dreaded neighbors outside the Great Wall, cannot be too highly rated.

Many of these fragments are plain taffeta weaves, some with traces of embroidery;

34

others are fancy gauzes. But there are also patterned fabrics, woven in a highly characteristic technique that has been called "warp cloth" or "Han binding" (*armure Han*). Designs of three, four, and more colors are woven in true shuttle weaving, with all the threads involved tightly fastened into the fabric. The change of color is produced by as many different warps; the wefts are completely hidden, their presence felt only as faint horizontal ridges. This warp-cloth technique was used even for a form of monochrome pseudo damask. There the design is woven on the surface as a warp cloth, on the back as a plain cloth; the ground is a tightly woven taffeta and the design is faintly visible on the back of the fabric.

The Chinese weavers knew and used an elaborate loom, probably not unlike the drawloom the weavers in western Asia now invented. Quite probably these unraveled many Chinese fabrics in order to find the secret formula. Thus, when Pliny and Lucian tell of Chinese silk being unraveled, and spun and woven again, the unraveling becomes intelligible. For quite naturally the precious material would be used again, perhaps more sparingly, with warps or wefts of some other fiber.

The Western weavers, accustomed from tapestry weaving to produce patterns with the wefts, tried the same procedure on the drawloom. Their earliest experiments must have tended toward completely covering the warps with the wefts. This was superseded by the use of the weft-twill technique, which in Western silks predominated for centuries. Eventually such twill-woven fabrics found their way back to China, whose weavers quickly realized the wider possibilities of weft patterns. The overelaborate warp-cloth technique must have fallen into disuse during the chaotic political situation that followed the decline of the Han dynasty.

V. THE EARLIEST WESTERN SILK FABRICS

Most of the earliest silk fabrics produced in weaving centers around the eastern Mediterranean have been discovered in the cemeteries of Egypt; others have survived among the treasures of churches in western Europe, wrapped around relics of saints and lining their caskets, or glued into bookbindings as "endpapers," sometimes sewn between *62, 67* the illuminated vellum pages.

The invention of the drawloom heralded a change in textile design and technique. Magnificent polychrome fabrics could now be produced to any desired length, with uniform repeats of the pattern; weft twill was the almost ideal technique for the glossy silk thread.

A large proportion of the silks from Egypt, found mainly at Antinoë and Akhmîm, is woven in two colors only, with the pattern in a light tan that may originally have been white, on a ground of greenish or grayish blue, light red, or purple. The designs are of two types. There are many variants of all-over diaper patterns, formed of separate small motifs or of leafy stems, enclosing foliated motifs. Then there are roundels with elaborate compositions of fantastic trees, animals, and figure subjects, in floral frames. These seem to be monochrome adaptations of polychrome patterns; of some of them the original as well as the copy have been preserved. Some of these especially well-designed and finely woven fabrics were probably imported from Syria, yet many of these silks may well have originated at the sites where they were found. They all have been cut up for the decoration of tunics.

56   Certain workshops seem to have specialized in silks designed to the various shapes required for such decorations. This could easily be accomplished with the drawloom; several shoulder bands would be woven side by side into the width of a plain fabric, which was then cut away before sewing the band into place. One of these shops signed its stuffs 54 with the name of the owner "Zachariou"; others are signed "Joseph." These signed silks from Akhmîm are the forerunners of certain Byzantine silks that are inscribed with the names of the ruling emperors or the superintendents of the imperial workshops.

    While Akhmîm was, during the Roman period, pre-eminently a Coptic town with many monasteries, Antinoë remained true to its character of worldly elegance, second only to Alexandria. So it is not surprising that many of the most important textiles, woolen as well as silken, have been preserved in its cemeteries.

57   Among the silks found at Antinoë there is a group of gaily colored fabrics of quite unusual design. They must have been very costly and greatly coveted, for there have 34 been found also copies or adaptations of them, tapestry woven in fine wool. Or these may have been special orders for use as wall hangings, for which purpose the silks would have been too delicately patterned. There are fantastic combinations of masks seen frontally or in profile, ostriches and ibises, lions and leopards, antelopes, horses, and zebras or the protomas of such creatures, and, holding together all this diversity, the most fanciful floral and geometric inventions. These extraordinary fabrics are proof of an exotic trend indulged in by the leaders of fashion, which might be called *persanerie;* as twelve hundred years later there was to be an equally exotic, equally charming fashion, *chinoiserie.* They were most likely imported from Mesopotamia or Syria.

    The industrial and cultural centers of the Late Roman Empire were Alexandria, in Egypt, and Antioch, in Syria. Both were taken by the Arabs before the middle of the seventh century, Antioch in 636, Alexandria in 641. Before this happened, the weavers 44, 47, of one or the other of these cities produced a group of polychrome fabrics of great beauty. 49 Otto von Falke, in 1913, assigned them to Alexandria. Even then this attribution was questioned, affinities with Syrian art were adduced, and the whole group was given to Antioch. The question will probably never be settled to everybody's satisfaction. Both cities produced beautiful fabrics; the *Liber Pontificalis,* the Book of the Popes, which contains lists of gifts to many churches by the popes of the eighth and early ninth centuries, mentions both *vela alexandria habentia homines et caballos,* "Alexandrian hangings with men and horses," and *vestem siricam cum rotas et orbiculis,* "Syrian altar hanging with wheels and circles," also repeatedly *vestis de tyreo*. Tyre, the ancient center of purple dyeing, was still active in textile production, although the center of Syrian weaving was the capital, Antioch. More decisive is perhaps the fact that practically all the fabrics of this group have been found in European reliquaries. Syro-Palestine was the center of a lively trade in relics, especially in bones of martyrs, which for better appearance and to raise their market value were wrapped in fine fabrics. Taking into account also certain affinities with Sassanian art, the attribution to Syria appears altogether safely founded. The term "Alexandrian" is still used to designate this particular group, without intending reference to the site of its origin.

In these fabrics the possibilities of the new medium, the drawloom, were tested and improved. The first symmetrical repeat designs show a hesitancy that was soon overcome; the designer learned to make a virtue of the unavoidable. He emphasized the center line of the overturn by placing between the two halves of the design—often hunters on horse-back—a stylized plant form or a tree, which is not necessarily the "Tree of Life."

For the construction of textile designs the roundel shape was found to be most service-able. Roundels could be placed side by side like disks; they could be interlaced, or con-nected with *orbiculi*, small disks, laid over them at the angles. The designers found the roundel most versatile. It looked good with a simple linear border, or framed with an elaborately patterned ribbon, or a string of beads. The "Alexandrian" group is distin-guished by a border ornament that at first glance looks like a fairly realistic floral garland. Closer examination reveals the fact that the delicate variations of these heart- or palmette-shaped blossoms are the result of the designer's imagination. This border, with only small differentiations, is used with all the diverse compositions that fill the roundels, and also with the two-color imitations of the polychrome silks. The most admirably designed of these silks is the panel with representations of the Annunciation and Nativity in the Vatican Museum (Lessing, pl. 6; Falke, fig. 68). But several beautiful specimens of this group are now in American collections.

VI. THE SASSANIAN EMPIRE

Everybody remembers the astounding story of Alexander the Great's conquest of the Persian empire, followed all too soon by his untimely death in Babylon. His successors could not keep his heritage intact; the empire was divided among his generals. The lion's share, practically all the Asian parts, fell to the Macedonian Seleucus, who married a Persian princess, Apame. Their descendants neglected their Iranian possessions and soon lost them to the Bactrians and Parthians, retaining only Mesopotamia and Syria. The Parthian period in Persia coincides with the Han period in China. As the middlemen be-tween East and West, the Parthians grew fat on the profits accruing from the silk trade. They called themselves Phil-Hellenes; their art was derived largely from Hellenistic art.

In the early third century a great personality arose, Ardashir, son of Pabak of the family of Sassan, a Mazdean priest from ancient Persepolis. He founded a new dynasty and for four hundred years, from A.D. 226 to 641, the kings of the Sassanian dynasty ruled over Persia and Mesopotamia, sometimes also over Syria and Egypt; their capitals were Persepolis, of Achaemenian fame, and Ctesiphon, on the Tigris, newly built by Shapur, the son of Ardashir. The new empire was proclaimed as the revival of the empire of Cyrus, with an aggressively nationalistic policy.

The Sassanian rulers patronized art as a means of glorifying their dynastic aims. All too little of the splendor of their great cities has survived the forces of destruction by nature and human endeavor, merely a façade and a few elaborately domed and vaulted shells of palaces. More fortunately, fragments of wonderful silk fabrics have been preserved in the graveyards of Egypt and in shrines of saints in Christian churches. And vessels of gold and silver have found a resting place in the treasure vaults of these same churches, while others remained hidden where they had been buried many hundred years ago in southern Russia and along the Danube. These textiles and silverworks, together with great rock-carved reliefs, make it possible to reconstruct the character of Sassanian art.

It was eclectic; but rather than merely following the Hellenistic canons, it assimilated them with its own traditions of old Persian art and thus created a truly national art of such virility that, in its turn, it soon exerted an active influence that was to become as far-reaching as Hellenism itself. Accepted first as a fashionable novelty by elegant Antinoë, Sassanian art made a more forceful entry into the art of the Byzantine empire and, through it, reached all Christian Europe, where a considerable portion of Romanesque ornament must be credited ultimately to Sassanian inspiration. It also was the source and fountainhead of much of Muhammadan art.

Most admirable of all monuments of Sassanian art are the huge reliefs, cut into the rocks along the roads in southern Persia, the original home of the Sassanian princes, to commemorate the king's investiture by Ormuzd, or his prowess as a warrior. Other reliefs, in the Kurdistan mountains at Tak-i-Bustan, near Kermanshah, illustrate the lighter pleasures of the ruler. In a large vaulted grotto Khusraw Parvis (reigned 590–628) is represented riding his famous black horse, Shabdiz. On the side walls are great scenes of stag and boar hunts, shallow-cut reliefs that only lack of color prevents from looking like tapestries. That such tapestries actually existed, that they even sometimes traveled to far countries, is well known. Both Ammianus Marcellinus, who accompanied the ill-fated Emperor Julian on his Persian war in 363, and his contemporary, Sidonius Apollinaris, the genial bishop of Clermont in France, describe Persian tapestries with hunting scenes. Plautus, the playwright, and Theophrastus, a writer of character sketches, mention Persian tapestries among the coveted curiosities in the houses of their wealthy personages. And some splendid fragments of such tapestries have actually been preserved.

Especially important are the many textile designs carved with minute clarity in these rock reliefs. There are endless variations of floral motifs; birds and animals, enclosed in

38

lozenges or in roundels, in staggered rows, or sedately walking in long files, often with fluttering ribbons tied to their necks or legs. Khusraw himself wears breeches of a thin material, obviously silk, elaborately patterned with square compartments framing a peacock-tailed, lion-legged winged monster, the *senmurv*. Two existing fabrics actually preserve this elaborate pattern; a green and gold damask shows the *senmurv* (London, Victoria and Albert Museum), a polychrome brocade the framework (Rome, Vatican). Around these two splendid silks, masterpieces of Sassanian design and weaving, several other fabrics can be grouped. All these belong to the sixth and seventh centuries, but earlier Sassanian fabrics may also exist, though none is known today.

The Arab author, Masudi, writing about the year 900, tells that the Sassanian king Shapur settled Aramaean silk weavers from Syria in the province of Khuzistan. This may have been either Shapur I (reigned 241–272) or Shapur II (reigned 309–379). Both waged war against the Roman Empire and both are said to have transferred entire populations of cities or villages to Persia. Before then weaving in Persia may have been merely a home craft; now it became a great industry. The weaving centers of Susa, Shushtar, and Gundeshapur survived the fall of the dynasty and continued to flourish under Arab rule.

The battle of Nehavend in 641 brought to an end the four hundred years of Sassanian rule.

VII. BYZANTINE SILKS

The Roman Empire, foremost in skill of organization and administration, toward the end of the third century was beset by many covetous enemies, but the enemy most feared was the eastern neighbor, the Parthian first and then the Sassanian. To hold him in check required constant vigilance; therefore, in A.D. 330 the Emperor Constantine transferred his court and the administration of the Empire from Rome on the Tiber to new Rome on the Bosporus. Here, on the easternmost point of Europe, Greek colonists had long ago built a fortified town, in order to safeguard their traffic with the peoples around the Black Sea. From the eighth century B.C. Byzantium had lived modestly through many vicissitudes; now it became enormously important, but it lost its name, its identity. Henceforth it was called Constantinopolis, "the city of Constantine," soon simply "the city," *eis ten polis*, Istanbul.

Constantinople was built on a vast scale, surrounded by magnificent walls and adorned with treasures contributed by many cities. In character it was quite different from its prototype Rome; it was Greek and it was Christian. The Christian Roman Empire endured for 1123 years; it witnessed the birth and helped the growth of all the nations of Europe, and remained true to its task of defending Christianity against the powers of Asia. In 1204 Constantinople suffered the greatest sack known to history, not from Turks or

Arabs but from fellow Christians; the fourth crusade shamelessly turned its efforts to the capture of Constantinople. Though badly crippled, the Empire survived for another two hundred and fifty years and even experienced a renaissance of all the arts. It succumbed finally before the onslaught of the Ottoman Turks. Besieged by land and water, Constantinople fell, after a defense of epic grandeur, on May 29, 1453.

Byzantine art was a fusion of many elements, chiefly Greek idealistic, Syro-Semitic didactic, and Eastern formalistic; and it was exclusively Christian. In textile design the influence of Sassanian art makes itself felt, at times so overwhelmingly that it is impossible to decide whether certain wonderful silk fabrics come from a Byzantine or a Sassanian workshop. The invention of the drawloom had resulted in a flood of incredibly complicated designs; human beings, animals, plants, inanimate objects, all were crowded together in a fantastic polychromy. But this initial exuberance, this joy of having overcome the limitations of the loom, did not last long; the fundamental urge toward pure ornament took the lead. A new trend in stylization toward the angular becomes noticeable toward the end of the sixth century. It heralds the advent of medieval art and is one of the most important changes that ever influenced textile design. Byzantine fabrics show more virility than the somewhat fussy silks of the late antique period. In keeping with the bold scale of the design, heavier borders are now preferred. The detailed floral ornament of the roundels disappears; heavy palmettes, guilloches, or large disklike beads take its place.

Constantinople, the capital of the Empire, only began to make itself felt as the industrial center in the production of figured silks when the two great rival cities, Antioch (in 636) and Alexandria (in 641) succumbed to the Arab onslaught. When they became Muhammadan, Byzantium got rid of her most dangerous rivals, in both trade and industry. Before the latter part of the seventh century even documents concerning Byzantine silk production are rare. The edicts of Valens and Valentinian (369), of Arcadius (406), and Theodosius (424) only prove that even then private workshops interfered with the imperial *gynecaiae*, the women's quarters, where apparently gold borders and purple cloths were produced. Although the ivory diptychs show the consul dressed in elaborately patterned robes, they are far from reliable witnesses because they hardly ever permit one to distinguish a shuttle-woven design from a tapestry or an embroidered pattern, and of course they never indicate the origin of the fabrics.

One of the earliest preserved Byzantine fabrics shows a griffin holding a bull in its
59 talons. It was found in the tomb of a daughter of Pepin, father of Charlemagne, and quite likely had been part of the gifts brought to the Frankish king by the ambassadors of Constantine V in 758. That the fabulous griffin retained its favor as a textile design is proved by several extant silk fabrics. Two hundred years after the death of Pepin's daughter, in 972, a Byzantine princess, Theophanu, married the German Emperor Otto II. To negotiate this marriage Otto I had sent to Nicephorus Phocas in 968 the bishop of Cremona, Liutprand. On reading his piquant account one feels that the honest bishop was

singularly unsuited as a diplomat, too critically outspoken, too lacking in sympathy and understanding. His irritation at all things Byzantine grew to the boiling point when, as he left the city after a few months of fruitless negotiations, the customs officers confiscated certain purple stuffs he had purchased, as prohibited for export. " 'Such garments can hardly be called unique,' I said, 'when with us streetwalkers and conjurors wear them.' 'Where do they get them from?' they asked. 'From Venetian and Amalfian traders,' I replied." Actually such fabrics were probably available in some black market, from private workshops at Constantinople and from other parts of the Empire.

A later embassy was more successful and Theophanu arrived at Aachen with a large retinue and a very fine trousseau, with many imperial silks. One of these, which practically repeats the griffin and bull pattern of Pepin's time, was used by the draftsman of the marriage charter to embellish his purple-stained parchment. Another silk was used by her son, Otto III, as a shroud for the time-worn relics of Charlemagne, when he opened the tomb of his ancestor in the year 1000. This shroud, the most famous of all Byzantine textiles, is patterned with large elephants, enclosed singly in roundels. It bears, inwoven, the names and titles of two unknown court officials. (Lessing, pls. 67–69; Falke, figs. 241, 242). More fortunately, two fabrics, both designed with lions walking processionally, are inscribed with the names of emperors and can thus be dated to the years 921–31 (Romanus I and Christopher) and 976–1025 (Constantine VIII and Basil). In the latter fabric the stylization is more advanced (Lessing, pls. 62–66; Falke, figs. 239, 240).

Besides griffins, lions, and elephants, the Byzantine textile menagerie contained basilisks, leopards, tigers, winged horses, and eagles. The eagle, as a symbol of strength, was common to the Orient and the Occident; the presence of this bird at critical moments was welcomed as a good augury. Some of the finest Byzantine silks show large eagles with widespread wings. They are represented within complete or partial circles, standing free on plinths, or holding a small beast, a feline or a doe, in their talons. Sometimes the eagle is double-headed, symbolic of the sun's rising and setting; this is also an almost ideal design for the weaver at the drawloom. The eagle silks belonged to the class of "imperial fabrics"; they are thus mentioned in medieval inventories.

These greatest of Byzantine silks were woven in the imperial workshops during the tenth to twelfth centuries. In 969 Antioch was recaptured from the Arabs; the Oriental influence may have received a new impetus. But the outstanding contribution of Byzantine textile design, a respect for the empty space, was by then firmly rooted—it is noticeable in the spandrel designs and the compact, well-centered rosettes. The lion and eagle silks also owe much of their grandeur to their excellent use of the empty space.

Byzantine weaving did not come to an end with the fall of Constantinople. Many weavers must have been absorbed by the local Turkish factories; others may have joined monastic settlements such as those on Mount Athos, which had submitted to the Sultan and were left unmolested. These weavers adjusted their craft to the requirements of the Orthodox Church and produced fabrics with representations of saints or Biblical scenes, as a less expensive substitute for embroideries. They continued using the same designs long after they had become static. The same happened to the Armenian weavers, who may have depended to some extent on designs obtained from the Byzantine artists at Trebizond, if not directly from Constantinople. This sad and depressing end of a once great craft simply proves that, however excellent the weaver's technique, it cannot thrive without the impetus imparted by great design.

VIII. ISLAMIC TEXTILES

Islamic art is the art of many countries, fused only superficially by the community of creed, the belief that "there is no God but Allah and Muhammad is His Prophet." The term "Islamic" designates the cultural structure, "Muhammadan" the religious belief. The Arab contribution to Islamic art was their language, the language of the Koran, the sacred book that records the revelations and exhortations of Muhammad. Innumerable copies of the Koran were written in two styles of calligraphy, a formal style with angular letters, called Kufic, and a cursive style with rounded letters, called Naskhi. Both styles of writing occur also in textile art, where benedictory phrases or quotations from the Koran are often used as the sole decoration or as a frame for the main composition. The study of Muhammadan textiles is closely connected with the study of Coptic, Sassanian, and Byzantine textile art. In the noble craft of weaving there are never brusque transitions; by slow steps the types of patterns and weaves change, new markets cater to the taste of new consumers. In his youth Muhammad had been a merchant, and so he did not object when the faithful combined trade with the pilgrimage to Mecca. Especially he liked strange fabrics, which the pilgrims brought to him from faraway countries, and thus the Prophet of Allah was himself a collector of textiles.

Muhammad died in A.D. 632. Ten years later his followers had conquered Syria and Palestine (638), Egypt (641), and Persia (642). In less than a hundred years the Arabs had subdued the Near East and Central Asia to the borders of China and penetrated along North Africa to the Atlantic Coast. They occupied Sicily and the greater part of Spain; but the threatened advance into the heart of Europe was checked on the battlefield of Tours in 732.

THE   The Muhammadan politics, secular and spiritual, were under the guidance *CALIPHATE* of the caliphs, the "successors" of the Prophet. The first caliph was Abu

Bakr, the friend and father-in-law of Muhammad. He was followed by Umar (634–644), Uthman (644–656), and Ali, the husband of Muhammad's daughter, Fatima. Ali was murdered in 661 and posthumously became the idol of the Shia sect, the great schismatic division of Islam. These four, the orthodox caliphs, were succeeded by the Umayyad caliphs, who ruled from 661 to 749 and set up their capital at Damascus, in

Syria. All too soon the men from Arabia succumbed to the luxury and sophistication of the wonderful city and forgot that the Koran promised them the daintier delights only for the life after death.

In 749 the rule of the Umayyad dynasty came to a sudden end. The entire clan of the descendants of Umayya was massacred by its enemies, the Abbasids. These were descended from Abbas, an uncle of the Prophet. Both dynasties belonged to the Kuraish tribe. Only one Umayyad, a young man, Abd-ar-Rahman, escaped; in time he reached Spain and founded there an independent Western Caliphate.

The victory of the Abbasids meant also the victory of Iranian culture. In 762 the second Abbasid caliph, Mansur (754–775), built a new capital, Baghdad, on the western bank of the Tigris, not far from the former Sassanian capital, Ctesiphon. Thus Baghdad was built on a navigable river, which brought within easy reach all the ports of the Indian Ocean, on a site where the ancient caravan road connected the Mediterranean with central Asia and China. All the arts contributed to the embellishment of the new city, *Daar al Salaam*, the City of Peace. Its beauty is mirrored in the *Tales of the Thousand and One Nights*, which refers to Harun ar Rashid (caliph 786–809), the caliph who sent to Charlemagne gifts of many fine silks and an elephant. The rule of Harun ar Rashid's son, Mamun (813–833), marks the golden age of the Eastern Caliphate. Baghdad, with two million inhabitants, flourished. Its libraries and academies attracted many great men, and industrial quarters were built outside the original walls. Attabi, the silk weavers' quarter just outside the Damascus Gate, survived the destruction of Baghdad by the Mongols. Marco Polo visited it in 1272 and wrote: "In Baudas they weave many different kinds of silk stuff and gold brocades, such as *nasich* and *nac* and *cramoisy*, and many another tissue richly wrought with figures of beasts and birds." In Italy Baghdad was known as Baldacco; the costly fabrics brought thence were called *baldacchino*. Later this term was used to designate the canopies made of such fabrics. The name Attabi has survived in "tabby," a plain cloth weave; it has become also the name of a certain brindled cat.

With Mamun's successors began the gradual weakening of the dynasty. In the ninth and tenth centuries many of the outlying provinces to east and west seceded from the Caliphate and set up independent dynasties, so that by the tenth century the caliphs' authority hardly extended beyond the city of Baghdad. Even worse were the forces of disintegration within the caliphs' household. The Turkish bodyguard, at first petted slaves, now became the real rulers; the caliphs were mere puppets, elected, deposed, and murdered at their oppressors' whim. Outwardly at least, the caliphs fared better when the Persian Buyids seized Baghdad in 945; better still when the Turkish Seljuks once more united all Muhammadan Asia under one ruler, in 1055. The deathblow came in 1258, when the Mongol Hulagu, the grandson of Genghis Khan, entered Baghdad and cruelly murdered Mustasim, last of the Abbasid caliphs. Part of the tribute exacted from the stricken city was paid in textiles. Although there is considerable literary evidence, very few existing early silk fabrics can safely be ascribed to Baghdad.   *65, 66*

The spiritual dignity of the Caliphate was kept alive by certain Abbasid refugees at the court of the Mamluk sultans in Egypt. When the Ottoman sultan, Selim I, conquered Egypt in 1516, he arrogated to himself and his descendants the right of succession to the Caliphate.

EGYPT   The first Arab conquest on non-Asiatic soil was Egypt, taken by Amr in 641.
AND   For two hundred years the important province was administered by gov-
SYRIA   ernors appointed by the Umayyad and early Abbasid caliphs. In 868 the
governor Ahmed ibn-Tulun, a Turk, founded the Tulunid dynasty and, in 897, added Syria to his sphere of government. The Tulunid dynasty, famous for its public works and the elegance of its capital city, Katai, was short-lived and came to an abrupt end in 904.

After a short interval Egypt and Syria were taken, in 969, by the Fatimids, a Shiite clan of Berber origin who claimed descent from Fatima, the Prophet's daughter, Ali's wife. This conquest was merely an extension of their North African empire, which now stretched from the Syrian desert to the borders of Morocco and included Malta, Sicily, and Sardinia. The Fatimids lost their Western provinces when they removed the seat of government from Kairwan, in Tunisia, to their new capital, Cairo, where they resided in an enormous, luxuriously appointed palace. They ruled for two hundred years, the greatest of the medieval Egyptian dynasties, as Shiite caliphs independent of the Eastern Caliphate. Many visitors to Fatimid Cairo have left fantastic accounts of its splendor and of the incredible luxury of the court. Thus Maqrizi tells how one princess left at her death thirty thousand pieces of Sicilian embroidery, another twelve thousand costumes complete with jewelry.

On a Friday in 1171 the faithful assembled in the great mosque of al-Azhar were amazed to hear the official prayer, the Kutba, offered in the name of the Abbasid caliph. The last Fatimid ruler lay on his deathbed and his vizier, Nasr Salah ad Din—whom the Crusaders called Saladin—thus officially proclaimed the advent of the Ayyubid dynasty and the return to the suzerainty of the Eastern Caliphate. The Ayyubid sultans ruled for eighty years. In 1250 they were ousted by their bodyguard of Turkish-Circassian slaves. Two Mamluk dynasties ruled until 1516, when the Ottoman sultan, Selim I, dispossessed them utterly and made of Egypt a Turkish pashalik.

When the Arabs conquered Egypt in 641, they found there a flourishing textile industry. The Coptic weavers were willing to work for their new lords and ready to adapt the decorative patterns to their liking. With the desert-born Arabs, clothing in the widest sense of the word ranked foremost as comfort and luxury. Even when they exchanged their tents for houses, the furnishing and interior decoration consisted almost entirely of hangings, cushions, and rugs. It was a far cry from the Bedouin's coarse mantle of black goat hair and brown and white sheep wool to the refinement of the delicately dyed, finely spun, and exquisitely woven fabrics of Egypt.

Early Islamic datable textiles are scant even in Egypt. This is natural; for only the name of a historically known person occurring in an inscription provides a secure date. Such inscriptions are more often embroidered than woven and are generally found on plain linen fabrics. Figured weaving was for a long time continued according to the old tradition. And it is impossible to disentangle the fabrics woven in Syria from those woven in Egypt during the period of the Umayyad and early Abbasid Caliphate.

The embroidered or woven, sometimes even painted, inscriptions were called *tiraz*. Then this term was used also for the ornamental bands of which such inscriptions formed an integral part, and for the garments decorated with such bands. Finally the weaving establishments were themselves called *dar at tiraz*, or just simply *tiraz*. Such factories may at first have been the prerogative of the caliphs, inspired by the similar institutions of the Byzantine and Sassanian courts. Soon every petty princeling in every province of the Muhammadan empire had to have his *tiraz* factory, which often was housed in the palace. There were also state factories controlled by the rulers, and private factories that supplied the open market.

In Egypt the really brilliant period of expansion in textile art came with the advent of the Fatimid dynasty, in the tenth century. Tapestry-woven borders were still fashionable, but the woolen thread was largely replaced by silk. With this medium very sharp outlines could be obtained, elaborate patterns of interlaced ribbons, interspersed with small, highly stylized plant forms, birds, and quadrupeds. These delicate calligraphic designs set off the beauty of the linen ground. There were several specialties, all in great demand for export to Syria, Iraq, and Persia: thus *dabiki* and *kasab*, so fine that a turban cloth might be a hundred yards long; *bukalemun* of changing color. Gold brocading occurs in fabrics of the tenth century; Maqrizi calls it "Iraqian gold thread." It is made of strips 69 of gilded vellum wound around a linen core and may possibly antedate the Byzantine invention of "Cyprian" gold thread. Maqrizi, the historian of Fatimid Egypt, describes a "Picture Map" that was woven for the Caliph Muizz (952–975). It showed the earth with its mountains, seas, and rivers, with the roads connecting the towns, all leading to Mecca. Each locality had its name woven in threads of silk, silver, or gold.

Tapestry technique continued through the Ayyubid into the early Mamluk period; it was then supplanted by drawloom-woven fabrics. Certain shuttle-woven silk stuffs can 67 be dated as early as the eighth or ninth century; they are closely related to the Sassanian and East Christian fabrics. Like these, they are weft twills and show the design in shades of buff or tan on a dark reddish or greenish ground. Sometimes there occurs a woven inscription in Kufic script. Fabrics such as these were probably woven in Syria, at Damascus and Antioch; but drawlooms must have been widely used also in Egypt. New techniques were elaborated. By the thirteenth century the influence of Persian Seljuk design becomes noticeable. In the fourteenth century the importation of Chinese fabrics, some of which have been found in Egypt, gave a new impetus to textile design.

Islamic textiles documented for Sicily during the Norman period will be described in the next chapter.

The Fatimid emirs of Sicily probably had a *tiraz* factory attached to their palace at Palermo. No specimen of the silk and gold woven fabrics that are mentioned by the chroniclers can today be distinguished from among the Fatimid output. It seems plausible that Sicily's fame was owing to her embroidered fabrics, such as those mentioned by Maqrizi as being collected by a Fatimid princess. If these were comparable to the documented embroideries, the imperial mantle of 1134 and the imperial alb of 1181, they must have been truly magnificent.

SPAIN Spain, westernmost of all countries that bowed to the forces of Islam, was the first province that renounced allegiance to the Caliphate.

  The Iberian Peninsula had been for centuries one of the most flourishing parts of the Roman Empire. In the fifth century it was overrun by several Germanic tribes, the Alans, the Vandals, and the Suebi. All these were ousted by the Visigoths, who remained as rulers for almost three hundred years, maintaining a court that rivaled in splendor that of the Byzantine exarchate of Ravenna. Dynastic jealousies brought their kingdom to an end. One faction asked the aid of the Arab governor of Morocco; the result was the Arab conquest of Spain in 712. Hordes of fugitive Visigoths were driven beyond the Cantabrian Mountains. They settled in Asturias and Galicia and in time rallied to the standards of the kings of Castile and León. The Arabs kept for themselves the best part of Spain, Andalusia, comprising the fertile valleys of the Tagus, Guadiana, and Quadalquivir, with many cities famous since Roman times, and Catalonia, with good ports on the Mediterranean. The new province was ruled by governors appointed by the caliph. But jealousy between the Arabs and the Berbers, to whose help the conquest was largely owing, quickly led to serious disturbances. The leadership of a strong man was needed to bring order out of the chaos, and at the right time such a man appeared. He was the Umayyad Abd ar-Rahman, the only survivor of the massacre of his family by the Abbasids. In 756 he founded the Umayyad emirate of Córdoba; soon this became the Umayyad Western Caliphate, entirely independent of the Abbasid Eastern Caliphate. Córdoba, the capital, was the most highly cultured city of medieval Europe, where many a future Christian ruler or statesman received his education. But eventually the Western caliphs, just like the Eastern and the Fatimid caliphs, became the tools and toys of their bodyguard. The Caliphate came to an end in 1031 and was followed by several short-lived dynasties, which in turn were ousted by the Berber dynasties of the Almoravides and Almohades. Meanwhile the Christian princes of Spain organized their crusade of reconquest. Catalonia had been torn away from Moorish Spain by Charlemagne as the result of several campaigns.

The great epic poem of France, the *Chanson de Roland*, describes one incident, the destruction of the rear guard at Roncesvalles, a valley in the Pyrenees. The deeds of the great hero of the reconquest, Ruy Díaz de Bivar, el Cid Campeador, were sung in romances even before his death in 1099. The *Poema del Cid*, which can be traced back to the twelfth century, contains many descriptions of Moorish textiles.

The last Muhammadan dynasty, the Nasrids of Granada (1232–1492), revived for a time the splendor of the great days of the Caliphate; they were ousted by the *reyes católicos*, Ferdinand and Isabella. The Moriscos, Muhammadans who by one means or another had been converted to Christianity, were tolerated for another hundred years. Their final banishment deprived Spain of many skilled craftsmen, weavers and potters especially, and of several hundred thousand agricultural workers. Large numbers of dispatriated Moriscos joined the Barbary corsairs of North Africa. The decline of Spain was inevitable and rapid.

Of all Islamic textiles those woven in medieval Spain rank foremost in interest today. Many fine specimens that were hidden in private collections and the treasuries of churches are now available to the student, in public collections. A number of tombs, such as those of the royal pantheon of the kings of Castile and León at Las Huelgas, near Burgos, have been examined scientifically and their contents published. The knowledge thus obtained helps to clarify many problems, assign to the looms of Spain a number of textiles of questionable origin and perhaps remove a few from the Spanish repertory.

Sericulture seems to have been unknown in Spain before the Muhammadan conquest. Yet shortly thereafter Spain was able to export raw silk in great quantity and woven fabrics of such beauty that they were in demand even in the eastern part of the Mediterranean. The creation of the Western Umayyad Caliphate gave new impetus to friendly relations with Syria; these led to an interchange not merely of goods but, more importantly, of ideas and fashions. Among these must have been the introduction of the *tiraz*. A very fine gauzelike fabric, preserved in the Royal Academy of History at Madrid, has an elaborate tapestry border woven in silk and gold thread, flanked by an inscription in Kufic letters referring to Hisham II, caliph of Córdoba (976–1009). Spanish textiles brocaded with silver are mentioned in the *Liber Pontificalis* for Gregory IV (827–844). Of the diverse centers of silk weaving Almería is mentioned first by the chronicler Razi (d. 932); in the thirteenth century this town was still considered "superior to any other in the world" for its many varieties of woven silks (ibn-al-Khatib). Of almost equal fame were Málaga, Murcia, Seville, and Granada. Silk weaving flourished also at Saragossa, in Aragon. That city was reconquered by Alfonso I, King of Aragon, in 1118; the weavers continued working for their new Christian clientele, probably adapting their designs to the change in taste. *Drap sarragoçois vermel ouvré á lioncels d'orfrois*, "red cloth of Saragossa with small lions of gold thread," mentioned in a French romance of the thirteenth century, seems to imply a fabric of heraldic, almost Gothic design.

Although there are many Hispano-Moresque fabrics designed with animals and
72-76 even a few with human figures, yet on the whole the textile design is limited to geometric
and arabesque patterns. The thirteenth century brings a wide variety of the star and
77-85 *lacería* patterns, which predominated then in all Moorish crafts. Their appeal is owing
largely to the jewellike quality of their colors. The fifteenth century, while still elaborating
horizontally striped geometric patterns, often combined with Kufic inscriptions in bands or
92-95 cartouches, ushered in the Mudejar style, which cunningly blended Moorish and Gothic
motives. This style survived the fall of Granada, while the pure Moorish style found a last
89-91 nostalgic expression in certain fabrics woven in Morocco in the sixteenth and seventeenth
centuries.

IRAN   Of greatest importance for the evolution of Islamic art was the conquest of
Iran in 642. The Persians helped the Abbasid clan to wrest the Caliphate
from the Umayyads, but in payment they demanded recognition of their
national pride. In the ninth and tenth centuries many of the governors of the outlying
provinces proclaimed their independence and set up several dynasties. Most important of
these, also for their contributions to the development of textile art, were the Samanids in
eastern Iran and Transoxiana and the Buyids in southern Iran and Mesopotamia. All
these national dynasties were absorbed by the Turkish Seljuks, who appeared in Khurasan
in 1037 and in less than twenty years overran the lands of the Eastern Caliphate. They
ruled until 1256, when they were swept away by the Mongols of Chinghiz Khan's grandson, Hulagu. One branch of the Seljuks formed an independent dynasty in Asia Minor and
remained in power until the end of the thirteenth century, when they yielded to the
Ottoman Turks.

In Persia Hulagu founded the Il-khan dynasty, which ruled over a territory bounded
by the Oxus, Indus, and Euphrates. Another great Mongol leader, Timur, appeared in
1370, destroying everything in his way and sparing only a number of craftsmen, who were
sent to Samarkand, his capital in Transoxiana. Timur advanced into Asia Minor, where,
in 1403, he took prisoner the Ottoman Sultan Bayazid I, and thus incidentally gave the
Byzantine empire another fifty years' span of life. Timur died in 1404 and was followed
by sons and grandsons. One of these, Babur, eventually founded the Mughal dynasty in
India. But medieval Islamic art comes to an end with the Timurids.

96   The early Islamic silk fabrics of western Persia show designs in the Sassanian tradition.
In Samanid eastern Persia, possibly in Transoxiana, a new type of design was evolved that
broke with the Hellenistic tradition and indulged in an almost surrealistic angularity. This
99-101 was achieved technically by a simplification of the arrangement of the pattern on the
drawloom. Instead of tying one single pattern warp thread to the corresponding draw cord,
two or even three pattern warps are tied to the one draw cord. This reduces the number
of the draw cords by one half or more, but the pattern is stretched out to double or treble
its width. An entirely new type of design was needed, which emphasized the angular

stepped outline. Mere technical simplification does not explain the sudden success of patterns of such almost ungainly rigidity; the fundamental reason must be sought in a change in taste. Sir Aurel Stein discovered many silk fabrics of this type in the caves of the Thousand Buddhas at Tun-huang, in Chinese Turkestan. He believed them to be woven in Sogdiana, possibly at Samarkand.

The Buyids, who seized Baghdad in 945, traced their ancestry to a Sassanian hero, Mihr-Narse, of the staff of Bahram Gur (420–440). Thus their rise to power, as mayors of the palace of the Abbasid caliph, who gave them the title of Amir-al-Umara, emir of emirs, satisfied the national pride of the Persians. "Without the Iranian interlude, represented by the Samanids in the East and the Buyids in the West, the Iranian tradition would have been broken; and Persia would have found it infinitely more difficult to reestablish her national conscience after so many shocks to which she had to bow, till the arrival of the Safavids" (Minorsky, *La Domination des Dailamites*, Paris, 1932). Until recently few silk fabrics were known that could safely be dated to the Buyid period (932–1055). The exploration at Raiy of Khou Nagareh Khan, a tomb tower distant about two miles from the sanctuary of Bibi Shar Banu, the traditional resting place of the Sassanian princess who became the wife of Husayn son of Ali, brought to light a goodly number of silk fabrics. A group of these shows an especially close relationship to Sassanian design; three of the fabrics are dated, A.D. 994, 998, and 1003. The group belongs to the Buyid period; the style of design and certain peculiarities of the technique make it probable that these silks were woven in Samanid workshops. Several of these beautiful fabrics can now be *103–110* studied in American collections. The textile style of the Seljuk period is thus seen as derived from the style evolved during the Buyid period. New is the full evolution of an abstract ornament, the arabesque. This is a transformation of the ubiquitous ornament of late classical art, the floral tendril. In the arabesque, stalk and leaf are merged into a con- *111–119* tinuous filament; the stalk expands into the leaf and the leaf again contracts into the stalk. The arabesque is the most versatile of all abstract ornaments.

The designs of these Persian textiles are breathtakingly beautiful. Designer and weaver work together as never before and rarely afterward. The limitations of the loom seem to stimulate rather than hamper the imagination of the designer. The material itself takes its part in this joyous revelry; never before were there so many fine graduations of colors, from palest apricot, green, and blue to glowing deep tones and the blackest black. The weaver is inspired to try out new techniques. Double cloth, not entirely new, is now used with such perfection, such even tension of the two simultaneously woven cloths, that there are no bulges between the design where the two cloths lie separately. A two-textured compound cloth shows the pattern twill-woven on the cloth ground. A new venture is a warp-twill where the warp threads almost completely cover the wefts. This leads to satin weaving in a transitory stage, somewhat rough, lacking the smooth, even surface of perfection. The American museums are rich in Seljuk textiles; most of the surviving patterns are represented by excellent, sometimes quite large, specimens.

Many of these beautiful silk fabrics were found at Raiy, a city near Teheran, flourishing in Buyid and Seljuk times, a heap of ruins since its destruction by the Mongols in 1221. Raiy is best known for the magnificent ceramic wares produced there, but it was also a noted textile center. The medieval chroniclers and geographers mention also many other cities and villages all through Persia that in their time were famed for their weaving and for sericulture. Certain cities, such as Merv, in Khurasan, and Gorgan, near the Caspian Sea, seem to have specialized in the export trade of "seed," the eggs of silkworms.

All this glory came to an abrupt end with the Mongol invasion. Thirty years after Chinghiz Khan's death (1227) two of his grandsons, Khubilay and Hulagu, became Supreme Khan and Provincial Khan, Khakhan of China and Il-khan of Persia. The magnificence of Khubilay's court at his new capital, Khan Baligh (Cambaluc, Peking), is well known from Marco Polo's account; he also tells how he escorted a princess of the Yüan House to Persia.

The linking up of China and Persia had important repercussions in the realm of textile art. Already during the rule of the T'ang dynasty (618–907) Persian textiles had been traded to China and Muhammadan weavers induced to settle there. Textiles woven in T'ang China, showing clearly the inspiration of Sassanian and early Islamic patterns, have been preserved in the Shoso-in at Nara, in Japan; others were found by Sir Aurel Stein at Tun-huang, in Chinese Turkestan. When Khubilay Khan founded the Yüan dynasty in 1280, these earlier immigrants had grown to a considerable population. These weavers were now Chinese in all but their hereditary knowledge of the Arabic script. No special weaving centers are known. They may have been near Peking and possibly also in eastern Turkestan, where sericulture had flourished since the time a princess of the Han dynasty had smuggled silkworm eggs in her coiffure to her betrothed, a prince of Khotan.

The new Chinese fabrics were highly prized throughout Islam and imitated from Persia to Spain. Probably only those brocaded with flat strips of gilded leather should be considered Chinese export ware. The most important contribution of Yüan China to textile art was a certain naturalism in design that inspired the Persian weavers of the fourteenth and fifteenth centuries. Only a few of the preserved silk fabrics are clearly of Iranian origin. How overwhelmingly the prevailing fashion was for Chinese imports can be seen in the illuminated manuscripts of the Mongol and Timurid periods. Not only are the fabrics depicted decorated with the Chinese fabulous fauna, dragons, khilins, and phoenixes, but the old Persian heroes in the *Shah-nama* wear armor of the Mongol type as described by that great traveler, Friar Guillaume Rubruquis, who watched the smiths at their work in the Great Khan's camp near Karakorum; and sometimes there are mandarin squares sewn to their jackets.

SAFAVID   For eight hundred and fifty years after the downfall of the Sassanian dynasty
PERSIA   Iran had been ruled in turn by Arabs, Turks, and Mongols, with only the
            short interlude of the Samanid and Buyid dynasties. At the end of the

fifteenth century the Safavid clan proclaimed its right to political and spiritual leadership. Tracing their descent to the seventh Imam Musa al-Kazim of the family of Husayn the son of Ali, and through Husayn's wife, a daughter of Yezdegerd, to the Sassanian kings, the Safavids were stanch supporters of the Shia confession, and were even to the strictest of their subjects the rightful successors of the truly national kings of Persia. The name of the dynasty refers to Shaykh safi of Ardebil, who had acquired a reputation of sanctity. The real founder of the greatness of his house was Ismail I (reigned 1502–1524), who made of his capital, Tabriz, a center of all the arts. As the result of several victorious campaigns, Ismail's dominions stretched from the Oxus to the Persian Gulf, from Afghanistan to Iraq.

Ismail's son, Shah Tahmasp (reigned 1524–1576), centered his efforts during a reign of fifty-two years on the building up of a new tradition of refinement and sophistication. He studied painting with Sultan Muhammad, one of the greatest artists of the day, and there is a tradition that Tahmasp himself designed some of the marvelous rugs that were woven for him, to be used for the embellishment of the ancestral shrine at Ardebil and other mosques, for his palaces and for gifts to certain princes of Europe. In 1561 Queen Elizabeth of England sent an ambassador, Anthony Jenkinson, to treat with the Shah "of Trafique and Commerce for our English Marchants" (Samuel Purchas, d. 1626).

Greatest of the Safavid rulers was Shah Abbas I (reigned 1587–1628). The many ambassadors and foreign merchants who came to Isfahan, the new capital of Persia, were impressed by the fact that Shah Abbas was not merely a great patron of all the arts, which flourished as never before, but also a serious student of the problems pertaining to agriculture and trade.

The three successors of Shah Abbas I maintained the political and economical power of Persia at a high level. Two Frenchmen, Tavernier and Chardin, wrote well-informed accounts of their visits to Persia. These entertaining travel tales were widely read and helped to create a fashion for Persian works of art in Europe.

Toward the end of the seventeenth century the already decadent Safavid dynasty weakened rapidly. A series of tribal insurrections culminated in the Afghan invasion of 1722 and the usurpation of the throne by Nadir Shah (1736–1747), who extended his conquests to Afghanistan and India.

Jean Chardin, who was in Persia in 1667, tells in his splendid record that the most important manufacture of the country was silk weaving. "Comme la soie est une matière abondante en Perse, les Persans sont particulièrement exercés à la bien travailler, et c'est à quoi ils réussissent le mieux." At Isfahan he found thirty-two weaving shops attached to the court, each employing about one hundred and fifty highly specialized craftsmen. But, he adds, he has been told that formerly (obviously in the time of Shah Abbas the Great) there had been more ateliers and more silk workers. These weavers enjoyed substantial privileges, sometimes even social prestige. Their fabrics were incomparably beautiful and so costly that Chardin wrote, "il ne se fait point d'étoffe si chère par tout le monde."

No new techniques were invented during the Safavid period, but those already existing were used with absolute perfection, from plain cloth to brocaded polychrome velvet. Two types of design were prepared by the court painters for the weavers, a wide variety of plants and flowers often combined with birds and butterflies, and figure subjects. These may illustrate scenes from the *Shah-nama* and the romances of Nizami, or they simply depict charmingly effeminate youths in landscapes full of strange creatures, rabbits and gazelles, lions and leopards, and all the flying beasts created by Allah and the *138* human mind. The simplest type of weaving, cloth, which makes possible sharp outlines and details, is but seldom used, although some of the finest preserved silks are thus woven. All too rarely also occurs that interesting technique, the double cloth, but when it is found it surprises with its esoteric refinement. Brocading, which has all the freedom of embroidery, is found more often, especially with the satin weaves. Sometimes very elaborate *132–137* figure subjects are woven as polychrome velvets, often over a ground of gold or silver. This is surely gilding the lily! Under Shah Abbas brocaded velvet was occasionally used for the weaving of large rugs. Chardin may have been told of the expense involved in such extravaganzas; but they had their uses as exceedingly impressive diplomatic gifts.

Certain weavers of the Safavid period have left their name inscribed on textiles produced by themselves or their workshops. Lists of such weavers and their preserved work are given by Phyllis Ackerman, in *A Survey of Persian Art*, London, 1939, III, 2094–2133; and by Mehmet Aga-Oglu, in *Safavid Rugs and Textiles, the Collection of the Shrine of Imam Ali at al-Najaf*, New York, 1941.

In the seventeenth century and later, wide sashes were an intrinsic part of the Persian costume. These sashes found favor with the Polish cavaliers and in the eighteenth century they were imitated in Poland, especially at Slutsk, where Prince Michael Casimir Radziwill founded a factory for silk weaving. The first weavers employed there are said to have been Armenian prisoners of Sobieski's wars against the Turks.

THE
MUGHAL
EMPIRE   The history of India is typical of all the states that border on the steppe regions of Central Asia. From time immemorial the great peninsula was overrun by wave after wave of invaders, which were absorbed and assimilated.

Across the sea came Arab pirates who had observed the steadiness of the direction of the monsoons that enabled them to cross the Indian Ocean in opposite directions at different seasons of the year. These piratical expeditions may go back to the time when the Queen of Sheba paid her visit to Solomon, and they continued during the early days of Islam.

But for the true conquest of India the road led through Afghanistan. This road was taken by Mahmud of Ghazna (reigned 998–1030), a mighty warrior, great statesman, and magnificent patron of literature, at whose court Firdausi wrote the *Shah-nama*, the "Book of Kings." Mahmud was the first of several rulers of Afghanistan who attempted the subjugation of the wonderful lands beyond the great river, the Indus, where temples full of treasure attracted raiders, where statues of Hindu deities made icon-breakers feel virtuous. Last of these Turkish conquerors was Babur, a descendant of Timur.

Zahir al-Din, surnamed Babur, "the Tiger," born in 1483, was driven from Fergana by the Uzbek Tartars and conquered Afghanistan in 1504. Twenty years later he descended from Kabul, his mountain stronghold, into the Punjab. In quick succession he took Lahore, Delhi, and Agra, but died in 1530. Like so many of Timur's descendants, Sultan Babur, the founder of the Mughal dynasty, was a true scholar. His admirable autobiography, the *Babur-nama*, is a precious document for the history of the last Timurid rulers and gives much valuable information concerning the quarrels and petty jealousies of the many sultans and rajas of India.

Babur's son, Humayun (reigned 1530–1556), tried valiantly to complete his father's work. After ten years of fighting and intrigue he was forced to seek refuge at the court of Shah Tahmasp at Tabriz. In 1555 he recovered Delhi, but died six months later.

Humayun had merely begun the work of reconquest. It was left to his son Akbar (1556–1605), born in exile in 1542, at his father's death not yet fourteen years old, to finish it. Akbar is the true founder of the vast Mughal empire; he deserves the name of the Great by his wise administration. He conciliated the Hindus by allowing them freedom of worship; he spent much thought on a plan of fusing the diverse religions of India into one universal creed. He established schools all through his empire for the education of both Hindus and Muhammadans. Abu'l-Fazl, his vizier, wrote the *Akbar-nama*, a chronicle of his life, and the *Ain-i-Akbari*, "Institutions of Akbar." These contain much useful information concerning the textile industry; there are lists of the different fabrics produced, cottons, woolens, silks, and cloths of gold or silver, about one hundred and twenty kinds in all. This impressive list became even larger during the reigns of Akbar's son and grandson, Jahangir (1605–1627) and Shah Jahan (1628–1658). This half century represents the period of greatest magnificence of the already proverbial splendor of the Mughal court. Trade with Europe was encouraged. To Jahangir's court came, in 1615, Sir Thomas Roe, bringing polite greetings from James I, and obtaining special privileges for the East India Company. This had been founded toward the end of the sixteenth century under charter of Queen Elizabeth. Shah Jahan is remembered popularly as the builder of Taj Mahal, the tomb of his wife, Mumtaz Mahal; it is the last of a series of noble mausoleums built for the Mughal emperors and their families.

Last of the first six Mughal emperors was Aurangzib (1658–1707). His intense bigotry and intolerance alienated the Hindus and the haughty Rajputs. His utter lack of interest in art amounted to hostility toward the artists and thus Mughal art rapidly declined. His successors were kept on the peacock throne until 1858 by the power of the English East India Company. The government of India was then assumed by the Crown of England, and in 1876 Queen Victoria was proclaimed Empress of India.

As ancient Egypt was the land of linen and Mesopotamia the land of wool, so India was the land of cotton, famous even before Alexander the Great's expedition for the production of fabrics woven from "wool that grew on trees," a term that has survived in the German *Baumwolle*. In Mughal times and probably long before, the finest muslin was produced at Dacca, in Bengal. The weaving of these fabrics could only be done during the rainy season, when the air was moist; they were distinguished by poetic names such as "running water" and "woven air." The Dacca muslins were used plain, sometimes finely pleated, or painted and printed, often with gold, for saris and headcloths and complete dresses.

No fabrics earlier than of Mughal times have been preserved. The designs of the silk brocades of the seventeenth and eighteenth centuries show a mixture of Persian and Hindu style, often on a solid ground of gold or silver. Another type of brocade weaving, which may reflect Rajput rather than Mughal taste, shows affinity with the Chinese *k'o ssu*.

144, 145   Most characteristic of all Indian fabrics is woolen twill tapestry. This was woven by the yard, to be cut up for garments, or in squares with borders all around, known as Kashmir shawls. This interesting type of weaving is often combined with embroidery; the design is an all-over pattern or rows of pear-shaped stylized motives.

OTTOMAN TURKEY   Last of the diverse Turkish tribes who left their original homes in Central Asia and migrated westward was the clan of Ertughril of the Oghuz tribe, which settled in Asia Minor about the middle of the thirteenth century. In 1299 Uthman, son of Ertughril, founded the Ottoman dynasty, which eventually became the greatest power in Mediterranean lands and the terror of Christianity. The Ottoman sultans set up their capital at Brusa and absorbed one by one the small Seljuk and Byzantine states in Asia Minor. In 1358 they crossed the Hellespont and started on their conquest of the Byzantine empire in Europe. In less than forty years they had taken possession of the entire Balkan peninsula. The defeat of Bayazid I (1389–1403) by Timur in 1402 was merely a temporary check. The near anarchy that tore to pieces Timur's empire after his death in 1404 made possible the reorganization of the Ottoman possessions by Muhammad I (1413–1421). Constantinople fell to Muhammad II (1451–1481) in 1453 and Hagia Sophia, "the mightiest church in Christendom" (William of Malmesbury), became the model for many beautiful Turkish mosques. The next hundred years saw victory after victory, till the Ottoman Empire included all Western Asia, North Africa from the Red Sea to the Atlantic Ocean, the Balkan peninsula, Moldavia and Hungary in Europe. Twice, in 1529 and 1683, the Turks even laid siege to Vienna. The three-hundred-year period of expansion came to an end with the death of Sulaiman I in 1566. The period of decline began with a naval defeat, the battle of Lepanto in 1571, which proved that the colossus was vulnerable and had feet of clay. Yet the Ottoman dynasty held on for another three hundred and fifty years, until 1924.

To the arts of Islam the Ottoman Turks made important contributions in the domain of architecture, ceramics, and textile art. The earliest textiles of the Ottoman period are known only through a few portraits of princes and noblemen, painted by Gentile Bellini of Venice during his sojourn at Sultan Muhammad II's court in Constantinople in 1479–1480. The earliest preserved fabrics do not antedate the sixteenth century. The chief center of weaving was Brusa, the old capital of the empire. Certain brocaded velvets of especially imaginative design may have been woven at Damascus, and there were other cities in Asia Minor, among them Scutari and Hereke, that had their share in the development of the textile industry.

The earliest Ottoman fabrics show undisguised borrowing from Persia and Venice. Yet very soon the Turkish designer threw off the yoke of such dependency and created a truly national style. The Turks were adherents of the Sunna, the orthodox creed, which, in opposition to the Shia, looks askance at the representation of living creatures. Their artists were limited to geometric and floral design; the first they used with commendable simplicity and directness, the latter they enriched by the introduction of the same flowers that also make their ceramic ware so pleasing, tulips, carnations, and hyacinths. The weavers translated these designs into a long series of gold and silver brocaded satins and velvets. The Ottoman silk fabrics of the sixteenth and seventeenth centuries may lack the intimate charm of the contemporary Persian fabrics, but theirs is a grandeur and a straightforwardness of their own.

IX. EUROPEAN TEXTILES

MEDIEVAL ITALY It is axiomatic to state that the art of weaving elaborate designs on drawlooms originated in the East and only slowly migrated westward. Italy was in an excellent position for absorbing suggestions. In the early Christian centuries the Church was the focal point; the papal inventories mention fabrics imported from the Byzantine and Sassanian empires, from Syria and Egypt. The rise of feudal power brought in its train a display of rare and costly things; fine textiles were of paramount importance for interior decoration, for the trappings of horses on parade and for the elaborate costumes of men and women. The expansion of trade led eventually to the creation of a new lesser nobility of merchants and bankers, and to the growth of the power of cities. And thus, when the importation of silk fabrics from the Near East became increasingly unreliable because of the catastrophe of the Mongol invasions, Italy, long known for her excellent woolen fabrics, resorted to silk weaving. The raw material was obtained from the Levant and Spain, and sericulture quickly became an important industry in Italy. The locally produced silk fabrics may at first have been traded as imported *d'outre mer;* yet soon they could stand on their own merit.

Little is known concerning the evolution of textile design from the twelfth to the fourteenth century. Sculptures and illuminated manuscripts are of scant help because the textile patterns are much simplified. More information can be gathered from paintings, but these are relatively late.

Thus the grouping of certain types as it is offered here is merely an attempt at clarification. It is possible that future research may change today's ideas, as these have changed since the late nineteenth century, when all medieval Italian silks were blithely assigned to the looms of Palermo.

SICILY The geographical position of Sicily, the island that forms a barrier between Europe and Africa, explains its historical position as the halfway house between the powers of the eastern and western Mediterranean. It was the granary of many nations, Phoenicia and Greece, Carthage and Rome. From A.D. 525 to 827 Sicily was a Byzantine province; the Greek language superseded Latin and was not entirely forgotten during the two hundred and fifty years of Arab overlordship. The reconquest came in the third quarter of the eleventh century, and reads like an epic rather than sober history. While the Duke of Normandy made ready for the conquest of England, one of his lieges, Roger of Hauteville, conquered for himself another, far more beautiful island. The conquest of Sicily was the result of a systematic series of campaigns that lasted thirty years (1062–1091). The chronicler Malaterra tells of Roger that "he was a youth of greatest beauty, most eloquent in speech and cool in council. He was far-seeing in arranging his actions, pleasant and merry with all his men, strong and brave in battle." His success as a ruler was largely owing to his policy of full toleration of Arabs, Greeks, and Jews. Roger, "great count of Sicily," died in 1101, in his seventieth year, and, after the death of his older son, Simon, was followed, in 1103, by his younger son Roger II, who was then only eight years old.

Roger II added to his inherited possessions the Norman parts of the Italian mainland and became Duke of Apulia and Prince of Capua. On Christmas Day, 1130, Pope Anacletus II crowned him King of Naples and Sicily. To his court at Palermo came visitors from far lands; among those who stayed on were the Arab geographer Idrisi, the Greek historian Nilus Doxopatrius, and the "admiral of admirals," George of Antioch, who made Sicily the greatest sea power in the Mediterranean. Roger II died in 1154 and was followed by his son, William I, a weak man who died in 1166. His son and successor, William II, inherited all his grandfather's excellent qualities but, unfortunately, died childless in 1189. Thus it happened that the kingdom of the Two Sicilies came to the Hohenstaufen emperor Henry VI, as the husband of Constance, last surviving legitimate descendant of the House of Hauteville. Henry died young, in 1197, Constance eighteen months later, leaving a four-year-old child, Frederick, first as King of Sicily, second as Emperor.

This much admired and much hated man made a deep impression on his contemporaries. Even now, seven hundred years after his death, scholars take sides for and against him, with a passion worthy of the Guelfs and Ghibellines in their most truculent mood. From babyhood Frederick was surrounded by intrigue and treachery, a pawn in the hands of his guardian, Pope Innocent III. A precocious boy, he learned early to enjoy the graces of Muhammadan culture and became familiar with the ecclesiastical squabbles of the Greeks and Romans. Later, Frederick kept Saracen troops as his bodyguard; they were devoted to him and indifferent to papal excommunication. The learned men of all creeds were welcome at his court, first at Palermo, then at Naples. In the latter place he founded a university, which quickly became as famous as those of Salamanca, Bologna, and Paris. Under Frederick II the Kingdom of the Sicilies became the first state ruled in the modern manner, with a staff trained for civil service. Trade and industry flourished, taxes were light. Frederick himself was a learned man and a poet; he wrote poetry like the troubadours, and so did his son Manfred—*pulcherrimus et inventor cantiorum.* They wrote in the young Italian language, which they then passed on to Petrarch and Dante. Those were halcyon days in Sicily's history. An earthquake shook Italy at the hour when Frederick expired in 1250. Sixteen years later, defending his patrimony against Charles of Anjou, Manfred died, the last scion of two great houses, Hauteville and Hohenstaufen. "Biondo era e bello e di gentile aspetto" (Dante, *Purgatory* III, 107).

From that day Sicily was the prey of contending adventurers until in 1860 it was annexed to Italy by Garibaldi.

It is possible, even plausible, that sericulture was introduced in Sicily during the Byzantine period, although actual proof is missing. The Saracen emirs had their *tiraz* attached to their palace at Palermo, and this was taken over by Roger I. His son, Roger II, much strengthened the weaving ateliers when, having taken the cities of Corinth, Thebes, and Athens in 1147, he brought back to Palermo the Greek silk weavers of those cities. Henceforth these worked side by side with the Saracenic weavers and embroiderers in the *tiraz* ateliers of the royal palace. That sericulture existed and raw silk was produced in Sicily is attested by Idrisi, who finished his "Geography" in 1154. A Latin chronicler, Hugo Falcandus, who wrote about 1189, gives some information concerning the silks woven at Palermo. "You will see there," he writes, "fabrics of one, two or three threads, not very costly and easy to weave, but also heavier fabrics of six threads. Here, the *diarhodon* hits the eye like fire; there, the greenish color of *diapistus* flatters the eye pleasingly; the *exarentasmata*, designed with a variety of circles, demand more material and greater skill and therefore are more expensive." He mentions the use of precious stones and whole pearls, which were "either set in gold casings or pierced and fastened with a thread, so elegantly that they make pictures." Two splendid garments thus embroidered, the mantle of King Roger I, dated 1134, and the alb of William II, dated 1181, have been preserved because they were later incorporated among the imperial vestments.

The basic fabric of both is *diasprum;* this is the first Western silk weave that shows the pattern and the ground in a different texture but of the same color. To achieve this, two warps and two wefts were required. The ground is woven in simple cloth weave, with fine wefts; for the pattern, a heavy weft is taken over two ground warps and one binder warp and under one binder warp; the effect is like that of a floated weave, sometimes almost like a weft twill, surrounded by sunken lines that look chiseled out. It is a fabric of esoteric charm, not at all spectacular. These diasprum fabrics have been generally assigned to Byzantium, yet the patterns, which range from small scrolls to large ogee compartments, seem too slender and unassuming to have emanated from a weaving center working for the court. Could it be possible that the diasprum was a specialty of the weaving centers in Greece, and that Roger brought the weavers from Corinth, Thebes, and Athens to Palermo because he wanted this very specialty to become his own? The distribution of vestments of diasprum, in treasuries and tombs of Austria and Germany, ranging over the eleventh and twelfth centuries, does not help answer this question. But diasprum survived in medieval Italy into the fourteenth century; the later specimens show parts of the design brocaded in gold.

All in all, it can be stated that the Sicilian silks of the Norman period are a happy blending of Muhammadan and Byzantine motifs. Important is the mantle of rose-red silk and gold in which the Emperor Henry VI was buried in 1197 in the Cathedral of Palermo. Horizontal bands of gazelles and parrots are counterbalanced by the strongly vertical effect of the long-stemmed slender arabesque trees between the animals. These continuous vertical stems are a main characteristic of the Palermitan designs. They occur again and *170* again, always in combination with horizontally disposed rows of animals, often peacocks or griffins. Most famous of peacock fabrics is the burial robe of Robert of Anjou, King of Naples, preserved at Toulouse. Here the horizontality is further emphasized by weaving the peacocks in alternate red and green bands. This fabric has been claimed for Almería, because of its perfection of design and weaving, but the long-stemmed arabesque tree is idiomatically Palermitan, and the arbitrarily colored bands also point to Sicily.

Another specialty of the Palermitan ateliers were *aurifrisia*, borders of gold with details of brightly colored silk. They were woven on small looms in a special form of tapestry technique; some look like elaborate tablet weaving. These very solid borders were used *156–158* for the trimming of curtains, for caps, shoes, and bags and for miters, stoles, and maniples.

Frederick II, in his *Book of Laws* promulgated at Melfi in 1231, describes himself as the master weaver who crosses the warp of justice with the weft of peace. When, in 1226, he transferred his administration from Palermo to Naples, the diverse ateliers attached to the palace followed there. But even before then the wise ruler had established sericulture and silk weaving in well-chosen centers on the south Italian mainland. There he also established certain families of Jews, probably from Syria or Greece, who held monopolies in the dyeing industry. Although documentary proof is scarce, the names of Capua, Benevent, Trani, Bari, and Cosenza are found mentioned. Such fabrics were exported as *bon cendal d'Adrie*, or *paille d'Adrie*. Certain preserved fabrics may belong to this group. They are thirteenth-century developments of twelfth-century Palermitan designs, but show a tendency toward accepting Gothic influence, thus paralleling the evolution in architecture and sculpture. They are imbued with a new spirit, the designs are more diversified, like

feelers thrown out in different directions. Besides strictly heraldic patterns, there are designs *168*
of elaborate devices that became fashionable in the thirteenth century; there are silks that
foreshadow in design and technique the linen and cotton runners of fourteenth-century *175*
Perugia; silks that point out the coming trends of Lucca and Venice, and others that are
unique, inspirations of the moment, rhapsodies in green. Frederick's passion had been
hunting, especially with falcons, and the green of his hunting attire became the color of
the Ghibelline party. The wars between Anjou and Aragon brought silk weaving and sericulture to a standstill. When, in the fifteenth century, the kings of Naples, Alfonso and
Ferrante, paid special attention to reviving sericulture, it was too late. By then the primacy
in silk weaving was firmly entrenched in the cities of Tuscany and in Venice.

LUCCA Foremost among the cities of Tuscany stands Lucca, famous since Roman
times for the production of fine woolen cloth. In the early Middle Ages
Lucca was the favorite residence of the margraves of Tuscany. In 1115, after
the death of the last of these, the famous Matilda, *la grandonna d'Italia*, Lucca became an
independent community, a city republic. Her neighbor Pisa, Ghibelline port par excellence, had always been in close relation with the Kingdom of the Sicilies. Thus it was only
natural that, after Manfred's death in 1266, his silk weavers should have turned to congenial Lucca. Soon the fame of the silks of Lucca spread across the Alps; in 1336 the Lucchese merchants in Paris formed a syndicate. Henceforth *samit de Lucques*, *drap d'or de
Lucques*, *cendal*, *siglaton*, and *baudequin* are mentioned in practically all inventories in France
and soon also in Burgundy. Lucca silks are depicted in paintings both in Italy and Flanders. They draped softly and thus enhance the beauty of the charming ladies in the *Triumph
of Death* that Traini painted on the wall of the Campo Santo in Pisa. Equally well they lent
themselves for wall coverings, as shown by Hubert van Eyck in the Ghent altar. The
triumph of the Lucca silks is easily explained: they brought a new type of textile design,
which broke entirely with the traditions of the Romanesque period.

The old style had organized the surface into firmly circumscribed compartments, a
type inherited from the Sassanian-Byzantine silks. The twelfth-century compositions took
the subject matter, addorsed or confronted animals or birds, out of the roundels and
placed them in rows in horizontal bands as an attempt at finding a way out of old servi-
tude. All this was now discarded in favor of a free disposition in diagonal rows, technically
achieved by the half overlap, but disguised by the use of at least three different motifs.

Animals are still the preponderant element, but they are changed fundamentally.
They are drawn realistically and, instead of quietly confronting each other in stately *192*
heraldic presentation, they are now full of life and motion, they run, fly, rush in assault, or
recoil. The floral ornament also succumbs to caprice; twisted trees with wind-blown crowns
grow from rocks or fenced enclosures. The stock in trade of motifs is immensely enlarged;
the powers of imagination seem inexhaustible; truly these are such stuffs as dreams are
made on.

The Italian silk style of the fourteenth century is a unique manifestation in Western art. It combines with absolute mastery the Gothic spirit of naturalism of representation with the Chinese spirit of aloofness.

Chinese textiles had been known since the time of the early Roman Empire. The Mongol conquests in hither Asia brought a new influx of Chinese motifs to the Mediterranean area; these may have reached Italy directly or through Persian adaptations, but in any case China was the source of the inspiration.

A group of Lucca fabrics that can be assigned to the early part of the fourteenth century shows almost direct copies of thirteenth-century Chinese satins, gold brocaded with lotus tendrils and phoenixes. More often the Chinese motifs are used in Western disguise. The phoenixes, pheasants, cranes are transformed into falcons, hawks, and swans, the khilin into a stag or gazelle, a dog or hunting leopard. Yet, tails ending in floral motifs or feathery tassels, certain curves of neck or body, and unnecessarily fluttering wings recall the Chinese origin. Flaming rays became a favorite motif of the Lucca weaver; they also belonged to the Far Eastern repertoire.

195   Toward the mid-fourteenth century a fashion for pseudo-Kufic lettering becomes noticeable. This may be owing to a direct influence of Hispano-Moresque textiles; more probably to the influx of Persian fabrics. About the same time appears a "modernized"
170–172 form of diasprum cloth. It is now often woven in two colors, but always shows the pattern woven with heavy, untwisted silk, the ground with thin, twisted silk; the heads and feet of the animals are brocaded in gold thread. The exorbitant price asked for these diasprum silks by the Lucchese merchants is preserved in French bills and the household accounts of the Dukes of Burgundy.

All these diverse influences were finally merged in a clearly Gothic, though still quite
199, 200 fantastic style. Here castles with domed or pointed roofs stand on luminous clouds or in
201, 202 floral ornaments. Huntresses appear, sometimes half hidden in snail shells, or between the wings of eagles, or leaning from trees, or drinking from fountains. In the second half of the fourteenth century there appear fabrics picturing religious subjects. They are mentioned first in the papal inventory of 1361, and several of these rare fabrics are preserved in
205, 206 American collections. They are brocaded satins showing, scattered over a light blue or green ground, figures of cherubim with flaming wings, angels swinging thuribles or carrying the instruments of the Passion. Sometimes there occur clouds shaped like curling ribbons; these are derived from the *Tchi*, which had found its way from China to Persia and thence may have become part of Christian representations in Armenia; or it may have reached Italy directly.

VENICE   While the merchants of Lucca traded mainly with western Europe—France, Burgundy, and England—the countries of central and eastern Europe— Germany, Austria, Poland, and the Balkan states—received their silks from Venice.

According to Muratori, silk weaving was introduced in Venice by weavers from Lucca who left their home town in 1314, fleeing from the tyrant Uguccione della Faggiuola, who had made himself the master of the little republic. But the papal inventory of 1295 mentions both cities as centers of silk weaving; repeatedly a fabric is called *venetico sive lucano*, Venetian or Lucchese. And Zanetti mentions a decree of the year 1258 concerning the weaving of cendal and cloth of gold in Venice. Thus it seems plausible that sericulture and silk weaving were brought to Venice directly from southern Italy by way of the Adriatic Sea, by weavers from Bari or Trani. This explains the fact that puzzled the compiler of the papal inventory, the similarity of the early fabrics of both cities. Probably, whenever either Lucca or Venice created a new design that appealed to the buying public's fancy, the other city would quickly follow with a similar composition. Very likely, Lucchese weavers came to Venice more than once, for at Lucca politics were unstable while the fame of Venice grew steadily, largely as the result of her stable government. On his deathbed in 1423, the eighty-year-old doge, Tommaso Mocenigo, told his friends how much had been accomplished during his tenure of office: "Now we have invested in our silk industry a capital of ten million ducats and we make two millions annually in export trade; sixteen thousand weavers live in our city."

The main characteristic that distinguishes the Venetian from the Lucchese textiles is a *213–216* lack of temperament, a greater stability. Instead of the nervous excitement of the Lucca designs, there is a clear, smooth draftsmanship. The Gothic spirit pervades the compositions; the plant motifs are stronger, a highly individual palmette tree occurs repeatedly, generally in combination with almost naturalistic plants.

In the sketch book of Pisanello (1397–1450), there are some "fashion plates," drawings of ladies and cavaliers in slightly exaggerated costumes, with the details of textile decoration carefully indicated; they look more like embroideries than woven designs.

The sketch book of Jacopo Bellini (*c.* 1400–1470) in the Louvre has ten pages of de- *217, 218* signs for brocade weaving. These were made by the young artist; later in life he lost interest in them and covered nine pages with a layer of gray painting ground, so that he could again use the good parchment. Thus only one page, with three designs, is preserved intact. Jacopo Bellini is no innovator; his motifs are the old ones, but their fusion to novel compositions shows the great artist. Several existing brocades show how far the weaver was able to follow the great painter's dream.

PERUGIA   Figure weaving was almost entirely confined to silk. In France, Flanders, *TOWELS*   and Switzerland woolen thread, beautifully spun and dyed, was finding a growing use for the weaving of tapestries. Plain linen was produced practically everywhere in Europe. Its superlative quality helped to give first place in the international markets to the linen from Reims, in northern France. The few actual specimens preserved are adorned with embroidery, or painted in black and red, sometimes in gold or silver, with patterns imitating those of Near Eastern or Lucchese silks. Neckerchiefs, veils, and wimples of gossamer fine linen are seen in many paintings.

61

Quite different from these fine linens are towels, patterned in horizontal stripes with floral and figural designs, woven with blue-dyed cotton thread. The rather coarse linen ground is generally woven in a fancy twill, the blue cotton wefts are floated, the pattern is reversible. Towels of this type may have been woven in widely distanced localities; one *176,177* especially well-designed group has been traced to Perugia, in Umbria. Here, in the fourteenth and fifteenth centuries, were woven *mantili* and *pannilini*, headcloths and towels. These are often mentioned in bills and inventories and are found represented in many guises in paintings from Duccio and Giotto to Ghirlandaio. The designs show animals and birds, confronted and addorsed, with the tree of life or with architectural structures that look not unlike the Fontana Maggiore or the Porta Eburnea, both well-known landmarks of the old hill town. Very often the griffin, the heraldic supporter of the arms of Perugia, is found. Inscriptions occur, generally strangely abbreviated, even misspelled.

178 *WOVEN* In the thirteenth and early fourteenth century the Church vestments were
ORPHREYS made of the wide variety of very beautiful, richly patterned fabrics that were then produced in the Near East, in Italy, and in Spain. Or, if made of a plain material, often damask or velvet, they were entirely covered with fine needlework. The orphreys were rather inconspicuous narrow borders with a purely decorative pattern. The later fourteenth century preferred to concentrate the decoration on wide orphreys, which then were embroidered with suitable subjects, the Crucifixion for the chasuble, the Annunciation and the Nativity for the dalmatic and the shield of the cope, single saints in an architectural framework for the vertical bands. Their exceeding costliness called for a less expensive substitute, and this was supplied in the form of woven orphreys. The endless repetition of the same scene from the New Testament or the same figure of a saint is not altogether successful as a makeshift for the diversity of the embroidered orphreys. Yet that the woven substitute was at least a passing fashion is proved by the fact that both chasubles and copes thus adorned are preserved among some of the most spectacular vestments of famous church treasures, such as those of Danzig and Halberstadt.

A Paris inventory of 1416 mentions "drap de Luques ovré à ymages de l'Annonciation Notre-Dame." Competitors of Lucca, for the designing and weaving of such orphreys, were Siena and Florence. They were woven in normal loom width, two, three, or more side by side and then cut into strips. In the early orphreys the design is woven in gold thread on red, rarely on green ground, the flesh parts are generally of white silk, small details of blue or green. In the latter part of the fifteenth century brocatelle is the preferred
207-209 technique; the surface of silk and gold is strengthened by a linen backing. The pattern stands out in yellow silk or gold twill on a red satin ground; the red warp threads are used also for the inner lines of the design. Scenes like the Resurrection of Christ and the Assumption of the Virgin were now preferred for the vertical borders: the figures could easily be arranged in tiers and were not so tedious as long rows of a single saint.

The designs were made by real artists, possibly by the assistants and pupils of great masters. The woodcut illustrations in the early books of Florence and Venice may also have been used.

PARIS AND The history of the evolution of silk weaving in the countries north of the
COLOGNE Alps is still a moot question. Precious fabrics for ecclesiastical vestments and
the costumes worn at court were imported from the Near East, Byzantium, and Italy. That there was a guild of silk weavers in Paris in the thirteenth century is positively documented by the *Ordenance du mestier des ouvriers de drap de soye de Paris*, dated 1260. But it is difficult to prove a possibly French origin for a group of preserved silk 184, 185 fabrics with scattered designs of plant forms, fleurs-de-lis, and rather heraldic-looking animals. An ivory group of the second third of the thirteenth century, in the Louvre, has been quoted as supporting the theory, but although the dress and mantle of the Virgin of the Coronation show traces of gold patterning, more pertinent proof is urgently needed. Little better is the documentation for the weaving of borders, which were produced in imitation of the famous Palermitan *aurifrisia*. Border weaving survived into the fifteenth century as a pastime for ladies. Thus it is depicted in manuscripts and tapestries, most delightfully in one of the great tapestries of the Life of the Virgin at Reims Cathedral. Here, in the very center of an allegorical representation of her Perfections, the young Mary is shown seated at a tablet loom, weaving an elaborately patterned border.

Another center of border weaving was Cologne on the Rhine. *Frixio de Alemania* is mentioned in a papal inventory of 1292; a hundred years later the King of France and his brother, the Duke of Burgundy, shared the services of a *Bordurwirker* (weaver of borders) from Cologne. The Cologne borders are more massive than those woven at Palermo and Paris, and many specimens have survived, mainly in the guise of orphreys of chasubles and copes. They are woven in a fancy compound twill, with linen warps, one linen weft that never appears on the surface and a ground weft in plain or herringbone twill of a locally produced, generally badly tarnished gold thread. Extra wefts of colored silks are introduced where they are needed for the design, and small details are sometimes added with the embroidery needle. The designs include birds and animals, trees and flowers, invoca- 187 tions of saints and sacred monograms, single figures of saints and simple compositions, such 195 as the Annunciation and the Crucifixion. Coats of arms are sometimes accompanied by 227 the donor's name. This industry flourished from the thirteenth to the fifteenth century.

THE A similar adulteration of a silk fabric with a linen backing is found in a 188, 189
"REGENS- group of textiles of the period of transition from Romanesque to Gothic.
BURG" The thrifty use of silk seems to point to a place of manufacture far from an
BROCADES easy supply of the raw material. As such a place Otto von Falke chose
Regensburg, chief center of the Danube trade with the Levant, connected with Venice by an excellent road across the Alps, by similar roads with all the Hanseatic

towns of the German empire. Falke reasoned thus: in the third quarter of the nineteenth century there was discovered in the chapel of the bishops' castle near Regensburg a strange fabric that ought to have been woven as a tapestry rather than on a shuttle loom. Woven to hang above an altar, it was later cut down for use as an antependium. Even so, the mutilated fabric measures more than a yard in height by almost three yards in width. Preserved is the Crucifixion with part of the right side and the entire left side. Here, next to St. Peter, is the kneeling donor, named in an inscription at his side as the bishop Henry (1277–1296), who, according to a contemporary chronicler, endowed the Cathedral of Regensburg with many fine altar furnishings. It seems plausible that this unique fabric was designed and woven at Regensburg, possibly in the monastery of St. Emmeram. To the same workshop may be assigned several other fabrics, with representations of the Nativity, the Virgin and Child with saints or angels, all designed in the style of about 1280 and preserved in German churches or monasteries. The figures of these fabrics are sturdy and show a relation to Byzantine provincial art.

But Falke did not accept the theory of production of this group of fabrics at St. Emmeram; for him the Regensburg industry assumed an international character, derived from Venice, introduced and periodically strengthened by immigrant Venetian weavers. This enabled him to assemble a strange medley of designs, provided the fabrics were woven in the characteristic technique. He adduced two literary sources: in the twelfth century in a statute of the Cluniacense order the Abbot Peter Venerabilis forbids his monks the use of *scarlatas aut barracanos vel pretiosos burellos qui Ratisponi fiunt;* and in the thirteenth century Wolfram von Eschenbach, the greatest poet of medieval Germany, praises the *zendel* fabrics of Regensburg. But the *barracanos* may have been brightly dyed woolen cloths; and *zendel, cendal,* was a strongly woven, thin silk fabric of light weight, used for banners and pennons and quilted linings. Both these types of fabrics were probably traded in the shops of Regensburg; but they are quite different from the stiff, linen-backed silk fabrics of Falke's classification. These may have been produced in several widely spaced weaving centers. The technical similarity with the Cologne borders gives plausibility to that city's claim. Falke himself makes it clear that apart from the characteristic technique he would find it difficult to assign to Regensburg rather than to Italy fabrics like the Falconer on Horseback (London, Victoria and Albert Museum), the Ascension of Alexander the Great (Berlin), and the Griffins in Roundels (Siegburg). Lately the royal tombs of Las Huelgas, Burgos, have yielded a number of such fabrics. This rather upsets the theory of a linen backing of silk fabrics for economy's sake; surely silk was not so scarce in Christian Spain in the period of the reconquest that the tomb vestments of princes and princesses should not have been made of pure silk brocades. The other type must have been a temporary fashion.

The "Regensburg" question has lately tended to become acrimonious. This is all the more regrettable as neither side has definite proof for its claims. At the very least, the theory of Otto von Falke has lifted from oblivion a group of rather inconspicuous and not-too-well-preserved fabrics, and drawn attention to the innate charm of their design.

RENAIS-
SANCE
AND
BAROQUE

The fifteenth century witnessed a change as fundamental as the breaking up of the Roman Empire had brought to pass a thousand years earlier. The old institutions had outlived their usefulness. The Church had grown from apostolic poverty to great splendor, but it had lost its spiritual prestige. Feudal society vainly clung to its prerogatives; it vanished before the rapid growth of civic power. Even though, in the eyes of the French or English nobility, the leaders of Florentine society were merely wool or silk merchants not to be treated as equals, it was from small city republics such as Florence that those ideas emanated which culminated in the Renaissance.

Italy

It was a period of exhaustless energy, which found its finest outlet in great works of art. The architects explored the principles of Vitruvius; the sculptors were inspired by the timely recovery of important works of the Hellenistic period; the painters once more looked on Man as the center of the universe. And all the arts came forward to cater to Man, surround him with the best in their power. Foremost was textile art. Confined through the Middle Ages to work to the bidding of the Church and a few ruling families, it was now the weavers' privilege to provide with fine apparel a good many men and women endowed with taste and wealth, even though sometimes lacking in the prerogatives of birth.

The new exuberance lasted well into the early part of the sixteenth century. Great artists created wonderful designs for the weavers and embroiderers. When the inevitable relaxation set in, these designs could be revamped endlessly. As already once before, when the Byzantine designers intentionally simplified the overelaborate compositions of the "Alexandrian" style, so now the Italian designers simplified the overelaborate compositions of the Lucca style. The fundamental urge toward pure ornament again took the lead. The designers selected the lotus palmette for a central motif and evolved a thousand and one varieties, which are generally summed up as the "pomegranate" pattern. This collective name was coined in the nineteenth century; it is only partly correct, better than the more recent name of "artichoke" pattern. The name given to these designs in old inventories, *pomme de pin* or simply *pomme*, is slightly better.

The pomegranate pattern of the Renaissance had its beginnings thousands of years earlier. The original lotus motif of early Egyptian art was changed into the more conventional palmette and used, side by side with the naturalistic pine-cone pattern, in Assyria, and thus inherited by Persia and Greece. Transplanted to China, it was reborn there as a more or less realistic lotus and as such incorporated into Islamic art. Thence it was brought to Italy, where it continued in full blossom all through the Gothic period. The Renaissance and Baroque brought the long evolution to a triumphant end.

The bold scale of these new designs made them especially suitable for velvet weaving. Destined to become the leading technique in the textile art of the sixteenth and seventeenth century, velvet appears first in the late Middle Ages. There are preserved several wonderful polychrome velvets of the latter part of the fourteenth century, and a few more are mentioned in bills and inventories. Thus King Edward III of England purchased in the year 1327 a *roba de panno velvetti viridis ad aurum*, and in 1363 the Duke of Normandy bought *deux veluiaux verdes ouvrez à arbres d'or*. These incredibly elaborate velvets were probably woven in Venice, although Lucca may have a claim to some of them. In 1421 the Venetian velvet weavers were separated into two groups, those weaving solid velvet and those weaving patterned and brocaded velvet; each group was submitted to different tests. Thirty years later, in 1452, the second group was subdivided into five categories, on complaints by the apprentices who told the guild masters that, while they could learn to perfection certain types of pattern weaving, it was impossible for them to master the whole craft.

In the latter part of the fifteenth century Florence began to compete successfully with Venice. In 1472 Benedetto Dei, chronicler of the city of Florence and a personal friend of Lorenzo de' Medici, records *Una lettera mandata a' Vinitiani*, an open letter to the Venetians who had spoken patronizingly of the Florentine merchants. The irate Florentine tells them that, "concerning silk cloths and gold and silver brocades, we make, have made, and shall always continue making much more than your city of Venice, Genoa, and Lucca together. . . . Find out from the banking houses of the Medici, Pazzi, Capponi, Buondelmonti, Corsini, Falconieri, Portinari, Ghini, of Ser Martino, Gian Perini, the Zampini, Martelli, Canigiani . . . that they do not trade in notions such as sewing thread, fringes, rosaries, glass beads, but in brocades and ducats."

The typical Renaissance textile design divides the composition into two distinct parts, an architectonic frame that builds up compartments of lanceolate arcs, and a floral decoration within the frame. Animals persist at first and appear now and then even in the sixteenth century, but the main interest of the designers rests clearly in the floral motifs. With the growth of wealth came the love for gardens. Many palaces were set in large formal gardens; but typical of the time is the *giardino segreto*, a walled-in space filled with flowers that were the owner's most private delight. To these secret gardens Persia and Asia Minor contributed their flowers, hyacinths and roses, carnations and tulips. In the portraits painted by great masters, men and women are shown holding a carnation in their hand; several painters used this flower for their signature. For textile design the carnation was found most suitable. It could be stylized more easily than any other blossom without losing its characteristic feathery silhouette.

Sometimes the velvets of the fifteenth century show only the architectural frame; the pattern is called *ferronnerie*, from a fancied similarity to wrought-iron work. Logically the gold brocaded velvets should be called *orfèvrerie*. These are often built up into compositions of undulating vertical bands that are overlaid with large leaflike motifs. From these bands grow boughs carrying pomegranates, thistles, or roses. This type of composition is exceedingly opulent, of great beauty in the hands of a true artist. The velvet is always cut, but interspersed with loops of gold thread, and the ground is generally a cloth of gold.

These diagonally designed patterns seem to have been especially favored in Burgundy; they are found in many paintings by Memling and his contemporaries.

In the sixteenth century the forms remain fundamentally the same, but tend to become heavier. The velvet shows a combination of cut and uncut loops, is ciselé. Some of the finest velvets are cut in delicate differentiation of height, pile on pile. No longer do great artists create new designs; whatever novel inspiration there is comes from the Near East, from Persia and Turkey.

Certain fabrics were made especially to the order of wealthy patrons, with coats of arms, monograms, armorial or sentimental devices.

In the seventeenth century the patterns become more tortuous. A greatly improved loom, invented by the Lyonnais Claude Dangon, facilitated the production of fabrics of most complicated effects; this resulted in an orgy of sheer technical accomplishment. Sometimes these fabrics emulate the relief effect of pressed leather. Such leather was then a magnificent but very expensive form of wall decoration. Sheets of well-tanned skins were covered with silver leaf and varnished with yellow lacquer. Then they were stamped with patterns in relief and these were painted in brilliant colors. In churches of the Baroque period leather antependia were fashionable; sometimes even chasubles were made of the heavy, stiff material. Toward the end of the seventeenth and all through the eighteenth century Italian weaving faced the suddenly successful competition of France. Venice again came to the front; this last spectacular period of her arts included her textiles, which technically emulate those of Lyons and, as works of art, often surpass them.

Spain During the long reign of Charles V (1506–1558), rich with the gold of Mexico and Peru, Spain inaugurated an era of prosperity and incomparable pomp. All the luxury industries profited, especially that of silk weaving. Very beautiful are the Mudejar fabrics, where the Muhammadan influence is still strong. Yet, largely owing to the shortsighted banishment of many master craftsmen, Spain was forced to import on a large scale silk fabrics from Italy. Many Italian fabrics of the sixteenth century are clearly designed to please the Spanish taste. The new generation of Spanish weavers copied them, often not too successfully. Yet one group of large-scale designs is magnificent; here the Spanish artist surrounds the ubiquitous pomegranate motif with elaborate arabesques, and gold and silver thread is used extravagantly, sometimes in large patches of loops. It is a clearly national style, which leads imperceptibly into Baroque, more congenial to Spanish taste than the harsh clarity of Renaissance design.   *263, 264*

The last quarter of the sixteenth century saw a fundamental change in dress fashion; the ample skirts of the ladies, the wide coats of the cavaliers, all so well suited for the display of large-patterned fabrics, gave way to rather ugly tubular skirts and skimpy tunics. These called forth a new type of textile design, small geometric or floral patterns powdered over the ground, often quite charmingly presented in cut, uncut, or ciselé velvet on satin ground. To alleviate monotony, the dyers' guilds created many new colors in subtle graduations; the weavers used these freely in often surprising combinations. This fashion lasted well into the seventeenth century.

Linen The countries north of the Alps contributed one great novelty to textile art,
Damask the weaving of linen damask for tablecloths and napkins. This was evolved in the early sixteenth century, in imitation of silk damask, in the flax-growing regions of Saxony, Flanders, and northern France. The early history of linen-damask weaving is obscure. One of the earliest references preserved mentions André Graindorge of Caen, whose linen damask was traded under the name of "Grand Caen." In the latter part of the sixteenth and all through the seventeenth century it was a very profitable industry in Flanders and Holland. How greatly the housewives esteemed their beautiful table linen can be seen in many paintings by Pieter de Hooch and others. Holland succumbed to the competition of Saxony, Belgium, and Ireland, where the weavers were paid smaller wages and often were recruited from among the inmates of monasteries and similar institutions.

281   A special style of design was evolved, possibly by borrowing from the early woodcuts of the Flemish and German schools. The subjects were chosen mainly from the Old and New Testaments and sometimes resemble the woven orphreys of Florence. Armorial de-
282 vices and trophies, sometimes accompanied by lengthy inscriptions, were woven to the order of wealthy patrons.

FRANCE About the middle of the seventeenth century France took the lead in textile
AND art. Magnificent tapestries were woven at the Gobelins', Beauvais, and
ENGLAND Aubusson; laces of unrivaled beauty were made at Alençon and Argentan.
IN THE 17th But of even greater importance were the silk fabrics woven at Lyons. All
AND 18th these improvements in national craft were owing to the genius of one man,
CENTURIES the minister of finance of Louis XIV, Jean-Baptiste Colbert (1619–1683).
    But the reason underlying all Colbert's endeavors, the fear of good money going abroad—in this case to the Netherlands for tapestries, to Italy for laces and silks—was much older. Rulers of vision, such as Louis XI (1461–1483), Francis I (1515–1547), and Henry IV (1589–1610), tried to stop it by extending their patronage to the home crafts. Louis XI chose first Lyons, then Tours, as the center of silk weaving, inviting Italian weavers and granting them many privileges. Francis I definitely established the silk industry at Lyons. The religious wars of the succeeding fifty years almost annihilated its progress, until Henry IV assured freedom of belief to the many Huguenot silk weavers by the promulgation of the Edict of Nantes in 1598. The revocation of this edict in 1685 caused many thousands of silk weavers to migrate to Switzerland, Holland, and especially to England, where in 1629 a corporation of Protestant weavers had been established at the village of Spitalfields, close to the eastern wall of London, by Jan van Stryp, a silk throwster of Brabant. Strype Street and Fleur-de-lys Street recall the Flemish and French refugees.

The weavers from Lyons quickly learned to adapt their designs to the English taste, and all through the eighteenth century they were fairly prosperous, selling their "brocade lutstring," "tobine," "flowered tabby," "four-combed damask," and other quaintly named silks to mercers and private patrons. 283–288

Their prosperity was short-lived. The early nineteenth century saw a steady decline. The younger men found better-paid work in the weaving districts of northern England. Only the elderly people remained who could not adapt themselves to work at power looms. The tradition of Spitalfields silk weaving was carried on, but the once gracious cottage industry came to its natural end when the last of the old weavers laid down his tools.

Lyons   In the eighteenth century Lyons became the center of silk production because the technical skill of the weavers was supported by the beauty of the designs, provided by artists who were in close touch with the industry. Jacques Savary, in his *Dictionnaire universel du commerce*, published in 1726, says that at Lyons a good designer was considered "the soul of the establishment." The great accomplishment of these designers was the introduction of flowers designed from life. In the period of Louis XIV (1643–1715), the flowers were larger than nature, sometimes of almost gigantic size and completely covering the surface. Yet for special occasions of state even these strongly colored, spectacular brocades were not deemed sufficient to serve as a background for the *Roi Soleil;* only the most resplendent gold and silver brocades would do. Madame de Sévigné, witty and observant, describes a dress worn by Montespan, the King's mistress, as "gold upon gold, embroidered with gold, overspun with gold, all combining to make the most divine material ever invented."

During the reign of Louis XV (1723–1774) flowers remained the chief element of the decoration of silk textiles; one great designer, Joubert de l'Hiberderie (1715–1770), even calls that period "The Empire of Flora." The flowers, culled from gardens and meadows and from the ever-growing literature of botany, were represented in their natural size and color. *Dans le goût des Gobelins*, Courteois called them; he died in 1750, but the good work was carried on by Ringuet (1721–1769). These artists used three tones of each color, the middle tone as *couleur locale*, the light and dark tones for giving plasticity. Meanwhile Jean Revel (1684–1751) invented a process of weaving called *point d'entré* or *point berclé*. This was the use of two tones of a color, freely as with an embroidery needle. The paler shade entered the darker at irregular intervals, with the effect of a light stroke of the painter's brush. Revel was a painter himself and specialized in designs of fantastic flowers. He is credited also with the invention of the *mise en carte*, the design painted on a graph paper where each line and square represents a warp and a weft thread. But geometrical charts showing the interplay of warp and weft threads must have been used ever since the invention of the drawloom; Revel may have given them a more spectacular appearance.

The designs interspersed among the flowers add greatly to the beauty of these brocades. Toward the end of the period of Louis XIV the robust masculinity of the silk designs shows a certain moderation. The years of the Regency (1715–1723) brought a foretaste of the gaiety that was to be the main characteristic of the Lyons silks of Louis XV. Then it was that all things charmingly effeminate were brought together, floating ribbons, laces curving between the bouquets, and, in honor of Queen Maria Leszczynska, even bands of fur and feather boas.

Chinese motifs became fashionable and, blended with the sea-shell curves of the Rococo, were travestied into *chinoiserie*. This latest fashion reached Lyons through the paintings and designs of Jean Pillement (1728–1808). For a time he was employed as a designer by the Manufacture des Gobelins; again he created the designs of some of the most beautiful and most amusing *toiles de Jouy*. His whimsical inventions have a charm and grace that make them delightful for all time. Pillement's influence went beyond France; he published album after album of his designs and through these reached the designers of textiles, wallpapers, and porcelains of all the countries of western Europe. But an art as artificial as *chinoiserie* could not last long; the magic world where men and women tried to look like porcelain figurines came to an abrupt end, even before the death of Louis XV.

Greatest of all the silk artists of Lyons was Philippe de Lassalle (1723–1803). His teachers were Daniel Sarrabat at Lyons, Bachelier and Boucher in Paris. Charryé, a designer-manufacturer, induced him to return to Lyons, where he became Charryé's partner and son-in-law. Later he joined the firm of Camille Pernon (1753–1808), who, among the silk manufacturers of Lyons, stands supreme as the champion of taste and quality. And now Lassalle designed wonderful brocades, for Louis XV and his father-in-law, the exiled King of Poland, Stanislas Leszczynski, for Louis XVI and Marie Antoinette, for Catherine the Great of Russia, and for the court of Spain. Louis XVI gave him the order of St. Michael, and everything must have looked rosy, when the Revolution brought absolute, complete ruin. Lassalle could not adjust himself to the changed taste of the Directoire and Empire, and for the last ten years of his life he eked out a miserable existence working on improvements of the loom in a garret allotted to him by the city of Lyons.

314–321 Philippe de Lassalle was the ideal combination of artist and craftsman; equally skilled as a designer and a weaver, he created his masterworks from the first pencil sketch to the finished fabric. He did not like the obtrusive gleam of metal thread and used only silks and chenille thread. He began with purely floral designs; then he interspersed his garlands, bouquets, and festoons with groups of musical instruments, birds and animals and pastoral motifs. To him the style of Louis XVI owes what it has of grandeur.

The exuberance of multicolored floral design had reached its apogee with the brocades of Philippe de Lassalle. The fashion prevailing in France in the years before the outbreak of the Revolution was toward an artificial simplicity, sponsored by the writings of Jean-Jacques Rousseau. Dress fashion still called for figured silks; but a less expensive type, striped patterns interspersed with scattered flowers on a small scale, superseded the spectacular designs of the Rococo period. Even these relatively simple silks suffered from the competition of the fashion for batiste and printed cottons, sponsored by Marie Antoinette.

The monochromy of the roller-printed *toiles de Jouy* cast a blight over the silk trade. For curtains and hangings Lyons devised a special technique, *lampas*, which showed the design *en camaieu*, in the manner of a cameo, on a brilliantly colored ground. Lampas looks somewhat like a two-color damask, but it is not reversible. It is a fancy compound satin, strengthened by a secondary warp, the design is in twill of two wefts, generally of slightly contrasting ivory shades. Lampas was well suited to the weaving of designs *à la grecque*. This fashion, which was owing to some extent to the excitement over the discovery of Pompeii and Herculaneum, even survived the Revolution. The neoclassic designs were greatly to the taste of the Directoire. Napoleon's government promoted silk weaving, which soon became one of the great sources of national wealth. But now it was changed from a craft to an industry, catering to a new type of customer, the well-to-do middle class. Huge quantities of lightweight, prettily patterned fabrics were produced on the Jacquard looms, especially when these were fully mechanized and power-driven.

But there remained hundreds of weavers who were too old to learn the new ways of working at the looms. It became the task of the great merchants and manufacturers to devise ways and means of keeping these last representatives of the great craft occupied. Among these manufacturers Camille Pernon stands supreme. At every court of Europe, *325* from Spain to Russia, his agents solicited and secured orders for magnificent fabrics, to be woven on hand looms. Another great manufacturer interested in upholding quality and distinction was Natalis Rondot (1823–1900), the historian of the great craft of Lyons, the founder of the magnificent Textile Museum of that city.

These manufacturer-merchants were supported by excellent designers. First among these ranks Jean François Bony (1754–1825). For the curtains and wall coverings of Napoleon's palaces of Saint-Cloud and Malmaison he designed a series of patterns in a neoclassic mode that helped in the creation of the Empire style. Palm leaves, lyres, vases, cornucopias, garlands of laurel and oak, bees and eagles, and, always prominently, the initial "N," were the ingredients of the new textile style. For dress fabrics patterns of a lighter vein were preferred. Sometimes they were printed on the warp before weaving; the floral designs by Antoine Berjon (1754–1843) lent themselves well for this technique, the *chiné* taffeta. Waistcoats and belts received the special attention of Pierre-Toussaint Déchazelle (1751–1833), whose miniature designs were woven in velvet, generally on a rep ground. Gaspard Grégoire (1751–1846) also specialized in a peculiar velvet technique, painting his designs on the velvet warps before weaving. This involved elaborate calculations and, since the artist destroyed his papers before his death, the charming velvet pictures known as "velours Grégoire" have remained unique.

CATALOGUE

1. WOOL TAPESTRY. A WOMAN'S HEAD

SYRIA OR EGYPT, 3RD—4TH CENTURY, POSSIBLY EARLIER. THE DETROIT INSTITUTE OF ARTS.

6¾ x 4¾ in. (17 x 12 cm.). No. 35.103. Provenance: Egypt. Exhibited: Brooklyn, 1941, cat. no. 231, pp. 46, 74; *Masterpieces of the Weaver's Art*, Grand Rapids, 1941, no. 1; Baltimore, 1947, cat. no. 820. Published: A. C. Weibel, "A Fragment of Hellenistic Wool Tapestry," *Bulletin* XV, 1936, p. 83; A. C. Weibel, "Hellenistic and Coptic Textiles," *The Art Quarterly*, XI, 1948, p. 106.

Linen warp, polychrome wool wefts, very finely woven. The woman's head, about half life size, is shown in practically front view, turned almost imperceptibly toward the right shoulder. This very slight turn receives a sharp accent by the deep-set golden-brown eyes, half veiled by heavy lids, turned to the extreme angle. The finely designed nose and the slightly open mouth, the shapely full chin, the wide low brow, all contribute to give to the picture the character of a portrait. The hair, chestnut with reddish lights, is parted in the center and arranged in a series of wavy locks covering the ears and forming a loop of the Apollo Belvedere type. A golden taenia set with a large red stone and a single earring with two pearls pendant bear out the general impression of fastidious moderation, a subtlety observed also in the simplicity of the dress, of which only one shoulder strap is preserved. The round nimbus marks the portrait as of the idealized rather than realistic type.

The modeling is achieved by imperceptible grades of shading, a perfect illustration of the old Roman term, *acu pingere*, with the reservation that it is not "needle painting," but "loom painting," a woven picture. The delicate violet and pinkish-purple accents around the neck and nose become more pronounced on the eyelids and, with the straight line of the lashes, give the portrait a tragic, almost sinister character. Our fancy strays to famous unhappy rather wicked great women known to history and legend, but we need not feel bound to attach any special name to the portrait.

Both technical and aesthetic reasons lead us to place this fragment very early. For an early date speaks also the refinement of almost impressionistic indetermination, a hankering toward Scopasian expression, the feeling of *Weltschmerz* so characteristic of the later Hellenistic period. Fabrics of such surpassing quality are always exceptional; but the tradition of shading from one color to another survived in Syria. Simple bands of two-shaded colors have been found at Palmyra and Dura-Europos.

2. WOOL TAPESTRY. ROSES

SYRIA, DURA-EUROPOS, BEFORE A.D. 256. NEW HAVEN, YALE UNIVERSITY ART GALLERY.

9 x 12½ in. (22.9 x 31 cm.). No. 1933.487, no. 140 in the catalogue. Published: *The Excavations at Dura-Europos*, conducted by Yale University and the French Academy of Inscriptions and Letters. Final Report IV, Part II, "The Textiles," by R. Pfister and Louisa Bellinger, New Haven, Yale University Press, 1945.

"Tapestry over one warp of tan wool. On a green ground staggered rows of shaded quatrefoil roses. The weaving is very fine. The rose petals are shaded from a dark red at the outside through two shades of pink to white and finally a blue or pink center surrounded by tan, the different shades being sharply defined. The shadings in the warp direction are straight; those in the weft direction curved. Next the warp cord, an apricot band 1.2 cm. wide. The elements of the pattern are later repeated in innumerable examples of textiles found in Egypt" (L. Bellinger).

3. WOOL TAPESTRY. NEREIDS

COPTIC, 5TH CENTURY. WASHINGTON, D. C., DUMBARTON OAKS RESEARCH LIBRARY AND COLLECTION, HARVARD UNIVERSITY.

32½ x 56¾ in. (82 x 144 cm.). No. 32.1. Provenance: Antinoë. Exhibited: Paris, the Louvre, 1931, *Exposition d'Art byzantin*, cat. no. 734; Worcester, 1937, cat. no.

138. Published: Peirce and Tyler, *L'Art byzantin*, I, 87, pls. 141 and 142; Dumbarton Oaks *Handbook*, 1946, no. 241.

The parts of three sides of a wide border frame a field where, on a brilliant red ground, two figures are confronted astride sea monsters. The border is designed with curving acanthus leaves, forming compartments where birds, quails, and quinea fowl are recognizable. The border is finished on both sides with a tassel ornament.

"The subject seems to be a confusion of the theme current in late antique art of Nereids riding on sea monsters and the story of Europa. Jupiter, as is well known, borrowed the form of a bull and swam, carrying off Europa, from Sidon to the island of Crete. This incident furnished to Nonnus, a native of Akhmîm, the opening scene of his *Dionysiaca*, a huge epic poem widely known in the fifth century. The other personage holds up a mirror. Perhaps she is Venus? Or, simply one of the Nereids of Europa's cortege?" (Peirce and Tyler). The latter theory seems more likely. Another fragment of the tapestry has been acquired by Dumbarton Oaks (no. 34.2). It shows, with a part of the same framing border, a Nereid holding up a jeweled torque. Thus the two figures are clearly marked as attendants of the princess Europa.

4. *WOOL TAPESTRY. ATTENDANT NEREID*

COPTIC, 4TH–5TH CENTURY. WASH-INGTON, D. C., DUMBARTON OAKS RESEARCH LIBRARY AND COLLEC-TION, HARVARD UNIVERSITY.

25½ x 23⅝ in. (58 x 50½ cm.). No. 34.2. For description see Fig. 3.

5. *WOOL TAPESTRY. MASK AND DUCK*

COPTIC, 4TH–5TH CENTURY. WASH-INGTON, D. C., DUMBARTON OAKS RESEARCH LIBRARY AND COLLEC-TION, HARVARD UNIVERSITY.

13 x 8¼ in. (33 x 20½ cm.). No. 46.16. Published: *Acquisitions*, 1946–47.

On rose ground a network of jeweled bands, framing the frontal head or mask of a woman, and a duck.

6. *WOOL TAPESTRY. PASTORAL SCENE*

HELLENISTIC, 3RD–4TH CENTURY. CITY ART MUSEUM OF ST. LOUIS.

13¼ x 13½ in. (33½ x 34 cm.). No. 48.39. Provenance: Akhmîm. Exhibited: Brooklyn, 1941, cat. no. 182. Published: Thomas Whittemore, "Two Coptic Cloths," in *Studies Presented to F. L. L. Griffith*, London, 1932, p. 384; City Art Museum of St. Louis, *Handbook of the Collections*, 1944, p. 5.

Linen warp, blue and red wool and linen wefts. A bearded man is milking a goat; her kid stands beside her. From a fairly naturalistic grapevine hangs an amphora-shaped vessel, possibly a milk jar. The uniform dark blue is accentuated by the red beaks and feet of the confronted birds in the border vine. The goat lacks one hindleg, probably because either the designer or the weaver decided that it would interfere with the clarity of the composition.

Pastoral scenes were a fashionable theme of Hellenistic art. The bucolic idyls of Theocritus and Virgil provided new themes for the sculptor and painter. In the guise of illustrations of Christ's parables, the bucolic element entered Christian art. On the other hand, the romantic appeal of the "simple life" occurs whenever a society becomes effete. As a spiritual companion to this pastoral scene, attention is called to the little lamb, so delightfully portrayed, possibly for Marie Antoinette, by Philippe de Lassalle (Fig. 320).

7. *SILK AND LINEN TAPESTRY. A HORSEMAN*

EGYPT, HELLENISTIC, 4TH–5TH CENTURY. BOSTON, MUSEUM OF FINE ARTS.

3¾ in. square (9½ cm.). No. 35.87. Exhibited: Brooklyn, 1941, cat. no. 201. Published: an identical specimen in the Victoria and Albert Museum, Kendrick, *Catalogue*, I, 66, pl. XIV; and Dalton, *Byzantine Art*, p. 81, fig. 46, there dated 6th century.

Square with fruits and water birds catching fish; in center a horseman. Ground, pale bluish green; design, red and white.

Very fine work.

8. *SILK TAPESTRY. A FALCONER*

SYRIA, 5TH–6TH CENTURY. THE CLEVELAND MUSEUM OF ART.

3 x 2¾ in. (7½ x 7 cm.). No. 41.293. Exhibited: Baltimore, 1947, cat. no. 764.

Red, green, buff, and black silks; silk warp. A youth, dressed in short tunic and flying scarf, Phrygian cap and high-laced boots, runs at top speed, looking backward and swinging a falconer's lure on a long string. On the ground lies a double ax; a cloud (?) motif serves as a space filler. The border is a broken wave.

It is possibly the contrast between this classical border and the baroque turmoil of the composition that makes this small medallion so pleasing. The colors are distributed in even proportions, as by a painter of enamels. It is a shock to see the figure rise almost to three-dimensionality, in a *contrapposto* so perfect that it bridges the thousand years to the youthful Michelangelo's first creation, *The Battle of Centaurs and Lapiths.*

This is also one of the earliest illustrations of falconry. The *arte venandi cum avibus* was the true sport of kings; it has inspired textile design to a far-greater extent than has any other form of sport. Here the last phase of the hunt is illustrated: when the falcon has seized his victim the huntsman swings the "lure"; the bird is trained to drop his prey and return to his master, where he will be permitted to eat the meat—generally a pigeon—fastened to the "lure."

9. *WOOL TAPESTRY. BUCOLIC SCENES*

HELLENISTIC, 5TH CENTURY. NEW YORK CITY, THE BROOKLYN MUSEUM.

4¾ x 4½ in. (12 x 11½ cm.). No. 44.143.C. Provenance: Said to come from Antinoë. One of four roundels.

Exhibited: Worcester, 1937, cat. no. 136; Baltimore, 1947, cat. no. 755. Mentioned by Adolf Goldschmidt in his review of the Worcester exhibition, *Parnassus*, IX, no. 3 (1937), 29. Published: Gerard Brett, "The Brooklyn Textiles and the Great Palace Mosaic," *Coptic Studies in Honor of Walter Ewing Crum*, The Byzantine Institute, Boston, 1950, p. 435.

Wool and linen tapestry on linen warps, extraordinary fine weave. Red ground; border a broken wave pattern, white on green. Colors of design: blue, tan, deep brownish-red, two shades of green and black. The designs are closely related to the illustrations in Virgil manuscripts. In the upper half a group of three figures is seen picnicking on the grass beneath trees. They are intently watched by a bird and two dogs; one of these sits up, begging. The lower half, the foreground, shows two servants, one of them tending a fire beneath a pot, the other dipping into a wine-skin; between them stands a wine cooler with the neck of a bottle protruding.

10. *WOOL TAPESTRY. BUCOLIC SCENES*

HELLENISTIC, 5TH CENTURY. NEW YORK CITY, THE BROOKLYN MUSEUM.

4⅞ x 4¼ in. (12¼ x 11 cm.). No. 44.143.B. Companion to no. 44.143.C., Fig. 9.

In the upper center a woman is seated cross-legged, nursing a child. She looks toward a well where a young man draws water to fill a trough. Cows are drinking; sheep are huddled in the foreground, awaiting their turn. An old man watches, leaning against a small tree.

11. *WOOL AND GOLD TAPESTRY. NECK ORNAMENT*

HELLENISTIC, 5TH CENTURY. BOSTON, MUSEUM OF FINE ARTS.

Total length 22½ in. (57 cm.). No. 46.401. Published: Gertrude Townsend, "Two Fragments of Late Hellenistic Tapestry," *Bulletin*, XLVI (1948), 12.

Warp, wool; wefts, gold thread and wool. "The gold thread appears to be a natural alloy of gold with approximately five per cent silver and one per cent copper. The metal is wound directly on a silk core." About fifteen warps to the centimeter, the designs woven in gold thread and a little color against a background of deep purple. "The fact that the pendant panels differ in size suggests the possibility that they were worn with one ornament hanging in front, the other behind." The connecting bands look like a very elaborate necklace. On each band a central ornament of three masks is flanked by ornaments that look like gold filigree. The central masks are crowned with ribboned wreaths and flanked by masks wearing Phrygian caps; perhaps this is a princess with her bodyguard of Amazons. The composition is framed by strings of beads and cabochon gems cased in gold. A similar arrangement of beads and gold-cased gems frames the composition of the smaller pendant (4¾ x 5 in.; 12 x 13 cm.) "Hatching, one of the chief technical resources of the tapestry weaver in medieval Europe, has been used to suggest the light and brilliance of precious stones." A sea-centaur swims through the waves, holding a rudder over his shoulder, watching intently something beyond the beholder's vision.

The larger pendant (6⅜ x 6 in.; 16 x 15 cm.) pictures a sea-thiasos. "One might be led to associate it with compositions on a much larger scale such as those found in surviving examples of wall paintings and mosaics in Pompeii, Herculaneum and Antioch. . . . Though this panel is worn, and though some parts have been torn, the subtle richness of the design and the skill of the weaver still bring wonder and delight. Nereids, a sea horse, attendant Tritons, Erotes and dolphins, woven chiefly in gold thread with touches of delicate fresh color, almost fill the panel, leaving only small patches of dark neutral purple as a background. There is no definite line between sea and air, but light on moving water is vividly suggested by wavy horizontal lines and small areas of color, and water running over the fingers of the Triton in the lower right

hand corner is indicated by the introduction of a few threads of the dark purple ground, thus breaking the continuity of the flesh. In the graceful curve of the drapery held by the figure in the upper left hand corner there is a suggestion of moving air. The delicate realism of the figures which compose this group is produced not by the modeling of flesh tones or by light and shade, for the flesh is all woven with gold thread. Even the hair is for the most part gold, and the features and the softness of flesh are suggested only by a sensitive fluid line. Color is sparingly used to enhance the subject, not to portray it literally" (G. Townsend).

12. *WOOL AND GOLD TAPESTRY. NECK ORNAMENT*

HELLENISTIC, 5TH CENTURY. BOSTON, MUSEUM OF FINE ARTS.

Total length 20 in. (51 cm.). No. 46.402. Published: Gertrude Townsend, "Two Fragments of Late Hellenistic Tapestry," *Bulletin*, XLVI (1948), 12.

Warp, linen; wefts, gold thread, wool, and a little silk. "The gold thread appears to be a natural alloy of gold with approximately five per cent silver and one per cent copper. The metal is wound directly on a silk core." About fifteen warps to the centimeter, the designs woven in gold thread and a little color against a background of deep neutral purple. "The fact that the pendant panels differ in size suggests the possibility that they were worn with one ornament hanging in front, the other behind. . . . A necklace of colored stones set in gold, and terminating with a loop and hook with which to fasten it, is represented on each of the connecting bands." The smaller panel is square (3½ in.; 8¾ cm.). An octagonal frame is formed by a narrow golden band, or stylized garland with palmette leaves. Magnificent is the bust portrait of Dionysus. He is clad only in the skin of a jaguar, but it is fastened at the shoulder with a hexagonal pin of a type known from consular diptychs. Over his flowing golden locks he wears a horned crown and a garland of leaves and flowers. He carries the thyrsus like a scepter.

The larger panel is octagonal in outline (4½ in.; 11½ cm.). "The scene represented can be identified by the names Ariadne and Dionysus in Greek letters woven into the background. The slender stylized figure of Dionysus crowned with vine leaves rises above the reclining figure of Ariadne, now, alas, headless. In this scene, represented repeatedly in painting and mosaic, Dionysus discovers Ariadne asleep on the island of Naxos. It is here that according to a popular legend the daughter of Minos, King of Crete, was abandoned by Theseus. Is the slender object in the hand of Dionysus the traditional staff or thyrsus, or has he picked up from the shore of Naxos the thread which Ariadne had given to Theseus to guide him from the Cretan labyrinth after he had slain the Minotaur?" (G. Townsend).

As specimens of supreme achievement in the oldest weaving technique, these two lovely examples of Hellenistic art are unsurpassed. The designs used by the weavers are quite different. The panels with the sea-thiasos and sea-centaur are neo-Attic. But to what school does the severe stylization combined with the sensuous attraction of the Dionysus and Ariadne panels belong? I call it Alexandrian simply because to me it embodies all the sophisticated luxury that magic name implies.

13. TWO FRAGMENTS OF A TAPESTRY HANGING. THE RUNAWAY PONY

COPTIC, 5TH CENTURY. THE CLEVELAND MUSEUM OF ART.

16½ x 12 in. (42 x 30½ cm.). No. 48.27. Published: Dorothy G. Shepherd, "A Sixth-Century Coptic Tapestry Roundel," *Bulletin*, XXXV (1948), p. 56; Peirce and Tyler, *L'Art byzantin*, Paris, 1934, vol. II, pl. 57a.

A horse, fully saddled and harnessed, on a red background with a free suggestion of landscape. Border of heart-shaped petals and two double crescent motives. Traces of fruit baskets on the beige ground, small parts missing.

14. TWO FRAGMENTS OF A TAPESTRY HANGING. THE RUNAWAY PONY

COPTIC, 5TH CENTURY. BALTIMORE, WALTERS ART GALLERY.

15½ x 17¾ in. (39 x 45 cm.). No. 83.461. Exhibited: Brooklyn, 1941, cat. no. 240.

An almost identical specimen, with one complete fruit basket and parts of two birds preserved. The left side of the roundel with the horse's tail is restored, probably with threads from yet another fragment.

These two horses obviously belonged to one large curtain or hanging, where the roundels were widely spaced. It must have been a delightful composition, by a good designer. But the real charm of the lovely creatures is probably the contribution of the weaver, who ingeniously varied their expression. The Baltimore pony has just run away and is tasting the sweetness of liberty; his stable mate in Cleveland sees the groom who will try to catch him. The pony continues running in full stride, but throws back his head with a startled look in his beautiful eye. This look is unforgettable. The two fragments belong to the most distinguished works of Coptic weaving.

15. WOOL TAPESTRY. BOAR HUNT

COPTIC, 4TH–5TH CENTURY. WASHINGTON, D. C., DUMBARTON OAKS RESEARCH LIBRARY AND COLLECTION, HARVARD UNIVERSITY.

37 x 32 in. (94 x 81½ cm.). No. 37.14. Provenance: Antinoitis. Published: Dumbarton Oaks *Handbook*, 1946, no. 247.

The composition is practically square, perhaps slightly elongated in the process of weaving. The red field is edged and horizontally divided by bands of stylized foliage, with quatrefoil blossoms at the corners and angles. A landscape is indicated by a few plants, which also serve as space fillers. Two hunting scenes are superimposed. Above, an archer raises his right hand, which may have held a knife, to ward off a rearing lion; in his left hand he holds his bow and two arrows. Below, the attacking boar faces at close range an arrow on drawn bow. The archer is blond and blue-eyed, like the Venus-Nereid (Fig. 4.). The archers wear short tunics over breeches, edged and banded with a contrasting fabric. One archer's shoes are preserved; with heels and straps across the instep, they look very fragile. The entire scene shows in its astonishing realism the influence of Sassanian prototypes. But the wide framing border is clearly Egyptian. It is a Nilotic scene with crawfish among aquatic plants, and fishes swimming in the greenish water.

16. LOOPED BROCADING. AN ACOLYTE

COPTIC, 5TH CENTURY. BOSTON, MUSEUM OF FINE ARTS.

50½ x 37¼ in. (128 x 94½ cm.). No. 49.313.

On a ground of brownish linen the design is woven in loops of wool, white, pink, two shades of red, two purples, three greens, yellow, and orange. The composition is complete. In an aedicula, consisting of a ceiled and gabled roof supported by columns with bases, capitals, and ornamental rings, stands a man, blue-eyed and blond-haired. The right hand holds a staff (emblem of office?), the left raises a libation bowl. He is dressed in a long-sleeved belted tunic, black and white leggings, and red shoes. The ground around him is spotted with roses.

The man may be a steward or a cupbearer; more likely he is an acolyte serving in a temple.

17. WOOL BROCADING. AN ORANT

COPTIC, 5TH CENTURY. THE DETROIT INSTITUTE OF ARTS.

27½ x 25 in. (70 x 63½ cm.). No. 46.75. Provenance: Akhmîm. Exhibited: *Tapis et Tapisseries d'Orient de haute époque*, Paris, 1934, cat. no. 150; Baltimore, 1947, cat. no. 793. Published: Jean Pozzi, "A propos de la récente exposition des Gobelins," *Gazette des Beaux-Arts*, October, 1934; Adèle Coulin Weibel, "Hellenistic and Coptic Textiles," *The Art Quarterly*, XI (1948), p. 106.

Curtains and hangings sometimes show the design raised over the linen ground in a shaggy cut pile. This is achieved by brocading the pile wefts in between the selvage-to-selvage wefts, as on this large fragment of a curtain. Between the columns of an arcade stands a young woman, almost a child, in the attitude of prayer. Thoughtfully she looks at the beholder, her hands are raised, her feet encased in black shoes grip the soil. On either side stand vases, each with one long-stemmed flower, probably a lily, of which mere traces remain. The arch and columns are richly polychrome with jewel effects, a favorite type of ornamentation in early Christian Egypt. The design is of red, dark-blue, yellow, green, and black wool and white linen cut pile. Red is the color prevailing in the costume, the ankle-length tunic with long sleeves, *tunica manicata*, and the cowl, *maphorion;* checkered black and white are the shoulder and wrist bands, and the fringe around the medallion at her neck. This may be a *bulla* of horn, such as have been found in many tombs in the cemeteries of Akhmîm. They show incised representations of the Nativity and Baptism of Christ and may have been worn as amulets. White also are the two blossoms that relieve the monotony of the simple headcloth.

The beautiful figure may represent the soul of the dead woman entering paradise in the attitude of praying, offering thanks to God. Or she may be *euche*, prayer personified. The noble gesture is very old; it occurs in Greek and Egyptian antiquity. Tertullian (*c.* 155–*c.* 222) sees in it a symbolic connection with the Crucifixion. The date of this important fabric rests somewhere between the fourth and fifth century. Remarkable both technically and aesthetically, it also has the advantage of a pedigree, since it is known to have been discovered in a tomb of the cemetery of Sheik Sayet near Akhmîm. Akhmîm is one of the very earliest known centers of weaving, whether as Khen-min in Pharaonic times, as Chemmis or Panopolis during the Ptolemaic and Roman period, or as the Coptic Schmin and finally the Arab Akhmîm.

18. *WOOL TAPESTRY. A PORTRAIT*

COPTIC, 4TH CENTURY. THE DE-TROIT INSTITUTE OF ARTS.

10½ x 7½ in. (26½ x 18¼ cm.). No. 46.76. Exhibited: Baltimore, 1947, cat. no. 782. Published: Adèle Coulin Weibel, "Hellenistic and Coptic Textiles," *The Art Quarterly*, XI (1948), p. 106.

Bust portrait of a man. He is dressed in a white tunic with dark blue clavi, of the severe type of *tunica angusticlavia;* a pallium of palest pink hangs over his shoulders. A napkin with red and blue stripes covers the hands, which hold a book with a red cover and jeweled ornaments. The portrait is severely frontal, the head turned slightly to the left but the eyes looking straight at the beholder. The pale face is framed by dark hair and a short round, slightly curled beard, joined to narrow mustaches. The enormous eyes with arched brows, the long narrow nose, and the pinched mouth give to the face an austere expression, while the nimbus is the mark of a saintly personage. This striking portrait stands out from a background of old rose and is contained within an oval frame, like the rim of pale gold of an enameled medallion. This rests on a ground of dark blue, with lotus blossoms of white and green in the corner spandrils.

Quite obviously it is the portrait of a once well-known personality, although we are not able to give it a name. Yet at least we can date it fairly closely. In the Roman period the elaborate embalming methods of Pharaonic Egypt were discontinued. Now the dead body was strewn with granular natron, traces of which are often preserved. It was then dressed in the garments it had worn in daily life, tied to a board of sycamore wood, and wrapped in shrouds, *pallia mortuorum.* In the case of burial of important persons, these shrouds are often adorned with large medallions of tapes-

try work. The center of the shrouds is often found destroyed by the pressure of the bandages tying it to the body, while the corner medallions are apt to be preserved. Over the dead face there was often placed the portrait of the defunct person, painted on a slab of wood in encaustic or tempera. A comparison with such painted portraits permits dating the tapestry portrait to the second quarter of the fourth century. This data is supported by the evidence of the coins with portraits of the sons of Constantine and, in monumental sculpture, by the Berlin fragment of a sarcophagus with Christ and Apostles. This remarkable medallion is too large to have been part of the decoration of a garment such as the "pictured tunic" that the emperor Gratian sent, in 379, to his former tutor, the poet Ausonius, on his accession to the consulship. It seems almost too important to have been a corner ornament of a shroud. Probably it belonged to the elaborate decoration of a hanging or curtain.

19. *WOOL TAPESTRY. "SAINT THEODORE"*

COPTIC, 5TH–6TH CENTURY. CAMBRIDGE, FOGG ART MUSEUM, HARVARD UNIVERSITY.

Two panels: (*a*) Head of a Saint, *c.* 12½ x 17½ in. (32 x 45 cm.); (*b*) Decorative Motifs, *c.* 18¾ x 14½ in. (48 x 37 cm.). No. 1939.112, gift of Mrs. John D. Rockefeller, Jr. Provenance: said to have been found at Akhmîm. Exhibited: *Exposition d'Art byzantin*, Paris, 1931, cat. no. 225; Brooklyn, 1941, cat. no. 243; Baltimore, 1947, cat. no. 783. Published: W. R. Tyler, "Fragments of an Early Christian Tapestry," Fogg Art Museum *Bulletin*, IX (1939), 1–13. Mentioned: Peirce and Tyler, *L'Art byzantin*, 1932, I, 92, pl. 155; Phyllis Ackerman, *Tapestry, the Mirror of Civilization*, 1933, p. 21; David Talbot Rice, *Byzantine Art*, 1935, p. 178, pl. 41; Regina Shoolman and Charles E. Slatkin, *The Enjoyment of Art in America*, 1942, pl. 219.

When the tapestry became the property of the museum, the several fragments were assembled rather haphazardly into one panel (illus. fig. 3, Fogg Art Museum *Bulletin;* pl. 41, D. T. Rice). The regrouping and mounting in two separate panels is all the more satisfactory since a few patches of material, dissimilar in texture and obviously not belonging to the original fabric, have been eliminated. One panel (*a*) now shows, framed by a wide nimbus, a well-designed head with large eyes, long nose, traces of wavy hair, and a long pointed beard. A few folds of a cloak, fastened with a round fibula on the right shoulder, is all that remains of the Saint's body, for the hand holding a long staff topped by a jeweled cross belongs to another figure. An equally enigmatic plain staff is visible at the other side of the Saint. A second panel (*b*) shows a vine-scroll border and a heavy jeweled band. This frames an approximately triangular space with the remains of an inscription: (H)AGI(OS) THEOD(OROS). A pearl-studded segment adds one more question mark to this already puzzling ensemble.

"The type portrayed has the long features and solemnity of expression which is found in monuments of the end of the fifth and in the sixth century. . . . Apart from its aesthetic appeal, the fragment of *Saint Theodore* is of great importance and interest in that it shows us a physical type which was to survive for nearly a thousand years, and which we think of as characteristically Byzantine. It is one of the earliest surviving manifestations of a cast of countenance whose emergence seems to be related to the spiritual influence of Christianity" (W. R. Tyler).

". . . The large blue eyes stare at an ultramundane focus. . . . The carmine lips hint of sensuality. . . . It is a high-keyed, somewhat neurotic personality for whom religion is an emotional excitement, asceticism an inverse self-indulgence" (Phyllis Ackerman).

20. *WOOL TAPESTRY. PASIPHAË*

COPTIC, 5TH–6TH CENTURY. NEW YORK CITY, THE BROOKLYN MUSEUM.

Diameter: 4 in. (10 cm.). No. 15.429. Provenance: Egypt Exploration Society excavations at Antinoë, 1913–14. Exhibited: Brooklyn, 1941, cat. no. 215. Published: John D. Cooney, *Late Egyptian and Coptic Art*, Brooklyn, 1941, p. 22, pl. 46.

Warps, linen; wefts, red, rose, green, blue, yellow, black, tan, and golden-brown wool, and white linen. The roundel was woven into a yellow woolen garment. It shows on red ground two female figures, seminude, with floating draperies. One of these embraces a bull; the other, her attendant, seems to be holding a bowl and ewer.

This is probably an illustration of the old Cretan story of Pasiphaë.

21. *WOOL TAPESTRY. DANCERS*

COPTIC, 5TH–6TH CENTURY. THE DETROIT INSTITUTE OF ARTS.

4¾ x 4½ in. (12 x 11½ cm.). No. 30.244.

Linen and wool tapestry. The design in purple, details in white, flying shuttle. Two dancers in a landscape, indicated by flowery tendrils. The male dancer is nude, the female has draperies around her. The roundel frame is enclosed in a square with tassels on all sides.

The deterioration of the human body, especially of the hands, seems to indicate a late dating.

22. *WOOL TAPESTRY. SACRIFICE OF ISAAC*

COPTIC, 6TH–7TH CENTURY. NEW YORK CITY, COOPER UNION MUSEUM.

5¼ x 11½ in. (14½ x 29 cm.). No. 1902–1–142. Excoll. Baron. Exhibited: Worcester, 1937, cat. no. 141; Brooklyn, 1941, cat. no. 253; Baltimore, 1947, cat. no. 801. Published: R. M. Riefstahl, "Early Textiles in the Cooper Union Collection," *Art in America*, III (1915), p. 300; R. Cox, *Soieries d'art*, 1914, pl. 19, IV, the companion piece in the Musée des Tissus, Lyons.

Sleeve ornament of a linen tunic, polychrome wool and undyed linen wefts. The scene of the Sacrifice of Isaac, complete with Hand of God and ram, on orange ground, is flanked by panels with a design of lozenges filled with birds facing toward the center and floral motifs, on red ground. Narrow border of detached petals.

Woven Bible scenes are rare. The representation, with landscape indicated by a tree and the well-placed ram, harks back to a better composition, a book illustration or a mosaic, or even a shuttle-woven silk fabric. The flanking panels are obviously adapted from a silk fabric. "Individual scenes from the Old Testament survived in Early Christian iconography as possessing a particular liturgical or theological significance. One of these is the Sacrifice of Isaac, typical of the Lord's Supper. This scene was a favorite in Early Christian art; its directly symbolical nature is emphasized in the sixth century, as in the mosaics of San Vitale at Ravenna" (O. M. Dalton, *Byzantine Art and Archaeology*, 1911, p. 651).

23. WOOL TAPESTRY FRAGMENT. A CROSS

SYRIA OR MESOPOTAMIA, 5TH–6TH CENTURY. NEW YORK CITY, THE BROOKLYN MUSEUM.

1¾ x 1½ in. (4½ x 4 cm.). No. 15.439. Provenance: Antinoë, Excavations of the Egypt Exploration Society, 1913–14. Exhibited: Brooklyn, 1941, cat. no. 244. Published: John D. Cooney, *Late Egyptian and Coptic Art*, Brooklyn, 1943, p. 22, pl. 46.

A fragment of a ribbon of *mulham*, a fabric with silk warp and linen weft, shows a design of a cross with looped arms. This is tapestry-woven in brown silk and yellow linen. Open slits, weft-locked in a few places.

The use of *mulham* points to Syria or Mesopotamia as the probable place of manufacture.

24. WOOL TAPESTRY. A JEWELED CROSS

COPTIC, 5TH–6TH CENTURY. NEW YORK CITY, THE BROOKLYN MUSEUM.

6⅜ x 5¾ in. (16 x 14½ cm.). No. 41.798. Exhibited: Brooklyn, 1941, cat. no. 247. Published: John D. Cooney, *Late Egyptian and Coptic Art*, Brooklyn, 1943, p. 21, pl. 41.

Tapestry woven into linen ground. The vertical bars of the cross are woven detached, with their ends woven again into the linen ground. A jeweled cross, polychrome on red ground.

25. WOOL TWILL. BIRTH OF CHRIST

SYRIA OR EGYPT, 5TH–6TH CENTURY. NEW YORK CITY, THE METROPOLITAN MUSEUM OF ART.

3¾ x 21¾ in. (9½ x 55 cm.). No. 90.5.11, gift of George F. Baker. Published: M. S. Dimand, "Early Christian Weavings from Egypt," *Bulletin*, XX (1925), 57; H. Peirce and R. Tyler, *L'Art byzantin*, Paris, 1934, II, 88, pl. 58, "Soierie."

Five fragments of a continuous band. Plain compound twill; warp undyed linen, wefts undyed linen; red, green, and dark-purple wool, no silk. The linen wefts have disappeared in patches, showing the warp threads. The design is of linen thread on red ground; the borders have a broken wave on purple between narrow green stripes. The fragments show the Annunciation; Bathing of the Child; Shepherds at the Manger; and Adoration of the Magi.

Annunciation: The Virgin Mary is seated on a high chair, her feet resting on a stool. She spins, distaff in left hand, spindle in a basket on the floor. Of the archangel enough is preserved to show the head, the right hand raised for the salutation, the left holding a staff. Bathing of the Child: The mother rests on a pallet, wrapped in a blanket that leaves uncovered one foot and the left hand. She looks down at her Son. Here, instead of the plants, should be the two women who, according to the Apocryphal gospel, bathed the newborn Child. The scene, as presented, is symbolic of Christ's sacrifice, the bathtub changed to a chalice, Christ's arms spread as in the Crucifixion. This scene is followed here by the Epiphany, the first official appearance of Christ. The Adoration of the Shepherds is placed at the end of the border. The Epiphany is presented in two fragments. The first, after a separate motif at the left for which I have no explanation, shows the third of the Magi, in Phrygian costume with pointed cap, mantle, and breeches, and part of the second Magus. The scene continues on the next fragment with the leg of the first, kneeling, Magus and parts of his arms, tending a gift to the Child. He is held by His mother; above Him appears the star of Bethlehem. The Adoration of the Shepherds begins on this fragment. It is clearly marked as a separate illustration and continues on the last fragment. One shepherd runs to the right; a second stands looking toward the manger, where the well-swathed Child is watched by ass and ox. The big star between these and a dog watching the shepherds finish the composition.

26. WOOL TAPESTRY. THE ASCENSION

COPTIC, LATE 6TH–EARLY 7TH CENTURY. NEW YORK CITY, THE BROOKLYN MUSEUM.

Diameter: 4¾ in. (12 cm.). No. 05.305. Exhibited: Brooklyn, 1941, cat. no. 251. Published: John D. Cooney, *Late Egyptian and Coptic Art*, Brooklyn, 1943, p. 23, pl. 52; Elizabeth Riefstahl, "A Coptic Roundel in the Brooklyn Museum," *Bulletin of the Byzantine Institute, Crum Memorial Volume*, Boston, 1950, p. 531.

Warp, white linen; wefts, red, rose, green and four shades of blue wool and unbleached linen. Within a border showing a jewel-studded guilloche on deep green, the design stands out on a ground of unbleached linen. The head, shoulders, and upraised arms of a nimbed man are seen above a top-shaped structure that stands on a triangular foot. Bars protruding from this structure pass between the hind legs of two animals, confronted, regardant. Two floral sprays with a four-petaled flower fill the space below; a plant motif or palmette that above.

The strangely disintegrated composition represents a charioteer in a *biga*, a chariot drawn by two horses. In her excellent analytical article, Mrs. Riefstahl discusses the possibility of the figure being a solar deity. "The palmette surrounding the halo may well have been suggested by the sun-rays of Helios. The upraised arms of the figure, reduced to little more than stubs between the nimbus and the heads of the steeds, end in spots of vivid red, perhaps vestiges of flaming torches. And the rearing steeds seem to be carrying the chariot aloft for a journey across the heavens." But the crossed nimbus, which from early times was a distinguishing attribute of Christ, leads her to the conclusion that the composition of the roundel is "the adaptation of an ancient pagan heavenly flight to represent the Ascension."

27. TAPESTRY ROUNDEL. A CAVALIER SAINT

COPTIC, 6TH–7TH CENTURY. NEW YORK CITY, COOPER UNION MUSEUM.

7¾ x 8½ in. (19½ x 21½ cm.). No. 1902–1–71. Ex-coll. Baron. Exhibited: Worcester, 1937, cat. no. 142; Brooklyn, 1941, cat. no. 252; Baltimore, 1947, cat. no. 813. Published: R. M. Riefstahl, "Early Textiles in the Cooper Union Collection," *Art in America*, III (1915), p. 308. For discussion of the cavalier saint: Josef Strzygowski, "Der koptische Reiterheilige und der heilige Georg," *Zeitschrift für Aegyptische Sprache*, XL (1902), pp. 49–60.

Warp linen, wefts polychrome wool and undyed linen. A nimbed figure with flowing mantle, holding cross-scepter and wreath, looks at the beholder while cantering to left. Below the horse a lioness, on either side a small nimbed figure in exaggerated attitude (marking devotion?). Floral sprays and traces of letters on the red background. Double border with plant forms.

28. WOOL TAPESTRY. DETAIL FROM A COMPLETE TUNIC

COPTIC, 7TH CENTURY OR LATER. NEW YORK CITY, THE BROOKLYN MUSEUM.

12 x 8½ in. (c.30 x 21 cm.). No. 41.523. Exhibited: Brooklyn, 1941, cat. no. 267. Published: John D.

Cooney, *Late Egyptian and Coptic Art*, Brooklyn, 1943, p. 23, pl. 49–50; Millia Davenport, *The Book of Costume*, New York, 1948, p. 37, fig. 114.

The body of the tunic is of yellow wool; the tapestry-woven borders are of dark blue-purple and mauve wool and unbleached linen. In the pictured detail the upper border shows a series of interlaced squares and roundels. The squares frame figures standing in niches, the roundels floral compositions. The lower border shows a personage standing between two animals, probably griffins, repeated six times with delightful variations.

"The motif of the figure between griffins may represent the legendary journey of Kai Khosrau or Alexander the Great to Heaven, a subject of Near Eastern folklore and art which was carried over into the Mohammedan period and found its way into medieval Europe. Iconographically it probably goes back to a period before the time of either king" (Elizabeth Riefstahl).

29. WOOL TAPESTRY. GOATS

MESOPOTAMIA OR EGYPT, 7TH CENTURY OR LATER. BOSTON, MUSEUM OF FINE ARTS.

11½ x 31¾ in. (29½ x 10½ cm.). No. 10.359. Provenance: Jerusalem.

Warp, linen; wefts, rose, white, and dark-brown wools. A rectangular compartment, framed by a checker pattern. On rose ground a procession of six goats in strict profile, one horn only visible.

Border of a hanging or curtain, with warps plaited into a looped fringe, with tassels attached. The design looks almost Sumerian.

30. WOOL TAPESTRY. IBEX

SASSANIAN, 6TH–7TH CENTURY. NEW HAVEN, YALE UNIVERSITY ART GALLERY, THE HOBART MOORE MEMORIAL COLLECTION.

14⅞ x 10¾ in. (37½ x 27 cm.). No. 1937.4604. Provenance: Egypt. Exhibited: *Persian Art*, New York, 1940,

cat. p. 358, no. 59; Baltimore, 1947, cat. no. 824. Published: Phyllis Ackerman, "A Sassanian Tapestry," American Institute for Persian Art and Archaeology *Bulletin*, IV (1935), 2. *Survey* I, p. 708, fig. 249; R. Pfister, "Le rôle de l'Iran dans les textiles d'Antinoë," *Ars Islamica*, 13/14, 1948, p. 72.

All wool, dovetailed and slit tapestry. On red ground a white ibex with polychrome markings is running with bent forelegs. His elaborate collar with large pearls is tied with light-blue ribbons and flies behind the head. Lotos and pomegranate palmettes and traces of quatrefoil flowers adorn the field.

"The Iranian absorption in animal forms here reaches its most commanding formal representation. The cosmological, yet very real creature is depicted with the concentrated vitality typical of Sassanian design at its best. The distinction and intense character of this one large fragment make a poignant demonstration of how grave has been the artistic loss in the disappearance of Sassanian tapestry" (Phyllis Ackerman, in *Survey*).

31. WOOL TAPESTRY. GOATS

EGYPT, PERSANERIE, 6TH–7TH CENTURY. THE CLEVELAND MUSEUM OF ART.

4¾ x 11½ in. (12 x 29½ cm.). No. 50.522. Ex-coll. Delmar.

Two fragments of a border. On somewhat faded, dark-red ground, the design in white and several shades of green. Three goats, wearing collars, walk in stately procession. Over their backs the space is filled with an ornament of fluttering ribbons. The border is finished at the top with a band patterned with beads and ribbons.

A comparison with the Sassanian ibex (Fig. 30) shows, combined with similar body ornaments, a difference in stylization, most noticeable in the heads. The long twisted horns of the ibex are changed to chubby ornaments; the elongated muzzle changes the expression from noble simplicity to derision. It seems plausible to see in this border a *persanerie* adaptation of a Sassanian original.

32. WOOL TAPESTRY. PICTORIAL PANEL

EGYPT, PERSIAN INSPIRATION, 6TH CENTURY. NEW YORK CITY, THE BROOKLYN MUSEUM.

40¾ x 58½ in. (103 x 148 cm.); H. of figures 11½ in. (29 cm.). No. 46.128. Published: R. Girshman, "Études Iraniennes II, Recherches sur les coutumes funéraires Sassanides," *Artibus Asiae*, XI (1948), pp. 292–310, esp. pp. 304–306.

Polychrome wool tapestry, fragmentary. Preserved are three sides of the border and two rows of a composition that may have continued upward with a third row and the border. This shows a ribbon, twisted to form a zigzag line, and bunches of flowers and leaves. An inner band has leaves and berries; the outer band is left plain. The field has two superimposed rows of arcades, ornamented with pearls, supported by columns with capitals and bases. In each intercolumnar space stands a personage. The lordly figure in the upper central arcades is probably a portrait of the owner of this fabric, repeated for the sake of balancing the composition. He alone wears ear ornaments and elegant slippers. The long sleeves of his ample coat cover his hands and hang down to the knees. He holds before him a casket. The other men seem to be his retinue. The two at the extreme left are dressed in close-fitted belted tunics and boots; the one above holds a bow and arrows; both may be arms-bearers. The four remaining figures are represented alike, barefoot, dressed in long tunics with a scarf tied at the right shoulder. They are servants, carrying fruit baskets and drinking vessels.

According to Girshman, the scene represents an outstanding event in the life of the man who commissioned the tapestry. Here a Persian nobleman offers to his suzerain a casket with presents. Mr. Girshman draws attention to these boxes, on which letters of the Pehlevi alphabet appear, possibly the initials of the name of the anonymous nobleman, who is represented with hands well covered in the attitude of respect demanded by the etiquette of the Iranian court. The tapestry may have been designed for wrapping the owner's bones before placing them into an ossuary for burial.

33. WOOL AND LINEN TAPESTRY. MASKS

COPTIC, 5TH–6TH CENTURY. BOSTON, MUSEUM OF FINE ARTS.

11¾ x 11½ in. (30 x 29½ cm.). No. 07.444.

Warps, linen; wefts, wool: violet for field, red for border, the design polychrome. The field is covered with staggered rows of masks with parted hair and a skullcap. The border is patterned with squares and stars.

The design shows such strong Sassanian influence that it might be classed as *persanerie*.

34. THE HORSE AND LION TAPESTRY

SYRO-MESOPOTAMIA OR EGYPT, 6TH CENTURY. WASHINGTON, D. C., DUMBARTON OAKS RESEARCH LIBRARY AND COLLECTION, HARVARD UNIVERSITY.

58¼ x 30¾ in. (148 x 78 cm.). No. 39.13. Provenance: unknown. Published: Ernst Kitzinger, "The Horse and Lion Tapestry, a Study in Coptic and Sassanian Textile Design," Dumbarton Oaks Papers, no. 3, 1946, pp. 3–71.

Wool, left twist throughout. The dark-blue field is covered with seven horizontal rows of pairs of addorsed half-lengths of lions and horses in alternate rows. They spring from a basis shaped like a cup-capital, which tops a stem rising from an acanthus scroll. The capitals are decorated with fruit baskets flanked by addorsed birds. Blossoms fill the spaces between the animals and are scattered over the field. The wide green border shows alternately red and blue roundels with horsemen armed with a spear or a missile. Between these roundels a lion with a flaming mane and a panther alternate, prancing toward the field but looking backward. Narrow bands with a red crest ornament on white ground finish the border.

Fragments of other wool tapestries of the *persanerie* type belong to the Boston Museum of Fine Arts (No. 27.566; Kitzinger, fig. 4) and the Brooklyn Museum (No. 15.435; Kitzinger, fig. 5).

35. COTTON AND WOOL TWILL. EAGLES

SASSANIAN, 6TH–7TH CENTURY. WASHINGTON, D. C., DUMBARTON OAKS RESEARCH LIBRARY AND COLLECTION, HARVARD UNIVERSITY.

19 x 18½ in. (48 x 47 cm.); figure, H. 11⅝ in. (29½ cm.). No. 36.43. Exhibited: New York, 1940, cat. no. 60, p. 359. Published: Dumbarton Oaks Handbook, 1946, no. 258; *Survey*, p. 706, fig. 248.

Unbleached cotton and red wool, compound twill, reversible. The fabric is mounted to show the design in red on the ivory-white ground. Incomplete. Two confronted eagles displayed are grasping a goat or ibex. The eagle's breast is decorated with seven disks, each containing an anchor. The anchors appear again on one wing above a beaded band.

"The anchor in this fully developed form is most uncommon at this period. It functioned as a sky symbol. The eagle had for many centuries been a sky bird in the Iranian plateau, reinterpreted as a sun bird, carrying as its victim a horned animal of the moon" (Phyllis Ackerman).

36. COTTON AND WOOL TWILL. BIRDS

SASSANIAN, 6TH–7TH CENTURY. THE CLEVELAND MUSEUM OF ART.

Two fragments, each c. 19½ x 3¾ in. (50 x 9½ cm.). No. 50.511. Ex-coll. Delmar. Provenance: Egypt.

Unbleached cotton and red wool, compound twill. Reversible. The two fragments are part of a large roundel with beaded border. Confronted birds (herons?) stand on curled twigs and grasp in their beaks twigs ending in palmettes. These twigs were probably part of a central tree.

37. WOOL CLOTH. A HUNTING SCENE

SYRIA, 3RD CENTURY. PHILADELPHIA MUSEUM OF ART.

14¼ x 7¾ in. (36 x 20 cm.). No. 33-50-1. Exhibited: Brooklyn, 1941, cat. no. 181; Baltimore, 1947, cat. no. 777. Published: an identical specimen in Berlin (present location unknown), Wulff-Volbach, *Spätantike und koptische Stoffe*, 1926, no. 6682, p. 135, color plate; Falke, I, 23–24, fig. 31. For the technique: J. F. Flanagan, "The Origin of the Drawloom in the Making of Early Byzantine Silks," *Burlington Magazine*, XXXV (1917), p. 167 ff.

A mounted hunter with a spear, followed by a dog, attacks a boar (only the head and one forefoot are shown). A second hunter, with chlamys flying from neck, kneels behind a tree and shoots an arrow at a lion. A third hunter, running with a spear held in both hands, is warding off a lioness; a deer runs away but looks backward. The hunting scene appears as a wild turmoil. The bearded hunters may represent barbarians. The design appears in green on red ground with a wide purple band at right, a narrow purple strip at left. No selvages.

This is an adaptation of the Chinese warp cloth (Figs. 39–41). The Syrian craftsman was used from tapestry weaving to produce his design with the wefts. These covered the warps entirely, while in the "Han binding" the wefts were covered by the warps. So the Syrian weaver working at the drawloom simply wove his design sideways. As a result, in the finished fabric the warps lie horizontally, the wefts vertically. Each length of picture weaving is followed by a band of plain purple. Their limited size marks these fabrics for use on cushions and bolsters. The so-called Sarcophagus of Alexander Severus (emperor from 222 to 235), in the Capitoline Museum in Rome, shows clearly a fabric of this type covering the mattress-bolster. The shallow relief shows a hunting scene alternating with plain woven bands (Alois Riegl,

Spätrömische Kunstindustrie, Vienna, 1927, fig. 23). These highly specialized wool fabrics were probably soon discontinued. They could not compete with the rising fashion for silk fabrics, woven on the fully elaborated draw-loom.

38. WOOL TWILL. HARES AND TREES

SYRIA, 4TH–5TH CENTURY. BALTI-MORE, WALTERS ART GALLERY.

17½ x 12½ in. (44 x 31½ cm.). No. 83.510. Provenance: Egypt.

Red warp, red and white wefts. Woven sideways like Fig. 37, the design is red on the white ground. This shows an attempt on the part of the designer to produce a fabric that could be enjoyed seen from either side. He drew his hares alternately upside down, the trees, indicating a landscape, lying on their sides. He changed the plain band at the side to a triple band of red and white with an interlocked pattern of broken waves.

This fabric is obviously slightly later than the Hunting Scene. This is indicated by the use of twill, then a novel technique.

39–43. SILK FABRICS FROM NOIN-ULA

CHINESE, HAN DYNASTY, 1ST CEN-TURY B.C. PHILADELPHIA MU-SEUM OF ART.

Exhibited: *2000 Years*, cat. nos. 1 to 4. Published: Eleanor B. Sachs, "Notes on the Weaves of a Group of Silk Fabrics from the Burial Mounds of Noin-Ula, Now in the Pennsylvania Museum of Art," Needle and Bobbin Club *Bulletin*, XX (1936), nos. 1 and 2, p. 75 (this issue of the *Bulletin* is devoted entirely to technical studies of all the textiles found by the Kozlov Expedition; of special interest is P. K. Kozlov, "Mongolian Silk Fabrics from the Excavations," p. 11); Otto Maenchen-Helfen, "From China to Palmyra," *The Art Bulletin*, XXV (1943), p. 358; R. J. Charleston, "Han Damasks," *Oriental Art*, I, no. 2, 1948 (subtitle: "Who breaks a butterfly on a wheel?" Alexander Pope, *Epistle to Dr. Arbuthnot*).

39. The Heron Silk. 3⅝ x 2½ in. (9 x 5¾ cm.). No. 34–2–2. A heron stands on a large scroll beside a Chinese character that reads: "Prosperity Ten Thousand Years." The design is tan (originally white?) outlined in brown (green?), the ground dark brownish-red. The warps cross regularly under one main weft and over three wefts (one main, two secondary). There is always one warp in use on the face of the fabric and two on the back, carried together. The color disposition is therefore different on front and back, where the design is somewhat blurred. The secondary wefts serve only to reinforce the fabric and produce the faint horizontal ridge so characteristic of the "Han binding."

40. The Cock Silk. 7½ x 8½ in. (19½ x 21¾ cm.). No. 34–2–1. A wide chevron, or half lozenge, supports a cock between small angular scrolls and triple-engaged lozenges. The design is red outlined by tan, the ground dark brown.

41. The Diamond Silk. 5½ x 4 in. (14 x 10 cm.). No. 34–2–4. Diamond shapes, subdivided into four compartments each containing a dot. The design is red, the ground tan.

42. Fancy Gauze. 3¼ x 2 in. (8 x 5 cm.). No. 34–2–6. Repeats of triple-engaged lozenges. Cream silk, exceedingly fine weave.

43. Fancy Gauze. 4¾ x 3⅛ in. (12 x 8 cm.). No. 34–2–7b. "The same in weave and in design, but the color is different, for it was smoothed out and dyed (after it was found), apparently with the original cinnabar dye" (E. B. Sachs).

Gauze and warp cloth are related techniques, for in both the pattern-producing role is given to the warps, while the wefts are merely subservient.

44. POLYCHROME SILK TWILL. SAMSON OR A GLADIATOR

SYRIA, 6TH–7TH CENTURY. WASH-INGTON, D. C., DUMBARTON OAKS RESEARCH LIBRARY AND COLLEC-TION, HARVARD UNIVERSITY.

37¼ x 16 in. (96 x 40½ cm.), four repeats. No. 34.1. Provenance: The Cathedral of Chur, Switzerland. Exhibited: *Exposition d'Art byzantin*, Paris, 1931, cat. no. 214; Worcester, 1937, cat. no. 144. Published: Dumbarton Oaks *Handbook of the Collection*, 1946, no. 228.

Twill weave, red, white, yellow, blue, and green silks. On the deep-red ground the all-over pattern appears in a series of horizontal rows. The design shows the figure of a Roman gladiator, clad in sandals, a white tunic, and a red chlamys across the chest and floating behind his back. He stands with right knee braced against the back of a rearing lion whose jaw he wrenches with both hands. The gladiator has been variously called Samson, David, or Hercules. A flowery plant beneath the lion indicates a landscape. This group is repeated, turned alternately to right or left. Each row is framed by two scalloped bands, segments of a roundel. These show on white ground rose stems with a blossom and two buds, and square-cut jewels, and are outlined by strings of beads.

Besides this large, well-preserved specimen, the Samson silk exists in smaller pieces. One was used as part of the binding of a ninth-century Gregorian Sacramentary (Giuseppe Gerola, *Il Sacramentario della Chiesa di Trento*, Dedalo, II [1921], 221).

45. SILK TWILL. MOUNTED AMA-ZONS

SYRIA OR EGYPT, 6TH–7TH CEN-TURY. WASHINGTON, D. C., DUM-BARTON OAKS RESEARCH LIBRARY AND COLLECTION, HARVARD UNI-VERSITY.

8¾ x 7½ in. (22 x 19 cm.). No. 46.15. Published: Dumbarton Oaks *Acquisitions*, December, 1946–November, 1947. Another specimen, Metropolitan Museum, exhibited: *2000 Years*, cat. no. 16.

Plain compound twill, buff on blue-purple silk. Roundel with two mounted addorsed Amazons, shooting arrows backward at leopards. The small horses stand with one hind foot on the leopard's shoulder. The Amazons are dressed in a close-fitting chiton that leaves one breast uncovered, a chlamys seen only as a fluttering scarf, and high boots. The border shows a design of heart-shaped and trefoil flowers seen in profile, and leaves, between bands of twisted ribbons. The roundels touch and are connected by disks. The spandril ornament is an octagonal star with small palmettes.

The polychrome "Alexandrian" original of this two-color adaptation is preserved. It is the shroud of St. Fridolin, who in the late sixth century was buried in his abbey church, the later cathedral of Säkkingen on the Upper Rhine. The tomb remained unopened until the nineteenth century; then the well-preserved precious fabric was wantonly cut up. Fragments are now preserved in the textile collections of Berlin and Zurich. The adaptation is very close to the original. The size of the roundel is slightly smaller, and the Amazons are bareheaded instead of wearing Phrygian caps. The outstanding characteristic, the difficulty the weaver found in the turnover, resulting in the empty space between the figures, is present in the original fabric.

46. SILK TWILL. SUCKLING ANTE-LOPES

SYRIA OR EGYPT, 6TH–7TH CEN-TURY. THE CLEVELAND MUSEUM OF ART.

8¾ x 9 in. (22 x 23 cm.). No. 47.192. Published: Dorothy Shepherd, "A Silk Fabric from Egypt," *Bulletin*, XXXIV, 1947, p. 196. Exhibited: (the Dumbarton Oaks, specimen) *2000 Years*, cat. no. 14; published: Dumbarton Oaks *Handbook*, 1946, no. 226.

White and red silks, faded to tan and pale crimson. Two antelopes, suckling their young, stand confronted on either side of a tree, nibbling its branches with heads turned backward, thus showing both lyre-shaped horns. The tree grows from a container; the boughs end in fig (?) leaves. The border, with its somewhat overstylized blossoms and leaves, is identical with the border of the Amazon silk (Fig. 45). The two fabrics can therefore be assigned to one workshop. A reconstruction of the spandril motive is not possible.

Miss Shepherd calls it "a lovely fabric," "an exquisite pattern." It is certainly one of the most delightful fabrics preserved for our enjoyment by the kindly soil of Egypt.

47. POLYCHROME SILK TWILL. THE DIOSCURI

SYRIA, EARLY 7TH CENTURY. NEW YORK CITY, THE METROPOLITAN MUSEUM OF ART.

10⅜ x 10⅞ in. (26 x 27½ cm.). No. 37.53.2. Provenance: Maastricht, church of St. Servatius. Published: M. S. Dimand, "Two Syrian Silk Weaves of the VII Century," *Bulletin*, XXXII (1937), p. 259; *Handbook*, 1944, p. 19. The Maastricht specimen: Falke, I, 58, fig. 77.

Plain compound twill. Warp, rose-red; wefts, white, dark red, dark green, olivegreen. Two figures stand on the abacus of a column, which at the base is decorated with a bucranium. The figures, Castor and Pollux, wear olive-green helmets and jackets over white tunics and hold spears and shields. Sacrificial bulls are forced to kneel by attendants; winged genii hold fluttering linen cloths. The roundels are connected by disks; both these and the border show large blossoms on a wavy tendril. A tree occupies the spandril.

St. Servatius, bishop of Tongern, died in A.D. 384. The Dioscuri silk must have been placed with his relics considerably later, possibly when these were placed in their new shrine made by Godefroid de Clare.

48. SILK TWILL, REVERSIBLE. BIRDS

SYRIA OR EGYPT, 6TH–7TH CENTURY. NEW YORK CITY, COOPER UNION MUSEUM.

6¼ x 11½ in. (16 x 29 cm.). No. 1902–1–210. Ex-coll. Miguel y Badia. Provenance: Antinoë (?). Exhibited: Baltimore, 1947, cat. no. 759.

Plain compound twill, reversible, brown and white silks. A procession of four different birds, pigeon, duck, peacock, and goose; the landscape is indicated by detached plant motifs.

Woven sideways, very fine weave.

49. POLYCHROME TWILL. LION HUNTERS

SYRIA, EARLY 7TH CENTURY. NEW YORK CITY, THE METROPOLITAN MUSEUM OF ART.

10⅜ in. square (26 cm.). No. 37.53.1. Published: M. S. Dimand, "Two Syrian Silk Weaves of the VII Century," *Bulletin*, XXXII (1937), 259; *Handbook*, 1944, p. 19; F. E. Day, "Silks of the Near East," *Bulletin*, IX (1950), 108.

Plain compound twill. Warp, rose-red; wefts, cream, dark-green, olive-green, orange, dark-red silks. This "Alexandrian" silk fabric illustrates the weaver's preoccupation with the problem of the overturn, demanded by a symmetrically repeated design on the drawloom. The difficulty of masking the center line is here partly solved by the introduction of the small palmette tree at the top. But beneath this inconspicuous motif, which foreshadows a splendid evolution, there yawns a gap from the drawn bows to the heads of the lions. The design stands out clearly from the typical red background. Pleasing are the hunters' eyes, veiled by the lids, not staring. The costume is rendered without folds; the long-sleeved tunic is patterned with heart shapes. A reversible material is indicated by the upturned corner of the tunic, where the pattern appears in reversed colors. The bare feet beneath the leggings are poorly designed. The horse's mane is dissolved into a coxcomb and fringe. The roundel frame has cornucopiae with floral strands tied by ribbons and squares and angles. The roundels are adjacent, not touching; the spandrils show a palmette tree.

50. SILK TWILL, REVERSIBLE. A HERDSMAN

SYRIA OR EGYPT, 5TH CENTURY. BOSTON, MUSEUM OF FINE ARTS.

3½ x 2¾ in. (9 x 7 cm.). No. 11.90.

Light tan (white?) and purple (faded) silks. A boy sits on the ground, watching his herd of sheep and gamboling lambs with the help of a dog. Small trees and flowery plants indicate landscape.

The design is closely related to classical art. It is instructive to notice the relief on the obverse, the flat appearance of the figures on the reverse side of this unique specimen, one of the earliest figured silk fabrics preserved.

51. SILK TWILL. PLANT MOTIFS

EGYPT, AKHMÍM (?), OR SYRIA, 6TH–7TH CENTURY. BOSTON, MUSEUM OF FINE ARTS.

13 x 23¾ in. (33½ x 60½ cm.). No. 15.385.

Rose and light yellowish tan. Roundels, adjacent but not touching, contain a lotus tree within a palmette frame. The spandrils have flowers growing from an eight-lobed stem that frames a disk.

The complete specimen shows the best part of six roundels.

52. SILK TWILL. LOZENGE DESIGN

EGYPT, AKHMÎM (?), 6TH–7TH CENTURY. THE DETROIT INSTITUTE OF ARTS.

6 x 5½ in. (15 x 13¾ cm.). No. 47.75. Ex-coll. Sangiorgi. Provenance: Akhmîm. Published: Falke, I, p. 46, fig. 66, Akhmîm, 6th to 7th century. Other specimens exhibited: *2000 Years*, cat. no. 15 (Metropolitan museum: Sassanian, 6th century); Baltimore, 1947, cat. no. 766 (Yale University, Moore Collection: Syria, 5th to 7th century).

Compound weft twill, red and tan (white?) silks. Wavy vine tendrils with heart-shaped leaves form an all-over lattice, with quatrefoil rosettes at the intersections. In alternate rows roundels with two birds facing a tree, and eight-lobed medallions with addorsed birds on the branches of a tree.

53. FRAGMENT OF A SILK CLAVIS

SYRIA OR EGYPT, 7TH CENTURY. THE CLEVELAND MUSEUM OF ART.

11¾ x 2¼ in. (30 x 5½ cm.). No. 39.505. Provenance: Akhmîm. Exhibited: *2000 Years*, cat. no. 11. Published: Falke, 1913, p. 46, fig. 63. This is possibly the companion clavis from the same tunic.

White and dark-green silks, plain compound twill. Design incomplete. In a landscape indicated by a stylized tree, a crouching rabbit, a snarling lion, and a hunter armed with a sword and small shield and clad in tunic and short mantle are placed one above the other. A second rectangle, shorter and not complete, shows the larger part of a palmette tree. The band is bordered with heart-shaped petals and rudimentary leaves.

This design has been called, wrongly, "St. Michael and the Dragon." It is rather an illustration of the parable of how the stronger preys on the weaker. This story is almost as old and as widespread as humanity; in this special case the design, and possibly the fabric itself, came from Syria, a stronghold of didactic teaching.

54. SILK TWILL. A "JOSEPH" SILK

EGYPT, 6TH–7TH CENTURY. THE CLEVELAND MUSEUM OF ART.

11⅛ x 7⅝ in. (28 x 19½ cm.). No. 47.143. Provenance: probably Akhmîm. Published: Dorothy Shepherd, "A Coptic Silk," *Bulletin*, XXIV (1947), 216. Another fragment of the same fabric: R. Forrer, *Römische und byzantinische Seidentextilien aus Akhmim-Panopolis*, 1891, pl. V, no. 1.

All silk, weft twill. On a field of faded purple the design stands out in tan (originally white?). Preserved is the central part and one end of a sleeve panel. The square central field is occupied by a large eight-lobed medallion, framing a smaller medallion. Connected with this motif is a wide ribbon adorned with pearl-studded circles; it cuts across the outer field, where each half shows the same design, reversed at right, direct at left. In a landscape indicated by rudimentary trees a horseman swings a mace to ward off a pedestrian with a raised lance. A crane below, a bird above, fill empty spaces. The name "Joseph" in Greek letters appears over the head of the rider. A border on each side has a palmette tendril.

The design occurs almost identically with the name "Zacharias." These names cannot refer to the cavaliers, since they are also found in the floral tendrils of purely ornamental designs. Miss Shepherd offers an ingenious interpretation: "Until now no very satisfactory explanation of these inscriptions has been made. It occurs to the writer, however, that these two names may refer to Joseph, the father of Christ, and to Zacharias, the father of John the Baptist. In a fourth century Coptic church at Deir Abu Hennis are frescoes depicting the Annunciation to Zacharias of his future fatherhood. In the same series are painted the Warning of Joseph and the Flight into Egypt. These representations do not seem to occur in Early Christian art outside of Egypt and may indicate that Zacharias and Joseph had a special importance to the Copts, which would account for their repetition in this group of textiles. This then provides further evidence that these textiles are the products of the local workshops of Akhmîm" (D. Shepherd).

55. WOOL TAPESTRY. A SET OF TUNIC ORNAMENTS

COPTIC, 6TH–7TH CENTURY. SE-ATTLE ART MUSEUM.

Two shoulder bands, each 28 x 3¾ in. (71 x 9½ cm.); two roundels, each 8 x 8½ in. (20½ x 21½ cm.); one sleeve panel, 9½ x 13 in. (24 x 33 cm.). No. 40.3, *E-C;* Eugene Fuller Memorial Collection. Exhibited: Baltimore, 1947, cat. no. 787; *Liturgical Arts*, Portland, Oregon, 1947.

Polychrome wool tapestry on linen warps. The design of each piece is centered on a human figure or bust. These are surrounded by a conglomeration of palmette motifs in an advanced state of disintegration, and bordered by triple bands with floral and geometric motifs.

This bare description does not do justice to the glowing effect of this extraordinary set of ornaments. The combination of reds and white gives the impression of a cornelian cameo. The designs are important as adaptations of silk fabrics of the "Alexandrian" type. The nimbed busts of the roundels hark back to Hellenistic prototypes, while the standing saints of the shoulder bands with their exaggeratedly big hands point with long fingers toward later medieval art, and bring to our minds such famous figures as the Angel of the Bamberg Apocalypse and the St. John of the Grünewald altar. The half-length figure in the jeweled roundel of the sleeve panel looks at first glance like an orant. But she is no Christian personification; she is much older, a nature-goddess, possibly Atargatis, holding up with both hands a scarf filled with the fruits of the earth. Luckily, the silk prototype of this design has been preserved among the relics of the tomb of St. Cuthbert (J. P. Flanagan, "The Nature Goddess at Durham," *Burlington Magazine*, LXXXVIII, 1946, p. 241). In the much larger and more elaborate design of the silk the goddess rises from water, which fills the bottom part of the roundel. There, and in the spandrils, are fishes and ducks. This explains the strange corner motifs of the tapestry; they are ducks, swimming on the dark-blue water.

56. SILK TWILL. TUNIC ORNAMENTS

SYRIA, 6TH–7TH CENTURY. NEW HAVEN, YALE UNIVERSITY ART GALLERY, THE HOBART MOORE MEMORIAL COLLECTION.

No. 1947.201 *A-G.* Provenance: Akhmîm, Egypt. Part of a set of nine trimming bands. Published: Margaret J. Rowe, *Textiles*, Yale University Art Gallery Picture Book No. 2, pl. 3.

Silk twill, colors very faded, probably red, yellow, white on a blue ground. The design is largely Byzantine, a conglomeration of many motifs. The shoulder band is bordered with palmettes connected by half circles. Candelabrum trees alternate with a full-length male figure standing frontally, richly dressed and wearing a crown, holding a flower in each hand. A small roundel, depending from a palmette-patterned ribbon, shows the bust portrait of a crowned female figure. The "emperor" appears again as a bust portrait in the center of the large roundel, in a circle of beads surmounted by a floral motif. This is surrounded by eight motifs that look like plumed helmets, and detached floral sprigs. The sleeve ornament—one half is here presented—is divided into rectangles and squares by a band of heart-shaped blossoms in profile with a calyx, and a band of floral motifs. The rectangles are occupied by squat candelabrum trees, the squares by bust portraits of the crowned female figure. That she is a nature goddess is supported by the border, where fishes swim amid water plants.

57. SILK TWILL. PERSANERIE

EGYPT, ANTINOË, 6TH CENTURY. BOSTON, MUSEUM OF FINE ARTS.

12¼ x 7½ in. (31 x 19 cm.). No. 04.1620. Published: (a similar specimen at Lyons) Falke, I, 35, fig. 38; Peirce and Tyler, *L'Art byzantin*, vol. II, pl. 50; R. Cox, *Soieries d'art*, 1914, pl. 22, 1.

Plain compound weft twill, very thin silks, dark blue, pale and golden yellow and light green. An all-over lozenge pattern of wavy tendrils with trilobate leaves and fruit (pears?), overlaid at the crossing points with disks framing a star or a flower. Inside the lozenges are two alternate patterns, a roundel with confronted birds (ibis?) holding in their beaks a ribbon that flutters over their heads, and a stylized motif that may be either a large blossom or a flower basket.

As a help to dating this rare specimen Falke mentions the consular diptych of Justinus, of 540, where pears are figured in the ornament. Peirce and Tyler mention the consular diptych of Philoxenus, of 525, for the trilobate leaves. They consider this silk an outstanding example

of the "fantastic imagination of the Antinoë designer."

58. SILK TWILL. A DUCK

PERSIA OR MESOPOTAMIA, SASSANIAN, 6TH–7TH CENTURY. NEW YORK CITY, THE METROPOLITAN MUSEUM OF ART.

8 x 5½ in. (20 x 14 cm.). No. 90.5.10, gift of George F. Baker. Published: M. S. Dimand, *Handbook*, 1930, p. 212; 1944, p. 18.

Silk. "Warp coral-orange, some lying loose on surface where wefts broken. Seven wefts (most are colors mixed), dark blue, white, blue and white, pink and white, blue and pink and white, pink and blue, dark and light blue, these floated across back at intervals. The pink in the wefts is a cyclamen or orchid tone, cold. The pattern light coral pink with deeper violet outlines, on a pale bluish ground" (analysis by Florence E. Day). Preserved is one complete roundel with parts of the disks at the angles, and parts of the spandril motif. Bands of dark blue cut across the ground. The duck stands on a low, beaded platform. The compact body is outlined by a guilloche (?) motif. The stumpy tail looks almost realistic; the wing feathers emanate from a beaded band and are curled upward. A jeweled collar hangs from the neck; another, or a string of pearls with a large pendant and long flying ribbons, is held in the duck's beak.

The roundel frame and spandril design are related to those of the famous cock silk of the Vatican (Falke, I, fig. 98; Reath and Sachs, no. 45). The duck is first cousin to the Vatican duck silk (Falke, I, fig. 99; Reath and Sachs, no. 46) and to the ducks, copies of Sassanian silks, painted on the wall of a rock temple at Kyzyl, Chinese Turkestan (Falke, I, fig. 100).

59. SILK TWILL. THE VIVENTIA FABRIC

BYZANTINE, 8TH CENTURY. BOSTON, MUSEUM OF FINE ARTS.

7¾ x 13¼ in. (20 x 34 cm.). No. 33.648. Ex-coll. Leopold Seligmann, Cologne, cat. 1930, no. 187. Provenance: the tomb of Viventia, daughter of Pepin, sister of Charlemagne, Church of St. Ursula, Cologne. Exhibited: *Byzantine Art*, Paris, 1931, cat. no. 286; *Arts of the Middle Ages*, Boston, 1940, cat. no. 81; Baltimore, 1947, cat. no. 769. Published: Falke, II, p. 3, fig. 213.

True reddish purple on neutral ground. Weft twill, uneven weave. A griffin on the back of a bull is repeated in alternate directions and framed by a heavy wreath of leaves. The oval medallions are overlaid by disks, adorned with pearls. Floriated rosettes fill the spandrils.

In 751 Pepin the Short founded the Carolingian dynasty, by dethroning Childeric III. The Byzantine emperor Constantine V (740–775) sent him congratulatory gifts including silks. Quite probably one of these silks was used as a shroud for his daughter Viventia, when she was buried in the early Christian Church of St. Ursula. But it is possible that the silk of the shroud is even older. It may have been a part of the treasure of the last Merovingian king, which fell into the hands of his major-domo when he arrogated to himself the crown of the Frankish kingdom. And Gregory of Tours tells that already Clovis (481–511) owned Byzantine silks of large size, *vela et cortines*. Silks patterned with animal combats must have been well known and greatly admired in western Europe. One such silk, possibly the shroud of Viventia, was actually the inspiration of the design of a woolen tapestry, fragments of which have been preserved in another church at Cologne, St. Gereon. This is the earliest tapestry woven in medieval Europe, and has been dated about A.D. 1000.

60. *SILK TWILL. DOUBLE-HEADED EAGLES*

BYZANTINE, 11TH–12TH CENTURY. NEW YORK CITY, THE METROPOLITAN MUSEUM OF ART.

24¾ x 18 in. (63 x 45½ cm.). No. 41.92. Ex-coll. Miguel y Badia. Provenance: said to have come from the tomb of San Bernardo Calvo, Bishop of Vich, 1233–1243.

Other specimens, same provenance: New York, Cooper Union Museum; The Cleveland Museum of Art; Berlin, Schlossmuseum; Paris, Musée des Arts Décoratifs. Published: Falke, II, 17, fig. 249; Lessing, pl. 77; Dorothy G. Shepherd, "The Hispano-Moresque Textiles in the Cooper Union Collection," *Chronicle*, vol. I, no. 10, 1943, fig. 2.

Plain compound twill; ground, dark red-purple, design, black with yellow (faded to tan) accents (the eagle's eyes and claws and the jewel in his beak). Between round arches, remnants of a roundel pattern, the twenty-inch-high eagles stand on addorsed lions. With three claws they clutch the back, with the fourth claw the hindquarters, of their prey. The turned-back lion's head is seen in profile, the tip of the hind ear just visible in the space between the wing and tail. Long lashes and strong brows mark the eyes. The mane is designed as a series of wavy lines between beaded bands. Shoulder and haunch are marked with palmettes, the leg joints with double rings. The tassel of the tail appears between the legs. The eagle's wings and tail are displayed, the feathers indicated as loops; the top of the wings is marked by an elaborate palmette. The lozenge diaper pattern on the breast shows heart-shaped flowers on long stems. A double string of pearls with a large jewel surrounds the neck, where the lozenge pattern of the body is repeated on a reduced scale, with a triple blossom, a fleur-de-lis. On the double head the yellow eyes are outlined with red markings. The strong beak holds a "Sassanian" jewel. The arched borders are covered with a geometrical interlocked pattern between beaded lines, and connected by disks with a quadruple palmette. A larger rosette is displayed in the spandril. Fig. 60A shows Lessing's reconstruction of the grandiose fabric.

The Roman inventory of 1295 (inv. no. 959) mentions: "dalmaticam rubeam de panno imperiali de Romania ad aquilas magnas cum duobus capitibus." It adds that the dalmatic had lost most of its ornaments; only at the sleeves remained traces of Anglican embroidery. It was obviously an old vestment, no longer in use, yet considered valuable.

61. *SILK TWILL. COCKS AND TREES*

BYZANTINE, 8TH–9TH CENTURY. NEW YORK CITY, COOPER UNION MUSEUM.

10 x 7 in. (25 x 18 cm.). No. 1902.1.212. Ex-coll. Miguel y Badia. Exhibited: Worcester, 1937, cat. no. 146; New York, 1940, cat. no. 62, p. 359, "Sassanian."

Plain compound weft twill, blue and yellow silks. Cross-tile motifs form an all-over network, with star octagons framing roundels. These contain alternately a cock and a palmette tree.

The "cross-tiles" are really four stylized peacock feathers emanating from a central rosette; the sharp corners are softened by heart-shaped petals. The placing of the small roundels in the star intervals shows the preoccupation of the Byzantine designer with the possibilities of the empty space. The cock and the tree are closely adapted from Sassanian prototypes. For dress wear small rather inconspicuously patterned fabrics, where the beauty of the colors was of great importance, were in steady demand. Since fabrics of this type were not highly valued, they are rarely preserved.

62. *SILK TWILL. BIRDS AND ROSETTES*

BYZANTINE, 8TH–9TH CENTURY. NEW YORK CITY, THE PIERPONT MORGAN LIBRARY.

13¾ x 10¼ in. (35 x 26 cm.). Inside front cover of M 1, Lindau or Ashburnham Gospels. Published: H. A. Elsberg, "Two Mediaeval Woven Silk Fabrics in the Binding of the 9th Century MS. 'The Four Gospels' in the Pierpont Morgan Library, New York City," Needle and Bobbin Club *Bulletin*, XVII (1933) No. 1, 3.

Red, dark-green, pale-green, and white silks. Two birds confronted, two birds addorsed, and on the red ground the faintly visible, badly rubbed remains of five rosettes. The birds, eagles or falcons, stand out in two shades of green; their feet are white with red claws. Around their necks are pearl collars tied with floating scarves, and in their beaks they hold jeweled rings. The birds are adapted from Sassanian art, but the rosettes are *diasprum*, a Byzantine invention, the first Western silk weave that shows the pattern and the ground of the same color but in a different texture. The somewhat uncertain use of this weave and also the purity of design of the birds point to an early date, probably the early part of the ninth century, possibly even earlier. By the end of the ninth and during the tenth century, *diasprum* was used for elaborate all-over designs in Byzantine plain-colored silk fabrics.

The date of the silk is confirmed by the evidence that it was part of the original binding. The "Four Gospels" were written and illuminated in the Benedictine Monastery of St. Gallen, Switzerland, about 825. The original cover was used as back cover when later in the ninth century a new front cover was added, a work of the monks of Saint Denis. According to tradition, this manuscript was a gift of Louis le Débonnaire, son of Charlemagne (emperor from 814 to 840), to the Chapter of the Noble Canonesses of Lindau, on Lake Constance. When the Abbey was dissolved in 1803, the manuscript became the property of the last abbess. After her death it was sold to the fourth Earl of Ashburnham; later it was acquired by Mr. J. Pierpont Morgan.

63. *SILK TWILL. THE SENMURV*

BYZANTINE, 8TH–9TH CENTURY. NEW YORK CITY, COOPER UNION MUSEUM.

12 x 6¼ in. (30½ x 15½ cm.). No. 1902-1-214. Ex-coll. Miguel y Badia. Exhibited: *The Dark Ages*, Worcester, 1935, cat. no. 145. Published: R. M. Riefstahl, "Early Textiles in the Cooper Union Museum," in *Art in America*, III, 1915, p. 253, fig. 3. Specimens of the same fabric: Brussels, Musée du Cinquantenaire, no. 609; Florence, Bargello, no. 629; London, Victoria and Albert Museum, no. 761–1892; Paris, Musée des Arts Décoratifs, no. 16,325. Compare: Falke, II, p. 11, "Byzantine 10th to 11th century"; Kendrick, 1925, no. 1005, p. 25, "Hither Asia, 9th century"; *Survey*, I, p. 711, no. 4, "Sassanian."

Compound weft twill, dark tones of blue, purple, green, and yellow silks. On the blue ground, purple roundels are framed by a twisted wreath of grapes and pomegranates. Disks, enclosing a four-petaled flower within a beaded circle, connect the roundels. Similar flowers, within a frame of pointed leaves, fill the spandrils. Along the bottom runs a purple end-of-run stripe with a band of yellow beads. Each roundel contains a winged dragon with the head, body, and two legs of a lion, the wings of an eagle, and an upcurved tail of peacock feathers.

This dragon is the Sassanian senmurv. As a textile pattern it occurs on the robe of the equestrian statue of Khusraw II at Tak-i-Bostan, and on a green and yellow silk twill preserved in London and Paris. The senmurv survived the fall of the Sassanian dynasty. It is used as the main motif in the present fabric, which is outspokenly Byzantine in every other respect, the color scheme, the drawing of the spandril rosettes and the roundel border, and the band of disks along the end-of-run. This last detail occurs also in two other famous Byzantine fabrics, the elephant silk at Aachen and the lion silk at Siegburg.

64. SILK TWILL. FANTASTIC ANIMALS

BYZANTINE, 11TH CENTURY. NEW YORK CITY, COOPER UNION MUSEUM.

20 x 12¾ in. (51 x 32½ cm.); diameter of roundels: 6¼ in. (16 cm.). No. 102.1.222. Ex-coll. Miguel y Badia. Provenance: Said to have come from the Monastery of Santa Maria de l'Estany, Catalonia. Exhibited: Worcester, 1937, cat. no. 147; Boston, *Arts of the Middle Ages*, 1940, cat. no. 84; Baltimore, 1947, cat. no. 772. Published: José Pascó, *Catalogue de la collection de tissus anciens de D. Francisco Miguel y Badia*, Barcelona, 1900, pl. 16; R. M. Riefstahl, "Early Textiles in the Cooper Union Collection," *Art in America*, III (1915), 239, fig. 5; Dorothy G. Shepherd, "The Hispano-Islamic Textiles in the Cooper Union Collection," *Chronicle*, I, 1943, fig. 1 (Spain?). The Berlin specimen: Falke, II, p. 11, fig. 237.

Plain compound weft twill, rose-red, blue, and dark-green silks. The rose-red ground is covered by roundels, adjacent, not touching. These show, framed by a pearl border, elephants, senmurvs, and winged horses. The spandril rosette is centered on a roundel with four heart-shaped petals.

The design is derived from a Sassanian model, but "the Byzantine origin is unmistakable; the spandril rosette and the fluency of the draughtsmanship are sufficient proof. The elephant has, in lieu of ears, an ornamental drapery, threefold like that of the great Aachen fabric" (Falke).

65. LINEN CLOTH, BROCADED. COCKS IN MEDALLIONS

MESOPOTAMIA, BAGHDAD, 9TH–10TH CENTURY. NEW YORK CITY, COOPER UNION MUSEUM.

7¾ x 6¾ in. (19½ x 17 cm.). No. 1948.24.31. Purchased in memory of Jacques Seligman.

Fine white linen cloth decorated with red, pink, orange, yellow, white, and three shades of blue silks. Gold thread is used as a flat foil, sometimes alone, sometimes apparently laid along a fine brown silk core; no vellum is discernible. The brocading seems to be done with a needle, as a form of loom embroidery.

The cock in the octagonal medallion is still quite Sassanian in type. The fabric is incredibly fine, like tissue paper.

66. SILK CLOTH, BROCADED. LIONS AND HARPIES

MESOPOTAMIA, BAGHDAD, LATE 11TH–EARLY 12TH CENTURY. BOSTON, MUSEUM OF FINE ARTS.

17¾ x 19¾ in. (45 x 50½ cm.). No. 33.371. Provenance: the tomb of San Pedro de Osma (d. 1109), Cathedral of Burgo de Osma. Published: H. A. Elsberg and R. Guest, "Another Silk Woven at Baghdad," *Burlington Magazine*, LXIV (1934), 270; Dorothy G. Shepherd, "The Hispano-Islamic Textiles in the Cooper Union Collection," *Chronicle*, I (1943), 357 (a fragment of the same silk).

Plain compound cloth, brocaded. Warp, light-brown silk; wefts, white, golden-yellow, red and green silks, and gold thread. Large tangent roundels enclose addorsed lions and human-headed birds, separated by a slender tree. The lions carry their tails between their legs and grasp the birds by a wing. These magnificent creatures stand calmly confronted, with one foot resting on the lion's haunch, the other touching the tree. The long tail cuts across the lion's body and disappears between the hind legs; the tip of a wing is visible between the forelegs. The face, with almond-shaped eyes, curved nose, firm chin, and narrow whiskers, is enclosed in a bonnet fastened with a beaded band. Two locks of hair ending in dragons' heads add a last fanciful touch to the strange creatures. Mr. Elsberg called them "human-headed eagles," for "with their bearded faces they can hardly be meant for harpies." Were there no male harpies? The roundel frame shows, four times repeated, a kneeling man grasping the forelegs of two griffins, eagle and lion-headed. This sheer fantasia is well balanced by severely designed spandril motifs and connecting disks. Both times a four-petaled flower forms the center. In the spandril it is surrounded by an octagonal star with four branches ending in palmettes and medallions containing rabbits; in the disk it forms the heart of a large rosette. Like the roundel, the disk is framed by a border within beaded bands. But this border is filled with an inscription: "This was made in the town of Baghdad, may God guard it" (read by Rhuvon Guest).

This is the second time Mr. Guest found the place name of Baghdad on a silk: (A. F. Kendrick and R. Guest, "A Silk Fabric Woven at Baghdad," *Burlington Magazine*, XLIX [1926], 261). That fabric was also discovered in Spain, in the Colegiata de San Isidoro at León; the inscription fills the border of the roundel. "It may be supposed that the fabrics on which the mark of the Baghdad manufacture was inscribed were made on purpose for export, and that when some of them reached Spain they were imitated there . . .

possibly by weavers coming from the East to practice their art there" (A. H. Elsberg). That is possible; yet the three fabrics of this group (Figs. 72, 73) look like the output of one atelier, perhaps the work of one master weaver.

67. COMPOUND TWILL. GRIFFINS AND BIRDS

SYRIA, 8TH–9TH CENTURY. NEW YORK CITY, THE PIERPONT MORGAN LIBRARY.

13¾ x 10¾ in. (35 x 27 cm.). Inside back cover of M 1, Lindau or Ashburnham Gospels. Published: H. A. Elsberg, "Two Mediaeval Woven Silk Fabrics in the Binding of the 9th Century MS. 'The Four Gospels' in the Pierpont Morgan Library, New York City," Needle and Bobbin Club *Bulletin*, XVII, no. 1 (1933), 3.

Grayish-blue, rose and yellow silks. On the blue ground the design stands out in yellow and rose with details of the blue silk. Two vertical motifs alternate and interlock. The central motif consists of a roundel that shows, in a beaded frame, a cone placed on a palmette between split palmettes; this motif may ultimately be derived from the Sassanian royal headdress. From this roundel grows a tree with pendant palmettes, possibly the stylization of a palm tree. This is flanked by two pairs of birds, addorsed beneath the tree, confronted on its upper branches. In the second motif a slightly smaller, slender candelabrum tree rises between eight-pointed stars filled with heart-shaped petals between the double outline and center. The tree is flanked by confronted griffins with the body of a lion and the head of a dragon.

Silks of this type, so closely following the Sassanian tradition, were woven in Syria and Baghdad in the early centuries after the Arab conquest. This date is confirmed by the position of the silk panel that was used as the inside lining of the back cover of the Lindau Gospels. This cover, a marvel of the goldsmith's craft, was probably made at St. Gallen between 825 and 850 (comp. no. 62).

97

68. COMPOUND CLOTH. GRIFFINS AND FOXES

SYRIA, AYYUBID, 13TH CENTURY. BOSTON, MUSEUM OF FINE ARTS.

19¾ x 13½ in. (50 x 34 cm.). No. 31.11, gift of Denman Ross. Provenance: said to be part of a tunic, found in a cemetery near Medinet el Fayyum. Published: (the Metropolitan Museum specimen) Florence E. Day, "Silks of the Near East," *Bulletin*, IX (1950), 111.

Two warps and two wefts, green, once dark, now mostly faded to medium, and creamy tan, undyed. Reversible. An intricate design of griffins, foxes, and birds frolicking among vine scrolls. These cover the whole ground, springing from two stems. The elegant fox has been unduly neglected by textile designers.

69. LINEN, SILK AND GOLD TAPESTRY

EGYPT, FATIMID, 11TH CENTURY. NEW YORK CITY, THE METROPOLITAN MUSEUM OF ART.

12¾ x 17 in. (32 x 43 cm.). No. 31.106.66, gift of George D. Pratt. Published: M. S. Dimand, "Egypto-Arabic Textiles," *Bulletin*, XXVII (1932), 94; *Handbook*, 1944, p. 254.

Linen cloth; warp, straw color; wefts, green; general effect pale green. Tapestry, woven on the cloth warp, white, pale-green, tan, medium- and dark-blue silks; gilded membrane on white silk core. The central band shows confronted falcons and palmettes, gold with white details on green tapestry ground. The outer bands show hexagonal cartouches, alternately green, tan, and blue, with leaves in gold, outlined in dark blue with white details. The narrow borders show inscriptions in Kufic letters, tan with white details on gold tapestry ground, in a purely decorative repeat.

"The style of the pattern is characteristic of the period of the caliph al Mustansir, who reigned from 1036 to 1094. Such fine fabrics decorated all over with gold tapestry may be identified with garments called *badana* made at Tinnis for the exclusive use of the caliph" (M. S. Dimand).

70. COTTON IKAT, WITH TAPESTRY INSET

ARABIA, YEMEN, AND EGYPT, 11TH–12TH CENTURY. THE DETROIT INSTITUTE OF ARTS.

9¼ x 8 in. (23½ x 20 cm.). No. 31.18, gift of Mrs. Dorothea Russell, Cairo.

The ground is of blue and grayish-white cotton ikat cloth. The pattern is produced by tying groups of warp threads in certain parts, then immersing them in a dye bath. As a rule, the woven fabric was then embellished with an inscription painted across the width, generally in gold.

This specimen differs in the mode of decoration. The weft threads were cut out in parts and replaced by tapestry weaving, obviously in Egypt.

71. "BYSSUS"

EGYPT, MAMLUK, 13TH–14TH CENTURY. WASHINGTON, D.C., TEXTILE MUSEUM.

10¼ x 11¼ in. (26 x 28½ cm.). No. 73.480. Exhibited: *2000 Years*, 1944, cat. no. 35.

Fancy compound cloth of byssus and silk. Byssus is the name of a thread formed by glandular secretion of a salt-water mussel. The fabric looks like fine linen and is dyed bright crimson. It is decorated with bands of small stereotyped patterns in green, yellow, and white silk.

True byssus is probably the rarest type of woven fabric; this is the only specimen known to me. The name "byssus" is sometimes used wrongly for very fine sheer linen or silk fabrics.

72. COMPOUND CLOTH, BROCADED. THE LION STRANGLER

HISPANO-MORESQUE (OR BAGHDAD), LATE 11TH–EARLY 12TH CENTURY. NEW YORK CITY, COOPER UNION MUSEUM.

19½ x 20¾ in. (49½ x 52½ cm.). No. 1902.1.220. Ex-coll. Miguel y Badia. Provenance: the tomb of St. Bernard Calvo, bishop of Vich (1233–1243). Published: As Fig. 73; another specimen in Cleveland: Dorothy G. Shepherd, "A Twelfth-Century Hispano-Islamic Silk," *Bulletin*, XXXVIII (1951), 59.

Detail. Warps, light-brown silk; wefts, white, yellow, red, and green silks and gold thread. Tangent roundels show a man strangling a lion in the crook of the elbow of each arm. Beneath the lions' feet are small animals, between the man's feet two small addorsed peacocks. The border shows, between pearl bands, eight pairs of confronted griffins. The spandrils are filled with large and small palmettes emanating from octagonal stars. At intervals the succession of roundels is interrupted by horizontal bands inscribed *al'amr* (the power) in Kufic letters.

The motif of the lion strangler is found on Babylonian and Assyrian seal stones and among the sculptures of the Achaemenid palace at Persepolis. In early Christian art it is often confounded with Samson or Daniel. In this silk fabric the type of the black-bearded, savage-looking man, dressed in a richly embroidered long tunic with a golden belt, belongs to the old Orient. The cowl or bonnet connects him with the harpies and sphinxes silks (Figs. 66, 73).

73. COMPOUND CLOTH, BROCADED. SPHINXES

HISPANO-MORESQUE (OR BAGHDAD), LATE 11TH–EARLY 12TH CENTURY. NEW YORK CITY, COOPER UNION MUSEUM.

13 x 12½ in. (33 x 31½ cm.). No. 1902.1.216. Ex-coll. Miguel y Badia. Provenance: the tomb of St. Bernard Calvo, Bishop of Vich, Catalonia (1233–1243). Pub-lished: José Pasco, *Catalogue de la collection de tissus anciens de D. Francisco Miguel y Badia*, Barcelona, 1900, no. 47, pl. V: "Tissue de Soie Orientale"; Falke, I, 117, fig. 189; R. M. Riefstahl, "Early Textiles in the Cooper Union Collection," *Art in America*, IV (1915), 43; Dorothy G. Shepherd, "The Hispano-Islamic Textiles," *Chronicle*, I (1943), 357; another specimen in Cleveland: Dorothy G. Shepherd, *Bulletin*, XXXVIII (1951), 74.

Plain compound cloth, brocaded; warp, light-brown silk; wefts, white, golden-yellow, red, and green silks, and gold thread. Preserved is one complete roundel and parts of the adjacent roundel and spandril motif. Two winged sphinxes sit confronted, with one forefoot raised and touching the slender tree between them. Their haunches are adorned with a palmette; the tails end in an elaborate split palmette. The wings are richly elaborated. The features are strongly marked, with eyes outlined by heavy brows. The head is covered by a bonnet. Beaded bands adorn neck, chest, and wing. The small animals at the sphinxes' feet are practically destroyed. The roundel is framed by a border with a palmette tendril between pearl bands.

Compare with Figs. 105 and 115, the winged sphinxes of the Buyid and Seljuk silks.

74. SILK AND GOLD TAPESTRY. DRINKING GIRLS

HISPANO-MORESQUE, ALMERÍA (?), 12TH–13TH CENTURY. NEW YORK CITY, COOPER UNION MUSEUM.

13¾ x 7 in. (34¾ x 17½ cm.). No. 1902-1-82, gift of J. P. Morgan. Ex-coll. Miguel y Badia. Published: Dorothy G. Shepherd, "The Hispano-Islamic Textiles," *Chronicle of the Museum*, I (1943), 383; R. M. Riefstahl, "Early Textiles in the Cooper Union Collection," *Art in America*, III (1915), 47, pl. 10; F. R. Martin, *A History of Oriental Carpets*, Vienna, 1908, p. 17.

Polychrome thread; tapestry. The design is incomplete. It seems to have consisted of ribbons, interlaced to form stars and spandril motifs and the framing of the roundels. These have an inner border encrusted with pearls, and are occupied by women seated on a low platform or bench. In one roundel the two young women appear toasting each other with goblets of wine; in the other roundel one of them holds a full goblet, the other a globular decanter with a high foot and long neck.

F. R. Martin assigned the fragment to Persia; R. M. Riefstahl says: "This conspicuously fine specimen is by far the most important relic of Fatimid tapestry-work that survives." But the tapestry technique relates this fabric equally well with clearly Spanish work, such as the "veil of Hisham" of the early eleventh century, preserved in Madrid, and the tapestry ornament of the San Valero dalmatic (Fig. 77). The design connects the fabric directly with the gold brocade from Vich (Fig. 75). The theme of two women passing the time pleasurably may have been far more elaborate in the complete tapestry. There may have been musicians like the tambourine players of the brocade, possibly others playing lutes, psalteries, or rebecs. Such musicians are preserved on the ceiling of the Capella Palatina at Palermo, painted before A.D. 1150 for King Roger II by Fatimid artists.

75. COMPOUND CLOTH. MUSICIANS

HISPANO-MORESQUE, ALMERÍA (?), 12TH–13TH CENTURY THE ART INSTITUTE OF CHICAGO.

4 x 5 in. (10 x 12½ cm.). No. 50.1, gift of Mrs. Walter B. Smith. Provenance: Vich. Exhibited: *2000 Years*, cat. no. 123. A companion piece, New York, Metropolitan Museum of Art, published: Joseph Breck, "A Hispano-Moresque Textile Fragment," *Bulletin*, XXIV (1929), 253; M. S. Dimand, *Handbook*, 1944, p. 276.

Red, green, blue, light-brown, and white silks, and gold thread. Compound cloth. The warps are light brown and white, used with the white wefts in a double-cloth technique. At a first glance the design appears as an all-over network of interlaced large and small roundels. A second glance reveals the fact that in the vertical the large roundels rest free from each other on the red ground. The small roundels are filled with stars of inter-laced golden ribbons on a white ground, with an eight-pointed star of blue silk in the center. The large roundels show, on gold ground, two women seated on a low platform or bench, playing tambourines. A lamp is suspended between them. This, the bench, the faces and hands are white; the dresses green and gold; the tambourines gold with red outlines. Red is used also for the hair, which hangs over the cheek in a long curl and down the back in a plaited tress. Red outlines all the golden bands.

The use of a thin line for limning the forms and separating two juxtaposed colors is a characteristic feature of the early Hispano-Moresque textiles. This brocade and the tapestry (Fig. 74) may be the work of one designer who experimented with the possibilities of *laceria*, both in curves and sharp angles, as a framework for his figure compositions. While for the tapestry various subjects may have been used, only one was selected for the brocade. But here the designer counteracted a static repetition by his astonishing solution of the strapwork pattern. He actually points to his daring innovation with accents in the figure composition, the verticals of the legs of the bench below, the swinging of the suspended lamp above.

"Music accompanied the Arab from the cradle to the grave, from the lullaby to the elegy. Almost every Arab of substance had his singing girls. Vocal music was especially appreciated; the instrumental accompaniment was furnished by the lute, psaltery or flute. With the women of Andalusia the tambourine was a special favorite" (H. G. Farmer, "Music," in *The Legacy of Islam*, Oxford, 1931).

76. DETAIL OF BORDER OF A LARGE PANEL

HISPANO-MORESQUE, 14TH CENTURY. NEW YORK CITY, THE HISPANIC SOCIETY OF AMERICA.

No. H.909. Published: Florence Lewis May, *Textiles*, *Handbook*, 1938, p. 275; Dorothy G. Shepherd, *Chronicle*, 1943, p. 383, fig. 18.

Plain compound cloth; red, dark-blue, green, and white silks, and gold thread. The ground has faded to a soft deep rose-red. The field is patterned with a complicated system of geometric interlacing of stars and rosettes. Across this field cuts a wide border edged by a series of four narrow bands, containing arabesques and Kufic inscriptions. The border, of which a detail is shown, has three rows of large and small roundels connected by framing ribbons. These interlace and form stars between the small roundels, which are filled with rosettes. The large roundels contain alternately addorsed antelopes with a meager tree between them, and two figures seated on a bench, holding in their raised hands a flower or a fruit.

This appears to be the last of the Hispano-Moresque textiles with representations of two women visiting. Obviously such fabrics were rare in their own time, and only the three specimens presented here are known today.

77–81. THE VESTMENTS OF SAN VALERO

HISPANO-MORESQUE, ALMERÍA (?), EARLY 13TH CENTURY.

The Berber tribes, who, after the fall of the Caliphate of Córdoba, swept over Andalusia in wave after wave, asserted their puritanism by upholding strictly the injunction against the representation of living beings. In the early thirteenth century their artists created a new style, the true Hispano-Moresque. They used geometric forms in a wide variety of combinations and added strength to their designs by a cunning use of strong colors: red, blue, green, yellow, and white. This style was applied to all the arts of decoration; the Alhambra at Granada is the best-known large-scale illustration. The Hispano-Moresque style was eminently suitable for textile design, and fortunately its very beginnings are preserved in a series of well-documented fabrics.

These are the vestments, a cope and two dalmatics, which tradition assigns to St.

Valerius, legendary bishop of Saragossa. But the fabrics of which these vestments are made were woven about nine hundred years after the saint's death. They may have been placed in his shrine when his relics were removed from the cathedral of Roda, which was destroyed by fire, to the cathedral of Lérida. The date of that translation of the relics is unknown. In the late nineteenth century the "vestments of San Valero" were sold by the authorities of the cathedral of Lérida to Don Luis Plandiura of Barcelona, at least that part of them which is now preserved in the Museum of Barcelona. Small pieces of the cope and dalmatics have found their way into several museums in Europe and America.

77. FRAGMENT OF A DALMATIC OF SAN VALERO

HISPANO-MORESQUE, ALMERÍA (?), EARLY 13TH CENTURY. THE CLEVELAND MUSEUM OF ART.

4½ x 5 in. (11¼ x 12½ cm.). No. 28.650. Exhibited: *2000 Years*, cat. no. 118. Published: Gertrude Underhill, "Two Hispano-Moresque Silks from the Vestments of San Valero," *Bulletin*, XVI (1929), 68.

Tapestry-weaving; white, red, rose, and blue silks and gold thread. The design is arranged in *Tiraz* fashion, in horizontal bands. Of these the widest has a pattern of interlacing lines of red silk with small patches of white and blue on gold ground. It is flanked by narrow bands. One of these has a figure-eight pattern of interlaced ribbons of gold with red outlines; the other a braided pattern in white and red on gold.

This fragment is part of an ornamental panel that was sewn to the breast of one of the dalmatics. It is much more fragile and may be considerably older than the other fabrics. Another specimen (Barcelona) is complete with the gold band in the center of which here only traces remain. It has a conventional inscription in Neskhi script, red silk. (Giorgio Sangiorgi, *Contributi allo studio dell' arte tessile*, Milan, n.d., fig. 1, color plate.)

78. FRAGMENT OF A DALMATIC OF SAN VALERO

HISPANO-MORESQUE, ALMERÍA (?), EARLY 13TH CENTURY. BOSTON, MUSEUM OF FINE ARTS.

7 x 10½ in. (17 x 26½ cm.). No. 28.326. The Cleveland Museum specimen published: Gertrude Underhill, "A Group of Hispano-Moresque Silks," *Bulletin*, XV (1928), 71.

Compound cloth, bright blue and rose-red silks, and gold thread with a core of pink and yellow silk twisted together. On blue ground eight-pointed stars frame pairs of lions rampant, addorsed, and a palmette tree, of gold with rose outlines. The cruciform spandrils are filled with arabesques. A line of six weft threads of the rose-red silk runs across the spandrils. The Boston fragment shows also part of a wide band with an inscription in Kufic letters, the staffs ending in palmettes. The letters are of white silk with rose-red outlines, on gold ground, separated from the field by narrow stripes of white, yellow, blue, and pink silk, and golden ovals on blue ground.

This fabric was used to patch one of the dalmatics. It may originally have been an entire vestment, cut up and used for repairs. The style of the design seems to mark it as slightly earlier than the fabrics that composed the body of the cope and dalmatics.

79. FRAGMENT OF THE COPE OF SAN VALERO

HISPANO-MORESQUE, ALMERÍA (?), EARLY 13TH CENTURY. THE CLEVELAND MUSEUM OF ART.

16 x 10¾ in. (40½ x 27 cm.). No. 28.648. Exhibited: *2000 Years*, cat. no. 115. Published: Gertrude Underhill, "Two Hispano-Moresque silks from the Vestments of San Valero," *Bulletin*, XVI (1929), 68. Small specimens also: Cooper Union Museum, New York (Dorothy G. Shepherd, "The Hispano-Islamic Textiles," *Chronicle of the Museum for the Arts of Decoration of the Cooper Union*, I, no. 10 (1943), 379, fig. 13); Metropolitan Museum (M. S. Dimand, *Handbook*, 1944, p. 275); Textile Museum, Washington, D. C., no. 84.26; Victoria and Albert Museum, London (A. F. Kendrick, *Catalogue of Muham-*

madan Textiles of the Medieval Period, London, 1924, pp. 58, 61, no. 988).

Compound cloth, white, red, blue, and green silks and thread of beaten gold applied to vellum and wrapped about a yellow silk core. The design is relatively simple. Horizontal rows of small squares are filled with rosettes and stars, based respectively on interlacing curved and straight lines. The squares are separated by narrow white bands in an exceedingly fine double-cloth technique. The golden interlacings are limned on both sides by a line of red silk; little patches of the blue, green, and white silk fill in the intervals of the design and look like enamel.

80. FRAGMENT OF A DALMATIC OF SAN VALERO

HISPANO-MORESQUE, ALMERÍA (?), EARLY 13TH CENTURY. THE CLEVELAND MUSEUM OF ART.

3 x 3⅞ in. (7½ x 9¾ cm.). No. 42.1077. Exhibited: *2000 Years*, cat. no. 117. Published: Gertrude Underhill, "An Early Hispano-Moresque Silk," *Bulletin*, XXX (1943), 100.

Compound cloth, blue, red, and green silks and gold thread. The blue silk, of purest azure tint, forms the ground of small squares, which are separated by interlaced bands of gold with green and gold ornament at the intersections. Within the squares are golden rosettes of four interlaced oval rings.

The "nailheads" in the corners of the squares and the emeraldlike motifs at the intersections, combined with the gold showing wherever the blue silk ground has worn off, give to this "cloth of gold" an effect of goldsmith's work.

81. FRAGMENT OF THE ORPHREY OF THE SAN VALERO COPE

HISPANO-MORESQUE (?), 13TH CENTURY. BOSTON, MUSEUM OF FINE ARTS.

4 x 2 in. (10 x 5 cm.). No. 26.293.

Plain compound weft twill. White, orange, and blue silks and gold thread. Heavy hempen warp. On white ground, on the branch of a simple, stylized tree, stands an eagle (one of a confronted pair). Tree and eagle are of gold, with orange outlines, beak, and feet. On both sides borders of narrow stripes of blue, white, and orange silk and gold thread.

Otto von Falke, in a letter of December 31, 1927, to Miss Townsend, considers the border probably Spanish, although woven in the "Regensburg" technique. "There is no analogy in the ornaments of Regensburg for the palmettelike little tree between the pairs of birds. It and especially the leaf shapes beneath the feet of the birds accord well with Spanish ornaments."

82–85. BROCADES FROM VILLASIRGA

HISPANO-MORESQUE, GRANADA (?), 13TH CENTURY.

A group of brocades was removed from the tombs of Don Felipe, infante of Castile and León, who died in 1274, and of his wife, Doña Leonor Ruiz de Castro, at Villalcázar de Sirga, or Villasirga, in the province of Palencia. All that is known concerning this younger son of King Ferdinand the Saint, his wife, and their burial attire has been collected and made the subject of an excellent article by Florence Lewis May, in *Notes Hispanic*, New York, III (1943), 119–134.

There are subtle differences between these brocades and those from Lérida (Figs. 77–81). The Villasirga group shows a more subdued color scheme and slightly more complicated designs. In their combination of a small-patterned field with bands of Kufic inscriptions they lead directly to the Hispano-Moresque designs of the fourteenth century. The Villasirga brocades may have been woven at Granada, where the Nasrid emirs held their court. They may have been presented to Don Felipe by his friend Muhammad I.

Brocades from Villasirga are in the collections of the Museum of Fine Arts, Boston;

the Cleveland Museum of Art; Cooper Union Museum; Museum of the Hispanic Society; and the Metropolitan Museum of Art, the last three in New York City.

82. FRAGMENT OF THE TUNIC OF DON FELIPE

HISPANO-MORESQUE, GRANADA (?), 13TH CENTURY. NEW YORK CITY, THE HISPANIC SOCIETY OF AMERICA.

17¾ x 13¾ in. (45 x 35 cm.). No. H 904. Ex-coll. Madrazo. Published: Florence L. May, "The Hispano-Moresque Brocades from Villasirga," *Notes Hispanic*, III (1943), 119.

Compound cloth, red, green, blue, and white silks, and gold thread. Across the field of cloth of gold cuts a wide triple band. This is framed and subdivided by plain bands of gold with, on either side, rows of pencil lines of red, white, and blue silk. The central band consists of two rows of quadrilobed medallions filled with rosettes, with eight-pointed stars in the spandrils. The outer bands have a Kufic inscription, white with red outlines on gold ground. It reads: *baraka*, a term of blessing. The letters are written both normally and in mirror reverse; the long shafts end in a half palmette.

83. FRAGMENT OF THE TUNIC OF DON FELIPE

HISPANO-MORESQUE, GRANADA (?), 13TH CENTURY. THE CLEVELAND MUSEUM OF ART.

22 x 15 in. (55½ x 38 cm.). No. 39.39. Ex-coll. Elsberg. Published: Gertrude Underhill, "Textiles from the Elsberg Collection," *Bulletin*, XXVI (1939), 143.

The design is built up on a simple trellis of vertical and horizontal lines, which, between the intersections, bend into V shapes and thus form octagonal stars. The space between the trellis is occupied by eight-lobed rosettes set in a diamond frame that intersects with the trellis. Small palmettes fill the spandrils.

In this large fragment of the field of cloth that is a part of the tunic of Don Felipe, the adaptability of *lacería* for textile design is beautifully demonstrated.

84. FRAGMENT FROM THE TOMB OF DON FELIPE

HISPANO-MORESQUE, GRANADA (?), 13TH CENTURY. THE CLEVELAND MUSEUM OF ART.

9¾ x 7½ in. (24½ x 19 cm.). No. 29.906. Ex-coll. Elsberg. Exhibited: *2000 Years*, cat. no. 120. Published: Gertrude Underhill, "Textiles from Spain and Portugal," *Bulletin*, XVI (1929), 183.

Fancy compound cloth; red, blue, pale yellow and tan silks, and gold thread. Very sheer and delicate fabric. Horizontal bands are framed by narrow ribbons with a chevron pattern of yellow and tan silks. The widest band shows a linear geometric design of blue wefts floated over the tan warps. The second band carries the repeated inscription "Praise be to God," in red with tan outlines on gold ground.

85. FRAGMENT OF THE MANTLE OF DONA LEONOR

HISPANO-MORESQUE, GRANADA (?), 13TH CENTURY. NEW YORK CITY, COOPER UNION MUSEUM.

10½ x 7¼ in. (26½ x 18 cm.). No. 1902.1.978. Ex-coll. Miguel y Badia. Published: Dorothy G. Shepherd, "The Hispano-Islamic Textiles in the Cooper Union Collection," *Chronicle*, 1943, p. 377, fig. 12.

Compound cloth; blue, red, and white silks, and gold thread. The Kufic inscription *baraka*, "Blessing," in white silk with red outlines on gold ground, is a variant of the inscription on Don Felipe's tunic (Fig. 82). In the complete fabric there were probably two inscription bands, with a central band showing the two rows of eight-lobed blue and

gold medallions and the cross-stars, laid across the field. The field is represented here by one row of octagonal stars set in medallions and the end-of-run, a checkered band.

86. COMPOUND CLOTH. COMPLETE PANEL

HISPANO-MORESQUE, GRANADA (?), 14TH CENTURY. THE DETROIT INSTITUTE OF ARTS.

60½ x 21 in. (151 x 53 cm.). No. 47.37.

Red, blue, green, and yellow silks. Plain compound cloth; both selvages, warp threads twisted to fringes. The design is built up from a central field, flanked on both sides by corresponding wide and narrow bands. The field, blue ground, has three staggered rows of red quatrefoils filled with yellow blossoms, separated by twisted and knotted cloud forms. Clouds occur also in one of the wide bands, but there on a green ground. The narrow bands are filled with semifloral and arabesque patterns.

No description can do justice to the shimmering beauty of this fabric. The strong colors are no longer placed side by side as they were in the enamellike Lérida silks. The new feeling will lead to the best in Mudejar textile art.

87. COMPOUND CLOTH. LACERIA DESIGN

HISPANO-MORESQUE, GRANADA (?), 14TH–15TH CENTURY. THE DETROIT INSTITUTE OF ARTS.

6¾ x 7 in. (17 x 17½ cm.). No. 44.144, gift of K. T. Keller. Exhibited: *2000 Years*, cat. no. 132.

Yellow, red, green, and white silks. Plain compound cloth. Yellow ribbons with red outlines are elaborately interlaced to form rosettes with stars. These are red and white, or green and red.

88. COMPOUND CLOTH, BROCADED

HISPANO-MORESQUE, 14TH—15TH CENTURY. THE CLEVELAND MUSEUM OF ART.

19 x 10 in. (48 x 25½ cm.). No. 39.35. Ex-coll. Elsberg. Exhibited: *2000 Years*, cat. no. 125. Published: Gertrude Underhill, "Textiles from the Elsberg Collection," *Bulletin*, XXVI (1939), 143.

On gold ground the design in white, green, and red silks consists of arabesques and leaf forms intertwined with braided Kufic letters reading "Success."

89. COMPOUND CLOTH. PANEL

NORTH AFRICA, 16TH CENTURY OR LATER. WASHINGTON, D. C., TEXTILE MUSEUM.

26 x 13 in. (66 x 33 cm.). No. 84.28. Exhibited: *2000 Years*, cat. no. 237.

Red, blue, green, yellow, and white silks. On white ground a tile pattern, centered on cross-shapes. Across this field runs a wide band with a blurred geometric pattern, bordered by three bands with a floral tendril, interlocked palmettes, and a zigzag line respectively.

90. SILK CLOTH. COMPLETE PANEL

MOROCCO, 17TH CENTURY OR LATER. NEW YORK CITY, THE HISPANIC SOCIETY OF AMERICA.

93½ x 60 in. (237½ x 152 cm.). No. H 921. Published: Florence Lewis May, "Textiles," *Handbook of the Collections*, 1938, p. 276.

Plain compound cloth; red, yellow, green, dark-blue, and white silks. The design runs symmetrically from the center to both ends in a series of wide and narrow bands. Amid the rows of stars, rosettes, trees, and inscriptions in cartouches in the Granadine style, there is one band with an entirely different design, an adaptation of Kufic letters combined with a flower-topped festoon.

This last motif indicates the origin of this fabric. It belongs to the repertoire of Moroccan embroidery. More or less degenerated, yet still recognizable, it can be found in many embroideries as late as the nineteenth century.

91. COMPOUND CLOTH

SPAIN OR NORTH AFRICA, 16TH CENTURY OR LATER. THE DETROIT INSTITUTE OF ARTS.

40 x 8 in. (101 x 20 cm.). No. 43.34. Exhibited: *2000 Years*, cat. no. 133.

Red, white, yellow, green, and black silks. Plain compound cloth, one selvage. The design, in alternately wide and narrow bands, is based on the ornament of the so-called Alhambra style: interlaced ribbons framing stars and rosettes; interlocked stepped triangles, arabesques, and cartouches inscribed: "Glory to our Lord the Sultan."

This type of silk continued in fashion for a long time among the Moors in North Africa, especially in Morocco (information received from Dr. Ernst Kühnel).

92. FANCY COMPOUND SATIN

SPAIN, MUDEJAR, 15TH—16TH CENTURY. NEW YORK CITY, THE HISPANIC SOCIETY OF AMERICA.

12 x 9 in. (30 x 23 cm.). No. H 985. Detail of a large panel.

Ground, red satin; the pattern in twill, yellow, white, and green silks. Large-scale palmettelike motifs with the top turned over, are combined with pairs of confronted, crowned lions that stand on either side of a tree motif.

There are several variants of this design, which seems to have been very popular.

93. BORDER, REVERSIBLE. HERALDIC DESIGN

SPAIN, MUDEJAR, 15TH CENTURY. BALTIMORE, WALTERS ART GAL-LERY.

Detail shown: 2½ x 9½ in. (6¼ x 24 cm.). No. 83.677.

Red silk and white linen, double cloth, reversible. At either side of a fountain, which is surmounted by griffin-heads, stand lions affronted. Castles, with a turret flanked by birds, finish the composition.

This is obviously the armorial blazon of Castile and León, but treated here as a badge, an impresa. It is almost entirely a Gothic design. Only the lions show an affinity with Islamic art in the treatment of their mane and tail and especially in the mannerism of changing the claws into floral motifs.

94. FANCY COMPOUND SATIN

SPAIN, MUDEJAR, 15TH–16TH CEN-TURY. NEW YORK CITY, THE HIS-PANIC SOCIETY OF AMERICA.

6¾ x 6 in. (17 x 15 cm.). No. H 932. Detail of a large panel.

Ground, red satin; the pattern in twill, green, yellow, and white silks. Hop blossoms are intertwined with large-scale arabesques and small patches of *lacería*.

95. FANCY COMPOUND SATIN. HERALDIC DESIGN

SPAIN, MUDEJAR, 15TH–16TH CEN-TURY. THE CLEVELAND MUSEUM OF ART.

4 x 21¾ in. (10 x 55 cm.). No. 39.48. Ex-Coll. Elsberg. Exhibited: *2000 Years*, cat. no. 141. Published: Gertrude Underhill, "Textiles from the Elsberg Collection," *Bulletin*, XXVI (1939), 143.

Ground, red satin; the design brocaded in gold thread. One selvage. Shields with the blazon of Castile and León are separated by palmette scrolls.

A Mudejar design of great distinction, which could be used as an all-over pattern or, as here, cut into strips for borders or belts.

96. PLAIN COMPOUND TWILL. ELEPHANT

PERSIA, 8TH–9TH CENTURY. NEW YORK CITY, COOPER UNION MU-SEUM.

22¾ x 19 in. (59 x 48½ cm.); diameter of roundel: 17½ in. (45 cm.). No. 1902.1.221. Ex-coll. Miguel y Badia. Provenance: a church in Aragón. Exhibited: Baltimore, 1947, cat. no. 770. Published: R. M. Riefstahl, "Early Textiles in the Cooper Union Collection," *Art in America*, III (1915), 231, fig. 1; Frances Morris, "Elephant Medallion Silk in the Cooper Union Museum," Needle and Bobbin Club *Bulletin*, XVII (1933), 40; Falke, I, 94, fig. 128 (the Berlin specimen).

On the golden-yellow ground, the tangent roundels appear in brick red. They are framed by guilloches between pearl bands and connected by disks with a rosette of heart-shaped petals. The spandril motif shows related but more elaborate forms. The glory of the fabric is the large elephant that fills the roundel without crowding it, leaving space only for a smallish plant above its back. The colors are yellow, yellowish-green, and white; a dark brown (black?) outlining thread has mostly worn away.

This noble fabric has repeatedly been claimed as Byzantine, even Hispano-Moresque. But a Persian origin has been advocated most convincingly. Falke omits it from his Sassanian group merely because documentation is lacking. Riefstahl sees "the continuation of the Sassanian tradition in Persia." Miss Morris places it in East Iran, 10th–11th century, by comparing it with certain silks found by Sir Aurel Stein in Turkestan. An earlier date seems logical on the basis of the realism of the representation: in order to show both ears as a splendid ornament, the designer chose the moment when the elephant tosses its head.

97. *PLAIN COMPOUND TWILL. THE ELEPHANT TAMER*

SYRIA OR PERSIA, 10TH CENTURY. WASHINGTON, D. C., DUMBARTON OAKS RESEARCH LIBRARY AND COLLECTION, HARVARD UNIVERSITY.

8 x 13¼ in. (20 x 33½ cm.). No. 27.1. Provenance: Raiy. Exhibited: London, 1931, cat. no. 380: "Seljuk, 10th–11th century"; *2000 Years*, cat. no. 19: "Byzantine, 10th century." Published: Peirce and Tyler, "Three Byzantine Works of Art," Dumbarton Oaks Papers, no. 2, 1941: "Elephant-Tamer Silk, 8th century"; Heinrich Schmidt, "Seldschukische Seidenstoffe," *Belvedere*, X (1931), 81: "Early Islamic, Persia, 10th century"; *Survey*, p. 1998, note 5: "Syria (?)"; Dumbarton Oaks *Handbook*, 1946, no. 230.

Plain compound twill; blue-purple, green, orange, and white silks. Fragmentary, slightly less than half a roundel and parts of spandrils.

In the roundel a crowned personage clasps with both hands the trunks of two elephants. The roundel is framed by a wide border with a palmette scroll between pearl bands. The overlaying disks at the angles show a crescent motif, the spandrils, traces of a bird and animal (eagle and lion?) motif.

This beautiful fabric is one of the most widely discussed textiles that have survived the ravages of time. Two Byzantinists of note have devoted to it one of their learned articles. Comparing it with the famous Sudarium of St. Victor at Sens, the so-called "Lion Strangler Silk," a gift of Bishop Willicarius in 769 (Falke, I, fig. 129), they place the "Elephant Tamer" in the same class and time. Yet it is just this comparison which proves all the difference. Quoting H. Schmidt: "Compared with the Sudarium of St. Victor at Sens, which shows the Lion Strangler in almost old-Oriental severity of form, the Elephant Tamer shows clearly the degeneracy of form and subject. The purely ornamental use of contour stands on a par with the Sgraffito technique of Guebri ceramics." And for just one detail: the hands, which Peirce and Tyler consider "expressively drawn" (p. 22), seem schematic and listless when compared with the fierce energy of the Lion Strangler's hands.

98. *PLAIN COMPOUND TWILL. LIONS*

MESOPOTAMIA OR PERSIA, 10TH–12TH CENTURY. BOSTON, MUSEUM OF FINE ARTS.

9⅛ x 12 in. (23 x 30½ cm.). No. 47.1459. Ex-coll. Claudius Côte. Provenance: from the relics of St. Regnobert, Church of Saint-Saturnin de Vergy, Côte d'Or. Published: Blanchet, *Notices sur quelques tissus*, Paris, 1897, I, 25.

Plain compound weft twill; ground, pale green, design, yellow (faded red?) silk. Roundels, connected by disks, are framed with a Kufic inscription. They contain rampant lions, addorsed, regardant, a slender central tree with palmette top and little goats between the lions' legs. The disks, bordered by pearl bands, show birds in the vertical line, rosettes in the horizontal. In the spandrils, two overlaid squares form a star, filled with a rosette and ending in floral tendrils.

The Buyid silk of the Textile Museum (Fig. 105) has a very similar spandril motif.

99. *PLAIN COMPOUND TWILL. PEACOCKS*

EAST IRAN, 8TH–9TH CENTURY. WASHINGTON, D. C., DUMBARTON OAKS RESEARCH LIBRARY AND COLLECTION, HARVARD UNIVERSITY.

10 x 8 in. (24½ x 20 cm.). No. 36.50. Exhibited: *2000 Years*, cat. no. 17. Published: Dumbarton Oaks *Handbook of the Collection*, 1946, no. 231.

On rose-tan ground horizontal rows of roundels with confronted peacocks in green, rose-tan, and brown; in the interspaces smaller roundels with eight-pointed stars. The beaded frame of the large roundels has been reduced to an indented outline in the star disks.

The use of stepped rather than curved outlines appears as an intentional breaking away from the soft contours of the late Hellenistic silk designs.

100. *PLAIN COMPOUND TWILL. LIONS*

EAST IRAN, 8TH–9TH CENTURY. BOSTON, MUSEUM OF FINE ARTS.

15¾ x 22¾ in. (41 x 58 cm.). No. 47.1457. Provenance: a church at Verdun-sur-le-Doubs. Ex-coll. Claudius Côte; Yulliot, Sens; Maixmarron, Dijon, 1867; Liénard, Verdun, *c.* 1860. The identical specimen, the Sudarium of Ste. Columba at Sens, has been published by Falke, I, pp. 99–100, fig. 190.

Yellow, white, light- and dark-blue silks. Flattened roundels are framed with triangles and a pearl band. Two lions confronted stand above a palmette; triple-rounded motifs indicate hilly soil. The horizontal rows of roundels are separated by slender trees and running dogs and foxes.

101. *PLAIN COMPOUND TWILL. HORSES*

EAST IRAN, 8TH–9TH CENTURY. THE CLEVELAND MUSEUM OF ART.

6 x 11 in. (13 x 28 cm.); diameter of roundel: 4½ in. (11½ cm.). No. 39.585. Ex-coll. Elsberg. Provenance: Sens; in 1896 two pieces of the same fabric were removed from the shrine of St. Paul. Exhibited: *2000 Years*, 1944, cat. no. 181. Published: Gertrude Underhill, "Two Early Iranian Silks," *Bulletin*, XXV (1938), pp. 42–43. For the companion piece: E. Chartraire, *Inventaire du Trésor de l'église primatiale et métropolitaine de Sens*, no. 40; Falke, I, 98–102.

"The silk has a design of small circular medallions placed close together in horizontal rows; within the medallions are pairs of confronted horses in silhouette. Pairs of confronted birds fill in the intervening space between the medallions. The drawing of the birds and horses is animated, barbaric, and grotesque. The disk studding, which appears here in the borders of the medallions, relates the silk to earlier Sassanian designs. Only four colors are used, red, green, yellow and violet. All of these appear in the horses; green with ornaments of red in the bodies, violet in the necks, and yellow in the heads. The figures and the medallion border are outlined by

contrasting colors. The silk is woven of untwisted threads in a weft twill weave" (G. Underhill).

102. *PLAIN COMPOUND CLOTH. PEACOCKS AND SPHINXES*

PERSIA, BUYID, 10TH–11TH CENTURY. THE CLEVELAND MUSEUM OF ART.

9 x 9 in. (23 cm.). H. of ogive 3 in. (7½ cm.). No. 39.506. Provenance: Raiy. Exhibited: *Persian Art*, London, 1931 (no. 72, the specimen of the Victoria and Albert Museum). Published: R. Koechlin and G. Migeon, *Oriental Art*, New York, n.d., pl. LXIIb; Reath and Sachs, pl. 20, the specimen of the Boston Museum of Fine Arts.

Faded, now golden-brown on tan. Plain compound cloth, reversible. Vertical rows of ogives, framed by double lines of Kufic lettering, enclose confronted peacocks whose tails meet in the center above a tree with arabesque foliage. The interspaces show addorsed winged sphinxes regardant, arabesque foliage, and a central tree motif that begins with a palmette and ends in a fleur-de-lis.

"There is a contrast between the close cloth binding of the ground and the looser cloth binding of the pattern, which makes a difference in texture between background and design, and brings the pattern into relief. This contrast in texture is new in this period, and it is a forward step in the development of the art of weaving" (Reath and Sachs, p. 21).

103. *PLAIN COMPOUND CLOTH. PEACOCKS*

PERSIA, BUYID, 10TH–11TH CENTURY. WASHINGTON, D. C., TEXTILE MUSEUM.

17 x 13 in. (43 x 33 cm.). No. 3.241. Provenance: Raiy. Published: Arthur Upham Pope, *Masterpieces of Persian Art*, New York, 1945, pl. 70; Gaston Wiet, *Soieries persanes*, Cairo, 1948, p. 48, no. 7.

Plain compound cloth, aubergine and yellow silks. The primary motif of the design consists of roundels and small disks, connected by an interlaced beaded ribbon. The roundels serve as a background for lozenges that are framed severely by a plain band. Within the lozenges peacocks, clutching small felines, stand confronted, their tails forming a pointed arch over the central tree. In the spandrils surrounding the lozenge, above, winged panthers with rosette on thigh; below, trees with wide-spreading branches; every remaining vestige of space is filled with a floral scroll. Details of the design vary in alternating rows of roundels. The secondary motif of the design consists of a sturdy tree with ogival top and large-leafed branches, growing from a jar. Again there are small differentiations in the design, even more conspicuously in the accompanying winged quadrupeds. In the top row the place of the disks with the Kufic inscription is taken by flying insects. A band of festoons surmounted by fleur-de-lis finishes the design.

"The insects are a refreshingly frivolous innovation. The extreme contrast between the close-meshed, complete coverage within the roundel and the open spacing of the secondary motive is daring but successful" (A. U. Pope).

104. PLAIN COMPOUND CLOTH. GRIFFINS AND IBEXES

PERSIA, BUYID, 11TH CENTURY. BOSTON, MUSEUM OF FINE ARTS.

27½ x 13½ in. (70 x 34 cm.). No. 50.3428. Provenance: Raiy. Published: Gaston Wiet, *Soieries persanes*, Cairo, 1948, p. 44, pl. VI.

Plain compound cloth; warp, purplish-brown (aubergine); wefts, the same and black. The design consists of segments of quadrilobed roundels, interlocked like overlapping scales. Each bend of the arches is accentuated by a palmette, formed by the framing band. The scenes pictured in both compartments are of the same type, animals confronting the tree of life, yet the interpretation is quite different. In the dark compartment the design is contained in a roundel, but in the light compartment it fills the space beautifully, without

crowding. Both times the design is black on light ground, while the accompanying inscription is confined to the dark compartments and therefore appears in aubergine color. Both the ibex and the griffin are sturdy animals, with leg joints marked by palmettes. Both wear necklaces, with fluttering ribbons tied to those of the griffins. An inscription in simple Kufic frames the roundel with the ibexes and continues on the black framing ground: "Order of the emir Ghiyat al-umma Diha al-milla Muhammad, son of Sa'id, son of Ali, al-Harithi, may God lengthen his life."

This very beautiful fabric may have been woven at Raiy; more probably it was produced in a weaving center in eastern Persia, possibly in Transoxiana or Afghanistan.

105. PLAIN COMPOUND CLOTH. SPHINXES

PERSIA, BUYID, 10TH—11TH CENTURY. WASHINGTON, D. C., TEXTILE MUSEUM.

13¾ x 13¾ in. (35 x 35 cm.). No. 3.256. Provenance: Raiy. Published: Gaston Wiet, *Soieries persanes*, Cairo, 1947, p. 51, pl. VIII.

Plain compound cloth; warp, light yellow; wefts, yellow, light- and dark-green silks. Almost tangent roundels are bordered with a floral wreath and a Kufic inscription. In the spandrils large and small palmettes issue from the points of a star of interlaced ribbons, filled with a filigree rosette. Eight little birds accompany the palmettes. In the roundel two sphinxes are seated confronted beside the tree of life. This grows from a cluster of palmettes and is topped by a lotus motif. The sphinxes have almond-shaped eyes, big curved noses, and prominent chins and jowls. They wear crowns and necklaces. Their lion's bodies are outlined by a crested motif; shoulders and haunches are marked by palmettes, the wingfeathers curl at the tips, the tail ends in a tassel. A bird flies above their backs

A comparison of the sphinxes of this Buyid fabric with those of the Seljuk silk in the same collection (Fig. 115) is fascinating and instructive.

106. *PLAIN COMPOUND CLOTH. DOUBLE-HEADED EAGLE*

PERSIA, BUYID, 11TH CENTURY. WASHINGTON, D. C., DUMBARTON OAKS RESEARCH LIBRARY AND COLLECTION, HARVARD UNIVERSITY.

5¾ x 4 in. (14½ x 10 cm.). No. 30.1. One of three specimens in the collection of Dumbarton Oaks; a fourth specimen: Musée de Cluny, Paris. Provenance: Raiy. Published: Leigh Ashton, "Textiles, Some Early Pieces," *Burlington Magazine*, LVIII (1931), 22; J. Heinrich Schmidt, "Persische Seidenstoffe der Seldjukenzeit," *Ars Islamica*, II (1935), 84; Reath-Sachs, no. 16; *Survey* I, p. 886.

Both the two warps and the two wefts are of cream-colored silk. The ground is in plain cloth weave with faint horizontal ribbing; the heavier weft threads are practically covered by the closely woven warp. For the design the extra weft is bound down more loosely by the extra warp. By this slight difference in texture the pattern stands out in relief against the ground. Reversible. A double-headed eagle supports in his claws a small winged human figure whose hands clasp a rope that encircles both its throat and that of the eagle. Through an error in weaving the left arm is produced twice. The richly dressed figure stands with legs close together and feet spread. The eagle's wings show, in a compartment at the top, a seated griffin with raised foreleg. Winged lions rampant fill the space between the wings and the fan-shaped tail. An inscription in flowery Kufic reads: "The glory through Allah"; a smaller inscription above the wings mentions the name of Alp Arslan (1063–1072), nephew and successor of Tughril Beg.

This design illustrates the survival of old Oriental motifs. The representation of a king characterized as Sassanian by his crown and bunchy locks of hair, carried off by an eagle, is most probably a mixture of the motif of Ganymede with that of Alexander the Great.

The legendary tale of his ascent to heaven had been revived by the *Iskander-namah*. The acclamation by the sun griffins and sun lions point to Alexander, who had vested himself with some of the attributes of the old divinities of the sky and sun.

107. *PLAIN COMPOUND TWILL. DOUBLE-HEADED EAGLES*

PERSIA, BUYID, 11TH CENTURY. WASHINGTON, D. C., TEXTILE MUSEUM.

15¾ x 8½ in. (40 x 21½ cm.). Each eagle 7⅛ x 4⅜ in. (18 x 11 cm.). No. 3.242. Published: Arthur Upham Pope, *Masterpieces of Persian Art*, New York, 1945, p. 72, pl. 75; Gaston Wiet, *Soieries persanes*, Cairo, 1948, p. 64, pl. X.

White warps, tan and white wefts. The ground is twill, the pattern cloth woven. In an all-over design the vertical candelabrum trees and the horizontal inscription bands form rectangular compartments. Each of these contains a double-headed eagle with a seated winged human figure before its chest. The body of the eagle is presented in a rigidly geometric stylization that fits beautifully into the framework. The wings are reduced to rectangular triangles bordered with an imbricated line and finished at the top with an inscription. The passively dangling legs accentuate the perfect oval of the body. The heads are magnificiently ornamental, from the jeweled collar around the neck to the huge eyes, the sharply curved beak, and the queer excrescences of the horns. The figurine is no Alexander, no Ganymede. It is a houri looking at the beholder from almond-shaped eyes, her beautiful little face surmounted by a headdress with dangling disks.

"Double-headed eagles, which manage by their abstraction to make their few inches seem colossal, are removed from the natural sphere by the impersonality of their arrogance" (A. U. Pope).

110

108. *PLAIN COMPOUND TWILL. FRAGMENT OF TOMB COVER*

PERSIA, BUYID, IITH CENTURY. THE DETROIT INSTITUTE OF ARTS.

21½ x 15¾ in. (54 x 40½ cm.); width of Kufic border 4½ in. (11½ cm.). No. 31.59, gift of Edsel B. Ford. Provenance: Raiy. Exhibited: London, 1931, cat. no. 39; New York, 1940, cat. no. 9, p. 475. Published: Adèle Coulin Weibel, "Seljuk Fabrics," *Bulletin*, XV (1935), p. 41; Heinrich Schmidt, "Seldschukische Seidenstoffe," *Belvedere*, 10 (1931), p. 85; *Survey*, pp. 2038 and 2080.

Dark-blue and white silks. Along one side of the dark-blue ground of twill, or irregular satin, runs a border. Here between two narrow lines a recurrent inscription is woven in twill bound down by an extra warp of white that occurs only here, between every four main warps. The inscription is woven in the classical wedge-shaped Kufic script, with very long shafts. It reads: "I have no recommendation to Thee save the hope and the grace of Thy forbearance; and then verily I am a Muslim."

In the Middle Ages *cendal* is often mentioned by poets and in inventories among the fabrics imported *d'outremer*. It is described as light of weight yet firmly woven, especially well suited for banners and pennons. The fabric here described answers at all points the medieval description of *cendal*, a noble fabric of severe beauty.

109. *PLAIN COMPOUND TWILL. TOMB COVER*

PERSIA, BUYID OR SELJUK, IITH–I2TH CENTURY. YALE UNIVERSITY ART GALLERY, THE HOBART MOORE MEMORIAL COLLECTION.

21¼ x 38 in. (54 x 96½ cm.). No. 1937-4614. Provenance: Raiy. Exhibited: New York, 1940, cat. p. 463, no. 24; *2000 Years*, cat. no. 48. Published: *Survey*, III, p. 2032, no. 17; VI, pl. 997.

Dark-blue ground, Kufic inscription in white against red foliation faded to tan: "In death is my distress, in the burial is my solitude, in the grave my terror."

The elegance of these slender shafts of flowery Kufic set against the arabesque background represents an ultimate in refinement.

110. *PLAIN COMPOUND TWILL. TOMB COVER*

PERSIA, BUYID, ABOUT A.D. I000. WASHINGTON, D. C., TEXTILE MUSEUM.

Large inscription, h. 5¼ in. (13 cm.); small inscription, h. 1 in. (2½ cm.). No. 3.116. Provenance: Raiy. Exhibited: London, 1931, cat. no. 73; New York, 1940, cat. no. 16, p. 454. Published: R. Guest and A. F. Kendrick, "Earliest-dated Islamic Textiles," *Burlington Magazine*, LX (1932), p. 185; Gaston Wiet, *L'Exposition Persane de 1931*, Cairo, 1933, p. 21; Reath and Sachs, no. 57, p. 101; *Survey*, pp. 2009 and 2031, no. 12.

Blue and yellow silks. End-of-run lines of white and light-green silk and warp fringe. The fabric, a tomb cover or hanging, had been made into a tunic (Reath and Sachs, pl. 51; *Survey*, pl. 984A). This has recently been corrected. The fabric is now mounted flat, showing all the parts of the inscription. The pattern on the dark-blue ground consists of wide and narrow plain bands, two quatrefoil rosettes, and the inscription in two sizes, all of yellow silk. The inscription reads: "Glory and prosperity to the king of kings: (Bah)ā ad-dawla Diyā 'l-milla, Ghiyāt al'-u(mma, Abu Nasr, son of 'Adud ad-da) wla Taj al-milla, may his life be long. Order of Abu Sa'id Zadan Farrukh son of Azadmard, treasurer" (read by Gaston Wiet).

The Buyid prince Baha ad-dawla died in A.D. I012. This fabric belongs to the small group of dated fabrics of the early Islamic period. It is a magnificent example of the epic grandeur of wedge-shaped Kufic writing.

111. *DOUBLE CLOTH. THE HORSES OF THE SUN*

PERSIA, SELJUK, IITH–I2TH CENTURY. THE CLEVELAND MUSEUM OF ART.

13¼ x 9 in. (33½ x 23 cm.); the horses 5¼ in. (13¼ cm.). No. 37.23. Provenance: Raiy. Exhibited: *2000 Years*, 1944, cat. no. 52. Published: Gertrude Underhill, "Two Early Iranian Silks," *Bulletin*, XXV (1938), p. 42; *Survey*, III, 2012 and 2035, no. 29.

Silk double cloth, blue and white, reversible. "The design is composed of two widths of lengthwise ornament bands placed between narrow bands of inscription. In the first band a pair of rampant winged horses is tied to the *hōm* tree, or tree of life. In the leafy foliage of the tree is a pair of confronted birds, and above, a pair of birds flying downward in opposite directions. In the narrower band is the motif of the Sun, a motif which appears, as the sun above the lion, in the constellation of Leo in Seljuk coins of the period, issued at Rūm (Asia Minor). The sun mask alternates with two other motifs, a bird and an ibex. The bands with Kufic inscriptions read, according to Florence E. Day: 'To the owner victory and kingdom, to the owner victory and prosperity.' The drawing of the figures is sensitive and animated, with high stylization and fineness of detail" (G. Underhill).

Dr. Ackerman beautifully explains the iconography of this wonderful composition: "Both the theme and, in certain respects, the style are so dominated by pre-Islamic traditions that there must have been a direct contact. Nor is this far to seek. The old religion still had many adherents in Persia, remaining dominant on the Caspian littoral until the eleventh century, and shrewd merchants would have found it worth their while to make a special appeal to this clientele. The pattern does homage to the Sun. Horses had long been dedicated to the sun; and that these are specifically Sun horses is shown by the scabbard hung from the tail strap, surely in itself an odd device. Verethraghna, the Iranian Sun divinity, when in human incarnation, carried a sword with a golden blade . . . but Verethraghna also took form as a white horse, golden eared. Here, then, is the equine avatar of Verethraghna wearing his mystic sword, and so Sassanian is the solid compact animal that it seems probable that it is the last of a long line which has remained faithful to type. Similarly the tree announces itself as the Sun Tree of Many Seeds, in which nest cosmological birds. And finally, the sun mask set in the rosette of its rays in the alternate stripe makes explicit the theme. The

eagle here is the old Sky bird, now usually associated with the sun. The deer, on the other hand, represents a gesture to the companion power, the moon."

Perhaps it is just this little diplomatic gesture from god to goddess, from Verethraghna to Anahit, which makes the delightful fabric so unforgettable.

112. *TRIPLE CLOTH, BROCADED. A FALCONER*

PERSIA, SELJUK, 11TH—12TH CENTURY. THE DETROIT INSTITUTE OF ARTS.

22¼ x 10¼ in. (56½ x 26 cm.). No. 44.113. Provenance: Raiy. Exhibited: *2000 Years*, 1944, cat. no. 60. Published: Adèle Coulin Weibel, "The Falconer and the Black Beast," *Bulletin*, XXIV (1944), p. 7; *Survey*, pp. 2013, 2035, no. 31, 2190; Heinrich Schmidt, "Persian Silks of the Early Middle Ages," *Burlington Magazine*, LVII (1930), p. 284; Gaston Wiet, *Revue des Arts Asiatiques*, X, 1936, pl. LVII. In the Detroit specimen the pattern is incomplete. The Textile Museum, Washington, D. C., has two specimens: one of the complete pattern, badly rubbed; the other, of one rabbit only.

White, pale-blue, and dark-brown silks, triple cloth brocaded, reversible. Triple cloth is produced on the same principle as double cloth. All three cloths are woven independently in three layers; the third cloth lies hidden between the two others. Thus, when the pale-blue cloth is on the face, the brown cloth is on the back, the white cloth between. Or, brown (face), white (back), blue (between); and white (face), blue (back), brown (between). The brown looks almost black in the design. The inscription is brocaded. Part of selvage at right. Ribbons ornamented with a floral tendril are elaborately interlaced to frame compartments. The large compartments contain horsemen on either side of a palm tree with pendant bunches of dates. The rider holds a falcon on one hand and points with the other hand to the inscription, which reads: "The illustrious Ispehbedh, may God sustain him." The pale-blue horse steps daintily, one forefoot lifted, the other touching a black panther with a swastika marking the muscle of the shoulder. The subordinate compartments contain four-petaled blossoms with pistils forming a flowery cross, with a hare in each quadrant.

The composition harks back to pre-Islamic times, when the Persians were ruled by the Sassanian dynasty and believed in the dual powers of Ahura Mazda and Ahriman. Clearly the shining horseman represents the Power of Good, the black monster the Power of Evil.

The title Isbahbadh—leader of armies— has been traced to the year 23 B.C., "when the artificial atticism of the Arsacid chancelleries gave way to the Iranian language" (W. Lentz, *Zeitschrift für Indien und Iran*, IV, p. 252). It was used by the princes of Tabaristan in the time of the caliph Mansur (754–775). Tabaristan and the entire Caspian littoral remained strongholds of Sassanian resistance as late as the eleventh century. Thus there may have been a demand there for fabrics designed in the heroic character of the Sassanian period.

A perfect description of the Seljuk hare occurs in Virginia Woolf's *Orlando*: "A hare startled, but obdurate; a hare whose timidity is overcome by an immense and foolish audacity; a hare that sits upright and glowers at its pursuer with great, bulging eyes; with ears erect but quivering, with nose pointed, but twitching."

113. *PLAIN COMPOUND CLOTH. FRAGMENT*

PERSIA, BUYID OR SELJUK, IITH– I2TH CENTURY. BOSTON, MUSEUM OF FINE ARTS.

8 x 5½ in. (20 x 14 cm.). No. 04.1621.

Plain compound cloth, warps and wefts black and white silks. A heavy untwisted white silk weft is used for the design. Running loosely over five warps, it has the appearance of a slight relief. Fragment of a very large roundel showing the triple border, the top of the central tree, and the head of a parrot.

For sheer magnificence of design and scale, this fragment must be compared with the Buyid silk from Raiy dated 393／1003 (Gaston Wiet, *Soieries persanes*, Cairo, 1948, no. IV).

114. *PLAIN COMPOUND CLOTH. GRIFFINS*

PERSIA (?) OR SYRIA (?), IITH– I2TH CENTURY. THE CLEVELAND MUSEUM OF ART.

15⅞ x 12 in. (40 x 30½ cm.). No. 41.292. Exhibited: *2000 Years*, 1944, cat. no. 20; Baltimore, 1947, cat. no. 771. Published: Gertrude Underhill, "A Tenth-Century Byzantine Silk from Antioch," *Bulletin*, XXIX (1942), p. 6; Phyllis Ackerman, "Medieval Silk-weaving from Antioch, Byzantine Work of a School Previously Islamic," *Illustrated London News*, August 15, 1936, p. 274; Florence E. Day, "Some Islamic Textiles, Probably Mesopotamian," in a paper read before the American Oriental Society at Yale University, April, 1949.

Compound cloth, very fine green warp and wefts. The design is produced by the extra weft of white floss, which, when not needed, is passed between the ground wefts. The fabric is almost sheer in appearance, of very light weight. The design is incomplete. Interlaced bands form an eight-pointed star and other compartments. In the star motif the band is accompanied by a palmette tendril, which frames a central medallion. This contains a four-petaled blossom, composed of three-lobed palmettes pointing inward, on continuous stems that are crossed in the center. Griffins occupy the corner compartments. The incomplete parts of the design show palmettes forming bands and rosettes and a part of another motif.

This beautiful fabric has been assigned to Byzantine or Islamic Syria, to Mesopotamia or Persia. One characteristic of Byzantine textile design of the tenth to twelfth century, the excellent use of the empty space, is absent. The elaborately interlaced framework connects the design with Seljuk Persia of the eleventh to twelfth century.

115. PLAIN COMPOUND CLOTH. SPHINXES

PERSIA, SELJUK, 11TH–12TH CEN-
TURY. WASHINGTON, D. C., TEX-
TILE MUSEUM.

24 x 9½ in. (61 x 24 cm.). No. 3.212. Exhibited: New York, 1940, cat. no. 1, p. 440; *2000 Years*, 1944, cat. no. 51. Published: *Survey*, pp. 2015 and 2035, no. 28; Ashton Leigh, "Some Early Textiles," *Burlington Magazine*, LVIII (1931), p. 22; Arthur Upham Pope, *Masterpieces of Persian Art*, New York, 1945, pl. 72.

Compound cloth, the pattern in twill; red (faded to a golden apricot tone) and green silks. Design incomplete. Polygonal compartments are framed by a triple band of two plain ribbons and a heavily foliated undulating stem. A fantastic scrolling tree fills the oblong compartment that springs from two—possibly from four—angles of an octagonal compartment. Here candelabrum trees of two varieties organize the field outside an eight-pointed star that contains a floral rosette. Winged sejant sphinxes lift one forepaw and appear to smile in greeting the neighbor. They wear torques with medallions and crowns tied with a ribbon.

"The silhouettes and articulations suggest bas-reliefs. The tree is a descendant of a type which makes its first Iranian appearance at Tak-i-Bostan, and the sphinx has a peculiarly pure classical quality. This silk demonstrates again how sophisticated the artists of this school were, and how perfectly in command of their resources, both as draftsmen and as weavers" (Phillis Ackerman).

116. DETAIL OF A TOMB COVER

PERSIA, SELJUK, 12TH CENTURY.
WASHINGTON, D. C., TEXTILE MU-
SEUM.

Detail, shown sideways: 12 x 15 in. (30 x 38 cm.); the entire specimen: 66¼ x 34 in. (168½ x 86½ cm.). No. 3.209. Other specimens: New York, Metropolitan Museum, and Paris, Musée de Cluny. Exhibited (the New York specimen): London, 1931, cat. no. 38a, and *2000*

Years, cat. no. 50; the Textile Museum specimen: New York, 1940, cat. no. 8, p. 453. Published: Reath and Sachs, no. 61; *Survey*, III, 2020, 2194; VI, pl. 991.

Plain compound satin, reversible; white and brown silks. All-over design of lozenges, separated by a ribbon patterned with hounds pursuing hares across a floral tendril. The lozenges contain in alternate rows an arabesque ornament and confronted ibexes inscribed: "Pardon and Mercy"; they are repeated feet to feet over scrollwork covering the ground.

"The combination of the rigid structure of the major composition and the swift and forceful movement of the scrolls . . . makes this one of the most powerful textile designs known, a strength that is enhanced by the exquisite elegance of all the details" (Phillis Ackerman). The tomb covers, Figs. 116 and 117 may be the work of one designer; they were probably woven in eastern Persia, for in both cases the scrollwork behind the animals shows Eastern affinity, and the doe-khilin of figure 117 is clearly of Chinese derivation.

117. DETAIL OF A TOMB COVER

PERSIA, SELJUK, 12TH CENTURY.
THE DETROIT INSTITUTE OF ARTS.

Detail, shown sideways: 22 x 19 in. (56 x 48 cm.); the octagon: 9 x 10¾ in. (23 x 27 cm.). No. 40.139. Provenance: Raiy. Exhibited: *2000 Years*, 1944, cat. no. 53. Published: Adèle Coulin Weibel, "A Persian Satin of the Seljuk Period," *Bulletin*, XX (1941), p. 34; *Survey*, pp. 2018 and 2040; Arthur Upham Pope, *Masterpieces of Persian Art*, 1945, pl. 71. Another specimen: Cleveland Museum of Art, no. 49.115.

Plain, compound satin, reversible; white, pale-blue, and rose-beige silks. End of run, two white lines on blue ground and a band of white satin, with vestiges of a warp fringe. At first glance the design looks like a combination of the two main systems of Islamic ornament, the geometric and the biomorphic. Closer examination reduces the floral ornament of the spandrils to a pure abstraction, while the geometric sturdiness of the octagons is abrogated by their flexibility, caused by the fact that the border, with its inscription in tall, sparsely foliated Kufic, is hardly differentiated from the background. Within this frame, against a thicket of leafy scrolls, are four pairs of animals, confronted and feet to feet. A leaping hare screams in terror, a big spotted creature, a doe-khilin, looks back startled at some lurking danger.

118. *PLAIN COMPOUND CLOTH. DUCKS*

PERSIA, SELJUK, LATE I2TH–I3TH CENTURY. WASHINGTON, D. C., TEXTILE MUSEUM.

14 x 25 in. (36 x 63½ cm.). H. of roundel *c.* 9 in. (*c.* 23 cm.). No. 3.199. Provenance: Raiy. Exhibited: London, 1931, cat. no. 38g; New York, 1940, cat. no. 19, p. 479; *2000 Years*, 1944, cat. no. 56. Published: *Survey*, pp. 2019, 2038, no. 43; Heinrich Schmidt, "Persische Seidenstoffe der Seldschukenzeit," *Ars Islamica*, II (1935), p. 84; Reath and Sachs, p. 76, pl. 19; Arthur Upham Pope, *Masterpieces of Persian Art*, New York, 1945, p. 73, pl. 73b. Another specimen: Museum of Art, Providence, R. I.

Plain compound cloth, both selvages; yellow, dark-blue, tan (faded green?), and dull orange (red?) silks. Yellow ground with dark-blue roundels, slightly flattened, framed with a Kufic inscription: "Be not secure from death in any place nor at any breath" (Minovi). Each roundel contains two pairs of cackling ducks, confronted and in mirror repeat, against scrolling vines. The spandrils show exiguous trees in outline; also in outline is the scrolling leaf pattern behind the inscription.

"The intricate enmeshing of the figures in an all-over ground foliation is extended even to the Kufic script which, without margins, defines the roundels. Yet the underlying band of foliation, though identical in structure with that of the interstitial lozenges, is kept distinct with a narrow vacuum between" (A. U. Pope).

119. *COMPOUND TWILL. PEACOCKS*

PERSIA, SELJUK, I2TH–I3TH CENTURY. NEW HAVEN, YALE UNIVERSITY ART GALLERY, THE HOBART MOORE MEMORIAL COLLECTION.

11½ x 15 in. (29 x 38 cm.). No. 1937–4617. Exhibited: New York, 1940, cat. no. 24, p. 480. Published: Margaret T. J. Rowe, *Picture Book No. 2*, Yale University Art Gallery, p. 7; *Survey*, III, pp. 2010, 2032, no. 15.

Red, beige (yellow?), and dark-blue silks. Weft twill over two warps; one selvage; end of run, white wefts cloth-woven, traces of warp fringe. Confronted peacocks and conventional foliage in yellowish beige with blue outlines on red ground.

"This panel is thicker than any other medieval silks, and has a very individual and striking pattern, unusually large in scale. Fantastic peacocks are confronted against foliage of the type characteristic of the period, but very broadly though strongly drawn" (Phyllis Ackerman).

120. *FANCY SATIN. CAMELS*

PERSIA, SELJUK OR IL-KHANID, I3TH–I4TH CENTURY. THE DETROIT INSTITUTE OF ARTS.

7½ x 30 in. (19 x 71 cm.), both selvages. Detail pictured: w. 10 in. (25 cm.). No. 31.60, gift of Edsel B. Ford. Provenance: Raiy. Exhibited: London, 1931, cat. no. 38q; New York, 1940, cat. no. 10, p. 475; *2000 Years*, 1944, cat. no. 59. Published: Adèle Coulin Weibel, "Seljuk Fabrics," *Bulletin*, XV (1935), 41; Heinrich Schmidt, "Seldschukische Seidenstoffe," *Belvedere*, X (1931), 84; *Survey*, p. 2041, no. 55, fig. 656b.

Green warps, yellow wefts, fancy satin, the pattern twill-woven. The ground is covered with leaf scrolls. Between these rise conventionalized trees of the lotus-palm type. They separate pairs of confronted camels regardant, inscribed in Kufic letters on their bodies: "Oh! Compassionate One." The terror expressed in their eyes and open mouths is rendered with astonishing reality.

Dr. Schmidt calls the animals "llamas." He says that "this very beautiful fabric belongs certainly to the end of the Seljuk period and shows the way to the Mongol period." Perhaps it is Il-Khanid; the Chinese influence is noticeable.

121. *COMPOUND TWILL, BROCADED*

PERSIA, SAFAVID, ISFAHAN, EARLY 17TH CENTURY. NEW HAVEN, YALE UNIVERSITY ART GALLERY, THE HOBART MOORE MEMORIAL COLLECTION.

Detail shown: 15¼ x 13½ in. (39 x 34 cm.). H. of motif: 7½ in. (19 cm.). No. 1937.4871.

Polychrome silks, silver and gilt metal threads, twill weave all through. On silver ground detached compact motifs are repeated in staggered rows, reversed. From a small mound rises a rosebush with two birds, brilliantly colored in yellow, green, and a sharp pink. Walking up the mound is a golden gazelle. The design is beautifully limned in black.

122. *PLAIN CLOTH, BROCADED, STAMPED*

PERSIA, SAFAVID, 17TH CENTURY. WASHINGTON, D. C., TEXTILE MUSEUM.

7⅛ x 7⅛ in. (18 x 18 cm.). No. 3.246. Provenance: Abiana, near Isfahan.

White and pink silks and gold thread. Staggered rows of iris, brocaded in gold with pink details, on the white rep ground. Diagonal lines stamped on the reverse of the fabric form a diamond-shaped frame for each flower.

The stamped secondary pattern remained fashionable all through the eighteenth century.

123. *DOUBLE CLOTH. FLOWERS AND CLOUDS*

PERSIA, SAFAVID, 17TH CENTURY. WASHINGTON, D. C., TEXTILE MUSEUM.

13¾ x 11¾ in. (35 x 30 cm.). No. 3.110. Exhibited: London, 1931, cat. no. 120m; New York, 1940, cat. no. 8, p. 398; Brooklyn, *5000 Years of Fibers and Fabrics*, 1946. Published: *Survey*, pp. 2201 and 2212; Reath and Sachs, example 37.

Deep-blue, white, and yellow silks. Double cloth; a white warp and a yellow weft are interwoven and appear as pale yellow. Large floral sprays and small cloud patterns in staggered rows. The petals of the flowers have a mauve tint because there the two cloths are interwoven, single lines of yellow alternating with single lines of blue.

124. *DOUBLE CLOTH, BROCADED*

PERSIA, SAFAVID, 17TH CENTURY. WASHINGTON, D. C., TEXTILE MUSEUM.

17 x 18 in. (43 x 45½ cm.). No. 3.52. Exhibited: *2000 Years*, cat. no. 289.

Polychrome silks and metal thread. Vertical rows of flowers, partly brocaded, alternate with bands where flaming lines in double-cloth technique are woven to look like warp-dyed ikat.

125. *DOUBLE CLOTH, BROCADED. SIGNED:* SALIHA

PERSIA, SAFAVID, 17TH CENTURY. WASHINGTON, D. C., TEXTILE MUSEUM.

16 x 13 in. (40½ x 33 cm.). H. of vase with flowers: 4½ in. (11 cm.). No. 3.135. Exhibited: New York, 1940, cat. no. 11, p. 399; Cleveland, *Islamic Art*, 1944. Published: *Survey*, p. 2210; Reath and Sachs, example 43.

Taupe-gray and pale-rose silks and gold thread. Symmetrical pattern of fluted vases with a bouquet, clouds, and a three-balls motif. The vase and four blossoms are brocaded in gold. The signature *Saliha* appears between the blossoms.

126. DOUBLE CLOTH, OBVERSE AND REVERSE

PERSIA, SAFAVID, YAZD, ABOUT A.D. 1600. THE DETROIT INSTITUTE OF ARTS.

9 x 5¾ in. (23 x 14½ cm.). H. of ship from keel to mast-finial, 2⅜ in. (6 cm.). No. 47.2, gift of Mrs. Owen R. Skelton. Ex-coll. Sangiorgi. Published: Adèle Coulin Weibel, "A Persian Silk Double Cloth," *Bulletin*, XXVI (1947), 60. Other specimens, all of small size, possibly from one garment, in several museums; Reath and Sachs, example 33; figure enlarged.

Red and white silks and silver thread. Very fine threads, double cloth closely woven. Ships with elaborate superstructures and dragon flags, with four figures, and boats rowed with square-ended oars, with three figures, ducks, and fishes. The smallest details are as precise as if engraved with the burin rather than woven with a shuttle. Yet this perfection of design was not enough for the weaver, who complicated his task of weaving a double cloth by using alternately wefts of white silk and of silver thread. It is impossible to decide which is the obverse, which the reverse. The effect of the white ships on crimson ground is as beautiful as are the red ships on the silvery ground.

Even more than any of the marvelous velvets and brocades of that great period this exquisite fabric demonstrates the priority of the Persian weaver over his brethren all over the world. Truly it is "small in scale, great in art."

127. DOUBLE CLOTH

PERSIA, SAFAVID, ABOUT A.D. 1600. BOSTON, MUSEUM OF FINE ARTS.

12¼ x 4¾ in. (31 x 12 cm.). No. 48.382.

Red and white silks. The design is divided into vertical stripes: a narrow stripe, with

cartouches framing alternately a spotted gazelle and a Neskhi inscription, is repeated and separates two wide stripes with patterns of vertical and horizontal rectangles. The horizontal compartments contain inscriptions and confronted birds (geese?); the vertical, a horseman, a man seated at a brook, two men standing beside a tree drinking, and a domed pavilion.

For its sheer technical perfection, this double cloth must be compared with Fig. 126.

128. COMPOUND CLOTH. A GARDEN SCENE

PERSIA, SAFAVID, 16TH CENTURY. HARTFORD, WADSWORTH ATHENEUM.

10¼ in. x 6½ in. (26 x 16½ cm.). No. 35.29.

Plain compound cloth, reversible; red and pale yellow silks. A prince is seated in a garden, indicated by a tree and a carnation. Two winged figures bring him their gifts. One, standing before him, offers him a cup; the other, flying overhead, with long trailing draperies, seems to hold a turban (?) adorned with a peacock feather. Cloud motifs.

129. COMPOUND SATIN. SIGNED: GHIYATH. LAILA AND MAJNUN

PERSIA, SAFAVID, 16TH CENTURY. BOSTON, MUSEUM OF FINE ARTS.

34½ x 34¾ in. (68 x 69 cm.). No. 28.17, gift of Denman Ross. Another specimen: Cooper Union Museum, New York. Published: Reath and Sachs, no. 65. For Ghiyath: Phyllis Ackerman, "Ghiyath, Persian Master Weaver," *Apollo*, 1933, p. 252; *Survey*, III, p. 2094.

Plain compound satin, black ground. The pattern wefts of white, yellow, pink, light-green, and light-blue silks are twill-woven. The design illustrates the immortal love story of Majnun and Laila from the *Khamsa* of Nizami. Majnun, a poet who with his songs charmed the wild animals, is pining away in a desert gay with the blossoms of spring and crowded with birds, stags, and does, ibexes and gazelles, lions, leopards, and jackals. The unhappy lover sits on the ground, clasping a gazelle to his bosom. He is frightfully emaciated and seems to awaken from a trance. Perhaps he hears the tinkling of the bells on the trappings of the camel that brings to him an unexpected visitor, Laila, in whose arms he will soon die. She bends forward from her seat in the howdah, one hand resting on its rim. It is covered by the long trailing sleeve of her white dust wrap; her hair is equally protected by a covering cloth. The driver turns in his stride and with raised stick orders the camel to squat. Presently Laila will alight. In a cartouche on the howdah is the signature *Amal Ghiyath*, "work of Ghiyath."

The name of Kwaja Ghiyath ad-din Ali, the *nagshband* (weaver of figured textiles), became known to Western art historians half a century ago, when this black satin was published (F. R. Martin, *Figurale Persische Stoffe*, Stockholm, 1899). Stylistically, the composition is related to Behzad; the design is perhaps by Aga Mirak, his disciple.

130. COMPOUND SATIN. FISHERMEN

PERSIA, SAFAVID, 16TH CENTURY. WASHINGTON, D. C., TEXTILE MUSEUM.

39½ x 9 in. (100 x 23 cm.). No. 3.259. Other specimens exhibited: London, 1931, cat. nos. 360 and 361. Published: A. J. B. Wace, "Some Safavid Silks," *Burlington Magazine*, LVIII (1931), 67; *Survey*, p. 2080.

Blue, red, green, and yellow silks and silver thread. Compound satin, pattern twill-woven. Across a meadow with seminaturalistic flower sprays flows a river. Three men are busy catching fish; a bearded man holds a full pail and one large fish; two young men display their catch of four fishes. The costumes, especially the style of the turbans, are those of the reign of Shah Tahmasp (1524–1576).

"A scene of fishermen calls to mind the work of Mir Sayyid Ali, who delighted to depict ordinary people at work and drew just such strongly characterized bearded men of the people" (Phyllis Ackerman).

131. COMPOUND SATIN. CUP-BEARER IN PARK

PERSIA, SAFAVID, 16TH CENTURY. THE CLEVELAND MUSEUM OF ART.

33¼ x 14¾ in. (84½ x 37 cm.). H. of youth, 10½ in. (26¾ cm.). No. 24.743. Exhibited: Pennsylvania Museum, 1926; New York, 1940, cat. no. 46, p. 42; Grand Rapids, 1941, cat. no. 229; *2000 Years*, cat. no. 258; Denver, 1945. Published: Cleveland Museum *Handbook of the Collections*, 1925, p. 65; 1928, p. 81; Regina Shoolman and Charles E. Slatkin, *The Enjoyment of Art in America*, 1942, pl. 83. Other specimens: Sarre-Martin, *Die Austellung von Meisterwerken Muhammedanischer Kunst in München, 1910*, vol. III, pl. 199; M. S. Dimand, *Handbook*, 1944; Reath and Sachs, example 64; *Survey*, 1938, III, p. 2084; VI, pl. 1011.

In a parklike landscape, where pheasants perch in cypresses and blossoming trees, a young man carrying a bottle and a cup walks calmly, not noticing a lion crouching beside a fish pond, and a leopard stalking a gazelle. The ground is yellow satin, the pattern, twill of six colors; the young man's gown is crimson or light orange in alternate bands. Black is used throughout for limning and for the folds of the white turban and the leopard's spots.

The Cleveland Museum assigns this beautiful fabric to Herat; the *Survey* places it in the Tabriz-Yazd group of Personnage fabrics. "The figure repeats almost exactly a portrait signed by Shah Muhammad (Boston, Museum of Fine Arts), but evidently represents an established school model" (Phyllis Ackerman).

132. POLYCHROME VELVET. A HUNTING SCENE

PERSIA, SAFAVID, 16TH CENTURY. BOSTON, MUSEUM OF FINE ARTS.

Diameter: 37½ in. (95½ cm.); width of velvet: 27½ in. (70 cm.). No. 28.13, gift of Mrs. Walter Scott Fitz. Ex-coll. Sanguszko, since 1683. Exhibited: London, 1931, cat. no. 146; New York, 1940, cat. p. 38, no. 36. Published: Gertrude Townsend, "A Persian Velvet," *Bulletin*, XXVI (1928), 24; Reath and Sachs, no. 84; *Survey*, III, p. 2090; VI, pl. 1023.

Foundation warp, cream-white silk; pile warps, black, deep wine-red, light and dark blue, several shades of green and yellow. Wefts, cream-white silk and flat strips of gilt metal. "These evidently once covered all the flat surfaces, passing unseen through the pile, from selvage to selvage. . . . Once the varied forms of hunters, animals, and rocks stood out in brilliant contrast to their background of shining gold. Today the design, subdued to a more subtle harmony, requires closer study to reveal the distinguished quality of its line and color" (G. Townsend). The circular shape with the hole in the center proves that the velvet was used for the ceiling decoration of a tent with a central supporting pole. In order to show more clearly the design of the complete width of the velvet, we omit the section that finishes the circular shape at the right side of the vertical seam. It is a patchwork of four irregular pieces that, apparently, were cut from the top and bottom at left.

Hunters, mounted and on foot, move through a rocky landscape in pursuit of their prey. The design, a miniature painting translated into a woven fabric, includes the section from the top to below the central hole. Here the movement is all toward the right; then suddenly, yet without abruptness, it swings to the left. The "overturn" is masked by subtle changes in the colors, by the many flowering plants between the figures, and by the group of the lion tearing down a doe. This last detail is a masterly invention; it combines the direction of the doe fleeing from the pursuing hunter with the opposite direction of the aggressor. The horseman at the top and his cheetah seated on a cushion behind the saddle look backward at a herd of deer in full flight. One of these has an arrow in its side, but of the pursuing hunter, only the arm holding the bow is visible above the forepart of his horse. This hunter appears complete below the central hole; here the herd swerves to the left; the hunter with the cheetah is partly cut off by the circle curving inward. A third mounted

hunter seems to be warding off another lion, but the central hole cuts off a large part of this contest. Behind the fleeing herd a hunter on foot struggles with a tiger. Another seems to be feeding a very lean hound; he sits on a boulder and behind him a fox and a mountain sheep look from their hiding places among the rocks. A third hunter crouches among rocks at the extreme left. His poised gun arouses the curiosity of an ibex, which bends over and looks into its muzzle. This hunter must be a superb stalker; neither the little bear at one side nor the leopard and the ptarmigan at the other side of the rocks are aware of him. The astonishing delicacy of draftsmanship is enhanced by the black outlines that subtly limn every detail.

Miss Townsend compares the velvet with the famous silk hunting rug in Vienna. The designer of both the rug and the velvet is Sultan Muhammad, chief painter at the court of Shah Tahmasp, and director of the school of painting at Tabriz.

The tent belonged, traditionally, to Sultan Sulaiman the Magnificent (1520–1566); the velvets used for the interior decoration of ceiling and walls are supposed to have been obtained by him during one of his several invasions of Persia, between 1534 and 1554. After Sulaiman's death the tent remained the property of succeeding sultans; it was used by Kara Mustapha Pasha at the siege of Vienna in 1683. After the rout of the Turks by the relieving army of John Sobieski, the tent fell to the lot of a Polish general, Prince Sanguszko (cf. Figs. 133–135).

132a. DETAIL OF FIG. 132

The herd of deer in flight. Below, emerging from a cliff, the head and forepaws of a little bear.

132b. DETAIL OF FIG. 132

The massive rocks below the deer herd. The little bear is seen at right; behind him emerges a leopard. A ptarmigan sits on the cliff. A hunter poises his gun; an ibex seems to inspect it.

133. POLYCHROME VELVET. HUNTER AND CHEETAH

PERSIA, SAFAVID, 16TH CENTURY. NEW HAVEN, YALE UNIVERSITY ART GALLERY, THE HOBART MOORE MEMORIAL COLLECTION.

18 x 18 in. (45½ x 45½ cm.). No. 1937.4624. Ex-coll. Sanguszko. Exhibited: *2000 Years*, cat. no. 247. Published: Margaret T. J. Rowe, Yale University Art Gallery, *Picture Book No. 2*, p. 8.

The gold brocading of the ground is badly rubbed. The design is in green, blue, red, yellow, brown, and black velvet. A hunter rides across a flower-bedecked valley between rocky hills. A cheetah stands behind him on a small rug.

Similar to the hunters of the Boston velvet (fig. 132).

134. POLYCHROME VELVET. ISKANDER SLAYING A DRAGON

PERSIA, SAFAVID, 16TH CENTURY. NEW YORK CITY, THE METROPOLITAN MUSEUM OF ART.

28 x 21 in. (71 x 53 cm.). No. 27.51, gift of V. Everit Macy. Ex-coll. Sanguszko. Companion Figs. 132, 133, 135. Published: M. S. Dimand, "Persian Velvets of the Sixteenth Century," *Bulletin*, XXII (1927), 108; *Handbook*, 1944, p. 266.

Cut voided velvet, wine-red, dark-blue, light-green, tan, brown, and black silks, on a gold ground of flat gilded silver strips on natural silk. In a landscape with pheasants on flowering shrubs, irises, and other plants stands a young man. He is Iskander, as Alexander the Great is called in the *Book of Kings*, and he is shown slaying a dragon with a huge stone.

"In the repetition of the design the weaver of this velvet changed the colors of costumes and other motives, giving thus a more vivid pattern. The colors are purely decorative, the trees and leaves are red, the dragons alternately red and light tan, the pheasants green or tan. . . . Velvets of this type were used for garments at the court of Persian Shahs and served also as gifts to rulers of Europe and Asia" (M. S. Dimand).

135. POLYCHROME VELVET. FLORAL DESIGN

PERSIA, SAFAVID, 16TH CENTURY. WASHINGTON, D. C., TEXTILE MUSEUM.

35 x 15½ in. (89 x 39½ cm.). No. 3.221. Ex-coll. Sanguszko. Companion Figs. 132–134. Exhibited: London, 1931, cat. no. 171. New York, 1940, cat. no. 65, p. 186. Published: *Survey*, III, p. 2098: "Style of Ghiyat."

Cut voided satin velvet, dark wine-red, dark-blue, light and dark tan (originally yellow and orange), and gray (originally white). The ground of yellowish-tan satin was originally covered with a metal thread of gilded silver lamellae. These have practically disappeared, but are preserved at the once-turned-in edges. Broad jeweled ribbons, overlaid with rosettes and peony palmettes, form ogival compartments. These are filled with a network of delicate floral stems that support a large lotus palmette, tulips, and roses.

136. POLYCHROME VELVET. THE FALCONER

PERSIA, SAFAVID, 16TH CENTURY. THE CLEVELAND MUSEUM OF ART.

30½ x 26¼ in. (77 x 67 cm.). H. of falconer, 6 in. (15 cm.). No. 44.239. Published: Gertrude Underhill, "A Shah Tahmasp Velvet," *Bulletin*, XXXI (1941), 157; the V. E. Macy specimen: Reath and Sachs, example 80.

On a ground of red velvet, stems brocaded in gold twill form an ogival framework around golden, six-lobed medallions. Here a falconer and his attendant stand in a landscape indicated by blossoming plants. On the stems are lion masks and serpents coiled around palmettes; small flowers fill the interstices. The design is altogether of cut velvet of nine colors: dark red, light and medium blue, orange, yellow, green, tan, black, and white.

Of this ravishingly beautiful velvet, which was probably woven at Kashan, very likely for Shah Tahmasp (1524–1576) himself, Dr. Ackerman writes: "Later, more ostentatious velvets will be woven, technically more remarkable because of their bold scale, but nowhere is this velvet surpassed for perfection of detail."

137. POLYCHROME VELVET, STYLE OF RIZA-I-ABBASI

PERSIA, SAFAVID, EARLY 17TH CENTURY. THE CLEVELAND MUSEUM OF ART.

61⅛ x 28½ in. (153 x 71 cm.). H. of figure, 22 in. (56½ cm). No. 32.42. One of three panels originally in the Jaipur State Treasury; the other panels: The Art Institute of Chicago and The Victoria and Albert Museum in London. Exhibited: *2000 Years*, cat. no. 250. Published, Gertrude Underhill, *Bulletin*, XIX (1932), 50; Reath and Sachs, example 89.

Over a foundation weave of yellow satin the voided background of the panel is brocaded in gold thread, the fish pond and the robe of the young man in silver thread. For the design eleven velvet warps have been used: two shades of green, two blues, two reds, two yellows, orange, black, and white. Of all these only the moss-green velvet warp used for the cypress tree runs throughout the length of the panel, all the others are used only for short stretches and then cut. The cut ends are held in place merely by the closeness of the weave. This velvet is the greatest technical accomplishment of the period.

The design, obviously inspired by Riza-i-Abbasi, shows a garden of roses, pinks, and hyacinths, cypress trees and fish ponds. Young men, elegantly dressed in robes of many colors, inhale pensively the perfume of a flower held in their hands.

138. COMPOUND CLOTH, BROCADED, STYLE OF RIZA-I-ABBASI

PERSIA, SAFAVID, EARLY 17TH CENTURY. THE DETROIT INSTITUTE OF ARTS.

9½ x 4⅝ in. (24 x 11½ cm.). No. 42.15. Ex-coll. Mrs. Christian R. Holmes. Exhibited: New York, 1940, cat. p. 186, no. 64; *2000 Years*, cat. no. 259. Published: Adèle Coulin Weibel, "A Riza-i-Abbasi Silk," *Bulletin*, XXII (1942), 3; *Survey*, III, p. 2118n, pl. 1058 (specimen Moore coll., Yale University).

Plain compound silk cloth, brocaded. On the rose-red ground a young man sits in a garden with aspen shrubs and flowering plants. He is dressed in a gown of azure blue with a sash of golden yellow; a band of the same material is tied across his white turban. Beneath the tunic appears a white vest with red buttons, and at the neck a trace of the sash material is visible. All folds are indicated by red lines. He wears orange-yellow slippers over white stockings. Brocaded in black silk are the almond-shaped eyes, eyebrows, two long curls, and the outlines of the hands.

"The cloth weave provides a smooth, even surface such as distinguishes the finest paper, and it is better adapted than any other to maintaining linear quality, so that the calligraphic character which was one of Riza's greatest assets is remarkably well conveyed" (Phyllis Ackerman).

139. DOUBLE CLOTH. SIGNED: ABD ALLAH

PERSIA, SAFAVID, 17TH CENTURY. WASHINGTON, D. C., TEXTILE MUSEUM.

14 x 8¼ in. (35½ x 21 cm.); pavilion h. 3¼ in. (8 cm.). No. 3.182. Exhibited: *2000 Years*, cat. no. 256. Published: Reath-Sachs, example 38; for Abd Allah, *Survey*, III, p. 2101.

Rose-red and yellow silks, double cloth, reversible. Two men are seated in a garden pavilion surmounted by a hexagonal dome.

Servants bring gazelles, holding them on leashes; monkeys sit in trees. The inscription "Abd Allah" appears beneath the pavilion.

Abd Allah was not a great master. Yet he introduces, in the four signed textiles known, details in a playful spirit, such as the monkeys in this double cloth.

140. CUT SOLID POLYCHROME VELVET

PERSIA, KASHAN, SAFAVID, EARLY 17TH CENTURY. SAN FRANCISCO, M. H. DE YOUNG MEMORIAL MUSEUM.

49 x 23 in. (124 x 58 cm.). Gift of Archer M. Huntington. Ex-coll. Bessélièvre. Exhibited: New York, 1940, no. 20A, p. 18; *2000 Years*, cat. no. 251. Published: Etha Wulff, "A Persian Velvet Brocade," *The Pacific Art Review*, I, 1941, 38; *Works of Art*, 1950, p. 137; E. Flemming, *Das Textilwerk*, 1927, pl. 296.

Red ground, polychrome design. A double network of wide and narrow stems, with ogival medallions, flowers, and pomegranates, is enriched by overlaying floral garlands and pairs of birds of two types.

141. CUT SOLID POLYCHROME VELVET

PERSIA, KASHAN, SAFAVID, EARLY 17TH CENTURY. THE DETROIT INSTITUTE OF ARTS.

21 x 13 in. (53 x 33 cm.). No. 36.40. Exhibited: *2000 Years*, cat. no. 252. Published: Adèle Coulin Weibel, "Persian Fabrics," *Bulletin*, XVI (1936), 28.

Four pile warps: light and dark blue; pink and golden yellow. Solid cut cloth velvet. On dark-blue ground an all-over trellis is formed by stems running in pairs, with blossoms and leaves. The compartments contain lotus flowers of two types, with tulips and bleeding hearts on delicately curved tendrils.

142. CUT VOIDED TWILL VELVET, BROCADED

INDIA, 17TH CENTURY. NEW HAVEN, YALE UNIVERSITY ART GALLERY, THE HOBART MOORE MEMORIAL COLLECTION.

28 x 28 in. (71½ x 71½ cm.). No. 1937.5326. Exhibited: *2000 Years*, cat. no. 424. Published: Margaret T. J. Rowe, "The Hobart Moore Memorial Collection of Textiles," Yale University Art Gallery *Picture Book No. 2*, p. 17.

Main warp, white silk; three pile warps, orange, blue, and green used throughout, other colors inserted where needed. Wefts white silk and silver thread. On the silver ground polychrome poppy plants alternate with blue pepper plants, with smaller flowers in the interspaces.

143. COMPOUND TWILL, BROCADED

INDIA, 17TH CENTURY. THE DETROIT INSTITUTE OF ARTS.

24½ x 8½ in. (62 x 21 cm.). No. 42.3, gift of Albert Kahn. Published: Adèle Coulin Weibel, "Indian Textiles," *Bulletin*, XXI (1942), 52.

The ground is of silver thread, the pattern of dark green and red silks.

The weaver goes beyond the intricacies of Safavid silks in the straightforwardness of placing his pattern, stylized palmette trees, in undeviating rows, all swerving to the right as in a soft breeze.

144. TWILL TAPESTRY. KASHMIR SHAWL

INDIA, 17TH CENTURY. BOSTON, MUSEUM OF FINE ARTS.

W. of shawl: 49 in. (125 cm.); h. of border: 6⅝ in. (16½ cm.). No. 45.540.

Long shawl with narrow border of pink blossoms all around. At each end a border, showing eleven polychrome plant motifs between the narrow borders. Warp fringe, very fine wool, reversible. Photograph shows obverse and reverse.

145. TWILL TAPESTRY. KASHMIR PANEL

INDIA, 18TH CENTURY. THE DETROIT INSTITUTE OF ARTS.

26 x 9 in. (66 x 22½ cm.). No. 42.4, gift of Albert Kahn. Published: Adèle Coulin Weibel, *Bulletin*, XXI (1942), 52. For the technique: Nancy A. Reath, *The Weaves of Hand-Loom Fabrics*, Philadelphia, 1927, p. 11; or Reath and Sachs, pp. 43 and 54.

Wool, warps white, wefts white and polychrome. All-over design of stems with fantastic flowers and leaves. The pattern is repeated with small changes in the color distribution.

An early indication concerning the commercial importance of Kashmir wool fabrics is found in the *Institutions of Akhbar*, written in 1570 by Abdul Fazl Allami: "shawls which are conveyed to all the parts of the world" (p. 126).

146. BORDER OF A SARI

INDIA, 18TH CENTURY. THE DETROIT INSTITUTE OF ARTS.

10 x 9¾ in. (25 x 24½ cm.). No. 42.88.

Tapestry, *chandheri*, red, pink, blue, green, brown, yellow, and white silk, and gold-metal thread. On gold-shot red ground the pattern is divided into six bands. On the chief band two stems with green leaves and red, pink, and white flowers form oval compartments with two yellow parrots feet to feet on a bough, and with peacocks in the spandrils. Narrower bands have single tendrils with smaller parrots and peacocks. There follows a narrow band with detached leaves and, at one side only, a guardband with trefoil leaves on a stem.

A border patterned with such contradictory elements would lend itself well for draping the sari, because one or the other set of birds would always appear upright.

147. FIVE-COLOR VELVET

SYRIA OR ASIA MINOR, SECOND HALF OF 15TH CENTURY. THE CLEVELAND MUSEUM OF ART.

17 x 9½ in. (43 x 24 cm.). No. 18.310. Exhibited: *2000 Years*, cat. no. 194.

White satin ground, the design in red, blue, green, and yellow velvet. A succession of floral motifs forms an all-over network, framing a six-petaled flower.

The seven dots in the heart of the flower have been compared to the *palle Medici*. If so, the fabric might have originated in Italy. The character of the design, though, places it clearly at the beginning of a line that culminated in the Brusa velvets of the sixteenth century.

148. THREE-COLOR VELVET, BROCADED

TURKEY, BRUSA, EARLY 16TH CENTURY. THE DETROIT INSTITUTE OF ARTS.

193 x 105½ in. (490 x 268 cm.); detail pictured: 53 x 40 in. (130 x 100 cm.). No. 48.137, gift of Mr. and Mrs. Eugene H. Welker. Ex-coll. Sangiorgi. Provenance: Villa Doria-Pamphilii at Rome. Published: Adèle Coulin Weibel, "A Turkish Velvet Hanging," *Bulletin*, XXVII (1948), 80.

White, red, and blue silks and gold thread; cut voided satin velvet, a complete panel, woven in four widths, with a border on all sides. The field consists of one hundred and ninety octagonal star motifs of tulips and carnations, separated by cross-motifs of trees emanating from rosettes. The border has octagonal floral motifs overlaid with large rosettes, tulips, and hyacinths, and separated by a geometric lozenge ending in carnations.

The hanging has an extraordinary pedigree. Until 1918 it belonged to the Princes Doria as a legacy from Andrea Doria (1466–1560), censor *in perpetuo* of the Republic of Genoa and admiral-condottiere in the service of the Emperor Charles V from 1528 to 1558. Tradition places the velvet as a throne hanging on the admiral's galley, the *Capitana*. As this galley was not only fast but built for comfort, the emperor liked traveling on it as the guest of his admiral.

149. FIVE-COLOR VELVET

SYRIA OR ASIA MINOR, LATE 15TH CENTURY. THE CLEVELAND MUSEUM OF ART.

82 x 16 in. (107 x 40½ cm.). No. 43.67. A chasuble of the same velvet was lent by the Art Institute of Chicago to the exhibition *2000 Years*, cat. no. 195.

White satin ground, the design in red, blue, green, and yellow velvet. An all-over network of alternately large and small rosettes frames a six-petaled flower.

This has also the seven dots in its seed pod. The more advanced stylization places it slightly later than Fig. 147.

150. CUT VOIDED VELVET, BROCADED

TURKEY, 16TH CENTURY. BOSTON, MUSEUM OF FINE ARTS.

60 x 23½ in. (152 x 59½ cm.). No. 17.600. Ex-coll. Denman Ross.

Red silk and gold thread. Two winding vertical stems with pomegranates and leaves on slender stems.

151. CUT VOIDED VELVET, BROCADED

TURKEY, 16TH CENTURY. BOSTON, MUSEUM OF FINE ARTS.

66 x 25 in. (167 x 63½ cm.). No. 04.1627. Ex-coll. Denman Ross.

Red silk and gold thread. On a ground of red velvet the entire pattern is of gold thread with a few accents of the red. In the loom width three vertical winding stems, enriched with openwork medallions, are overlaid with leaves and pomegranates on slender stems.

152. CUT VOIDED VELVET, BROCADED

TURKEY, 16TH CENTURY. NEW YORK CITY, THE METROPOLITAN MUSEUM OF ART.

66 x 52 in. (167½ x 132 cm.); two loom widths sewed together. No. 17.29.10. Published: M. S. Dimand, "Turkish Art of the Muhammadan Period," *Bulletin*, XI (1944), 216; *Handbook*, 1944, p. 270; Florence E. Day, "Silks of the Near East," *Bulletin*, IX (1950), 117.

Crimson velvet ground; the pattern in silver and gilded thread; twill-woven. Palmettes of lanceolate leaves, overlaid with sprays of carnations, roses, and hyacinths, frame a central pine cone.

153. TWO-COLOR VELVET, BROCADED

TURKEY, DAMASCUS (?), 16TH CENTURY. THE DETROIT INSTITUTE OF ARTS.

42½ x 25½ in. (108 x 64½ cm.). No. 46.305, gift of Robert H. Tannahill. Ex-coll. Sangiorgi. Published: Adèle Coulin Weibel, "Turkish Velvet of the Sixteenth Century," *Bulletin*, XXVI (1947), 61.

The red velvet ground is almost entirely overlaid with gold. Pale-blue velvet outlines a medallion, ogival above, heart-shaped below, framing a formal bouquet of five blossoms. From the medallion depend blue leaf shapes that are overlaid with flowers and connected by a floral tendril.

Damascus, the chief city of Syria, had long been a center of silk weaving. Even the fact that, about the year 1401, the Mongol Timur transferred silk weavers from Damascus to his capital, Samarkand, merely affirms the superiority of these craftsmen. It cannot have caused the industry to come to an end.

154. TWO-COLOR VELVET, BROCADED

TURKEY, EARLY 17TH CENTURY. NEW YORK CITY, THE METROPOLITAN MUSEUM OF ART.

62 x 50 in. (151 x 126 cm.); two loom widths sewed together. No. 17.22.9.

Two velvet warps, red and pale bluish-green. Binding warp, white. Filling weft, thick white cotton. Two metal pattern wefts, twill-woven. Silver strips on white-silk core, and gilt strips on yellow-silk core. The background and small details are red velvet; the small flowers green. Gilt metal is used for the ogival bands, the central rosette, and the base of the large palmette, which is of silver.

155. COMPOUND TWILL, BROCADED

TURKEY, 16TH–17TH CENTURY. THE CLEVELAND MUSEUM OF ART.

43 x 26¼ in. (109 x 66 cm.). No. 46.419. Ex-coll. Sangiorgi.

Red, blue, and white silks and gold-metal thread. On the red ground, bands of gold form an all-over ogival network. Each compartment contains a golden medallion. Tulips, carnations, hyacinths, and roses fill the frames and medallions.

156. TABLET-WOVEN GOLD BORDER, BROCADED

SICILY, PALERMO, 12TH CENTURY. THE CLEVELAND MUSEUM OF ART.

6¾ x 6½ in. (17½ x 14 cm.). No. 31.444, gift of C. S. Reber. Ex-coll. Seligmann. Exhibited: *2000 Years*, cat. no. 66. Published: *Die Sammlung Dr. Leopold Seligmann*, Cologne, 1930, fig. 193; Fritz Witte, *Die liturgischen Gewänder . . . des Schnütgen Museums*, Cologne, 1926, p. 12, a similar specimen.

Tablet-woven; fancy twill in Cypriote gold thread. The design is incomplete: trapezoid forms of narrow bands are enlivened with small pennants; birds are spaced over the field; on one side a small border.

The red and white silks gleam like enamel on the still-luminous gold ground. The excellent preservation is owing to the fact that the border, used as an orphrey on a chasuble, was at a later date covered by a wider embroidered orphrey. It was discovered toward the end of the nineteenth century and was then shared by the Schnütgen Museum and Dr. Seligmann.

157. TABLET-WOVEN GOLD BORDER

SICILY, PALERMO, 11TH–12TH CENTURY. THE CLEVELAND MUSEUM OF ART.

3 x 2 in. (7½ x 5 cm.). No. 39.46. Ex-coll. Elsberg. Exhibited: *2000 Years*, cat. no. 67. Published: Gertrude Underhill, "Textiles from the H. A. Elsberg Collection," *Bulletin*, XXVI (1939), 143.

Two borders are joined together; they are patterned in brown, buff, and green silks on gold ground. Tablet-woven. Both show a continual wavy tendril, with birds and lions and trefoil ornaments within the scrolls.

Narrow borders like these had many uses; a notable example is the sandals, which may have been part of King Roger II's costume at his coronation in 1130; they have survived with the robes of the Holy Roman emperors (M. Dreger, fig. 75c).

158. GOLD-BROCADED ORPHREY

SICILY, PALERMO, 12TH CENTURY. BOSTON, MUSEUM OF FINE ARTS.

Detail of the orphrey of a chasuble, no. 33.676. Published: Gertrude Townsend, "A Twelfth Century Chasuble," *Bulletin*, XXXIII (1935), 5.

Main warp and wefts, orange silk, brocaded with true gold thread—gold wire beaten flat, wound around a silk core. The gold thread goes only to about a millimeter of the edge of the satin selvages. "If it continued to the edge the sewing in place of the bands would be very difficult, for they are so solid that it would be hard to pierce them with a needle" (G. Townsend). The gold is woven in fancy twill, suggesting a basket weave. Groups of small balanced figures are twill-woven in white, green, orange, and purple silk. Of the ten groups, four are represented on this detail of the orphrey: birds, lions, and deer beneath trees, and a pair of horned creatures beside a rosette. Not represented here are elephants, dragons, and griffins. Narrow tablet-woven golden bands accompany the main orphrey.

These orphreys belong to one of the few preserved bell-shaped chasubles of the Middle Ages. According to a Latin distich embroidered in gold thread around the bottom, the noble vestment was the gift of "Heinrich the Sinner" to the altar of St. Peter. This Heinrich was the abbot of the monastery of St. Peter in Salzburg from 1167 to 1188.

159. SATIN, BROCADED. GRIFFINS AND BEARS

SICILY, PALERMO, LATE 12TH CENTURY. THE CLEVELAND MUSEUM OF ART.

Two fragments, one narrow strip missing: 4½ x 5½ in. (11 x 14 cm.) and 4¾ x 3½ in. (12 x 9 cm.). No. 43.394. Exhibited: *2000 Years*, 1944, cat. no. 68.

Brocaded satin; a wide purple and a tan stripe are separated by narrow white stripes. The purple stripe is divided by narrow bands with small geometric patterns into squares filled with an octagonal star, and rectangles with confronted griffins and bears alternately. The white (faded light blue?) stripe shows a bird (pelican?) and a fish among foliage (water lilies?); the tan stripe, only partly preserved, seems to be filled with floral scrolls.

Even in its fragmentary state, this fabric is a very important document. The griffins are

directly copied from the wide border of the imperial alb of 1181. Surely this once-splendid fabric was also woven for the use of King William II, or possibly for the Princess Constance, his successor on the throne of the kingdom.

160. FRAGMENT OF THE SHROUD OF GUY DE LUSIGNAN

SICILY, PALERMO, 12TH CENTURY. BOSTON, MUSEUM OF FINE ARTS.

21 x 12½ in. (53 x 32 cm.). No. 40.53. Ex-coll. Elsberg. Provenance: Famagusta, Cyprus.

Double cloth, reversible; yellowish-tan and dark-blue silks; a tape of ribbed cloth of the same date is sewed to the edge of the fabric. Bands forming zigzag rows are edged with a pseudo-Naskhi inscription and ornamented with fleurs-de-lis.

Guy de Lusignan, a handsome French adventurer with a checkered career, died in 1194 as King of Cyprus.

161. COMPOUND TWILL. PARROTS AND TREES

SICILY, PALERMO, 12TH CENTURY. BOSTON, MUSEUM OF FINE ARTS.

5¾ x 5 in. (15 x 13 cm.). No. 48.379. Provenance: a tomb in the Cathedral of Palermo.

Woven sideways. Warp, thin yellow silk; wefts, untwisted brown and yellow silk. Trees, with diverse forms of foliage and rings around the slender stems, are interspersed with parrots, confronted and addorsed.

162. COMPOUND TWILL. DOUBLE-HEADED EAGLES

SICILIAN OR HISPANO-MORESQUE, 11TH–12TH CENTURY. NEW YORK CITY, COOPER UNION MUSEUM.

9 x 17 in. (23 x 43 cm.). No. 1902-1-244. Ex-coll. Miguel y Badia. Published (the Berlin specimen): Lessing, pl. 44c; Falke, I, 122, fig. 202; Flemming, p. 30.

Plain compound weft twill. Warp, neutral yellow; wefts, same yellow and dull-green silks. Design incomplete. Horizontal row of bicephalous eagles with eyes surrounded by a rosette. Body and wings outlined by beaded bands, across the latter an inscription: "Blessing," in Kufic letters. The eagles hold lions with gazelles in their grip. They are separated by slender trees, emanating from palmettes, topped by pine cones with palmette tendrils; rings encircle the stems and the split roots. A single blossom is used as a space filler above the lion's head.

It is impossible to speak with absolute certainty, yet Sicily seems preferable to Spain.

163. COMPOUND TWILL. HERALDIC EAGLES

ITALY, 13TH CENTURY. HART-FORD, WADSWORTH ATHENEUM.

8¾ x 9½ in. (22 x 24 cm.). No. 33.343.

Plain compound twill, cream, tan, and rose-red silks. Star octagons and cross-shaped compartments. Eagles displayed, turned alternately to right and left; floral palmettes, rosettes, and fleurs-de-lis.

The eagles are still in Romanesque stylization; the heraldic lily is a motif beloved in medieval Italy. The design is adapted from an Islamic prototype.

164. COMPOUND TWILL, REVERS-IBLE. EAGLES

SOUTHERN ITALY, 13TH CENTURY. BOSTON, MUSEUM OF FINE ARTS.

9 x 10 in. (23 x 25 cm.). No. 40.39. Ex-coll. Elsberg.

Warp, yellow; wefts, yellow and green. Horizontal rows of eagles.

The color combination marks this light-weight silk fabric as suitable for hunting attire, the stylization of the eagles as belonging to the last years of Frederick II or to the reign of Manfred.

165. COMPOUND TWILL. HERALDIC EAGLES

ITALY, 12TH–13TH CENTURY. NEW YORK, COOPER UNION MUSEUM.

5 x 7¾ in. (12½ x 19½ cm.). No. 1902-1–240. Ex-coll. Miguel y Badia.

Plain compound twill, reversible; warp, terra-cotta-red silk; wefts, same and silver thread. Eagles displayed, turned to left and right alternately, are framed by circles contained in squares. Stylized floral motif in the corners.

The influence of Mamluk armorial badges of office is clearly seen in this handsome Romanesque design.

166. FANCY COMPOUND SATIN, BROCADED

ITALY, 13TH CENTURY. WASHING-TON, D. C., DUMBARTON OAKS RE-SEARCH LIBRARY AND COLLEC-TION, HARVARD UNIVERSITY.

8 x 10½ in. (20 x 25½ cm.). No. 33.45. Exhibited: *2000 Years*, cat. no. 124. Published: *Handbook*, 1946, no. 240.

Blue, yellow, and green silks and gold thread. The light-blue ground is covered by an all-over pattern of vertical and horizontal bands framing rosettes, zigzags, and small animals. This pattern is overlaid by medallions with a brocaded lion crouching beneath a tree.

167. COMPOUND SATIN. HERALDIC ANIMALS

ITALY, 13TH CENTURY. NEW YORK CITY, COOPER UNION MUSEUM.

4½ x 8 in. (11½ x 20½ cm.). No. 1902.1.235. Ex-coll. Miguel y Badia.

Plain compound satin. The dark-blue ground is overlaid by green palmette tendrils forming lozenges with white quatrefoil rosettes at the crossings. Within this framework appear lions rampant and ravens, both of yellow silk.

The raven replacing the ubiquitous eagle is new. The design belongs to the transition from Romanesque to Gothic.

168. FANCY TWILL. CROWNED MONOGRAM

ITALY, 13TH CENTURY. BOSTON, MUSEUM OF FINE ARTS.

9½ x 9 in. (24 x 23 cm.). No. 47.1039. Exhibited: *2000 Years*, cat. no. 85.

Warp, purple; weft, white silk. Quatrefoil compartments are framed with bands of palmette tendrils. They contain a rose tree growing from a crenellated enclosure with an arched opening, and surmounted by a crowned monogram AA. The spandrils are filled by a cruciform rosette of lotus palmettes emanating from a central star of two interlaced cross shapes. Four well-designed birds, hoopoes and parrots, introduce a note of Gothic naturalism into the otherwise rigidly stylized composition.

169. SILK DAMASK. LOTUS FLOWERS

ITALY, 14TH CENTURY. BOSTON, MUSEUM OF FINE ARTS.

5¼ x 8½ in. (13 x 21½ cm.). No. 48.384.

This is a true damask, a combination of satin and twill, reversible. The obverse shows the design in yellow twill on the yellowish-green satin ground.

The design—of which this is a mere fragment—seems to have consisted of diagonal lines of curved stems, overlaid with lotus blossoms. Those preserved are of three sizes: one quite small, another of medium size, and one fairly large. This is the fairy-story house of the enchanted princess of the animal kingdom, a most delightful gazelle.

170. COMPOUND CLOTH, BROCADED. PARROTS AND GAZELLES

SICILY, PALERMO, 12TH CENTURY. THE CLEVELAND MUSEUM OF ART.

32 x 10 in. (81 x 25 cm.). No. 26.507. Other specimens in several collections (Cooper Union Museum, Detroit Institute of Arts, etc.); woven as a border, exhibited: *2000 Years*, 1944, cat. no. 71 (collection Mrs. K. P. Loewi).

Green and tan silks and gold thread, cloth weave. Alternate horizontal rows of confronted parrots and gazelles are separated by slender stems overlaid with pointed oval medallions. The alternate stems and medallions are delicately yet pronouncedly different, and thus their importance in the design is accentuated. The heads and feet of the animals, and patterned disks at the root of the parrots' wings, are brocaded in metal thread.

In 1197 the Emperor Henry VI was buried in the Cathedral of Palermo, wrapped in a mantle of red and gold. The design of that robe is practically identical with that of the fabric here presented. Another specimen was found in the tomb of Pierre Lombard, Archbishop of Paris, who died in 1160. The design, so well documented for the twelfth century, seems to have retained its favor throughout the thirteenth century. In the fourteenth century it was revamped and "modernized," probably at Lucca.

The charming pose of the gazelle, with one foreleg raised and crossed over the other, was adopted by the Church for the representation of the Lamb of God; it becomes maudlin when it clutches a cross.

171. COMPOUND CLOTH, BROCADED. PARROTS IN ROUNDELS

ITALY, 13TH CENTURY. NEW YORK CITY, THE METROPOLITAN MUSEUM OF ART.

18 x 8¼ in. (45½ x 20½ cm.). No. 46.156.30. Ex-coll. Sangiorgi. Exhibited: *Mostra del tessile nazionale*, Rome,

1937–38 cat. p. 23, no. 14, fig. 21. Published: Falke, II, 31, fig. 274, the Victoria and Albert Museum specimen.

Plain compound cloth, brocaded, red and green silks and gold thread. On the green ground the design, woven in untwisted red silk, stands out in slight relief. Adjoining roundels are connected by disks with rosettes; larger rosettes fill the spandrils. Within the roundels, which are bordered by floral tendrils between beaded bands, two parrots stand confronted at either side of a tree. Their heads and feet, and the central star of the spandril rosette, are brocaded in gold.

A papal inventory of 1295 mentions: "Item unum diasprum lucanum ad aves rubeas in rotis, cum capitibus ad aurum."

172. COMPOUND CLOTH, BROCADED. PARROTS AND DRAGONS

ITALY, 13TH–14TH CENTURY. NEW YORK CITY, THE METROPOLITAN MUSEUM OF ART.

20 x 15 in. (50½ x 38 cm.). No. 46.156.27. Ex-coll. Sangiorgi.

Fancy compound cloth, brocaded; ground, pale-green silk; design, pale-green, white, black, and red silks, and gold thread. Palmette trees form vertical lines; confronted parrots and bat-winged, snake-tailed dragons form horizontal lines. The heads and feet of the animals are golden, also the parrots' wing-shield and a band across the breast. The eyes are white with black centers. The dragons' crest is of red silk.

173. DAMASK. HERALDIC DESIGN

ITALY, 14TH–15TH CENTURY. PROVIDENCE, MUSEUM OF ART.

17⅜ x 10⅝ (44 x 26½ cm.). No. 47.419. Exhibited: 2000 years, cat. no. 113 (Collection Mrs. K. P. Loewi).

Blue warps, yellow wefts, reversible. Hexagonal compartments enclose in alternate rows a lion climbing a ladder and a dove with olive bough alighting above three balls.

An unusually charming combination of two devices; possibly made for a wedding.

174. PLAIN COMPOUND SATIN. GRASSHOPPERS

ITALY, 14TH–15TH CENTURY. BOSTON, MUSEUM OF FINE ARTS.

5 x 3½ in. (12½ x 9 cm.). No. 35.79.

Double satin, reversible, pale-yellow and light-blue silks. Fragment only. Two ears of wheat, grasshoppers, a dog, a mouse (?), and a butterfly.

175. SILK FANCY TWILL, REVERSIBLE

ITALY, UMBRIA (?), 13TH–14TH CENTURY. BOSTON, MUSEUM OF FINE ARTS.

10½ x 13¾ in. (26½ x 35 cm.). No. 40.43.

Across the unbleached silk ground runs a band of red silk patterned with yellow peacocks confronted, and bordered by narrow stripes of silver and gold thread.

Fabrics of this discreetly luxurious type are rare. They may well be the product of one weaving shop. The ground of small-patterned fancy twill, the reversible design of the band, are possibly pointers toward the evolution of the "Perugia towels."

176. LINEN AND COTTON TWILL. PART OF A TOWEL

ITALY, PERUGIA, 15TH CENTURY. BLOOMFIELD HILLS, MICHIGAN, CRANBROOK ACADEMY OF ART MUSEUM.

19¾ x 10¼ in. (50 x 26 cm.). No. 1927.307.

Into a ground of fairly coarse white linen, figural borders are woven in heavy blue cotton thread. Reversible. The fragment shows one wide border flanked by narrow bands, and a secondary border not quite complete. The wide border shows full-length figures dancing. Bagpipes and shields hang on the wall. The flanking band shows birds facing a plant. The last border has unicorns confronted rearing, plants, and birds.

177. *LINEN AND COTTON TWILL. BORDERS OF A TOWEL*

ITALY, PERUGIA, 15TH CENTURY. BLOOMFIELD HILLS, MICHIGAN, CRANBROOK ACADEMY OF ART MUSEUM.

12¼ x 10 in. (31 x 25½ cm.). No. 1927.308.

White linen and blue cotton, reversible. The wide border shows cocks confronted, between stylized trees and plants with small birds.

178. *LINEN, SILK, AND GOLD TWILL. RUNNER*

ITALY, UMBRIA, 15TH CENTURY. PROVIDENCE, MUSEUM OF ART.

31 x 16 in. (78½ x 40½ cm.). No. 47.331.

Into a plain ground of brown linen, bands of different width are woven in black silk and gold thread. The main band shows a Gothic tower, possibly the Turre Eburnea of Perugia, and a tree with four birds.

The design relates this fabric to the fifteenth-century Perugia towels, the choice of material to the small group of their silk-woven forerunners, which were produced in the thirteenth and early fourteenth centuries, possibly by Palermitan weavers on the Italian mainland.

179. *PLAIN COMPOUND SATIN. PHOENIXES*

ITALY, 14TH CENTURY. NEW YORK CITY, COOPER UNION MUSEUM.

15½ x 8¾ in. (39½ x 22 cm.). No. 1902.1.271. Ex-coll. Miguel y Badia.

Deep-blue satin ground, the design in gold thread. The stems of a grapevine form ogival arches, surmounted and filled by vine leaves and arabesques. These support pairs of phoenixes, addorsed and confronted.

A closely connected group of fabrics shows the design woven almost in relief with a heavy thread of gilt membrane wound over a linen core, on a generally dark-blue satin ground of thin twisted silk. Both Chinese and Iranian influence is obvious; the designs share a clear-cut, rather harsh quality that differentiates them from the Seljuk textiles. Lately the group has been called Hispano-Moresque. It seems best to give them to an Italian, not necessarily Lucchese, workshop.

180. *PLAIN COMPOUND SATIN. RAMPANT HARES*

ITALY, 14TH CENTURY. THE CLEVELAND MUSEUM OF ART.

8 x 13 in. (20 x 33 cm.). No. 39.44. Ex-coll. Elsberg. Published: Gertrude Underhill, *Bulletin*, XXVI (1939), 143.

Dark-blue silk and gold thread. An ogival network of lotus boughs frames multilobed oval medallions, which are outlined with curly leaves. The medallions contain pairs of hares rampant, addorsed, but turning their heads and screaming at each other across a small plant motif.

A design of this type is mentioned in an inventory quoted by Falke (II, 58); *panno tartarico ad pineas auri cum leporibus in eis*. Falke assigned the entire group to Il-Khanid Persia.

181. *PLAIN COMPOUND SATIN.* *GRIFFINS AT FOUNTAINS*

ITALY, 14TH CENTURY. NEW YORK CITY, COOPER UNION MUSEUM.

18½ x 8½ in. (46½ x 21½ cm.). No. 1902.1.273. Ex-coll. Miguel y Badia.

Dark-blue silk and gold thread. Winged griffins, half eagle, half lion, stand confronted at a fountain. Vine tendrils emerge from it and rise, forming an arch, which frames a small bird.

182. *PLAIN COMPOUND SATIN.* *DRAGONS AT FOUNTAINS*

ITALY, 14TH CENTURY. NEW YORK CITY, COOPER UNION MUSEUM.

No. 1902.1.272. Ex-coll. Miguel y Badia.

Dark-blue silk and gold thread. The ground is covered with arabesques, framing ogival compartments. These are occupied by winged dragons clinging to and drinking from a fountain.

With its crowned masks embedded among the arabesques, this is perhaps the most Italianate design of this group.

183. *SILK AND GOLD TAPESTRY.* *PART OF A RELIQUARY BAG*

FRANCE, PARIS (?), LATE 13TH CENTURY. THE CLEVELAND MUSEUM OF ART.

4¼ x 7¼ in. (11½ x 18 cm.). No. 39.37. Provenance: Cologne. Ex-colls. Elsberg; L. Seligmann. Published: Gertrude Underhill, "Textiles from the H. A. Elsberg Collection," *Bulletin*, XXVI (1939), 143 ff; *Die Sammlung Dr. Leopold Seligmann*, Cologne, 1930, no. 209, the textiles catalogued by Otto von Falke. Another part of this same reliquary bag: Fritz Witte, *Die liturgischen Gewänder . . . des Schnütgen Museums*, Cologne, 1926, p. 17, pl. 45.5.

"A fine silk and gold tapestry, a larger section of which is preserved in the Schnütgen Museum in Cologne, was part of a reliquary bag from a church of that city. It bears a heraldic design of four coats-of-arms (repeated), between which are rosettes and conventionalized bird forms. In the upper row there are, alternately: De Chatillon comte de Blois, and France (6 fleurs-de-lis); in the lower row, Flanders, and De Dreux duc de Bretagne. Around the upper edge is an exquisite narrow border. The colors are an azure blue, now faded to violet, cream and brown, with touches of green silk, and Cypriote gold thread" (G. Underhill).

184. *SILK REP, BROCADED.* *PARROTS AND TREES*

FRANCE, PARIS, LATE 13TH CENTURY. BOSTON, MUSEUM OF FINE ARTS.

7¾ x 10¾ in. (19½ x 26 cm.). No. 35.89. A closely related specimen: Falke, II, 39, fig. 298.

Ground, light-green silk rep; design, gold thread; in alternate rows parrots addorsed and small plants, and large plants or trees and eight-petaled flowers.

185. *SILK REP, BROCADED.* *GRIFFINS AND LILIES*

FRANCE, PARIS, LATE 13TH CENTURY. BOSTON, MUSEUM OF FINE ARTS.

13½ x 6½ in. (34½ x 16 cm.). No. 33.649. A closely related specimen: Falke, II, 39, fig. 301.

Ground, bluish-green silk rep. Design, gold thread, fleurs-de-lis and griffins. These are turned to right or left in alternate rows, and brocaded in right and left twill.

186. TABLET WEAVING, BROCADED

GERMANY, RHINELAND (?), 12TH–13TH CENTURY. THE DETROIT INSTITUTE OF ARTS.

15½ x 3¼ in. (39½ x 8 cm.). No. 50.37. Detail: reverse, natural size.

Lappet of a miter. Red silk and metal thread (the gilding almost disappeared). The fabric is woven in two layers with twisted warps and invisible wefts. The design, palmettes, stars, and part of a bird walking to the left, is twill-brocaded.

This is an unusually elaborate variant of tablet weaving.

187. HORIZONTAL BORDER

GERMANY, COLOGNE, 14TH–15TH CENTURY. THE CLEVELAND MUSEUM OF ART.

4½ x 16 in. (11 x 40½ cm.). No. 18.306. For comparison: Ernst Scheyer, *Die Kölner Bortenweberei des Mittelalters*, Augsburg, 1932, especially nos. 6, 11, and 19.

Three motifs brocaded on gold ground. A four-lobed rosette with a leaf motif in the corners contains a stylized flower; the petals, alternately red and white, are marked with crosses and divided by long pistils. Two trees grow from meadows with red and white daisies. The tree with the bell flowers is of local invention; the tree with the feathery leaves may have been adapted from a Palermitan border design.

188. SILK AND LINEN, BROCADED. LIONS

GERMANY, REGENSBURG, 13TH CENTURY. THE ART INSTITUTE OF CHICAGO.

22⅞ x 23⅞ in. (58 x 60½ cm.). No. 07.806. Provenance: Rhineland. Published: Dreger, pl. 77d; Errera, no. 7 and book-cover design; Lessing, pls. 100 and 101; Falke, II, 43, fig. 311. Falke mentions three specimens of large size: Berlin, Brussels, and Chicago.

Ground, green silk; design, gold thread rubbed down to the linen core; eyes yellow and white, teeth white silk. Reversible. Bands patterned with palmettes form a square compartment. This contains two lions addorsed regardant, a central tree, and two small animals in the corners below the lions. The lions' haunches are marked by a split palmette on a long stem, the ankles by figure-of-S spirals.

This is the most beautiful and best designed of the Regensburg fabrics.

189. A FRAGMENT OF THE BIURA COPE

GERMANY, REGENSBURG, 13TH CENTURY. THE DETROIT INSTITUTE OF ARTS.

6 x 18¼ in. (17 x 46 cm.). No. 46.313. Provenance: San Cugat del Valles, near Barcelona.

Twill weave; warp, linen; wefts, green and white silk and skin-gold thread. Roundels with pairs of addorsed lions are enclosed in hexagonal compartments. These are accompanied at top and bottom by framing ribbons, and thus form wide horizontal bands across a field covered with a diaper ornament. This main motif is supported by a secondary motif of vertical lines formed by a succession of serrated leaves. The fabric is much rubbed; in some places the silk threads have disappeared, exposing the linen warp.

Fragments of this fabric are preserved in many museums of Europe and America. Most of these specimens can be traced—probably they all belonged—to a complete cope. According to tradition, this cope was worn by Arnaldo de Biura, abbot of San Cugat (or Cucufate) del Valles, when he was assassinated at the altar in 1351.

In 1898 Alan Cole wrote of this fabric (*Ornament in European Silks*, p. 50): "The designer was neither a Byzantine nor a Saracen. . . . more or less remote from such immediate Saracenic influences as Sicily or Spain, and equally remote from Byzantium. It is possible that it may be a specimen of early French weaving."

In 1913 Falke assigned the Biura cope to Regensburg. Neither of them knew the large specimen of the Barcelona Museum. There the design is completed by a wide border, with a band of pseudo-Kufic letters. According to Miss Dorothy G. Shepherd, this "points towards a center in closer contact with Islamic influences than was probable in 13th century Regensburg, and one is inclined to look to Northern, i.e., Christian Spain." According to Gomez-Moreno, seven of the burials at Las Huelgas (his numbers 37 to 43) have yielded fabrics of the "Regensburg" type. These burials extend from 1242 to 1321. He suggests Christian Spain as the probable place of manufacture of the entire group.

190. COMPOUND SATIN. GRAPE-VINES AND MASKS

SOUTHERN ITALY, LATE 13TH CENTURY. THE CLEVELAND MUSEUM OF ART.

4 x 6 in. (10 x 15 cm.). No. 43.51. Exhibited: *2000 Years*, 1944, cat. no. 83. Published: Gertrude Underhill, "Gifts of the Textile Arts Club," *Bulletin*, XXXIII (1946), p. 24.

Compound satin, black and yellow silks. Spirals of vine tendrils, twisting and curving and branching off, with large and small leaves and grapes. Masks of fauns form narrow horizontal zones between the wider zones formed of leaves and grapes.

The very slightly twisted yellow silk stands out well from the black satin ground. It is surprising that masks do not appear more often in vine-leaf compositions, into which they fit naturally. This fabric may have been woven at Bari.

191. SATIN, BROCADED. GRAPE-VINE TENDRILS

ITALY, LUCCA, MID-14TH CENTURY. THE CLEVELAND MUSEUM OF ART.

8½ x 9 in. (21½ x 23 cm.). No. 26.509. Exhibited: *2000 Years*, 1944, cat. no. 91.

Green satin brocaded with gold thread. Symmetrically curved strong stems form interlocked ogival compartments, heart-shaped at the top. The compartments are filled with well-designed leaves, with a small rosette in the center.

The clear stylization suggests Persian inspiration. Fabrics of this type must have appealed greatly to the members of the Ghibelline party.

192. SATIN, BROCADED. FLYING PHOENIXES

ITALY, LUCCA, EARLY 14TH CENTURY. THE DETROIT INSTITUTE OF ARTS.

9½ x 11¼ in. (24 x 28½ cm.). No. 41.88. Exhibited: *Mostra del tessile nazionale*, Rome, 1937–38, cat. no. 17, pl. 36; *2000 Years*, 1944, cat. no. 84. Published: Adèle Coulin Weibel, *Bulletin*, XXI (1941), p. 12.

Ground, purple satin; design, skin-gold thread with touches of pink silk. Between diagonal, wavy tendrils with spiky leaves and three distinct groups of lotus flowers, long-tailed birds—phoenixes adapted from the Chinese—fly up and swoop down.

193. SATIN, BROCADED. EAGLES, DOGS, AND GAZELLES

ITALY, LUCCA, MID-14TH CENTURY. THE CLEVELAND MUSEUM OF ART.

10½ x 13 in. (21½ x 33 cm.). No. 42.1078.

Gold-brocaded satin, rose faded to tan. The design is divided into alternating wide and narrow horizontal bands. The wide band shows an eagle pecking at a plant and a collared dog clawing and barking at a tree. The narrow band has a design of leaf scrolls forming cartouches, which frame gazelles running to left.

This is an excellent illustration of the interpenetration of Chinese and European motifs. The general distribution and the animals are borrowed from the Far East; the eagle retains the head and something of the pose of the phoenix, while both the dog and the gazelle look so much like khilins that one is tempted to call them by that name. The feet of both animals show a tendency to merge into floral scrolls. The finely drawn cartouche scroll and the tree with its sharp-pointed leaves are Gothic. Delightfully uncertain is the small border motif between the bands.

194. SATIN, BROCADED. LOTUS PALMETTES AND ANIMALS

ITALY, LUCCA, SECOND HALF OF 14TH CENTURY. THE CLEVELAND MUSEUM OF ART.

c. 14 x 18½ in. (35½ x 47 cm.). No. 19.17a. Ex-coll. Dudley P. Allen. Exhibited: *2000 Years*, cat. no. 89. Published: Falke, II, 82, fig. 435; W. Mannowski, *Der Danziger Paramentenschatz*, Berlin, n.d. (1931), I, no. 7.

Ground, faded purple satin; design, gilded silver thread and touches of orange silk. Ribbons with pseudo-Kufic inscriptions form scalloped lines. From their points rise lotus palmettes, which are surmounted by sheaves of wheat. The palmettes are designed very imaginatively; in one row they are filled with floral arabesques and two dragons, in the next row (here incomplete) they are enlivened by four eagles. At the sides of the wheat motif sit confronted dogs and cheetahs, both wearing collars. Palmettes of two pairs of eagle's wings, and a Kufic motto surmounted by bat wings, finish this delightful composition.

Several fragments of this satin are preserved in the cathedral treasure of Danzig; the speci-

mens in Berlin, London, and Cleveland belonged originally to the same vestment.

195. PART OF A CHASUBLE

SATIN, BROCADED: ITALY, LUCCA, SECOND HALF OF 14TH CENTURY. ORPHREY: COLOGNE, 14TH CENTURY. THE CLEVELAND MUSEUM OF ART.

42 x 29 in. (106 x 68½ cm.). No. 28.653. Exhibited: *2000 Years*, 1944, cat. no. 97. Published: Gertrude Underhill, "A Textile of the 14th Century," *Bulletin*, XVI (1929), p. 51.

Satin ground faded to a greenish-ivory tone; design, all Cyprian gold thread. Large birds (herons?) have alighted on a flowery meadow and, curving their long necks downward, seem to inspect a motif composed of a few pseudo-Kufic letters. They are watched by cheetahs seated on mounds of earth. The orphrey consists of a Cologne border of the early Gothic type, with the design widely spaced on the gold ground. The holy name MARIA alternates with a stylized tree, a rosette, and a pelican feeding three fledglings. This border is accompanied and outlined by narrow bands of floral embroidery in polychrome silks and gold.

196. SATIN, BROCADED. BIRDS AND ANIMALS

ITALY, LUCCA, 14TH CENTURY. BOSTON, MUSEUM OF FINE ARTS.

No. 48.378. Exhibited (a complete specimen): *Mostra del tessile nazionale*, Rome, 1937–38, cat. no. 23, fig. 34.

On green satin ground, the design in gold thread, incomplete. Lions, dogs wearing a ducal crown around their body, eagles, and small birds are perched on a slender floral tendril.

197. SATIN, BROCADED. FALCONS WITH PREY

ITALY, LUCCA, 14TH CENTURY. BOSTON, MUSEUM OF FINE ARTS.

26 x 7 in. (66½ x 17½ cm.). No. 35.33.

On a ground of faded rose-red satin, the design is brocaded in gold thread. Large falcons, with a bell attached to the tail, stand in profile, grasping with one foot their prey. This is a small quadruped, perhaps a gazelle, possibly a khilin. Behind it rises a fantastic palmette tree; rain falls on it from three clouds. Smaller plants and flowers fill the space.

198. SATIN, BROCADED. LIONS IN SUNBURSTS

ITALY, LUCCA, SECOND HALF OF 14TH CENTURY. NEW YORK CITY, COOPER UNION MUSEUM.

17¾ x 12¾ in. (45 x 32½ cm.). No. 1902.1.275. Ex-coll. Miguel y Badia.

Faded green satin ground, design in gold-metal thread. On a ground covered with trailing ivy huge birds—phoenixes changed to eagles or herons (?)—screech wildly because their prey, little gazelles, is snatched from them by lions emerging from tunnels or tubes. These tunnels are outlined by a fringe of peacock feathers and flaming sun rays.

In this design the Westernization of Chinese motifs is fairly advanced. The Italian designer is responsible for the clear spacing, the arrangement in two zones, and the trefoil leaves of the ivy, where, for good measure, he has put an entirely unrequired, forlorn-looking little bird. The "sunburst" motif is used ingeniously.

199. DOUBLE TWILL, BROCADED. CASTLES AND KHILINS

ITALY, LUCCA, 14TH CENTURY. BOSTON, MUSEUM OF FINE ARTS.

12½ x 5¾ in. (31½ x 14½ cm.). No. 35.84.

The warps are a faded pinkish-yellow and a light bluish-green; the wefts are orange, yellowish-green, light-blue, and white silks; the brocading thread is a brownish-silvered membrane on a linen core. Castles, with four watchtowers, rise on hillocks, where mice sit upright, addorsed, with long ears and tails. Over the castles fly fantastic quadrupeds, obviously khilins, though their heads look like a hound's head of Gothic Europe. Between the castles cartouches have been brocaded in metal thread. They frame a pseudo-Kufic inscription, and from them dangles a palmette flower.

200. SATIN, BROCADED. CASTLES AND BASILISKS

ITALY, LUCCA, SECOND HALF OF 14TH CENTURY. THE DETROIT INSTITUTE OF ARTS.

8½ x 15½ in. (21½ x 39 cm.). No. 48.268.

On red satin ground faded to an amber tone, the design is twill-woven in gold thread. The fabric is reversible. The pattern is almost complete; the top of the castle appears below, between the basilisks. These are confronted, standing on a large fantastic floral motif from which emanate two plumes. Above these stands the castle. From its turreted walls spring forth huge dogs. They wear heavy collars and are chained. Lotus tendrils fill the space between the castles.

The design belongs to the period when the Gothic elements began to oust those obtained from the East.

201. SATIN, BROCADED. HUNTRESSES AT A FOUNTAIN

ITALY, LUCCA, LATE 14TH CENTURY. THE CLEVELAND MUSEUM OF ART.

15¾ x 10¾ in. (40 x 27 cm.). No. 40.1194. Published: Gertrude Underhill, "Two Fourteenth Century Italian

135

Silks," *Bulletin*, XXVIII (1941), 138; a similar specimen in Boston: Gertrude Townsend, "Four European Textiles of the Thirteenth and Fourteenth Centuries," Museum of Fine Arts *Bulletin*, XXV (1927), 4.

On faded-red satin ground the design is brocaded in gold thread with touches of white and pale-blue silks. Young women in close-fitting dresses stand by a fountain in a forest of oak trees and dip for water to quench their thirst. They carry rabbits tied to a stick and hold a leash with a dog coupled with a leopard, both wearing jeweled collars. They strain at the leash to drink from the lower basin. Between the figures rises an oak tree with roots, leaves, and acorns; ivy trails on the ground. The faces, shoulders, and hands of the huntresses are of white silk; the water of the fountain, the eyes and collar ornaments of the dogs, of blue silk; all the rest of the design is brocaded in gold thread.

This is Gothic art at its most enjoyable. Here is one of those fountains which, according to minstrels and troubadours, appear magically in the midst of forests and deserts. It shows its Eastern origin by the huge pine cone that tops its column and the dragons with prickly bat wings. But the Italian designer puts them to work; they hold in their mouth the rope with the small water bucket. Possibly this very fabric is mentioned in an inventory of the Cathedral of Prague of 1387: *cappa in rubeo habens puellas cum faciebus albis, haurentes aquam,* "a red cope with white-faced maidens ladling water."

202. DOUBLE TWILL, BROCADED. A HUNTRESS

ITALY, LUCCA, 14TH CENTURY. BOSTON, MUSEUM OF FINE ARTS.

5¾ x 7½ in. (14½ x 18½ cm.). No. 35.88.

Warps, blue (faded) silk; wefts, blue, yellowish-green, white, and light pinkish-yellow. The gold thread is of gilded silver on a very thin membrane, much rubbed. Fragment only. From a tree emerges a young woman in a close-fitting dress and cap. On her left,

gauntleted hand stands her falcon, with bells on both legs. His wings are spread wide; he looks up at the food the huntress presents to him. This is the lure; the long string to which it is tied passes over her left arm and hangs below in an elaborate knot. Behind the falcon appears a lotus blossom on a long stem with three groups of leaves.

203. PLAIN COMPOUND TWILL. CHERUBS

ITALY, SIENA, FIRST HALF OF 15TH CENTURY. NEW YORK CITY, THE METROPOLITAN MUSEUM OF ART.

14 x 18½ in. (35½ x 46½ cm.). No. 46.156.79. Ex-coll. Sangiorgi. Published: Giorgio Sangiorgi, *Contributi allo studio dell' arte tessile*, Milan, Rome, n.d., p. 96, fig. 7.

Plain compound twill; ground green silk, design in gold thread with details in white and salmon silks. All-over design of cherubs and stylized flowers. On one side a narrow border with a small flower between leafy stems.

204. PLAIN COMPOUND TWILL. CHRIST BLESSING

ARMENIA, 16TH CENTURY. THE ART INSTITUTE OF CHICAGO.

4½ x 12½ in. (11 x 31½ cm.). No. 16.378, Martin A. Ryerson Collection.

Plain compound twill, brocaded. Ground, gold thread; design, red, white, blue, and black silks. Adjacent roundels frame the half-length figure of Christ blessing; Greek crosses in the spandrils.

Fabrics of this type could be used for the body of vestments, or be cut up for orphreys.

205. SATIN, BROCADED. NOLI ME TANGERE

ITALY, LUCCA OR FLORENCE, 14TH CENTURY. BOSTON, MUSEUM OF FINE ARTS.

10½ x 14 in. (26½ x 35½ cm.). No. 04.1640.

The ground is partly satin, partly twill, faded coral-pink silk. The design is in white silk faded to light brown, and gold thread.

206. SATIN, BROCADED. THE ANNUNCIATION

ITALY, LUCCA OF FLORENCE, LATE 14TH CENTURY. THE CLEVELAND MUSEUM OF ART.

9¼ x 18¼ in. (23 x 46½ cm.). No. 31.61, Dudley P. Allen Collection. Exhibited: *2000 Years*, 1944, cat. no. 102. Published: Gertrude Underhill, "Two Fifteenth Century Brocades," *Bulletin*, XVIII (1931), 69.

Blue and white silks and gold thread. The design is woven in gold thread; the faces and hands are brocaded in white silk. The Virgin is kneeling with hands crossed over her breast. The archangel, also kneeling, delivers his message with right hand raised, holding in the left a wand topped by a lily. Two birds with boughs in beak hover above and beside the Virgin. A landscape seems to be indicated by a narrow border with flowers at the lower edge.

"In Lucca biblical subjects do not appear until about 1370. It is possible that the Annunciation silk was woven during the first quarter of the fifteenth century, but whether in Florence or Lucca it is difficult to say. The design lacks some of the freer movement of the earlier Lucchese products." (G. Underhill).

207. SATIN, BROCADED. THE NATIVITY

ITALY, SIENA OR FLORENCE, SECOND HALF OF 15TH CENTURY. NEW YORK CITY, THE METROPOLITAN MUSEUM OF ART.

9¼ x 8 in. (23½ x 20 cm.). No. 46.156.75. Ex-coll. Sangiorgi. The museum owns another piece of the same orphrey showing the Flight into Egypt (no. 46.156.82).

Plain compound satin, brocaded. Ground red satin, design in gold, details in blue, white, and green silks. Between borders with a cres-cent motif, the newborn Christ is adored by the Virgin and St. Joseph.

208. BROCATELLE. THE ANNUNCIATION

ITALY, FLORENCE, LATE 15TH CENTURY. THE DETROIT INSTITUTE OF ARTS.

22 x 8 in. (56 x 20 cm.). No. 29.281. Published: Adèle Coulin Weibel, "Woven Orphreys," *Bulletin*, XVI (1937), 96.

On amber satin ground, the design in yellow and amber twill shows a portico in an enclosed garden. The Virgin is seated; the angel kneels before her.

Style of Andrea del Sarto.

209. BROCATELLE. THE ASSUMPTION

ITALY, FLORENCE, LATE 15TH CENTURY. THE DETROIT INSTITUTE OF ARTS.

Repeat: 17½ x 9¼ in. (44½ x 23½ cm.). No. 29.283. Published: Adèle Coulin Weibel, "Woven Orphreys," *Bulletin*, XIV (1937), 96.

Brocatelle, woven in normal loom width, then cut into strips for orphreys. Ground red satin, pattern yellow twill, the red warp used also for the inner lines of the design. This is built up in three tiers: on a flowery meadow, before the open sarcophagus, kneels St. Thomas about to receive the girdle that, according to old tradition, the Virgin threw down to the apostle while she was being carried to heaven. She is shown here seated on a cloud, supported and adored by four angels. God the Father holds a crown over her head, and two cherubs bring the composition to an end.

Since orphreys were of narrow width, a scene that lent itself to a composition in height was especially suitable. The designs were made probably by the same artists who prepared the woodcut illustrations of the early printed books, sometimes also by assistants of great masters. The Assumption shows the style of Alessio Baldovinetti (1425?–1499). The relic of the *Sacra Cintola* is preserved in the treasury of the Cathedral of Prato, near Florence. It had been brought back from the Holy Land by a knight of Prato in 1130.

210. *SATIN, BROCADED. FALCONS*

ITALY, LUCCA OR VENICE, LATE 14TH CENTURY. THE CLEVELAND MUSEUM OF ART.

15¾ x 9¾ in. (40 x 24½ cm.). No. 43.283. Exhibited: *2000 Years*, 1944, cat. no. 101. Published: Friedrich Fischbach, *Die wichtigsten Webeornamente*, pl. 93, fig. 6, is probably this specimen. Others: I. Errera, cat. no. 34; W. Mannowsky, *Der Danziger Domschatz*, 1931, vol. I, no. 4, pl. 10.

Faded-rose satin ground, the design in gold thread. Pairs of falcons stand on the lure. This consists of a bird's wing to which a piece of meat is fastened; the huntsman swings the lure to call the falcons off their prey. This incident of the falcon hunt is pictured on a Tournay tapestry in the Minneapolis Museum of Art. Between these groups of falcons are bouquets of flowers in small containers placed on top of a latticework ornament. The motif filling the space between the latticework and the falcons of the next row looks like a bunch of ostrich plumes with an agraffe.

This is one of the rarest and most delectable of all late Gothic inventions. It may have been designed for a special commission, perhaps for a Burgundian nobleman.

211. *COMPOUND TWILL, BRO-CADED. BURGUNDIAN HATS*

ITALY, VENICE, EARLY 15TH CENTURY. THE CLEVELAND MUSEUM OF ART.

9½ x 9½ in. (24 cm.). No. 50.5. Exhibited: *2000 Years*, cat. no. 86, "Italy or Burgundy (?)." Published: Friedrich Fischbach, *Die wichtigsten Webeornamente*, pl. 109b; Lessing, pl. 161a; Falke, II, 80 (note 3: Cyprus [?]).

White silk twill brocaded in gold thread and two shades of blue silk. Peaked caps are slit at the top to permit the secure fastening of a huge panache of plumes and feathers. The caps are surrounded by crowns. Tasseled strings are held together by rings; they spread out and form an all-over network.

The well-organized design, the absence of merely space-filling details, point to Venice. It looks like an impresa and may have been woven as a special commission.

212. *SATIN, BROCADED. HERALDIC MOTIF*

ITALY, VENICE, 14TH–15TH CENTURY. NEW YORK CITY, COOPER UNION MUSEUM.

17¼ x 18¾ in. (44 x 48 cm.). No. 1902–1–281. Ex-coll. Miguel y Badia.

Fancy compound satin, brocaded; dark-blue silk and gold thread. A twisting vine covers the ground and forms oval compartments for the gold-brocaded winged leg of a griffin, the armorial motif of the Patala family.

213. *SATIN, BROCADED. THE GONDOLA*

ITALY, VENICE, LATE 14TH CENTURY. GERMANY, DANZIG.

It is often difficult, even impossible, to decide the question that already puzzled the compilers of the medieval inventories: Lucchese or Venetian? One fabric, part of the treasure of vestments of the Cathedral of Danzig, Germany, is unmistakably Venetian. Otto von Falke was first to realize this and to point out other fabrics with designs related to, sometimes practically copied from, this black and gold brocaded satin.

On water peopled with swans and ducks, a gondola is propelled by a falcon with a bell fastened to its tail. He stands on the high stern, on one foot, and with the other manipulates the long oar. His passenger is a runaway dog, with broken chain dangling from collar. Behind the gondola rises an elaborately curved tree with pomegranates growing on its boughs and a huge palmette from its top. From the patch of water dangles a large blossom and a branching tendril with sharply-pointed straight and curved leaves.

214. SATIN, BROCADED. LIONS, DOGS, AND BIRDS

ITALY, VENICE, EARLY 15TH CENTURY. THE CLEVELAND MUSEUM OF ART.

25½ x 12 in. (64½ x 30 cm.). No. 47.294. Published: Dorothy G. Shepherd, "A Fifteenth Century Italian Textile," *Bulletin*, XXXV (1948), 46.

Plain compound satin. Two warps, one very fine deep blue for the satin ground and a tan binder warp; coarse, dull-purple wefts. The design is entirely in metal thread. Heavy stems with lotus palmettes rise in diagonal lines, which are counterbalanced by narrow horizontal bands of continuous half palmettes. A dog and a lion jump about; a falcon flies toward two ducks on a patch of water. Flowers and leaves fill the remaining space.

"The transitional character of the textile is indicated by the presence of the large-scale undulating branch with its monumental stylized leaves, and although the traditional animal motives are still present, they have lost the vitality and realism that characterized such motives in the earlier patterns. Falke illustrates a group of related examples that serve clearly to demonstrate this evolution in style and to show the relative position of the Museum's piece in the series" (D. Shepherd.)

215. SILK DAMASK. FALCON AND DOG

ITALY, VENICE, EARLY 15TH CENTURY. THE CLEVELAND MUSEUM OF ART.

8 x 9 in. (20 x 22½ cm.). No. 44.458, gift of the Textile Arts Club. Exhibited: *2000 Years*, cat. no. 108. Published:

Gertrude Underhill, "Gifts of the Textile Arts Club," *Bulletin*, XXX (1946), 24.

Damask, green and white, woven as a horizontal band. A falcon grasps a mace (or a musical instrument?), decorated with a tasseled cord. He looks down at a dog, which seems to be chained to a palmette tree. The dog's forefeet look like floral motifs, blending with the irrational flora of the background.

216. SATIN, BROCADED. FALCONS AND LIONS

ITALY, VENICE, MID-15TH CENTURY. BOSTON, MUSEUM OF FINE ARTS.

15¾ x 6¾ in. (40 x 17 cm.). No. 04.1689. Published (the Düsseldorf specimen): Falke, II, 91, fig. 477.

White, faded to light tan, the gold thread now gray. Reverse of fabric shown here. Heavy stems form pointed ovals, with bunches of carnations and magnificent palmettes above, a triple-moon motif below. Lions drink from a pool; falcons are poised above them, basking in rays emanating from the moons.

Falke sees in the carnations and the triple moon signs of the preoccupation of the Venetian weaver to produce a fabric suitable for the Levantine trade.

217. SATIN, BROCADED. AFTER JACOPO BELLINI

ITALY, VENICE, MID-15TH CENTURY. THE DETROIT INSTITUTE OF ARTS.

Irregular, 18 x 15 in. (34 x 25 cm.). No. 34.31. Exhibited: *2000 Years*, cat. no. 111. Published: Adèle Coulin Weibel, "A Late Gothic Brocade," *Bulletin*, XIV (1934), 27. For the Bellini thesis, see Falke, 1913, II, 93–95, figs. 484 to 488; also V. Golubew, *Les Dessins de Jacopo Bellini*, Brussels, 1908, vol. II, pl. 95.

Compound satin, brocaded, pink, green, and white silks and gold thread. The fragment shows the curved band with running animals of Bellini's design, and parts of the two ogival compartments with an eagle and a gazelle and a small part of a tree in one, a large part of the tree and small parts of a lion and an antelope in the other. The originally pink ground is faded to a tone of old ivory. The design is in a mellow green with touches of white; the animals and the swirling rosettes of the band are gold-brocaded.

The fabric belongs to a small group of brocades woven in Venice around the middle of the fifteenth century. The design is inspired by sketches of Jacopo Bellini (c. 1400–c. 1470). Three designs for brocade weaving are assembled on a page of his sketchbook, which is preserved in the Louvre. These designs are an artist's dream; for the exigencies of the draw-loom they had to be reassembled.

218. COMPOUND TWILL. PHOENIXES

ITALY, VENICE, MID-15TH CEN-TURY. BOSTON, MUSEUM OF FINE ARTS.

6¾ x 5¾ in. (17 x 14½ cm.). No. 31.128.

Compound warp and weft twill. Warp, coral-pink silk (mostly faded to tan); wefts, green, with additional white for details (center of wings, flowers, and small ogives, all in one line). Ogives, containing confronted phoenixes framed in bands with pointed leaves, are surrounded by flowery branches, which at the angles form figures of eight. Similar interlaced motifs occur also among the floral arrangement in the spandrils.

The imaginative design shows the influence of the sketches by Jacopo Bellini (Falke, II, fig. 484). There the phoenixes stand singly on slender boughs, interlaced to figures of eight and growing from a vertical stem outlined by leafy bands.

219. PLAIN COMPOUND TWILL. SAILS AND ANIMALS

ITALY, VENICE, MID-15TH CEN-TURY. NEW YORK CITY, THE MET-ROPOLITAN MUSEUM OF ART.

24 x 6 in. (35½ x 15 cm.). No. 46.156.38. Ex-coll. Sangiorgi. Exhibited: *Mostra del tessile nazionale*, Rome, 1937–38, cat. p. 24, no. 20, fig. 20, "style of Jacopo Bellini." Published: Giorgio Sangiorgi, *Contributi allo studio dell' arte tessile*, Rome, Milan, n.d., p. 115, fig. 12; Falke, II, 25, fig. 446 (a similar piece), "Venice, 15th century."

Plain compound twill; ground, tan silk (faded rose-pink?); design, gold thread (metal worn off showing the purple-silk core). Rocks and pools rise from golden-rayed clouds. On the top of the rocks sit magnificently designed stags, at their base dogs with jeweled collars. Both turn their heads to look at pouncing birds (herons?). In the pools stand swans with sails tied to their collars. The sails are driven by the wind over the back of the next bird, which pokes its head through the canvas and holds the spar in its beak.

220. VOIDED SATIN VELVET. DEER AND LIONS

ITALY, VENICE, SECOND HALF OF 14TH CENTURY. PROVIDENCE, MU-SEUM OF ART.

63 x 39½ in. (159½ x 100 cm.). No. 35.005.

Crimson (faded) and tan silks. Fantastic trees are topped with lotus and carnation palmettes. A spurious zigzag effect is obtained by the placing of seated lions and walking deer.

221. POLYCHROME VELVET. AN IMPRESA

ITALY, EARLY 15TH CENTURY. THE CLEVELAND MUSEUM OF ART.

8 x 10½ in. (20 x 26½ cm.). No. 39.43. Ex-coll. Elsberg. Published: Gertrude Underhill, "Textiles from the H. A. Elsberg Collection," *Bulletin*, XXVI (1939), 143.

Solid cut velvet. "A small design of eagles with spread wings holding calves' heads in their talons and vine tendrils and blossoms in their beaks. Three colors are used in the velvet pile: dark blue for the ground; red for the eagles, blossoms, and tendrils; cream for the centers of the blossoms, eagles' beaks, and calves' heads" (G. Underhill). The cream is faded pale blue.

This fabric was probably woven as a special order; the strange design is an impresa, one of those semiheraldic devices which were so fashionable in the Gothic age. It is impossible to assign fabrics of this kind to any special weaving center. Lucca appears to have produced velvet toward 1400; the household bills of the Burgundian court mention in 1412 and 1416 *veluiau de Lucques broche d'or*. Polychrome velvets do not occur in these inventories. Venice specialized in voided velvets of three, four, even five colors in the second half of the fifteenth century. It seems plausible that solid cut polychrome velvet may have preceded there the elaborate masterpieces of the early Renaissance.

222. FIVE-COLOR VELVET. PART OF A CHASUBLE

ITALY, VENICE, FIRST HALF OF 15TH CENTURY. THE CLEVELAND MUSEUM OF ART.

31½ x 22½ in. (80 x 57 cm.). No. 43.66. Ex-colls. Figdor; Nemes. Exhibited: *2000 Years*, cat. no. 158. The back half of the chasuble: William Rockhill Nelson Gallery of Art, Kansas City. Published: *Sammlung Dr. Albert Figdor*, sales catalogue Vienna, 1930, vol. I, no. 111, pl. XXXIII; *Sammlung Marczell von Nemes*, sales catalogue, Munich, 1931, vol. II, no. 118, pl. 45, both pieces.

Solid cut velvet. The black pile of the ground is slightly rubbed in parts. The design, in green, red, blue, and white velvet, is arranged in two horizontal rows. Addorsed gazelles squat beneath a tree in an enclosure; a fountain, from which grows a tree with large leaves and white and blue flowers, is flanked by peacocks; floral motifs fill the interstices. This is the largest preserved specimen of

Italian polychrome velvet with animals. It is unequaled in beauty both of design and color distribution.

223. FIVE-COLOR VOIDED VELVET

ITALY, VENICE, MID-15TH CENTURY. THE CLEVELAND MUSEUM OF ART.

12 x 17½ in. (30½ x 44½ cm.). No. 40.369, gift of the Textile Arts Club. Exhibited: *2000 Years*, cat. no. 199. Published: Gertrude Underhill, *Bulletin*, XXX (1946), 24.

Green satin ground, cut velvet red, blue, yellow, and white. The vertically curved stems are overlaid by a six-lobed pomegranate motif. The space between the stems has a fanciful pattern evolved around two curled leaves.

224. FIVE-COLOR VOIDED VELVET

ITALY, VENICE, MID-15TH CENTURY. THE CLEVELAND MUSEUM OF ART.

18 x 12 in. (45½ x 30 cm.). No. 40.370, gift of the Textile Arts Club. Exhibited: *2000 Years*, cat. no. 170. Published: Gertrude Underhill, *Bulletin*, XXX (1946), 24.

Cut voided velvet, blue, yellow, white, and red on green satin ground. Horizontal rows of connected wide oval medallions; pointed above and below, they contain a trefoil with an eight-petaled flower. These rows are separated by a continuous tendril with a scroll ornament and two palmette flowers.

The exquisite fabric was probably designed for export to Turkey. The type is found in the paintings of Gentile Bellini.

225. FIVE-COLOR VOIDED VELVET, BROCADED

ITALY, VENICE, LAST QUARTER OF 15TH CENTURY. THE CLEVELAND MUSEUM OF ART.

44 x 13 in. (111½ x 33 cm.). No. 46.74. Ex-coll. Figdor. Exhibited: *2000 Years*, cat. no. 177.

Red and green cut voided velvet, light-purple satin, gold and silver brocading. Seven-foiled compartments are connected vertically by a subsidiary ogival motif. Three versions of the pomegranate motif and small pseudo-naturalistic flowers fill the ground.

In this beautifully balanced design the pomegranate motif has attained the apex of its evolution.

226. *CUT VOIDED VELVET. FER-RONNERIE*

ITALY, MID-15TH CENTURY. THE CLEVELAND MUSEUM OF ART.

26 x 22½ in. (66 x 57 cm.). No. 40.604, bequest of James Parmelee.

Red silk, *ferronnerie* velvet. Small compact pomegranate in the center of an ogival leaf. Designed in staggered rows, slightly overlapping.

227. *COMPLETE COPE*

VELVET: VENICE, MID-15TH CENTURY. ORPHREY: GERMANY, COLOGNE, 15TH CENTURY. THE DETROIT INSTITUTE OF ARTS.

No. 30.36, gift of Mr. and Mrs. Edsel B. Ford. Exhibited: *2000 Years*, cat. no. 182. Published: Adèle Coulin Weibel, "A Gothic Velvet Cope," Detroit Institute of Arts *Bulletin*, XI (March, 1930), 83.

Cut voided satin velvet, deep sapphire blue. Horizontal rows of two interlocked ogival compartments. They contain two variants of simple pomegranates, each with four small flowers. The upper ogive is surmounted by a flower with thistle leaves. The shield is pieced together of six fragments of a similar but smaller-patterned velvet of the same shade of blue. The orphrey consists of two bands of cloth of gold patterned in polychrome silks with inscriptions of *Ihesus* and *Maria*, and stars, rosettes, and stylized trees. Such borders were woven in Cologne from the thirteenth to the fifteenth century.

228. *DETAIL*

An additional interest is given to this cope by the fact that it was first used as a mantle. Hidden by the shield is a semicircular cut, now patched with a piece of plain blue velvet. This, and the fact that the shield is obviously a later addition for which velvet of the same color and a related pattern had to be obtained with some difficulty, make it plausible that a highly valued garment was donated to a church, presumably after the first owner's death.

229. *PILE-ON-PILE SUMPTUARY VELVET*

ITALY, VENICE, ABOUT 1500. THE ART INSTITUTE OF CHICAGO.

Detail of a complete, semicircular mantle. No. 51.52, the Lucy Maud Buckingham Collection. Exhibited: *2000 Years*, cat. no. 188.

Deep-crimson silk, very firm weave, the design cut with scissors. Intertwined branches are held together by crowns and support large lotus rosettes. Smaller rosettes fill the spandrils.

Velvet of this special type and quality was reserved for the use of the senate of the Venetian republic. Red was worn by the procurator, blue by the senators, velvet on cloth of gold by the Doge.

230. *CUT VOIDED SATIN VELVET, BROCADED*

ITALY, VENICE, MID-15TH CENTURY. BOSTON, MUSEUM OF FINE ARTS.

22¼ x 7¼ in. (56½ x 18½ cm.). No. 04.1666.

Satin and pile warps crimson silk, brocaded with true gold thread. The unusual design consists of many different palmettes.

231. PILE-ON-PILE VELVET, BRO-CADED

ITALY, VENICE, SECOND HALF OF 15TH CENTURY. THE CLEVELAND MUSEUM OF ART.

59 x 19¼ in. (149½ x 48½ cm.). No. 31.63. Exhibited: *2000 Years*, cat. no. 171. Published: Gertrude Underhill, "Two Fifteenth Century Brocades," *Bulletin*, XVIII (1931), 64.

Deep purple, pile-on-pile velvet, with broad undulating band of gold leaves and detached pomegranates in the curves; true gold thread.

232. CUT VOIDED SATIN VELVET, BROCADED

ITALY, VENICE, SECOND HALF OF 15TH CENTURY. NEW YORK CITY, THE METROPOLITAN MUSEUM OF ART.

30 x 16 in. (76 x 40½ cm.). No. 46.156.132. Ex-colls. Sangiorgi, Besselièvre. Exhibited: *Mostra del tessile nazionale*, Rome, 1937–38, cat. p. 32, no. 104, fig. 74. Published: Molmenti, *La Storia di Venezia nella vita privata*, Bergamo, 1922, p. 383; Fanny Podreider, *Storia dei tessuti d'arte in Italia*, n.d., p. 124, fig. 134.

Lobed rosettes with leaves and pomegranates in red velvet. Brocaded in gold are floral motifs in the center of the rosettes, flying birds and crouching dogs in the interstices.

233. CUT VOIDED VELVET, BRO-CADED

ITALY, VENICE OR FLORENCE, 15TH CENTURY. NEW YORK CITY, THE METROPOLITAN MUSEUM OF ART.

52½ x 23 in. (132 x 58 cm.). No. 44.54.2. Ex-coll. Werner Abegg.

Cut voided dark-blue velvet; ground cloth of gold, details in brocaded bouclé gold thread. Two vertical stems, undulating and

crossing, are enriched with branches ending in pomegranates and acanthus leaves.

234. CUT VOIDED VELVET, BRO-CADED

ITALY, VENICE OR FLORENCE, LATE 15TH CENTURY. KANSAS CITY, WILLIAM ROCKHILL NELSON GALLERY OF ART.

37½ x 22¾ in. (95 x 57 cm.). No. 31.110. Ex-coll. Nemes, sales cat. no. 139.

Blue silk pile, gold thread for brocading and loops. The ground is of sapphire-blue cut velvet, the pile enriched by loops of the gold thread. A broad ribbon of gold curves vertically. It is overlaid by a velvet stem that ends in a large golden fruit motif, a pomegranate surrounded by blossoms and surmounted by a bunch of five flowers. This motif rests on a velvet leaf form that is outlined by a golden garland. From this central motif diverge branches with thistle blossoms, six-petaled roses, and leaves of fantastic shapes.

235. CUT VOIDED VELVET, BRO-CADED. ARMORIAL DESIGN

ITALY, VENICE OR FLORENCE, SECOND HALF OF 15TH CENTURY. NEW YORK CITY, THE METROPOLITAN MUSEUM OF ART.

26½ x 22 in. (67 x 56 cm.). No. 46.156.141. Ex-coll. Sangiorgi. Exhibited: *Mostra del tessile nazionale*, Rome, 1937–38, cat. p. 31, no. 88, fig. 71. Published: Giorgio Sangiorgi, *Contributi allo studio dell' arte tessile*, Milan, Rome, n.d., p. 70, fig. 12.

Pile-on-pile cut voided cloth velvet, brocaded. Ground gold, with design in red velvet pile in two heights, details brocaded in gold and silver bouclé. From a winding vertical stem branch out secondary stems with acanthus leaves and artichoke (?) motifs. The large rosette on the principal stem contains a coat of arms, brocaded twill, green in base, gold in chief, charges outlined in red pile with details in gold bouclé.

The arms are: party per fess, or and vert, in chief a dog passant proper, base powdered with unidentified charge (truffles?). They have been thought to be those of Alemanni, Lopez, or Biliotti, but are not definitely identified. Possibly the design on the bucranium-shaped shield is merely an impresa.

236. *CUT SOLID POLYCHROME VELVET, PILE-ON-PILE*

ITALY, PROBABLY FLORENCE, LATE 15TH CENTURY. THE ART INSTITUTE OF CHICAGO.

20½ x 8½ in. (52 x 21½ cm.). No. 95.847, Martin A. Ryerson Collection. Published: Fanny Podreider, Bergamo, n.d., p. 154, fig. 175.

Pile-on-pile velvet, white, green, and red pile warps. The design is raised over the white velvet ground. From branches forming an oval network there grows a profusion of naturalistically rendered pomegranates. They frame a palm frond with a ribbon, inscribed: "Justus ut palma florebit."

This is the device of the Soderini family. The velvet may have been made for Piero Soderini (1450–1513), who was elected gonfalonier for life in 1502 by the Florentines.

237. *CUT SOLID POLYCHROME VELVET, PILE-ON-PILE*

ITALY, VENICE, LATE 15TH– EARLY 16TH CENTURY. NEW YORK CITY, THE METROPOLITAN MUSEUM OF ART.

Chasuble, detail shown: 18 x 21 in. (45½ x 53 cm.). No. 41.87, gift of George and Mary Ann Blumenthal. Ex-coll. De Kermaingant.

Four-color velvet, two shades of green, red, and white. On the pale-green velvet ground an all-over diaper is formed by emerald-green twisted and interlaced ropes. Each compart-

ment contains confronted birds (herons?), of crimson pile at left, white at right, both with details of green pile.

This quite unusual design is probably an impresa, designed and woven for a special order.

238. *CUT VOIDED SATIN. VELVET. HERALDIC DESIGN*

ITALY, FLORENCE, EARLY 17TH CENTURY. THE DETROIT INSTITUTE OF ARTS.

11½ x 10½ in. (47 x 26½ cm.), detail shown. No. 38.83, gift of E. and A. Silberman.

Cut voided velvet, sea-green on golden-yellow satin. A shield containing a conventional eagle is suspended from the neck of a double-headed eagle, with lions rampant as supporters. The group is surmounted by a canopy with an elaborate finial, flanked by large birds. These canopies emerge from a foliated mask that is surmounted by a complicated device of baskets, grapes, and cupids.

If the bunch of twenty-five pellets is not merely a grape but a reference to the *Palle Medici*, the rather incongruous pattern becomes the device of a grand duke of Tuscany. The kneeling cupids, proffering a crown and a jewel depending from a chain, indicate an alliance by matrimony with a member of the arch-house of Austria, represented by the double-headed eagle with the lions. Such a marriage took place in June, 1608, between Cosimo II and Maria Magdalena, a sister of the emperor Ferdinand II.

239. *COMPOUND SATIN. HERALDIC DESIGN*

ITALY, 16TH CENTURY. BOSTON, MUSEUM OF FINE ARTS.

35¾ x 19¼ in. (91 x 49 cm.). No. 48.1256. Compare: Tettoni and Saladini, *Raccolta Araldica*, Milan, n.d., vol. II, "Borromeo."

Green satin ground, the design outlined in yellow silk and filled in with green and yellow silks in bouclé effect. The elaborate design shows a combination of several heraldic motifs belonging to the noble families of Borromeo and Visconti, both of Milan. The somewhat crowded composition of flowers and leaves is obviously centered on the inscription "humilitas." The long shafts of the *h* and *l* are terminated with palmettes and support a crown. Below this group two camels squat, addorsed, on baskets. Their humps are hidden by a crown-shaped container from which emerge bunches of acanthus leaves. These motifs, as well as the rearing, confronted unicorns with not-quite-Sassanian fluttering scarves, tied around the neck, are Borromeo property. To the Visconti belong the serpent swallowing a child, the three interlocked rings, and the cones surmounted by the sun and a tree. Fastened with ribbons to some convenient boughs are rectangular objects, perhaps musical instruments. This diversity of rather unrelated motifs is cleverly held together by tendrils forming compartments. They are adorned with fantastic leaves and flowers.

240. *FANCY SATIN, BROCADED. FLOWERS AND BIRDS*

ITALY, VENICE, LATE 15TH–EARLY 16TH CENTURY. NEW YORK CITY, THE METROPOLITAN MUSEUM OF ART.

114 x 23½ in. (288 x 59½ cm.). No. 46.156.143. Ex-coll. Sangiorgi.

Damask ground of white silk, forming broad oval medallions. Each of these frames a brocaded design of pink, light-blue, and green silks, of a vase containing carnations and feathery leaves. Between these large motifs run three smaller designs: bunches of strawberries, a pine cone surrounded by flowers, and a small vase flanked by birds.

241. *FANCY SATIN REVERSIBLE. DAMASK*

ITALY OR SPAIN, FIRST HALF OF 16TH CENTURY. NEW YORK CITY, THE METROPOLITAN MUSEUM OF ART.

75¾ x 22½ in. (192 x 57 cm.). No. 26.231.18. Exhibited: *2000 Years*, cat. no. 152.

Fancy satin, all violet silk. Two curving stems with heart-shaped pointed leaves are surmounted by a crown; they frame a pomegranate of the "artichoke" type.

242. *SILK DAMASK, EMBROIDERED*

ITALY, LATE 16TH CENTURY. PROVIDENCE, MUSEUM OF ART.

15 x 10¾ in. (38 x 27 cm.). No. 47.420.

Blue silk for the damask, light-green, light-rose, and tan silks, gold thread and gilt spangles, for the embroidery. The relatively simple design of stylized flowers and feathery leaves is greatly enhanced by the adroit application of contrasting colors with the embroidery needle. The outlines of gold thread and the sparingly used spangles, which are fastened with French knots, give to the fabric an effect of well-balanced richness.

"In my opinion the fabric demands such outlining and additions in embroidery. I cannot imagine that damasks of this kind were made without having such a finishing process in mind" (Rudolf Berliner, in a letter).

243. *PLAIN COMPOUND CLOTH, LINEN. BORDER*

ITALY, 16TH CENTURY. NEW YORK CITY, THE METROPOLITAN MUSEUM OF ART.

21½ x 1¼ in. (54½ x 3 cm.). No. 46.156.71. Ex-coll. Sangiorgi.

Plain compound cloth, ground white, design light-brown linen. Lions confronted at a fountain, between them a stylized plant.

The museum owns another piece with the same design in red (35.19), and a piece of Italian sixteenth-century drawnwork with a similar design (06.476). As a pattern suitable for embroidery and lace, it was published by G. B. and M. Sessa, *I Frutti*, Venice, 1564, leaf II. A lacis of the same design was published by Elisa Ricci, *Old Italian Lace*, 1913, I, 25; a buratto, Leopold Iklé Collection, sales catalogue, Zurich, 1923, no. 395.

244. *FANCY COMPOUND CLOTH, WOOL AND COTTON*

ITALY, LAST QUARTER OF 16TH CENTURY. PROVIDENCE, MUSEUM OF ART.

35½ x c. 18½ in. (90 x c. 47 cm.). No. 11.070, gift of Mrs. Gustav Radeke.

The design of red wool is a grotesque of the classical type, in staeredgg vertical rows.

245. *PLAIN COMPOUND CLOTH, SILK AND COTTON. BORDER*

ITALY, 16TH CENTURY. NEW YORK CITY, THE METROPOLITAN MUSEUM OF ART.

7½ x 1¾ in. (18½ x 4½ cm.). No. 36.90.1497, gift of the United Piece Dye Works. Ex-coll. Besselièvre.

Plain compound cloth; ground, red silk; design, white cotton. Cupids support a garland with, astride it, a third cupid.

A pattern like this could be used also for embroidery.

246. *CISELÉ VOIDED VELVET*

ITALY, GENOA (?), EARLY 17TH CENTURY. PROVIDENCE, MUSEUM OF ART.

8½ x 17 in. (21½ x 43 cm.). No. 06.099.

Yellow satin ground. The design in blue velvet, a leaf and blossom in staggered, overturned rows.

247. *CISELÉ VOIDED VELVET*

ITALY, EARLY 17TH CENTURY. PROVIDENCE, MUSEUM OF ART.

15½ x 10½ in. (29 x 25½ cm.). No. 06.411.

Ground, ivory satin. The design of maroon and green velvet consists of detached boughs of diverse flowers and pomegranates. These are interspersed with seated lions and hens calling attention to their new-laid eggs.

Interesting is the presence of small diagonal motifs that have no relation to the design, but recall the slashed silks of the period.

248. *SLASHED SILK REP, BROCADED*

ITALY, SICILY (?), EARLY 17TH CENTURY. PROVIDENCE, MUSEUM OF ART.

23¼ x 9½ in. (59 x 24 cm.). No. 47.188.

The rep ground is purple silk shot with silver, the brocaded design a pale-yellow silk, gold-wrapped. The slashes are indicated by purple and yellow silk.

249. *CISELÉ VOIDED VELVET*

ITALY, GENOA (?), FIRST HALF OF 17TH CENTURY. PROVIDENCE, MUSEUM OF ART.

17½ x 9½ in. (44 x 24 cm.). No. 06.140.

Ground, tan silk rep shot with silver; design, ecru silk. An all-over trellis of seminaturalistic oak boughs with leaves and acorns.

250. CISELÉ VOIDED VELVET

ITALY, GENOA (?), FIRST HALF OF
17TH CENTURY. PROVIDENCE, MU-
SEUM OF ART.

14½ x 11½ in. (37 x 29 cm.). No. 47.351.

Purple velvet on light-blue ground. A ribbon motif and small acanthus leaves form an all-over network of irregular meshes. These are enlivened by two types of floral bouquets and by leaves twisted into a fleur-de-lis motif.

251. BROCATELLE

ITALY OR SPAIN, LATE 16TH–EARLY
17TH CENTURY. THE DETROIT IN-
STITUTE OF ARTS.

19¾ x 9¾ in. (50 x 24½ cm.). No. 31.88.

On the green satin ground, the pattern is woven of undyed linen and stands out in slight relief. Acanthus leaves, emerging from a palmette, form ogival compartments. These contain two different floriated motifs.

252. BROCATELLE

ITALY OR SPAIN, 17TH CENTURY.
PROVIDENCE, MUSEUM OF ART.

19 x 14⅛ in. (48 x 36 cm.). No. 06.265

Green silk and white cotton; acanthus motifs, stylized flowers (tulips?), and peacocks.

253. CISELÉ VELVET ON GOLD-SHOT GROUND

ITALY, GENOA, LATE 17TH CEN-
TURY. THE DETROIT INSTITUTE OF
ARTS.

129 x 25 in. (253 x 63½ cm.). No. 45.31, gift of Mrs. Graham John Graham. Published: Adèle Coulin Weibel, *Bulletin*, XXV (1946), 67.

Green ciselé velvet on gold-shot ground. The symmetrical design is centered on a gadrooned flower container, framed by floral and strap scrolls and surmounted by a canopy. Little elves play their lutes to invisible fairies; large and small birds and rampant lions complete the grotesque ornament. The technique of ciselé velvet is admirably suited for the elaborate design. The great masses of cut loops glow like emeralds, and lines of uncut loops frame them and add small details in a delicate celadon shade.

Foremost among the artists who inspired the textile designers of the baroque period stands Jean Louis Bérain (1637–1711), *arbiter elegantiarum* of the court of Louis XIV. The influence of this oracle of taste was not confined to France; in Italy especially, where the competition of the Lyons looms began to be felt, Bérain's ornament engravings were studied thoroughly. The Italian designer then often added warmth and a new vitality to the coldly elegant French pattern.

254. CUT VOIDED VELVET ON CLOTH OF GOLD

ITALY, VENICE, 1ST QUARTER 18TH
CENTURY. THE DETROIT INSTITUTE
OF ARTS.

78 x 24 in. (198 x 61 cm.). No. 29.232.

On gold shot ground the design stands out in cut red velvet. Ribbons, patterned with small rosettes, are tied into bows and overlaid with garlands and bouquets of peonies, tulips and small flowers.

This fabric is used for curtains in one of the salons of Ca' Rezzonico, the Museum of eighteenth-century art in Venice.

255. SATIN, BROCADED. FANTASTIC FLOWERS

ITALY, VENICE, EARLY 18TH CEN-
TURY. THE DETROIT INSTITUTE
OF ARTS.

73 x 21 in. (184 x 53 cm.), detail only. No. 29.285. Published: Adèle Coulin Weibel, "Italian Textiles," *Bulletin*, XI (October, 1929).

On bottle-green satin ground, the design consists of symmetrically placed large, fantastic flowers growing from small tufts; from these spring also groups of small, fairly realistic blossoms and leaves. Two greens, four reds, three blues, and a metallic gold thread.

Patterns of this type can often be traced to the ornamental designs Daniel Marot published in Holland in 1710. Marot was a French Huguenot who, like many thousands of excellent craftsmen, left France after the Revocation of the Edict of Nantes in 1685. Contrary to other French designers of the period, Marot does not break with but rather develops the traditional baroque trend in design. In Venice his ornament prints were widely adapted by the weavers.

256. SATIN, BROCADED. ABSTRACT DESIGN

ITALY, VENICE, EARLY 18TH CENTURY. BOSTON, MUSEUM OF FINE ARTS.

98½ x 19¼ in. (290 x 48½ cm.). No. 50.310, gift of Mrs. Bliss Knapp.

Detail of a panel made up of two lengths seamed together. Salmon-pink satin ground with self-figure. Most of the design silver, with some gold. Details brocaded in white, pink, orange, dark- and light-blue, and green silks. Altogether a shimmering effect of utmost beauty.

257. FANCY SATIN, BROCADED

ITALY, VENICE, MID-18TH CENTURY. THE DETROIT INSTITUTE OF ARTS.

80 x 21 in. (202 x 53 cm.). No. 29.284. Published: Adèle Coulin Weibel, "Italian Textiles," *Bulletin*, XI (October, 1929).

On the brick-red satin ground polychrome flowers such as carnations and daisies grow from golden stems; large golden leaves and pine cones complete the pattern.

258. FANCY CLOTH, BROCADED. DETAIL OF A WAISTCOAT

ITALY, VENICE, MID-18TH CENTURY. THE DETROIT INSTITUTE OF ARTS.

Detail shown: 18 x 13 in. (45½ x 33 cm.). No. 49.519, gift of Francis Waring Robinson.

The azure ground has a small all-over pattern and detached flowers brocaded in flat and crinkly silver thread. The border design of silver and gold is enriched with detached bouquets of polychrome silks. The pockets show garlands; the buttons are overspun with the metal thread.

The fabric was designed and woven for this special purpose.

259. SATIN, BROCADED. SHIPS AT SEA

ITALY, VENICE, MID-18TH CENTURY. THE DETROIT INSTITUTE OF ARTS.

33½ x 21½ in. (85 x 54½ cm.). No. 50.185. Published: Adolph Cavallo, "A Venetian Brocaded Satin of the 18th century," *Bulletin*, XXX (1951), 68.

Plain compound satin, polychrome. On dark-brown ground, oval cartouches, like windows, afford a view of ships at sea. The cartouches are framed by pilasters and palm boughs. Shells and fantastic flowers fill the ground.

260. FANCY SATIN, BROCADED. THE DRUMMER BOY

ITALY, VENICE, MID-18TH CENTURY. THE DETROIT INSTITUTE OF ARTS.

32 x 21½ in. (81 x 54½ cm.). No. 42.7, gift of Mr. and Mrs. Albert Kahn. Exhibited: *Mostra del tessile nazionale*, Rome, 1937–38, cat. no. 221; *2000 Years*, cat. no. 364. Published: Adèle Coulin Weibel, "The Drummer Boy," *Bulletin*, XXII (1942), 16.

It is one of the rare, utterly fantastic, exquisitely frivolous designs with figures of that last great period of textile art. Although vaguely reminiscent of the ubiquitous fashion of the day, *chinoiserie*, there is nothing of the nostalgic artificiality that so often pervades the contemporary French *chinoiserie* fabrics. The Venetian designer and weaver unite in presenting to us a fabric of solid gaiety in the spirit of the *feste e maschere* that made Venice so attractive to travelers from foreign lands.

A fountain surmounted by dolphins, steps leading up a rock, a wind-blown tree with gnarled trunk, huge leaves and magnificent blossoms, an island tied to it by a garland of fruits and flowers, these are the ingredients of a landscape that make us forget the laws of gravity and symmetry, all the limitations of mere logic. In such a landscape figures are apt to become merely *staffage*, like the little girl looking over the rock at the fountain. But the Drummer Boy is more than that; he is a real personality. In his three-cornered hat and blue uniform, golden sticks in raised hands, he stands firmly behind his glittering kettledrums, absolutely master of his universe. The strong colors of the brocading silks contrast pleasingly with the background of white corded silk and the glimpses of gold.

260A. DETAIL
(frontispiece)

The panel pictures to perfection the high spirit and geniality of Venice in the last heydey of her glory, the eighteenth century, which "with its thousand corruptions, its elegances, its sprightly wit and its carelessness of tomorrow, in the most luxurious frame, on the most fantastic background, has ever baffled the poet's imagination and defied the painter's palette" (Théophile Gautier).

261. SATIN, BROCADED. CHINOISERIE

ITALY, VENICE, MID-18TH CENTURY. BOSTON, MUSEUM OF FINE ARTS.

19¾ x 30¼ in. (50 x 76½ cm.). No. 50.2478.

Detail of a lambrequin. Ground, dark-green satin; design brocaded in white, light-yellowish-green and pink silks and gold-metal thread. Huge birds stalking on long legs over tents and parasol-shaped roofs, water falling into little pools from the mouth of horned monster-masks, odd bits of architecture, and bunches of flowers are combined in a delightfully fantastic design.

262. DAMASK. CHINOISERIE

ITALY, TURIN, MID-18TH CENTURY. THE DETROIT INSTITUTE OF ARTS.

29 x 21 in. (73½ x 53 cm.). No. 44.202, gift of Adolph Loewi. Exhibited: *2000 Years*, cat. no. 400. The Metropolitan Museum owns a damask of the same design but woven so that the two figures are in the center, the pagodas at the corners; published in the Metropolitan Museum's handbook: *The China Trade and Its Influence*, 1941, fig. 20.

Damask, deep golden yellow, tone on tone. The design shows curved bands of driftwood (?) and flowers. These form compartments that are occupied alternately by two pagodas, and figures carrying parasols.

263. BROCATELLE

ITALY, 16TH CENTURY. NEW YORK CITY, THE METROPOLITAN MUSEUM OF ART.

78 x 21 in. (198 x 53 cm.). No. 38.77. Ex-coll. Elsberg.

Golden-yellow and crimson silks and a filler warp of hemp. Strong boughs, with pomegranates and feathery leaves, bend and form ogival compartments. These are occupied, in alternate rows, by flower vases surmounted by a crown, and a large floral motif.

The Spanish designer of the Toledan brocatelle (Fig. 264) must have known this fabric. He used certain elements, such as the vase and crown, with little change, but conformed to the Spanish taste by adding birds and lions, both drawn on a much smaller scale.

264. BROCATELLE

SPAIN, TOLEDO, 16TH CENTURY.
THE DETROIT INSTITUTE OF ARTS.

130 x 18½ in. (328 x 46½ cm.). No. 29.289. Published: Adèle Coulin Weibel, "Italian Textiles," *Bulletin*, XI (October, 1929).

The ground is yellow twill, the pattern red satin and white and light-blue twill. Slender stems with vine leaves, grapes, and lotus blossoms are held together by crowns and form ogival compartments. These contain a vase with a bouquet of fantastic flowers. Eagles and leopards occupy prominent places.

Of this fabric Alan Cole wrote: "This is the kind of crimson and yellow brocatelle which represents a good class of stuff for regular trade purposes in the late 16th and early 17th century. The collared leopards almost take one back to 14th century Lucca; but the gadrooned vase, which is a reflex of Italian pottery fashionable at the time, brings one back to the 16th century" (*Ornament in European Silk*, p. 113).

265. ARMORIAL BROCADE

SPAIN, 16TH CENTURY. THE DE-
TROIT INSTITUTE OF ARTS.

18 x 11 in. (45½ x 27½ cm.). No. 31.101.

Red silk and gold thread. Plain compound cloth. Garlands of leaves form ogival compartments that contain double-headed eagles. These are surmounted by a crown and display on the breast the monogram A M, "Ave Maria."

266. ARMORIAL DAMASK

SPAIN, 16TH CENTURY. THE DE-
TROIT INSTITUTE OF ARTS.

12½ x 7 in. (31½ x 17½ cm.). No. 31.79.

Red and yellow silks, plain compound satin, reversible. Ogival compartments, formed by double ribbons and rings, contain in alternate rows confronted crowned lions and pelicans, and pomegranates and four-petaled rosettes.

267. LINEN DAMASK

SPAIN, 16TH CENTURY. THE DE-
TROIT INSTITUTE OF ARTS.

9¾ x 4½ in. (24½ x 11 cm.). No. 31.238.

Scarlet and white linen thread. Plain compound satin, reversible. The pattern is twill-woven. One continuous wavy bough with small leaves and bunches of berries, and slender birds with crests (hoopoes?). The second motif is incomplete; it may be the continuation of the branch with the berries.

268. DAMASK, SILK AND COTTON

PORTUGAL OR SPAIN, 17TH CEN-
TURY. PROVIDENCE, MUSEUM OF
ART.

26½ x 19 in. (67 x 48 cm.). No. 06.275, gift of Mrs. Gustav Radeke.

Yellow silk and blue cotton. Stylized floral motifs, palmettes, and confronted birds.

269. DOUBLE CLOTH, SILK, WOOL, AND LINEN

SPAIN, 16TH–17TH CENTURY. NEW
YORK CITY, COOPER UNION MU-
SEUM.

12¼ x 9 in. (31 x 23 cm.). No. 1949.64.4.

Double cloth, reversible. Brown silk warp with terra-cotta-red wool weft, and beige silk warp with natural linen weft. One selvage turned over, on right side of dark view. The three fibers are used with complete mastery. Interlaced ribbons form heart-shaped petals, each adorned with a floral palmette. These "cross-tiles" frame star octagons containing heraldic lions. Empty spaces are filled by leaves growing from the framework.

The white design on the red ground appears

slightly heavier than in the reversed colors. This is an optical illusion.

270. DAMASK, WOOL AND LINEN

ITALY OR SPAIN, EARLY 17TH CENTURY. PROVIDENCE, MUSEUM OF ART.

13½ x 8 in. (34 x 20½ cm.). No. 46.499.

Warp white linen, weft red wool. Slender stems form heart-shaped compartments with peacocks and rampant lions, diverse palmettes, leaves, and berries.

271. COMPOUND CLOTH, LINEN

SPAIN, 16TH CENTURY. THE DETROIT INSTITUTE OF ARTS.

10 x 7½ in. (25 x 19 cm.). No. 31.239.

Blue, yellow, tan, and white linen thread. Plain compound cloth. The heavy blue ground wefts cover three of the thin warp threads; the pattern is satin-woven. The lions and birds are yellow, the flowers white, the leaves tan.

272. CHENILLE BROCADE. THE PAGAN PARADISE

PORTUGAL OR ANDALUSIA, C. 1700. THE DETROIT INSTITUTE OF ARTS.

36 x 32 in. (91½ x 81 cm.). No. 45.80. Exhibited: *2000 Years*, cat. no. 341. Published: Adèle Coulin Weibel, "The Pagan Paradise," *Bulletin*, XXIV (1946), 66.

In the last years of the seventeenth and into the early years of the eighteenth century, there worked, somewhere in Portugal or possibly in Andalusia, a weaver of great ingenuity. Nothing is known of him, yet his personality stands out clearly in a few preserved brocades. He has a tendency to crowd his compositions and is absolutely uninhibited in the relative size of his plants or animals. He is a good craftsman and uses chenille sparingly with fine results. Most alluring of his brocades is *The Pagan Paradise*. This is woven as a horizontal border

with narrow finishing bands, to be used for covering a wall above a high, paneled dado. In a landscape of palm trees and cypresses, between enormous flowers and fountains surmounted by dolphins and crested snakes, Hercules fights the Nemean lion. Rabbits, unicorns, and panthers, peacocks and turkeys, wander about and listen to the music of Apollo's lyre. Pegasus has just stamped his hoof on a pretty little Mount Helicon; the Hippocrene gushes forth merrily. The colorful composition looks like a backdrop for a ballet of fairies and pixies.

These brocades stand alone, outside the regular evolution of textile design from baroque to rococo.

273. CHENILLE BROCADE. THE SMOKER

PORTUGAL OR ANDALUSIA, C. 1700. THE DETROIT INSTITUTE OF ARTS.

26¾ x 25 in. (68 x 63½ cm.). No. 48.24, gift of Mrs. E. S. Fechimer. Ex-coll. Elsberg.

A man smoking a Dutch clay pipe sits calmly at the edge of a little pool and watches a lion gamboling and a pheasant scolding from a treetop. A detail of a composition, which includes a Portuguese hunter with a shotgun, and a fully rigged ship poised on a huge flower.

This is another brocade by the anonymous Portuguese weaver, the Master of the Pagan Paradise. It is badly patched, part of a jacket of which another equally fragmentary part is owned by the Musée des Arts Décoratifs in Paris.

274. CHENILLE BROCADE. MYTHOLOGICAL SCENES

PORTUGAL OR ANDALUSIA, C. 1700. BOSTON, MUSEUM OF FINE ARTS.

35⅖ x 22¾ in. (91 x 58 cm.). No. 96.409.

Ground white twill, the brocading in silks, chenille, and frisé thread. Woven as part of a continuous band, with borders at top and bottom. The design in three horizontal rows shows the Rape of Ganymede, Narcissus at a fountain, and a Centaur and a Nymph. As in all his compositions, the playful designer improves upon his models. Thus he provides the shepherd Ganymede with two dogs rearing and barking in a charming landscape, and Narcissus is accompanied by a big, hungry-looking lion. The trees are huge flowers, and there is a peacock looking at a snail almost as large as the bird.

275. METALLIC TWILL, BRO-CADED. SELENE AND ENDYMION

PORTUGAL OR ANDALUSIA, LATE 17TH CENTURY. THE CLEVELAND MUSEUM OF ART.

14 x 11 in. (35½ x 28 cm.), detail of a panel. Complete: 46 x 22 in. (117 x 56 cm.). No. 16.829, gift of Mr. and Mrs. J. H. Wade. Exhibited: *2000 Years*, cat. no. 342.

The design is brocaded in polychrome silks on gold metallic ground. In a landscape with fantastic huge flowers Selene approaches the sleeping Endymion. She is accompanied by two Erotes, one poising an arrow, the other holding in leash two peacocks drawing the chariot. A second scene shows a woman carrying on her head a basket with a bird, accosted by a hunter with a piebald hound. She points toward farm buildings or a well in the courtyard. A third scene shows a mounted hunter pursuing three leopards.

276. METALLIC TWILL, BRO-CADED. SAMSON AND DELILAH

PORTUGAL OR ANDALUSIA, LATE 17TH CENTURY. THE CLEVELAND MUSEUM OF ART.

Another detail of panel no. 16.829.

In the court of a large building, at the side of an elaborate fountain, Delilah is cutting Samson's hair with huge shears; a group of Philistines watches the performance. The scene below is baffling: a palace with a fountain on a terrace, two riderless horses, a bird of the relative size of the roc but probably a mere pigeon, and some human figures. All this may illustrate some incident of the adventures of Rinaldo and Armida from Tasso's *Gerusalemme liberata*.

The Cleveland panel by the anonymous artist, the Master of the Pagan Paradise, is probably slightly earlier than the Boston and Detroit silks. The design is a sheer extravaganza of playful imagination, somewhat crowded. The weaver has used no chenille.

277. FANCY SATIN, SILVER-BRO-CADED

SPAIN, 17TH CENTURY. THE DETROIT INSTITUTE OF ARTS.

22 x 9½ in. (55½ x 24 cm.). No. 31.99.

Black silk and silver thread. Fancy satin, brocaded. The ground is patterned with small rosettes. Two detached motifs are brocaded, a sprig of hollyhocks and a plant with serrated leaves and bulbous flowers, both seminaturalistic.

The Berlin portrait of Countess Olivares by Velazquez shows her wearing a dress of material of this type.

278. CLOTH OF SILVER, BROCADED

SPAIN OR ITALY (NAPLES), LAST QUARTER OF 18TH CENTURY. PROVIDENCE, MUSEUM OF ART.

49 x 21 in. (124 x 53 cm.). No. 47.423.

Warps of grayish silk, wefts blue-gray silk and silver thread. The slender floral tendrils are brocaded in white, pink, and red silks and silver lamé.

279. COMPOUND SATIN, POLY-CHROME

PORTUGAL OR ANDALUSIA, C. 1800. PROVIDENCE, MUSEUM OF ART.

30 x 21 in. (76 x 53 cm.). No. 50.155.

Flower vases are framed by garlands of tulips, roses, carnations, grapes, and wheat ears, with doves holding olive twigs, in green, buff, salmon, purple, blue, and yellow, on white ground.

280. CUT AND UNCUT VOIDED SATIN VELVET

SPAIN, LATE 18TH OR EARLY 19TH CENTURY. PROVIDENCE, MUSEUM OF ART.

27 x 21½ in. (68½ x 54½ cm.). No. 49.037.

On black satin ground, the design in white cut and black uncut velvet. All-over design of stripes and small flowers, wide border with two men dueling on a terrace, and two men fishing beneath a bridge.

281. BLUE AND WHITE LINEN DAMASK

DUTCH, LATE 17TH CENTURY. PROVIDENCE, MUSEUM OF ART.

22 x 20½ in. (55½ x 52 cm.). No. 50.156.

Blue and white linen, reversible. A garden house is indicated by two stone pilasters supporting volute shapes, and a curved balustrade. Gourd vines climb at the sides; a plane tree stands in the center. In front of this tree stands a heavy round table, laid with a coffee or chocolate service. Behind the table, at either side of the tree, two ladies are seated, drinking from deep bowls. They are elegantly dressed; a snood tied with a ribbon covers their hair and gives an air of intimacy to the scene. The ladies face their husbands, who sit comfortably with legs spread wide, right beneath very large gourds. But their heads are protected by their beaver hats, which are gay with ribbons. They smoke long clay pipes, and their cups in deep saucers stand untouched.

This is a delightful conversation piece.

282. LINEN DAMASK NAPKIN

FLEMISH, THIRD QUARTER OF 17TH CENTURY. THE DETROIT INSTITUTE OF ARTS.

49½ x 34¾ in. (125½ x 38 cm.). No. 38.95, gift of Miss Elisabeth Sunderstrom.

A cavalier on a richly caparisoned prancing horse raises his baton of command. In the background a platoon of soldiers armed with lances marches toward a walled town. This scene is framed by military trophies and a coat of arms displayed between flags and guns. Below, an inscription gives the owner's name and titles. He was Don Juan Domingo de Zúñiga y Fonseca, Count of Monterrey and Fuentes, Marquis of Tarazona and Baron of Maldegem in Flanders. There follows the date, 1667.

The designer was probably a Spanish painter. The scene of the soldiers with their lances shows that he knew and was influenced by *The Surrender of Breda* by Velazquez.

283. SATIN, BROCADED

ENGLAND, SPITALFIELDS, SECOND QUARTER OF 18TH CENTURY. BOSTON, MUSEUM OF FINE ARTS.

Detail of dress. No. 43.415. Provenance: a dress worn by an ancestress of Miss Townsend.

Vertical curved design of a scroll motif with swathes of leafy boughs and flowers.

284. *SATIN, POLYCHROME, GOLD-BROCADED*

ENGLAND, SPITALFIELDS, SECOND QUARTER OF 18TH CENTURY. BOSTON, MUSEUM OF FINE ARTS.

Detail of dress. No. 43.1642. Gift of Miss Elizabeth Day McCormick. Provenance: a dress worn by Lydia Catharine, Duchess of Chandos. Published: Gertrude Townsend, "Costumes from the McCormick Collection," *Bulletin*, XLIII (1945), 28 and 29.

Polychrome silks and gold thread. A beautifully curved tree with fantastic flowers, leaves, and fruits grows from a small patch of soil.

285. *SATIN, BROCADED*

ENGLAND, SPITALFIELDS, MID-18TH CENTURY. BOSTON, MUSEUM OF FINE ARTS.

Detail of dress. No. 43.1639. Gift of Miss Elizabeth Day McCormick.

Satin ground; design, curved motifs of intertwined ribbons and bouquets of fantastic flowers, white and polychrome.

286. *RIBBED SILK, BROCADED*

ENGLAND, SPITALFIELDS, MID-18TH CENTURY. BOSTON, MUSEUM OF FINE ARTS.

27½ x 20 in. (70 x 51 cm.). No. 46.279, gift of Miss Amelia Peabody and Mr. William S. Eaton.

Detail of a dress. On the slightly ribbed cream silk ground the self-colored design of shell serpentines is interspersed with polychrome brocaded sprays of flowers.

287. *SATIN, BROCADED*

ENGLAND, SPITALFIELDS, MID-18TH CENTURY. BOSTON, MUSEUM OF FINE ARTS.

Detail of dress. No. 43.1641. Gift of Miss Elizabeth Day McCormick. Published: Gertrude Townsend, "Costumes from the McCormick Collection," *Bulletin* XLIII (1945), 27.

A river crossed by a bridge, with groups of trees, buildings, and some fantastically large flowers.

288. *FAILLE SILK, BROCADED*

ENGLAND, SPITALFIELDS, THIRD QUARTER OF 18TH CENTURY. THE DETROIT INSTITUTE OF ARTS.

25 x 21 in. (63½ x 53 cm.). No. 49.5. Detail of a gown that in the 1770's belonged to Sarah Ayscough Malcolm of New York, great-great-grandmother of the donors, Miss Edith Malcolm White and Miss Ruth Gordon White, Morristown, New Jersey. Published: Adèle Coulin Weibel and Francis Waring Robinson, "An Eighteenth Century Costume," *Bulletin*, XXVIII (1949), 93.

White faille woven with two vertical bands of satin in the center of each width and one near each selvage. Four different sprigs of anemones are brocaded in various combinations of red, blue, yellow, and green.

The almost haphazard disposition of the flowery sprigs is well suited to the draped effects demanded by the fashion of the period. The design is possibly adapted from the "Vingt-quatre bouquets champêtres" by Charles Germain de Saint-Aubin (1721-1786), a protégé of Madame de Pompadour. Saint-Aubin's albums were widely circulated and probably known to the designer of the Spitalfields weaving establishment.

289. *COMPOUND SATIN*

FRANCE, LYONS, FIRST QUARTER OF 18TH CENTURY. PROVIDENCE, MUSEUM OF ART.

30½ x 20 in. (77½ x 50½ cm.). No. 44.230.

On the green satin ground the design stands out in two tones of tan.

The grandiose yet quite static design is characteristic of the last years of Louis XIV.

290. COMPOUND SATIN

FRANCE, LYONS, FIRST QUARTER OF 18TH CENTURY. PROVIDENCE, MUSEUM OF ART.

39 x 22 in. (99½ x 55½ cm.). No. 47.097.

White and salmon pink. Both selvages. Certain details of this design seem to foreshadow a new trend in textile design.

291. SATIN, BROCADED

FRANCE, LYONS, SECOND QUARTER OF 18TH CENTURY. PROVIDENCE, MUSEUM OF ART.

36 x 16½ in. (91½ x 41½ cm.). No. 47.095.

A design of small landscape motifs in the green satin ground is overlaid by twill-brocaded garlands in buff, salmon, pink, light blue, yellow, and black.

292. SATIN, BROCADED

FRANCE, LYONS, FIRST QUARTER OF 18TH CENTURY. BOSTON, MUSEUM OF FINE ARTS.

Detail of dress. No. 43.647. Gift of Miss Elizabeth Day McCormick. Published: Gertrude Townsend, "Some Notes on Fashions in France during the 17th and 18th Centuries," *Bulletin*, XLIV (1946), 9, fig. 8.

Ground, deep-brown satin; design, rich heavy flowers and fruit.

"A handsome example of the style in which shading is suggested by an intermingling of colors, which was said to have been introduced early in the eighteenth century by Jean Revel" (G. Townsend).

293. TAFFETA, BROCADED

FRANCE, LYONS, SECOND QUARTER OF 18TH CENTURY. PROVIDENCE, MUSEUM OF ART.

36 x 21 in. (91½ x 53 cm.). No. 47.093.

Polychrome silks, gold and silver thread, brocaded on taffeta with floated ground patterns. The design is symmetrical.

This is the finest period in the evolution of the dyer's craft. Even after long exposure to light and air the colors on the surface are hardly different from those unexposed on the reverse.

294. TAFFETA, METAL-BROCADED

FRANCE, LYONS, MID-18TH CENTURY. THE DETROIT INSTITUTE OF ARTS.

19 x 23½ in. (48 x 59½ cm.). No. 48.17, gift of Mrs. E. S. Fechimer. Ex-coll. Elsberg.

White, red, light-blue, and purple silks and metal thread. On white taffeta ground, over a floated pattern, floral tendrils with stems and leaves of gold curve symmetrically.

Possibly from a design by Jean-Pierre Ringuet of Lyons (1728–1767 or '71).

295. FANCY SATIN, BROCADED

FRANCE, LYONS, MID-18TH CENTURY. PROVIDENCE, MUSEUM OF ART.

17¾ x 22 in. (45 x 55½ cm.). No. 43.365. Another specimen with aubergine ground, Philadelphia Museum of Art.

On medium-blue ground, bands of miniver twist casually, like a fur boa, across and between floral garlands of yellow, blue, pink, and green silks.

296. SATIN, BROCADED

FRANCE, LYONS, MID-18TH CENTURY. THE DETROIT INSTITUTE OF ARTS.

45 x 25 in. (114 x 63 cm.). No. 48.16, gift of Mrs. E. S. Fechimer. Ex-coll. Elsberg. Exhibited: *2000 Years*, cat. no. 381.

Wavy bands of black feathers and miniver frame small polychrome landscapes; white ground.

Fur, especially miniver, a black-spotted ermine, was introduced into the design of textiles woven for Queen Maria Leszczynska, wife of Louis XV, daughter of the former King of Poland, Stanislas Leszczynski.

297. SATIN, BROCADED. FURS AND FLOWERS

FRANCE, LYONS, MID-18TH CEN-TURY. NEW YORK CITY, THE MET-ROPOLITAN MUSEUM OF ART.

41½ x 40 in. (103 x 100 cm.). No. 46.156.109. Ex-coll. Sangiorgi. Exhibited: *Mostra del tessile nazionale*, Rome, 1937–38, cat. p. 43, no. 222, fig. 134 (called: Venice, 18th century). Published: N. N. Sobolev, *Outline of the History of Textile Design*, Moscow, 1934, p. 281, fig. 181 (a piece with similar motifs in Nizhni-Novgorod Museum, called French, 18th century).

Plain compound satin, brocaded. Ground, yellow silk with lattice pattern enclosing rosettes brocaded in flat silver thread. Design of bands of miniver in white and light-brown silks and black chenille; sprays of small flowers in two shades of blue and black silks.

Probably made for Queen Maria Leszczynska.

298. FAILLE, BROCADED

FRANCE, LYONS, MID-18TH CEN-TURY. THE DETROIT INSTITUTE OF ARTS.

39 x 20 in. (99 x 50½ cm.). No. 49.521.

Pale-blue, white, rose, and green silks. On light-blue faille ground, bands of lace are twisted vertically and interspersed with bunches of flowers.

299. SATIN, BROCADED. THE COCK-ATOOS

FRANCE, LYONS, MID-18TH CEN-TURY. THE DETROIT INSTITUTE OF ARTS.

55 x 27 in. (139 x 68½ cm.). No. 44.201, gift of Adolph Loewi. Exhibited: *2000 Years*, cat. no. 354.

White satin, brocaded. White and pink cockatoos with red crests and alternately blue and green, or yellow and green, wings and tails stand on boughs of trees with pink, yellow, and white foliage and fruits.

The slender design owes much to the anonymous ornithologist whose painting of the tropical bird may have graced one of the many publications on travel and natural history. It owes something also to J. B. Pillement, whose inventive genius was not entirely limited by *chinoiserie*.

300. FANCY TAFFETA, BROCADED. CHINOISERIE

FRENCH, LYONS, MID-18TH CEN-TURY. PROVIDENCE, MUSEUM OF ART.

34½ x 21½ in. (87½ x 34½ cm.). No. 47.069.

Undulating vertical lines of twisted ribbons, bunches of flowers, and little landscapes with figurines combine to give a charming illustration of the style of Pillement.

301. TAFFETA, BROCADED. CHINOISERIE

FRANCE, LYONS, MID-18TH CEN-TURY. THE CLEVELAND MUSEUM OF ART.

40 x 21 in. (101 x 53 cm.). No. 37.21, gift of the Textile Arts Club. Published: Gertrude Underhill, "Gifts of the Textile Arts Club," *Bulletin*, XXXIII (1946), 24.

The white ground is overlaid with a thin diaper of metallic threads of gold and silver.

These are used also for the vertically twisted tendrils with fantastic leaf forms. A second pattern shows diagonally curved tendrils with small flowers, and bunches of larger, fantastic flowers. The brocading silks are of several tones of blue, violet, rose, yellow, and green.

Style of Pillement.

302. FAILLE, BROCADED. CHINOISERIE

FRANCE, LYONS, MID-18TH CENTURY. THE CLEVELAND MUSEUM OF ART.

21 x 19 in. (53 x 48 cm.). No. 37.22. Ex-coll. Elsberg.

The ground is a golden-yellow ribbed silk overlaid with small floated, vaguely floral, forms. Over this a symmetrical design of purely imaginary flowers and leaves is brocaded in blue, rose, violet, and green silks.

Style of Pillement.

303. SATIN, BROCADED. CHINOISERIE

FRANCE, LYONS, MID-18TH CENTURY. NEW YORK CITY, THE METROPOLITAN MUSEUM OF ART.

76 x 21¼ in. (193 x 59 cm.). No. 41.182. Exhibited: 2000 Years, cat. no. 371. Published: Raymond Cox, *Musée historique des Tissus, Soieries et Broderies*, Paris, n.d., pl. 42.

Plain compound satin, brocaded. Ground, golden yellow; the design in white, lavender, green, blue, and two shades of pink, with black accents throughout. Garlands of roses, anemones, chrysanthemums, and fantastic flowers form oval compartments, framing a rococo motif of doves, bows, and quivers. At the foot of palm trees growing from the garlands sit Chinese figurines. The fabric is slightly cut at both sides.

Probably from a design by Jean-Baptiste Le Prince (1734–1781).

304. TAFFETA, BROCADED

FRANCE, LYONS, THIRD QUARTER OF 18TH CENTURY. PROVIDENCE, MUSEUM OF ART.

37½ x 21½ in. (95 x 34½ cm.). No. 22.233.

Large and small flowers form garlands and bouquets in a symmetric design.

This fabric illustrates one of many attempts to replace the fantastic flowers of the mid-eighteenth century with blossoms culled in the fields and gardens of France, and indicates a growing preference for small flowers.

305. CORDED SILK AND METAL THREAD, BROCADED

FRANCE, LYONS, THIRD QUARTER OF 18TH CENTURY. THE CLEVELAND MUSEUM OF ART.

24 x 21½ in. (61 x 54½ cm.). No. 39.34. Ex-coll. Elsberg. Published: Gertrude Underhill, "Textiles from the H. A. Elsberg collection," *Bulletin*, XXVI (1939), 142.

The ground consists of vertical groups of stripes of gold and silver metallic thread. Across these stripes undulating sprays of small flowers and feathery leaves are brocaded in polychrome silks.

306. TAFFETA, SILVER-BROCADED

FRANCE, LYONS, THIRD QUARTER OF 18TH CENTURY. THE CLEVELAND MUSEUM OF ART.

23 x 22 in. (58½ x 56 cm.). No. 40.474. Ex-coll. Elsberg. Exhibited: 2000 Years, cat. no. 406.

On white taffeta ground a group of three vertical stripes is shaded from yellow to green. Across these stripes a garland of flowers and leaves is brocaded in silver thread. The taffeta ground is dotted with groups of silver disks forming lozenges.

307. TAFFETA, BROCADED

FRANCE, LYONS, LAST QUARTER OF 18TH CENTURY. THE CLEVELAND MUSEUM OF ART.

16 x 20 in. (40½ x 51 cm.). No. 19.108.

On lavender taffeta ground, the design of floral motifs in vertical rows is brocaded in polychrome silks. These rows are separated by a group of three narrow green stripes festooned by small sprigs of wild roses.

308. SILK REP, BROCADED

FRANCE, LYONS, LAST QUARTER OF 18TH CENTURY. PROVIDENCE, MUSEUM OF ART.

60 x 21½ in. (152 x 54½ cm.). No. 47.191.

Polychrome silks and silver thread. Undulating garlands ignore the vertical ribbons and floated sprigs beneath them; but they need the help of separate little trees growing from grass mounds to offset their own meagerness.

309. CHENILLE AND METAL BROCADE

FRANCE, LYONS, SECOND HALF OF 18TH CENTURY. THE CLEVELAND MUSEUM OF ART.

15¾ x 15¾ in. (40 x 40 cm.). No. 40.485. Ex-coll. Elsberg.

On striped metallic ground, the design is woven in blue chenille and silk. Ribbons wave in zigzag lines, small birds hold hearts in their beaks, single flowers fill the spaces.

310. CUT VOIDED VELVET

FRANCE OR ITALY, LATE 18TH CENTURY. PROVIDENCE, MUSEUM OF ART.

4¾ x 6½ in. (12 x 16½ cm.). Diameter of roundels: ½ in. (1¼ cm.). No. 13.1539.

Light- and dark-brown silks, the ground shot with silver.

311. CUT VOIDED TWILL VELVET

FRANCE, LYONS, LATE 18TH CENTURY. PROVIDENCE, MUSEUM OF ART.

16¼ x 10¾ in. (41 x 27 cm.). No. 47.421.

Cream twill ground, pale-blue and black cut velvet for the design. This is arranged in two alternating horizontal bands slightly less than 2½ inches wide. One of these shows a charming group of domestic fowls visited by a peacock, with blackbirds flying overhead. The design of the other band is far more ambitious: to Venus, seated in a bower, comes Cupid announcing a visitor, an elegant young man clad lightly in a flowing scarf. His cockleshell carriage is drawn by butterflies.

A fabric of such delicate charm must have had an immediate appeal for many possibilities of interior decoration, foremost probably the lining of a sedan chair.

312. PLAIN COMPOUND SATIN. PARTS OF A WAISTCOAT

FRANCE, ALSACE (?), SECOND HALF OF 18TH CENTURY. NEW HAVEN, YALE UNIVERSITY ART GALLERY.

35½ x 21½ in. (90 x 54½ cm.). No. 1939.517. Exhibited: *2000 Years*, cat. no. 411.

Plain compound satin, all parts of a man's waistcoat, woven in one piece and never used. Dark-gray satin, green, white, and polychrome design. The front has small detached flowers and borders with a garland that is continued on the collar. At the lower end there is a scene, repeated in overturn, of Justice with scales and whip driving away a group of men. The pockets are marked with separate garlands and the flaps show a Victory blowing a trumpet. Twelve buttons are also provided.

The two waistcoats pictured may have been produced by the same workshop. Uncut specimens are quite rare. It is interesting to see that they were actually woven in a diversity of length, for taller and shorter men.

313. PLAIN COMPOUND SATIN. PARTS OF A WAISTCOAT

FRANCE, ALSACE (?), SECOND HALF OF 18TH CENTURY. THE DETROIT INSTITUTE OF ARTS.

28½ x 21½ in. (82 x 54½ cm.). No. 44.141. Exhibited: *2000 Years*, cat. no. 410.

Plain compound satin, all parts of a man's waistcoat, woven in one piece and never used. The green ground is patterned with white ribbons tied into bows; polychrome garlands outline the front, a fair in the manner of Teniers the lower edge. The flaps for pockets and collar have bouquets, the buttons small rosettes.

314. "LE PANIER FLEURI," BY PHILIPPE DE LASSALLE

FRANCE, LYONS, c. 1770. THE DETROIT INSTITUTE OF ARTS.

52½ x 37 in. (133 x 94 cm.). No. 48.18, gift of Mrs. E. S. Fechimer. Ex-coll. Elsberg. The fabric was cut and used to cover a *bergère*.

Polychrome silks and chenille. Ribbons of two tones of blue flutter over the ground of cream silk *dauphiné*. They frame a basket filled with flowers and hold together bouquets and a garland.
On May 16, 1770, the dauphin Louis married the archduchess of Austria, Marie-Antoinette. This gay fabric may have been designed for that occasion. The ground weave of small chevrons, called *dauphiné* in contemporary bills and descriptions, may have been named in her honor. Lassalle must have liked the effect of a play of light and shadow in his

backgrounds, for even in his earlier fabrics he seems to have preferred a ground of faille to one of taffeta or satin. The *panier fleuri*, woven about 1770, inaugurates the unique series of magnificent silk brocades that are due to the collaboration of Philippe de Lassalle and Camille Pernon.

315. CHAIR BACK, BY PHILIPPE DE LASSALLE

FRANCE, LYONS, CAMILLE PERNON ET CIE C. 1770. NEW YORK CITY, THE METROPOLITAN MUSEUM OF ART.

34¼ x 22 in. (87 x 56 cm.). No. 38.182.7. Ex-coll. Elsberg.

Plain satin, brocaded. Ground white, with stripes shaded pink, red, and yellow; design brocaded in pastel colors. A blue vase containing roses, tulips, carnations, and peonies is supported between branches that issue from the border stripes. The ormolu handles of the vase form the letter L (Louis?).

316. A STILL LIFE, BY PHILIPPE DE LASSALLE

FRANCE, LYONS, CAMILLE PERNON ET CIE, C. 1770. NEW YORK CITY, THE METROPOLITAN MUSEUM OF ART.

28½ x 22 in. (72½ x 56 cm.). No. 38.182.5. Ex-coll. Elsberg.

Plain compound twill, brocaded. On a pale-green field lies an oval medallion of white satin framed by a garland of roses and containing a flower basket, lute, and music book resting on a segment of a garden. The medallions are connected by trailers of cornflowers; bunches of petunias fill the remaining space.
Cut up as a chair back. Fig. 317 belongs to the same design, but is woven in a different color scheme.

317. THE BAGPIPE PLAYER, BY PHILIPPE DE LASSALLE

FRANCE, LYONS, CAMILLE PERNON ET CIE, C. 1770. NEW YORK CITY, THE METROPOLITAN MUSEUM OF ART.

32 x 22 in. (81 x 56 cm.), loom width. No. 38.182.6. Ex-coll. Elsberg.

Another medallion of the design of Fig. 316, but woven with a pale-blue ground. The medallion contains an alternating composition: a boy playing the bagpipe, and a dancing dog, in a garden with an arcaded building in the background.

Cut up as a chair back.

318. "LES PERDRIX," BY PHILIPPE DE LASSALLE

FRANCE, LYONS, CAMILLE PERNON ET CIE, C. 1780. NEW YORK CITY, THE METROPOLITAN MUSEUM OF ART.

98½ x 31 in. (250 x 78½ cm.). No. 50.8a. From a bedroom at Peterhof, Catherine the Great's summer palace near St. Petersburg. Another specimen on rose-red ground in the Detroit Institute of Arts.

The light-blue ground is woven in *dauphiné*, a form of basket weave. The design, of polychrome silks and chenille, is centered on a large wreath of summer flowers tied casually with a white scarf. A sheaf of golden wheat is placed across the wreath and serves as a frame for a little idyllic scene, three partridges looking out from their refuge among cornflowers and poppies.

With this composition Lassalle reached the highest pinnacle in the art of textile design.

319. "LES PERDRIX," BY PHILIPPE DE LASSALLE. DETAIL

FRANCE, LYONS, C. 1780. THE DETROIT INSTITUTE OF ARTS.

Detail of a panel from a bedroom at Peterhof.

320. SATIN, BROCADED. THE PET LAMB

FRANCE, LYONS, C. 1780. THE CLEVELAND MUSEUM OF ART.

97 x 21½ in. (255 x 54½ cm.). No. 32.37. Exhibited: *2000 Years*, cat. no. 401.

Stripes of yellow satin are overlaid with an undulating garland of roses that extends onto the ground of white satin as a curved spray. It frames an idyllic scene: a shepherdess has tied her lamb to a rosebush. A shepherd has left there his bagpipes. The brocading is of red, pink, white, yellow, green, and blue silks, and brown and tan chenille.

This fabric stands close to "The Partridges," even closer to the wall hangings of Marie Antoinette's bedroom. Neither the design nor the *mise en carte* seems to have been preserved. The quality of the composition points to the one and only Philippe de Lassalle. It is the perfect illustration of the dying rococo.

321. CATHERINE THE GREAT, BY PHILIPPE DE LASSALLE

FRANCE, LYONS, CAMILLE PERNON ET CIE, *c.* 1777. NEW YORK CITY, THE METROPOLITAN MUSEUM OF ART.

40 x 29 in. (100 x 73½ cm.). No. 41.78. Ex-coll. Mrs. Henry Walters.

The oval profile portrait of Catherine II, Empress of Russia from 1762 to 1796; woven separately in several tones of *camaïeu* and applied to a larger panel forming a frame. The garland is woven in pinks, blues, greens, and citron yellow; the bow in white, pink, citron, and darker green; the background in greenish-golden satin. The inscription is embroidered in satin stitch of white silk: "Du Nil au Bosphore l'Ottoman frémit, son peuple l'adore, la terre applaudit." The signature is also embroidered.

322. *LAMPAS*

FRANCE, LYONS, LAST QUARTER OF 18TH CENTURY. THE DETROIT INSTITUTE OF ARTS.

114½ x 56½ in. (289 x 143 cm.). No. 44.284. Published: Adèle Coulin Weibel, "Lampas," *Bulletin*, XXVI (1947), 4.

The design of this lampas is so large in scale that it required two widths of the fabric. On the red satin ground, bouquets and garlands, rambling morning-glories and sheaves of wheat, and especially two well-designed herons continue the tradition of Philippe de Lassalle, while vases and a trophy surmounted by an eagle announce the trend toward the antique. The design at the top is incomplete; a narrow band sewed to the fabric seems to indicate the original presence of yet another motif to the repeat of the composition.

The noble fabric must have been woven in the last years before the outbreak of the Revolution. The continuous design, with details such as the tips of one heron's wings and the other's tail overlapping on to the adjoining panel, proves that this lampas was intended to mask an entire wall, somewhat in the manner of painted wallpaper imported from China.

323. *LAMPAS*

FRANCE, LYONS, LAST QUARTER OF 18TH CENTURY. THE DETROIT INSTITUTE OF ARTS.

84 x 21¼ in. (214 x 54 cm.). No. 45.9, gift of Mrs. Emma S. Fechimer. Published: Adèle Coulin Weibel, "Lampas," *Bulletin*, XXVI (1947), 4.

On celadon-green satin ground, nymphs, naiads, and Erotes, and medallions framing a genre scene or an amphora, are wreathed in slender garlands and strings of beads.

This lampas illustrates the fully evolved style *à la grecque*, according to the formula that had its roots in the art of recently rediscovered Pompeii and Herculaneum. These neoclassic designs were greatly to the taste of the generation that came to power after the Revolution, the Directoire.

324. *LAMPAS*

FRANCE, LYONS, FIRST QUARTER OF 19TH CENTURY. PROVIDENCE, MUSEUM OF ART.

43½ x 22 in. (109 x 56 cm.), width of fabric. No. 47.195. Two widths, seamed together.

Fancy compound satin, not reversible, green and ivory silks. Acanthus scrolls frame a medallion with two acolytes preparing a sacrifice at an altar, and support a console with chained seated griffins.

The equivocal airs and graces of Pompeiian art have given way to a sturdy, somewhat cold design that in the Napoleonic period was supposed to be characteristic of Roman imperial art.

325. *SATIN, BROCADED. THE PHEASANTS, BY J. D. DUGOURC*

FRANCE, LYONS, CAMILLE PERNON ET CIE, EARLY 19TH CENTURY. THE ENTIRE SPECIMEN: PROVIDENCE, MUSEUM OF ART. THE DETAIL: THE CLEVELAND MUSEUM OF ART.

Providence, No. 47.194; Cleveland, No. 35.237. Both specimens: 93 x 18 in. (236 x 45½ cm.); detail: L. 32 in. (81 cm.). Exhibited: *2000 Years*, cat. no. 376. Published: Gertrude Underhill, "Two Eighteenth Century French Silks," *Bulletin*, XXIII (1936), 36.

Polychrome silks on white satin; touches of embroidery of the period. On a vase-shaped console stands an empty birdcage with open door. It is wreathed in small flowers, with details added in embroidery. This motif is enclosed in a garland of roses with looped ribbons and strings of pearls. From the console rise slender rods that support tall baskets. On each of these a pheasant has alighted, magnificently designed with crested head and long tail feathers. Confronted, these birds hold in their beaks the strings of a pearl necklace. These pearls, together with floral garlands and ribbons, lead the attention to a jeweled staff that connects with a third motif. A tall vase is

161

filled with a bouquet of asters. Delicate handles rise from its mouth, curve up and bend down, and end in leafy garlands. These follow the contour of the vase with elaborate curves and trail around supporting rods. The almost unbelievably elaborate design leads gently from the style of the rococo to that of the Empire.

The designer was Jean-Démosthène Dugourc (1749–1825), a Parisian. In 1780 Dugourc became *dessinateur de Monsieur*, the Duke of Orleans; three years later he was made designer of costumes and stage decorations of the opera; in 1784 designer of the Garde-Meuble and superintendent of the buildings of "Monsieur." In 1790 he was given the important job of Inspector General of the manufactories of France. He then started in a business of his own, producing wallpapers from his designs, and playing cards. After an interval at the Spanish court, as *architecte du Roi*, he settled in Paris, where until his death in 1825 he held the job of *dessinateur de la Couronne et des Menus-Plaisirs*. Dugourc was the outstanding interior decorator of his period. He made the design of this ravishingly beautiful fabric for the walls of a room in the Royal Palace in Madrid, probably commissioned by François Grognard, the partner of Camille Pernon and his representative at the court of Spain. The satin was then woven for Camille Pernon. A collection of Dugourc's drawings for woven and embroidered textiles is still preserved by Pernon's successors, Châtel et Tassinari, at Lyons. In records of the firm of Camille Pernon et Companie the Pheasant brocade is described as "Verdures du Vatican," referring to the inspiration on Dugourc of the *Loggie* of Raphael.

326. *PLAIN COMPOUND SATIN, BROCADED*

FRANCE, LYONS, SÉGUIN ET CIE, EARLY 19TH CENTURY. NEW YORK CITY, THE METROPOLITAN MUSEUM OF ART.

42½ x 21½ in. (107½ C 54½ cm.). No. 38.182.33. Ex-coll. Elsberg. Published: Frances Little, "Textiles from the Elsberg Collection," *Bulletin*, XXXIV (1939), 144.

Ground of crimson silk, design of large and small rosettes brocaded in plain and crinkled gold thread.

Ordered by Napoleon I for the wall hanging of a salon in the palace of Fontainebleau. Made by Séguin et Cie, Lyon, 1805–1815.

327. *PLAIN COMPOUND CLOTH, BROCADED*

FRANCE, LYONS, SÉGUIN ET CIE, 1811. NEW YORK CITY, THE METROPOLITAN MUSEUM OF ART.

24 x 23½ in. (61 x 59½ cm.). No. 38.182.32. Ex-coll. Elsberg. Published: Frances Little, "Textiles from the Elsberg Collection," *Bulletin*, XXXIV (1939), 144.

Complete panel. Ground, oyster-white silk; design brocaded in gold thread. Rosettes and a border with palmettes.

Made by Séguin et Cie, Lyon, 1811, for the layette of Napoleon's son, the King of Rome.

328. *CUT SOLID VELVET, CHINÉ. A DECORATIVE BAND, BY GASPARD GRÉGOIRE*

FRANCE, AIX-EN-PROVENCE, EARLY 19TH CENTURY. NEW YORK CITY, COOPER UNION MUSEUM.

2¼ x 11½ in. (5½ x 29 cm.). No. 1939.15.2, gift of the estate of H. A. Elsberg.

Warp painted in shades of red, brown, green, and black. Lotus rosette and stems with laurel leaves.

A "petite bande avec rosace" such as this pleasing specimen was used for covering small boxes or etuis. It shows at its best the possibilities and limitations of this ephemeral technique, the *velours Grégoire*.

329. CUT SOLID VELVET, CHINÉ. PORTRAIT OF NAPOLEON I, BY GASPARD GRÉGOIRE

FRANCE, AIX-EN-PROVENCE, EARLY 19TH CENTURY. NEW YORK CITY, THE METROPOLITAN MUSEUM OF ART.

8¾ x 6¾ in. (22 x 17 cm.). No. 38.182.9. Ex-coll. Elsberg. Published: (the Lyon specimen) R. Cox, *Soieries d'art*, 1914, pl. 95.

Cut solid cloth velvet, *chiné;* dark-gray background, the portrait in tones of tan, brown, and red. Made by Gaspard Grégoire from a portrait of Napoleon painted by Jacques-Louis David.

330. CUT SOLID VELVET, CHINÉ. PORTRAIT OF LOUIS XVIII, BY GASPARD GRÉGOIRE

FRANCE, AIX-EN-PROVENCE, EARLY 19TH CENTURY. NEW YORK CITY, THE METROPOLITAN MUSEUM OF ART.

7¾ x 6½ in. (19½ x 16½ cm.). No. 38.182.10. Ex-coll. Elsberg.

Cut solid cloth velvet, *chiné;* purple background, the portrait in pink, white, and purple, the ribbon in green. Made by Gaspard Grégoire, from the portrait of Louis XVIII, painted by François Gérard in 1814.

331. FANCY COMPOUND CLOTH. PORTRAIT OF GEORGE WASHINGTON

FRANCE, LYONS, MATHEVON AND BOUVARD, 19TH CENTURY. BOSTON, MUSEUM OF FINE ARTS.

22½ x 17¾ in. (57½ x 45 cm.). No. 42.548.

Woven, probably, from an engraving by James Heath after the Lansdowne portrait by Gilbert Stuart.

One of the last handwoven textiles from the Lyon looms. Most of these portraits were woven in much smaller size, in ribbons, on Jacquard power looms at Basel or Coventry. This may be taken as the prototype of the power-woven examples and like them is in black-and-white.

BIBLIOGRAPHY

GENERAL

Algoud, Henri: *Grammaire des arts de la soie*, Paris, 1912.

Ciba Review: Published by the Society of Chemical Industry in Basle, from September, 1937. A wide variety of articles on the history of dyeing, printing, tanning, weaving, etc.; very valuable for students.

Chartraire, Eugène: *Inventaire du trésor de l'église principale et métropolitaine de Sens*, Paris, 1897.

Cole, Alan Summerly: *Ornament in European Silk*, London, 1899.

——: Articles in *Encyclopædia Britannica*, 11th ed., especially: "Brocade," vol. 4, p. 620; "Gold and Silver Thread," vol. 12, p. 200; "Weaving (Archaeology and Art)," vol. 28, p. 448.

Cox, Raymond: *L'Art de décorer les tissus d'après les collections de la Chambre de Commerce de Lyon*, Paris, 1900.

——: *Les Soieries d'art, depuis les origines jusqu'à nos jours*, Paris, 1914.

Dreger, Moritz: *Künstlerische Entwicklung der Weberei und Stickerei innerhalb des europäischen Kulturkreises, von der Spätantiken Zeit bis zum Beginne des XIX. Jahrhunderts*, 3 vols., Vienna, 1904.

Dupont-Auberville, A: *L'Ornement des tissus*, Paris, 1877.

Errera, Isabelle: *Catalogue d'étoffes anciennes et modernes*, Musées Royaux des Arts Décoratifs de Bruxelles, 2nd ed., Brussels, 1907.

Falke, Otto von: *Kunstgeschichte der Seidenweberei*, 2 vols., 613 illus., Berlin, Ernst Wasmuth, 1913. All references are to this edition.

——: *Decorative Silks*, New York, 1922. A translation of the 2nd, abbreviated, edition of *Kunstgeschichte der Seidenweberei*, Berlin, 1921.

Fischbach, Friedrich: *Die Geschichte der Textilkunst*, Hanau, 1883.

——: *Ornamente der Gewebe, gezeichnet von F. F.*, 4 vols., Hanau, 1874–80.

Flemming, Ernst: *Das Textilwerk. Gewebeornamente und Stoffmuster vom Altertum bis zum Anfang des XIX. Jahrhunderts*, Berlin, 1927.

——: *An Encyclopedia of Textiles*, New York, 1927.

Grisar, Hartmann: *Die römische Kapelle Sancta Sanctorum und ihr Schatz*, Freiburg im Breisgau, 1908.

Heiden, Max: *Handwörterbuch der Textilkunde aller Zeiten und Völker*, Stuttgart, 1904.

——: *Die Textilkunst des Altertums bis zur Neuzeit*, Berlin, 1909.

Hennezel, Henri, Comte d': *Le décor des soieries d'art anciennes et modernes. . . . du Musée Historique des Tissus de Lyon*, Paris, n.d.

——: *Decorations and Designs of Silken Masterpieces*, New York, 1930.

Heyd, Wilhelm von: *Geschichte des Levantehandels im Mittelalter*, Stuttgart, 1879.

——: *Histoire du commerce du Levant au moyen âge. Edition française, refondue et considérablement augmentée par l'auteur*, 2 vols., Leipzig, 1885–86; new ed., 1923.

Hunter, George Leland: *Decorative Textiles*, Philadelphia, 1918.

Lessing, Julius: *Die Gewebe-Sammlung des K. Kunstgewerbe-Museums, Kgl. Museen*, Berlin, 1900–09. 330 pls. in 11 portfolios.

Linas, Charles de: *Anciens vêtements sacerdotaux et anciens tissus conservés en France*, Paris, 1860.

Mannowsky, Walter: *Der Danziger Paramentenschatz Kirchliche Gewänder und Stickereien aus der Marienkirche*, 4 vols., Berlin, Brandus'sche Verlagsbuchhandlung, n.d. (1932).

Michel, Francisque: *Recherches sur le commerce, la fabrication et l'usage des étoffes de soie, d'or et d'argent, et autres tissus précieux en occident, principalement en France, pendant le moyen âge*, 2 vols., Paris, 1852 and 1854. A unique compilation of medieval literary references from chronicles, inventories and poetical works.

Migeon, Gaston: *Les Arts du tissu*, Paris, 1909.

Pariset, Ernest: *Histoire de la soie*, 2 vols., Paris, 1862–65.

——: *Les Industries de la soie*, Paris, 1890.

Reath, Nancy Andrews: *The Weaves of Hand-Loom Fabrics*, Philadelphia Museum of Art, 1927.

Riegl, Alois: "Textilkunst," in Bruno Bucher, *Geschichte der technischen Künste*, vol. III, Stuttgart, 1893.

Rock, Daniel: *Textile Fabrics*, London, 1870.

Rohault de Fleury, Robert: *La Messe*, 8 vols., Paris, 1883–89. Of greatest importance for the study of vestments.

Sangiorgi, Giorgio: *Contributi allo studio dell'arte tessile*, Milan, n.d.

Savary des Bruslons, Jacques: *Dictionnaire universel du commerce* (Edition augmentée par C. Philibert), 5 vols., Copenhagen, 1756–66.

Volbach, Wolfgang Friedrich: *I Tessuti del Museo Sacro Vaticano*, Città del Vaticano, 1942.

Bréhier, Louis: *La sculpture et les arts mineurs byzantins*, Paris, 1936.

Dalton, Ormando Maddock: *Byzantine Art and Archaeology*, Oxford, 1911.

———: *East Christian Art*, Oxford, 1925.

Diehl, Charles: *Manuel d'art byzantin*, Paris, 1925.

Dimand, Maurice: *Die Ornamentik der ägyptischen Wollwirkereien*, Leipzig, 1924.

Forrer, R: *Römische und byzantinische Seiden-Textilien aus dem Gräberfelde von Achmim-Panopolis*, Strassbourg, 1891.

Gayet, Albert Jean: *L'art copte*, Paris, 1902.

Gennep, A van, and G. Jéquier: *Le Tissage aux cartons et son utilisation décorative dans l'Egypte ancienne*, Neuchâtel, 1916.

Gerspach, Edouard: *Les Tapisseries coptes*, Paris, 1890.

Hirth, Friedrich: *China and the Roman Orient*, Leipzig, 1885.

Kendrick, Albert Frank: *Catalogue of Textiles from Burying Grounds in Egypt*, I—"Graeco-Roman Period"; II—"Transition and Christian Emblems"; III—"Coptic Period," London, 1920–22.

Pfister, R: *Textiles de Palmyre*, vols. I–III, Paris, 1934, 1938, 1940.

———: *Tissus coptes du Musée du Louvre*, Paris, 1932.

———, and Louisa Bellinger: *The Textiles; The Excavations at Dura-Europos*, final report IV, part II, New Haven, 1945.

Peirce, Hayford, and Royall Tyler: *L'Art Byzantin*, 2 vols., Paris, 1932–34.

Riegl, Alois: *Die ägyptischen Textilfunde im k.k. Oesterreichischen Museum*, Vienna, 1889.

Wulff, Oskar: *Altchristliche und byzantinische Kunst*, 2 vols., Berlin, 1914.

———, and Wolfgang Friedrich Volbach: *Spätantike und koptische Stoffe aus ägyptischen Grabfunden in den staatlichen Museen . . .* , Berlin, 1926.

Yates, James: *Textrinum antiquorum; an account of the Art of Weaving among the Ancients*, London, 1843. A valuable and learned work of reference.

NEAR EAST

Ackerman, Phyllis: "Textiles through the Sāsānian Period"; "The Textile Arts," *A Survey of Persian Art*, London and New York, 1939, vol. I, pp. 681–715; vol. III, pp. 1995–2220.

Aga-Oglu, Mehmet: *Safawid Rugs and Textiles, the Collection of the Shrine of Imam 'Ali at Al-Najaf*, New York, 1941.

Baghat, Aly Bey: *Les Manufactures d'étoffes en Egypte au moyen age*, Cairo, 1904.

Dimand, Maurice: *A Handbook of Muhammadan Art*, 2nd ed., revised and enlarged, New York, The Metropolitan Museum of Art, 1944.

Geijer, Agnes: *Oriental Textiles in Sweden*, Copenhagen, 1951.

Herzfeld, Ernst: *Am Tor von Asien*, Berlin, 1920. Important for Sassanian textiles.

Kendrick, Albert Frank: *Catalogue of Muhammadan textiles of the medieval period in the Victoria and Albert Museum*, London, 1924.

Koechlin, Raymond, and Gaston Migeon: *Oriental Art.* (Textiles, by G. Migeon), New York, n.d.

Kühnel, Ernst: *Islamische Stoffe aus ägyptischen Gräbern in der islamischen Kunstabteilung und in der Stoffsammlung des Schloss-museums*, Berlin, 1927.

———: *Maurische Kunst*, Berlin, 1924.

Lamm, Carl Johan: *Cotton in Medieval Textiles of the Near East*, Paris, 1937.

Le Strange, Guy: *The Lands of the Eastern Caliphate*, Cambridge, 1930.

———: (editor) *Clavijo, Embassy to Tamerlane*, London, 1928.

Martin, Fredrik Robert: *Figurale Persische Stoffe aus dem Zeitraum 1550–1650*, Stockholm, 1899.

———: *Die persischen Prachtstoffe im Schlosse Rosenborg in Kopenhagen*, Stockholm, 1901.

Migeon, Gaston: *Manuel d'art musulman; Arts plastiques et industriels*, 2nd ed., revised and enlarged, 2 vols., Paris, 1927.

Pfister, R: "Les Premières Soies sassanides," *Etudes d'orientalisme publiées par le Musée Guimet*, vol. II, Paris, 1932.

Pope, Arthur Upham: *Masterpieces of Persian Art*, New York, 1945. Especially "Seljuq Textiles," p. 72; "Safavid Textiles," p. 185.

Prisse d'Avennes: *L'art arabe d'après les momuments du Kaïre*, Paris, 1877.

Reath, Nancy Andrews, and Eleanor B. Sachs: *Persian Textiles and their Technique from the Sixth to the Eighteenth Centuries, including a system for general textile classification*, New Haven, 1937.

Sarre, Friedrich: *Die Kunst des alten Persien*, Berlin, 1922.

———, and F. R. Martin: *Die Austellung von Meisterwerken der Muhammedanischen Kunst in München, 1910*, Munich, 1912.

166

Survey of Persian Art, from Prehistoric Times to the Present, Arthur Upham Pope and Phyllis Ackerman, editors, 6 vols., London and New York, 1938–39. See also Ackerman, Phyllis.

Sykes, Sir Percy (editor): *Sir John Chardin's Travels in Persia*, London, 1927.

Tavernier, Jean-Baptiste: *Voyages en Perse* (edited by P. Pia), Paris, n.d. (1930).

Terrasse, Henri: *L'Art hispano-mauresque des origines au XIIIᵉ siècle*, Paris, 1932.

Wiet, Gaston: *Soieries Persanes*, Cairo, 1948.

EUROPE

Bock, Franz: *Geschichte der liturgischen Gewänder des Mittelalters*, 3 vols., Bonn, 1856–71.

——: *Die Kleinodien des heiligen römischen Reiches deutscher Nation*, Vienna, 1864.

Braun, Joseph: *Die Liturgische Gewandung im Occident und Orient*, Freiburg im Breisgau, 1907.

Duchesne, Louis Marie Olivier: *Etude sur le Liber Pontificalis*, Paris, 1877. The textile entries have been collected by Stephan Beissel and published in *Zeitschrift für Christliche Kunst*, 1934, pp. 357 ff.

Dumonthier, Ernest: *Etoffes d'Ameublement de l'Epogue Napoléonienne*, Paris, 1909.

Ebersolt, Jean: *Orient et Occident*, Paris, 1928.

Ferrari, Vittorio: *Tessuti Decorativi, Galloni, Nastri, Bordure, Fiocchi*, 2nd ed., Milan, 1944.

Gay, Victor: *Glossaire archéologique du Moyen Age et de la Renaissance*, 2 vols., Paris, 1872.

Hald, Margrethe: *Olddanske Tekstiler (Ancient Danish Textiles)*, with English summary and captions, Copenhagen, 1950.

Kendrick, Albert Frank: *Catalogue of early medieval woven fabrics in the Victoria and Albert Museum*, London, 1925.

Leroudier, E: *Les Dessinateurs de la Fabrique lyonnaise au XVIIIᵉ siècle*, Lyons, 1908.

Podreider, Fanny: *Storia dei Tessuti d'Arte in Italia*, Bergamo, 1927.

Réal, Daniel, *Tissus espagnols et portugais*, Paris, 1925.

Scheyer, Ernst: *Die Kölner Bortenweberei des Mittelalters*, Augsburg, n.d. (1932).

EXHIBITIONS QUOTED IN ABBREVIATION:

Baltimore, 1947:   *Early Christian and Byzantine Art, An exhibition held at the Baltimore Museum of Art, organized by the Walters Art Gallery, 1947*

Brooklyn, 1941:   *Pagan and Christian Egypt. Egyptian art from the first to the tenth century,* A.D., *Brooklyn Museum, 1941*

London, 1931:   *International Exhibition of Persian Art, Royal Academy, London, 1931*

New York, 1940:   *Exhibition of Persian Art, The Iranian Institute, 1940*

2000 Years, 1944:   *2000 Years of Silk Weaving. An exhibition sponsored by the Los Angeles County Museum in collaboration with the Cleveland Museum of Art and The Detroit Institute of Arts, 1944*

Worcester, 1937:   *The Dark Ages. Loan exhibition of pagan and Christian art in the Latin West and Byzantine East. Worcester Art Museum, 1937*

PHOTOGRAPHS THROUGH THE COURTESY OF THE FOLLOWING MUSEUMS:

PLATES

ALL reproductions are by courtesy of the Museums, the owners of the textiles. Many are here published for the first time by special permission. This generous collaboration is hereby acknowledged gratefully.

2. Wool Tapestry. Roses

SYRIA, DURA-EUROPOS, BEFORE A.D. 256

New Haven, Yale University Art Gallery

3. Wool Tapestry. Nereids
COPTIC, 5TH CENTURY

*Washington, D. C., Dumbarton Oaks Research Library
and Collection, Harvard University*

4. Wool Tapestry. Attendant Nereid
COPTIC, 5TH CENTURY

*Washington, D. C., Dumbarton Oaks Research Library
and Collection, Harvard University*

5. Wool Tapestry. Mask and Duck

COPTIC, 4TH–5TH CENTURY

*Washington, D. C., Dumbarton Oaks Research Library
and Collection, Harvard University*

6. Wool Tapestry. Pastoral Scene
HELLENISTIC, 3RD–4TH CENTURY
City Art Museum of St. Louis

7. Silk and Linen Tapestry. A Horseman
HELLENISTIC, 4TH–5TH CENTURY
Boston, Museum of Fine Arts

9. Wool Tapestry. Bucolic Scenes
HELLENISTIC, 5TH CENTURY
New York City, The Brooklyn Museum

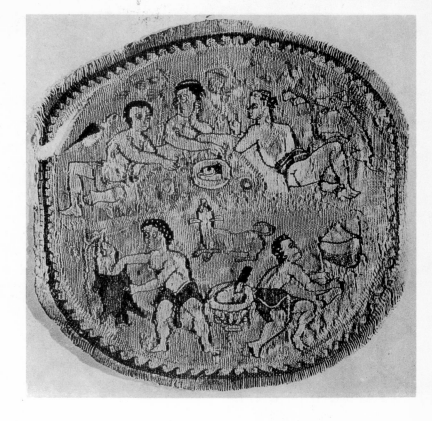

8. Silk Tapestry. A Falconer
SYRIA, 5TH–6TH CENTURY
The Cleveland Museum of Art

10. Wool Tapestry. Bucolic Scenes
HELLENISTIC, 5TH CENTURY
New York City, The Brooklyn Museum

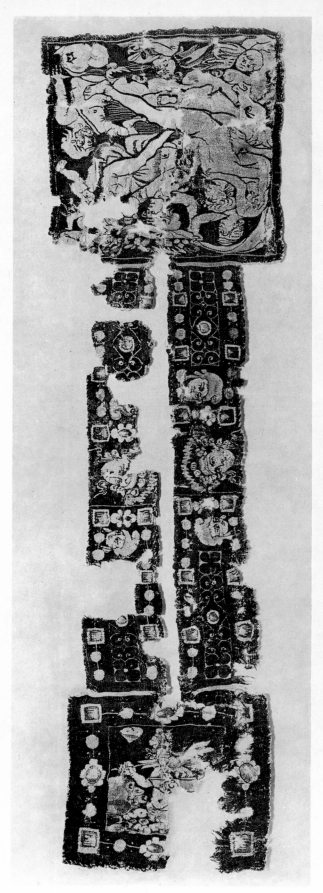

11. Wool and Gold Tapestry.
Neck Ornament
HELLENISTIC, 5TH CENTURY
Boston, Museum of Fine Arts

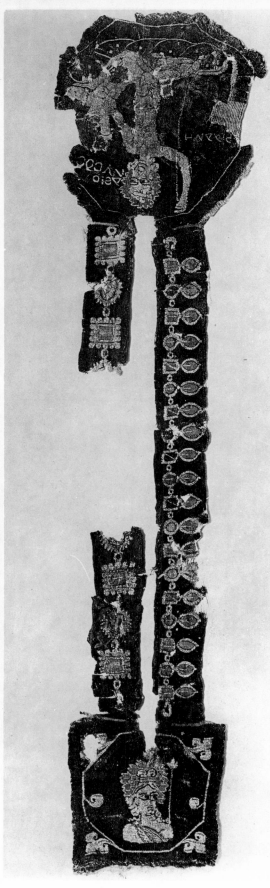

12. Wool and Gold Tapestry.
Neck Ornament
HELLENISTIC, 5TH CENTURY
Boston, Museum of Fine Arts

11a. Detail: A Sea-Thiasos

12a. Detail: Dionysus
and Ariadne

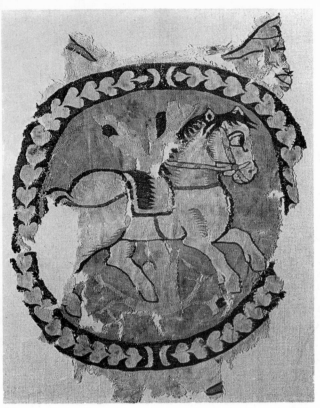

13. Wool Tapestry. The Runaway Pony
COPTIC, 5TH CENTURY
The Cleveland Museum of Art

14. Wool Tapestry.
The Runaway Pony
COPTIC, 5TH CENTURY
Baltimore, Walters Art Gallery

15. Wool Tapestry. Boar Hunt

COPTIC, 4TH–5TH CENTURY

*Washington, D. C., Dumbarton Oaks Research Library
and Collection, Harvard University*

16. Looped Brocading. An Acolyte

COPTIC, 5TH CENTURY

Boston, Museum of Fine Arts

17. Wool Brocading. An Orante

COPTIC, 5TH CENTURY

The Detroit Institute of Arts

18. Wool Tapestry. A Portrait

COPTIC, 4TH CENTURY

The Detroit Institute of Arts

19. Wool Tapestry.
"Saint Theodore"

19a. Wool Tapestry. Decorative
Motifs and Inscription
COPTIC, 5TH–6TH CENTURY
Cambridge, Fogg Art Museum,
Harvard University

20. Wool Tapestry. Pasiphaë
COPTIC, 5TH–6TH CENTURY
New York City, The Brooklyn Museum

21. Wool Tapestry. Dancers
COPTIC, 5TH–6TH CENTURY
The Detroit Institute of Arts

22. Wool Tapestry. Sacrifice of Isaac
COPTIC, 6TH–7TH CENTURY
New York City, Cooper Union Museum

23. Wool Tapestry. A Cross
SYRIA OR MESOPOTAMIA, 5TH–6TH CENTURY
New York City, The Brooklyn Museum

24. Wool Tapestry. A Jeweled Cross
COPTIC, 5TH–6TH CENTURY
New York City, The Brooklyn Museum

25. Wool Twill. Birth of Christ

SYRIA OR EGYPT, 5TH–6TH CENTURY

New York City, The Metropolitan Museum of Art

26. Wool Tapestry.
The Ascension
COPTIC, LATE 6TH–EARLY 7TH CENTURY
New York City, The Brooklyn Museum

27. Wool Tapestry.
A Cavalier Saint
COPTIC, 6TH–7TH CENTURY
New York City,
Cooper Union Museum

28. Wool Tapestry. Detail from a Complete Tunic

COPTIC, 7TH CENTURY OR LATER

New York City, The Brooklyn Museum

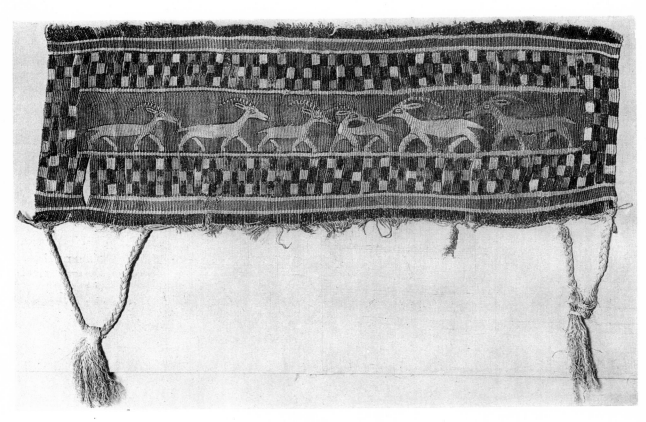

29. Wool Tapestry. Goats

MESOPOTAMIA OR EGYPT, 7TH CENTURY OR LATER

Boston, Museum of Fine Arts

Wool Tapestry. Ibex
SASSANIAN, 6TH–7TH CENTURY
New Haven, Yale University Art Gallery,
Hobart Moore Memorial Collection

31. Wool Tapestry. Goats
EGYPT, PERSANERIE, 6TH–7TH CENTURY
The Cleveland Museum of Art

32. Wool Tapestry. Pictorial Panel
EGYPT, PERSIAN INSPIRATION, 6TH CENTURY
New York City, The Brooklyn Museum

33. Wool and Linen Tapestry. Masks
COPTIC, 5TH–6TH CENTURY
Boston, Museum of Fine Arts

34. The Horse and Lion Tapestry
SYRO-MESOPOTAMIA OR EGYPT, 6TH CENTURY
Washington, D. C., Dumbarton Oaks Research Library
and Collection, Harvard University

35. Cotton and Wool Twill. Eagles

SASSANIAN 6TH–7TH CENTURY

*Washington, D. C., Dumbarton Oaks Research Library
and Collection, Harvard University*

36. Cotton and Wool Twill. Birds

SASSANIAN, 6TH–7TH CENTURY

The Cleveland Museum of Art

37. Wool Cloth. A Hunting Scene

SYRIA, 3RD CENTURY

Philadelphia Museum of Art

38. Wool Twill. Hares and Trees

SYRIA, 4TH–5TH CENTURY

Baltimore, Walters Art Gallery

39. The Heron Silk
CHINESE, HAN DYNASTY, 1ST CENTURY, B.C.
Philadelphia Museum of Art

40. The Cock Silk
CHINESE, HAN DYNASTY, 1ST CENTURY, B.C.
Philadelphia Museum of Art

41. The Diamond Silk
CHINESE, HAN DYNASTY, 1ST CENTURY, B.C.
Philadelphia Museum of Art

42. Fancy Gauze, White Silk
CHINESE, HAN DYNASTY, 1ST CENTURY, B.C.
Philadelphia Museum of Art

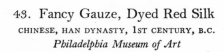

43. Fancy Gauze, Dyed Red Silk
CHINESE, HAN DYNASTY, 1ST CENTURY, B.C.
Philadelphia Museum of Art

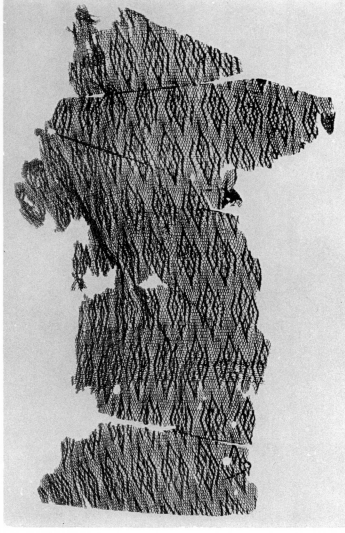

44. Polychrome Silk Twill. Samson or a Gladiator

SYRIA, 6TH–7TH CENTURY

Washington, D. C., Dumbarton Oaks Research Library
and Collection, Harvard University

45. Silk Twill. Mounted Amazons
SYRIA OR EGYPT, 6TH–7TH CENTURY
*Washington, D. C., Dumbarton Oaks Research Library
and Collection, Harvard University*

46. Silk Twill.
Suckling Antelopes
SYRIA OR EGYPT, 6TH–7TH CENTURY
The Cleveland Museum of Art

47. Polychrome Silk Twill. The Dioscuri
SYRIA, EARLY 7TH CENTURY
New York City, The Metropolitan Museum of Art

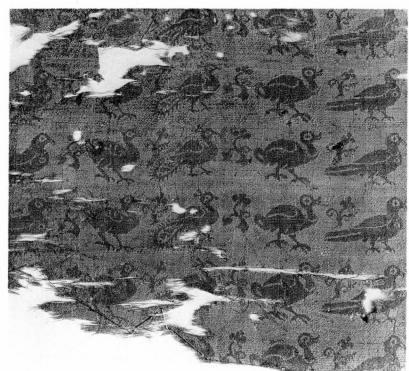

48. Silk Twill, Reversible. Birds
SYRIA OR EGYPT, 6TH–7TH CENTURY
New York City, Cooper Union Museum

**49. Polychrome Silk Twill.
Lion Hunters**

SYRIA, EARLY 7TH CENTURY
*New York City, The Metropolitan
Museum of Art*

50. Silk Twill, Reversible. A Herdsman

SYRIA OR EGYPT, 5TH CENTURY
Boston, Museum of Fine Arts

51. Silk Twill. Plant Motifs
EGYPT, AKHMÎM (?), OR SYRIA, 6TH–7TH CENTURY
Boston Museum of Fine Arts

52. Silk Twill. Lozenge Design
EGYPT, AKHMÎM (?), 6TH–7TH CENTURY
The Detroit Institute of Arts

54. Silk Twill. A "Joseph" Silk
EGYPT, 6TH–7TH CENTURY
The Cleveland Museum of Art

53. Fragment of a Silk Clavis
SYRIA OR EGYPT, 7TH CENTURY
The Cleveland Museum of Art

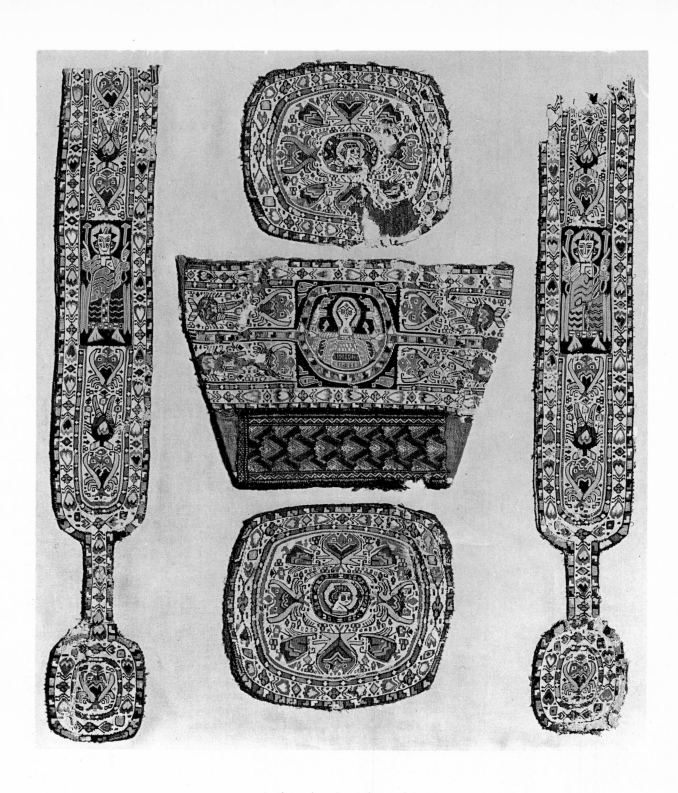

55. Wool Tapestry. A Set of Tunic Ornaments

COPTIC, 6TH–7TH CENTURY

Seattle Art Museum

56. Silk Twill. Tunic Ornaments
SYRIA, 6TH–7TH CENTURY
New Haven, Yale University Art Gallery,
The Hobart Moore Memorial Collection

57. Silk Twill. Persanerie
EGYPT, ANTINOË, 6TH CENTURY
Boston, Museum of Fine Arts

58. Silk Twill. A Duck

PERSIA OR MESOPOTAMIA, SASSANIAN, 6TH–7TH CENTURY
New York City, The Metropolitan Museum of Art

59. Silk Twill. The Viventia Fabric
BYZANTINE, 8TH CENTURY
Boston, Museum of Fine Arts

60a. The Double-Headed Eagles
RECONSTRUCTION AFTER LESSING, PLATE 77

60. Silk Twill. Double-Headed Eagles
BYZANTINE, 11TH–12TH CENTURY
New York City, The Metropolitan Museum of Art

61. Silk Twill. Cocks and Trees
BYZANTINE, 8TH–9TH CENTURY
New York City, Cooper Union Museum

62. Silk Twill. Birds and Rosettes

BYZANTINE, 8TH–9TH CENTURY

New York City, The Pierpont Morgan Library

63. Silk Twill. The Senmurv
BYZANTINE, 8TH–9TH CENTURY
New York City, Cooper Union Museum

64. Silk Twill. Fantastic Animals

BYZANTINE, 11TH CENTURY
New York City, Cooper Union Museum

65. Linen Cloth, Brocaded. Cocks in Medallions

MESOPOTAMIA, BAGHDAD, 9TH–10TH CENTURY

New York City, Cooper Union Museum

66. Silk Cloth, Brocaded. Lions and Harpies

MESOPOTAMIA, BAGHDAD, LATE 11TH–EARLY 12TH CENTURY

Boston, Museum of Fine Arts

67. Compound Twill. Griffins and Birds

SYRIA, 8TH–9TH CENTURY

New York City, The Pierpont Morgan Library

68. Compound Cloth. Griffins and Foxes

SYRIA, AYYUBID, 13TH CENTURY
Boston, Museum of Fine Arts

69. Linen, Silk and Gold Tapestry
EGYPT, FATIMID, 11TH CENTURY
New York City, The Metropolitan Museum of Art

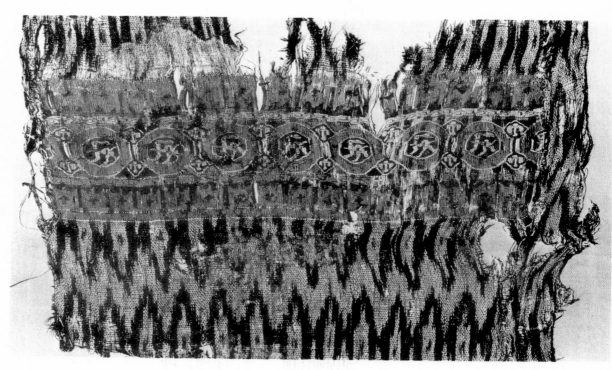

70. Cotton Ikat, with Tapestry Inset
ARABIA, YEMEN, AND EGYPT, 11TH–12TH CENTURY
The Detroit Institute of Arts

71. Byssus

EGYPT, MAMLUK, 13TH–14TH CENTURY
Washington, D. C., Textile Museum

72. Compound Cloth, Brocaded. The Lion Strangler

HISPANO-MORESQUE OR BAGHDAD, LATE 11TH–EARLY 12TH CENTURY

New York City, Cooper Union Museum

73. Compound Cloth, Brocaded. Sphinxes

HISPANO-MORESQUE OR BAGHDAD, LATE 11TH–EARLY 12TH CENTURY

New York City, Cooper Union Museum

74. Silk and Gold Tapestry. Drinking Girls

HISPANO-MORESQUE, ALMERÍA (?), 12TH–13TH CENTURY

New York City, Cooper Union Museum

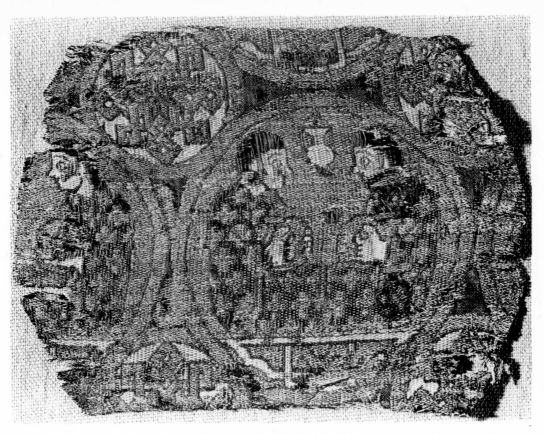

75. Compound Cloth. Musicians

HISPANO-MORESQUE, ALMERÍA (?), 12TH–13TH CENTURY

The Art Institute of Chicago

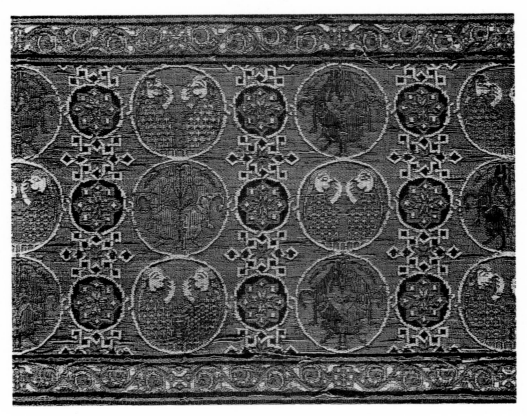

76. Detail of Border of a Large Panel

HISPANO-MORESQUE, 14TH CENTURY

New York City, The Hispanic Society of America

77. Fragment of a Dalmatic
of San Valero
HISPANO-MORESQUE, ALMERÍA (?), EARLY
13TH CENTURY
The Cleveland Museum of Art

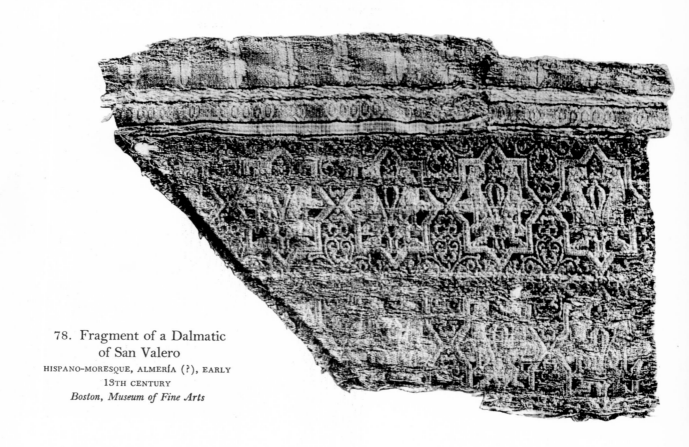

78. Fragment of a Dalmatic
of San Valero
HISPANO-MORESQUE, ALMERÍA (?), EARLY
13TH CENTURY
Boston, Museum of Fine Arts

79. Fragment of the Cope of San Valero

HISPANO-MORESQUE, ALMERÍA (?), EARLY 13TH CENTURY

The Cleveland Museum of Art

80. Fragment of a Dalmatic
of San Valero

HISPANO-MORESQUE, ALMERÍA (?), EARLY
13TH CENTURY

The Cleveland Museum of Art

81. Fragment of Orphrey of
the San Valero Cope

HISPANO-MORESQUE (?), 13TH CENTURY

Boston, Museum of Fine Arts

82. Fragment of the Tunic of Don Felipe

HISPANO-MORESQUE, GRANADA (?), 13TH CENTURY

New York City, The Hispanic Society of America

83. Fragment of the Tunic of Don Felipe

HISPANO-MORESQUE, GRANADA (?), 13TH CENTURY

The Cleveland Museum of Art

84. Fragment from the Tomb of Don Felipe

HISPANO-MORESQUE, GRANADA (?), 13TH CENTURY

The Cleveland Museum of Art

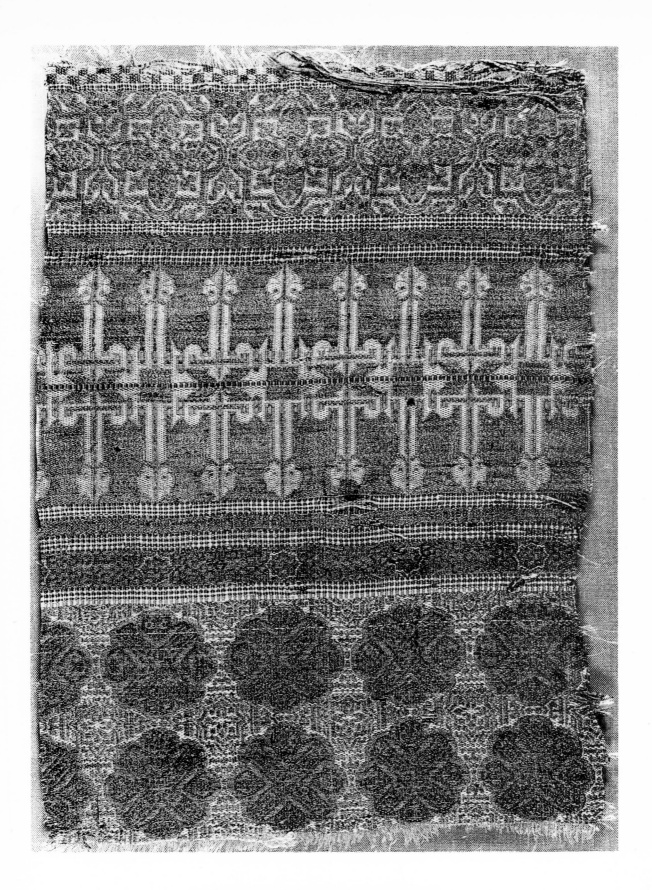

85. Fragment of the Mantle of Doña Leonor
HISPANO-MORESQUE, GRANADA (?), 13TH CENTURY
New York City, Cooper Union Museum

86. Compound Cloth. Complete Panel

HISPANO-MORESQUE, GRANADA (?), 14TH CENTURY

The Detroit Institute of Arts

87. Compound Cloth. Lacería Design

HISPANO-MORESQUE, GRANADA (?), 14TH–15TH CENTURY

The Detroit Institute of Arts

88. Compound Cloth, Brocaded

HISPANO-MORESQUE, 14TH–15TH CENTURY

The Cleveland Museum of Art

89. Compound Cloth. Panel

NORTH AFRICA, 16TH CENTURY OR LATER

Washington, D. C., Textile Museum

90. Compound Cloth. Complete Panel

MOROCCO, 17TH CENTURY OR LATER

New York City, The Hispanic Society of America

91. Compound Cloth

NORTH AFRICA, 16TH CENTURY OR LATER

The Detroit Institute of Arts

92. Fancy Compound Satin
SPAIN, MUDEJAR, 15TH–16TH CENTURY
New York City, The Hispanic Society of America

93. Border, Reversible. Heraldic Design
SPAIN, MUDEJAR, 15TH CENTURY
Baltimore, Walters Art Gallery

94. Fancy Compound Satin
SPAIN, MUDEJAR, 15TH–16TH CENTURY
New York City, The Hispanic Society of America

95. Fancy Compound Satin. Heraldic Design
SPAIN, MUDEJAR, 15TH–16TH CENTURY
The Cleveland Museum of Art

96. Plain Compound Twill. Elephant

PERSIA, 8TH–9TH CENTURY

New York City, Cooper Union Museum

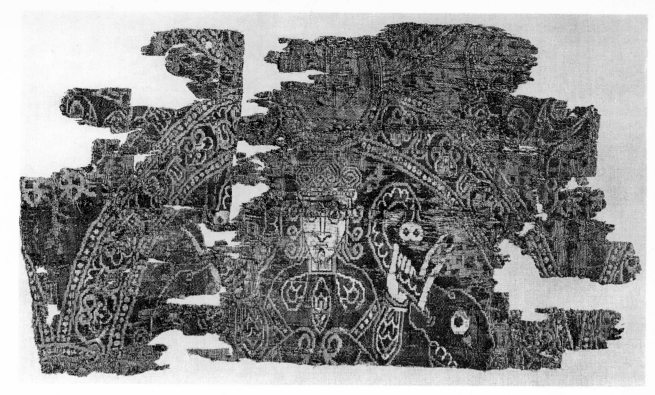

97. Plain Compound Twill. The Elephant Tamer
SYRIA OR PERSIA, 10TH CENTURY
*Washington, D. C., Dumbarton Oaks Research Library
and Collection, Harvard University*

98. Plain Compound Twill. Lions
MESOPOTAMIA OR PERSIA, 10TH–12TH CENTURY
Boston, Museum of Fine Arts

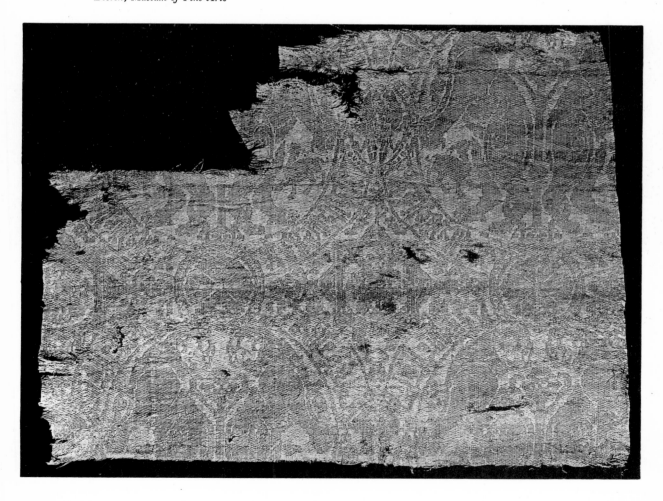

99. Plain Compound Twill. Peacocks
EAST IRAN, 8TH–9TH CENTURY
*Washington, D. C., Dumbarton Oaks Research Library
and Collection, Harvard University*

100. Plain Compound Twill. Lions

EAST IRAN, 8TH–9TH CENTURY

Boston, Museum of Fine Arts

101. Plain Compound Twill. Horses

EAST IRAN, 8TH–9TH CENTURY

The Cleveland Museum of Art

102. Plain Compound Cloth. Peacocks and Sphinxes
PERSIA, BUYID, 10TH–11TH CENTURY
The Cleveland Museum of Art

103. Plain Compound Cloth. Peacocks and Griffins

PERSIA, BUYID, 10TH–11TH CENTURY

Washington, D. C., Textile Museum

104. Plain Compound Cloth. Griffins and Ibexes

PERSIA, BUYID, 11TH CENTURY

Boston, Museum of Fine Arts

105. Plain Compound Cloth. Sphinxes
PERSIA, BUYID, 10TH–11TH CENTURY
Washington, D. C., Textile Museum

106. Plain Compound Cloth. Double-Headed Eagle

PERSIA, BUYID, 11TH CENTURY
*Washington, D. C., Dumbarton Oaks Research Library
and Collection, Harvard University*

107. Plain Compound Twill. Double-Headed Eagles

PERSIA, BUYID, 11TH CENTURY

Washington, D. C., Textile Museum

108. Plain Compound Twill. Fragment of Tomb Cover
PERSIA, BUYID, 11TH CENTURY
The Detroit Institute of Arts

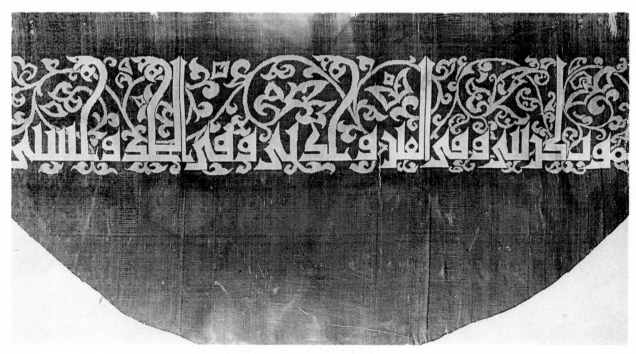

109. Plain Compound Twill. Tomb Cover
PERSIA, BUYID OR SELJUK, 11TH–12TH CENTURY
New Haven, Yale University Art Gallery,
The Hobart Moore Memorial Collection

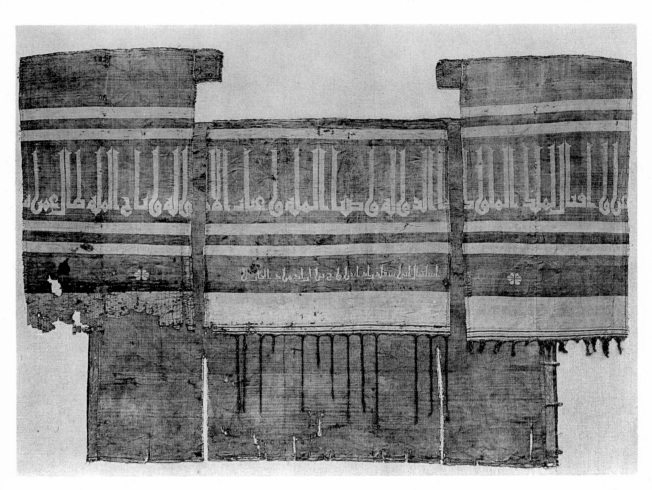

110. Plain Compound Twill. Tomb Cover

PERSIA, BUYID, ABOUT A.D. 1000

Washington, D. C., Textile Museum

111. Double Cloth. The Horses of the Sun
PERSIA, SELJUK, 11TH–12TH CENTURY
The Cleveland Museum of Art

112. Triple Cloth, Brocaded. A Falconer
PERSIA, SELJUK, 11TH–12TH CENTURY
The Detroit Institute of Arts

113. Plain Compound Cloth. Fragment
PERSIA, BUYID, OR SELJUK, 11TH–12TH CENTURY
Boston, Museum of Fine Arts

114. Plain Compound Cloth. Griffins

PERSIA (?) OR SYRIA (?), 11TH–12TH CENTURY

The Cleveland Museum of Art

115. Plain Compound Cloth. Sphinxes
PERSIA, SULJUK, 11TH–12TH CENTURY
Washington, D. C., Textile Museum

116. Detail of a Tomb Cover
PERSIA, SELJUK, 12TH CENTURY
Washington, D. C., Textile Museum

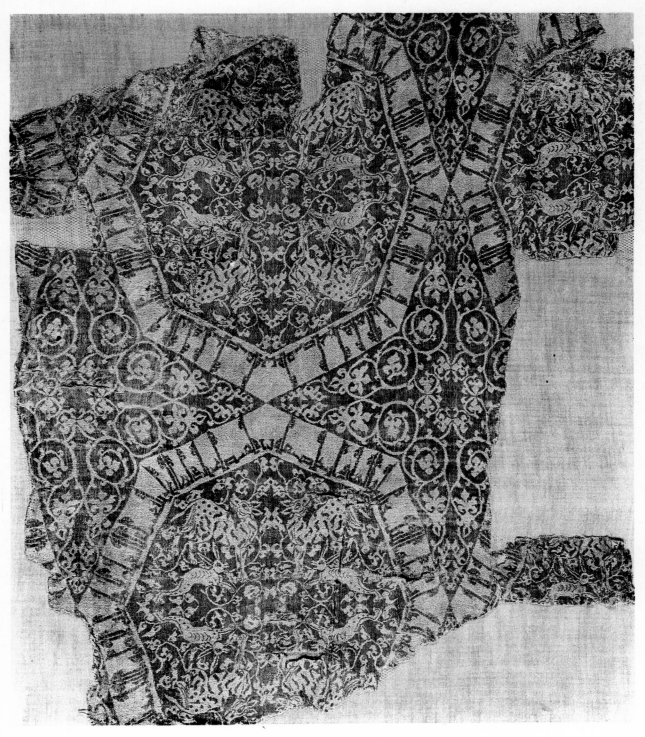

117. Detail of a Tomb Cover

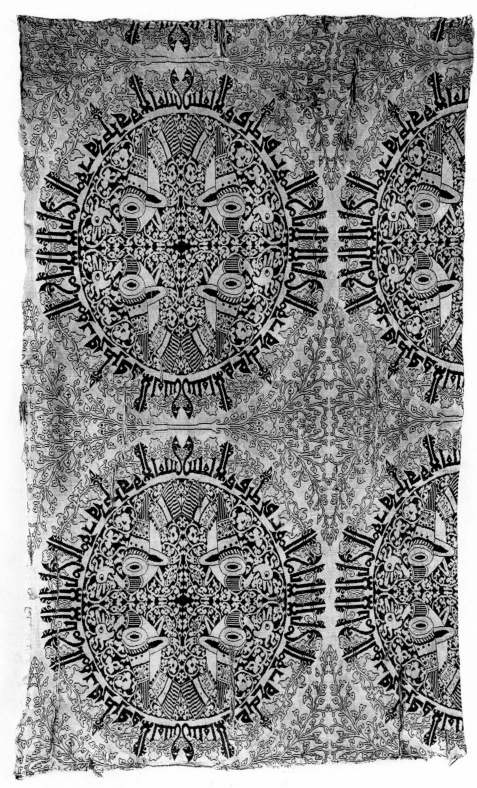

118. Plain Compound Cloth. Ducks

PERSIA, SELJUK, LATE 12TH–13TH CENTURY

Washington, D. C., Textile Museum

119. Compound Twill. Peacocks
PERSIA, SELJUK, 12TH–13TH CENTURY
New Haven, Yale University Art Gallery,
The Hobart Moore Memorial Collection

120. Fancy Satin. Camels
PERSIA, SELJUK OR IL-KHANID, 13TH–14TH CENTURY
The Detroit Institute of Arts

121. Compound Twill, Brocaded
PERSIA, SAFAVID, ISFAHAN, EARLY 17TH CENTURY
New Haven, Yale University Art Gallery,
The Hobart Moore Memorial Collection

122. Plain Cloth, Brocaded, Stamped

PERSIA, SAFAVID, 17TH CENTURY

Washington, D. C., Textile Museum

123. Double Cloth. Flowers and Clouds
PERSIA, SAFAVID, 17TH CENTURY
Washington, D. C., Textile Museum

124. Double Cloth, Brocaded
PERSIA, SAFAVID, 17TH CENTURY
Washington, D. C., Textile Museum

125. Double Cloth, Brocaded. Signed: *Saliha*

PERSIA, SAFAVID, 17TH CENTURY

Washington, D. C., Textile Museum

126. Double Cloth,
Obverse and Reverse
PERSIA, SAFAVID, ABOUT A.D. 1600
The Detroit Institute of Arts

127. Double Cloth

PERSIA, SAFAVID, ABOUT A.D. 1600

Boston, Museum of Fine Arts

128. Compound Cloth. A Garden Scene

PERSIA, SAFAVID, 16TH CENTURY

Hartford, Wadsworth Atheneum

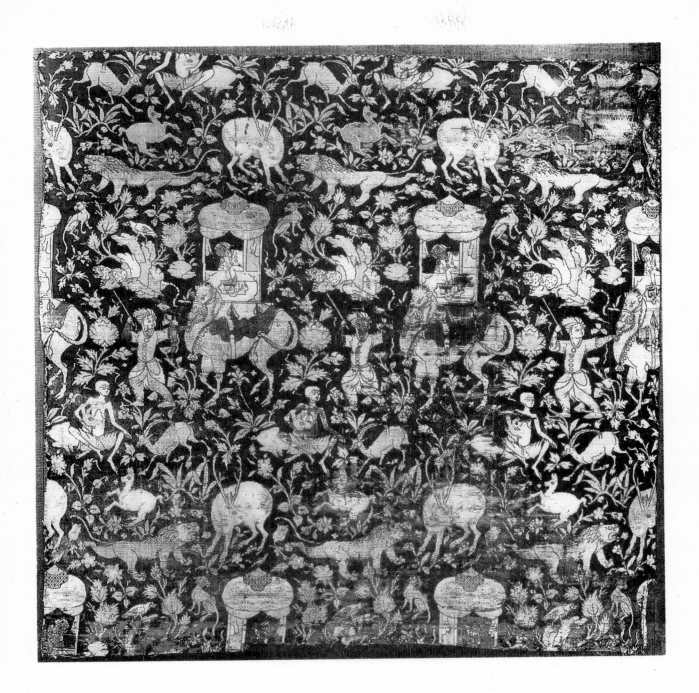

129. Compound Satin. Signed: *Ghiyath*. Laila and Majnun

PERSIA, SAFAVID, 16TH CENTURY

Boston, Museum of Fine Arts

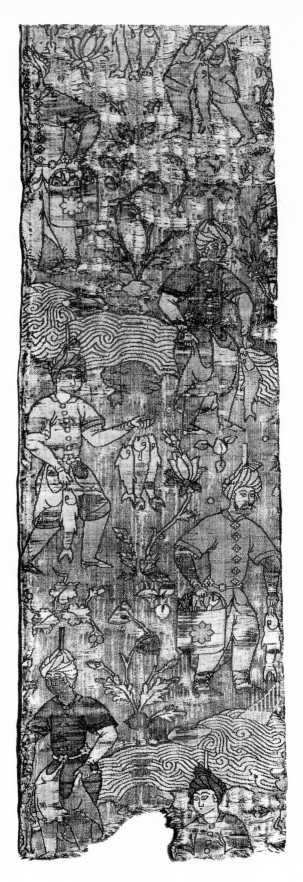

130. Compound Satin. Fishermen
PERSIA, SAFAVID, 16TH CENTURY
Washington, D. C., Textile Museum

131. Compound Satin. Cupbearer in Park
PERSIA, SAFAVID, 16TH CENTURY
The Cleveland Museum of Art

132. Polychrome Velvet.
A Hunting Scene
PERSIA, SAFAVID, 16TH CENTURY
Boston, Museum of Fine Arts

132a. Detail of Hunting Scene: The Deer Herd in Flight

132b. Detail of Hunting Scene: The Curious Ibex

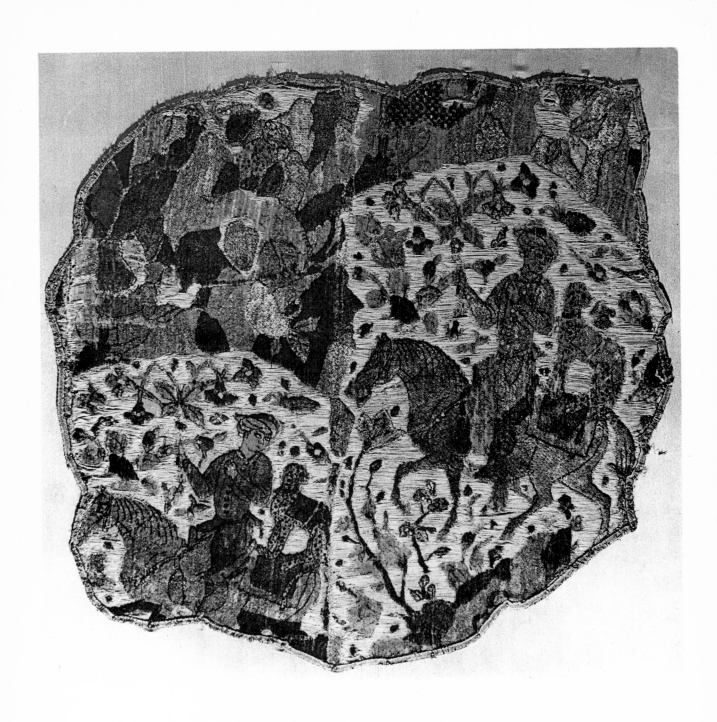

133. Polychrome Velvet. Hunter and Cheetah

PERSIA, SAFAVID, 16TH CENTURY

New Haven, Yale University Art Gallery,
The Hobart Moore Memorial Collection

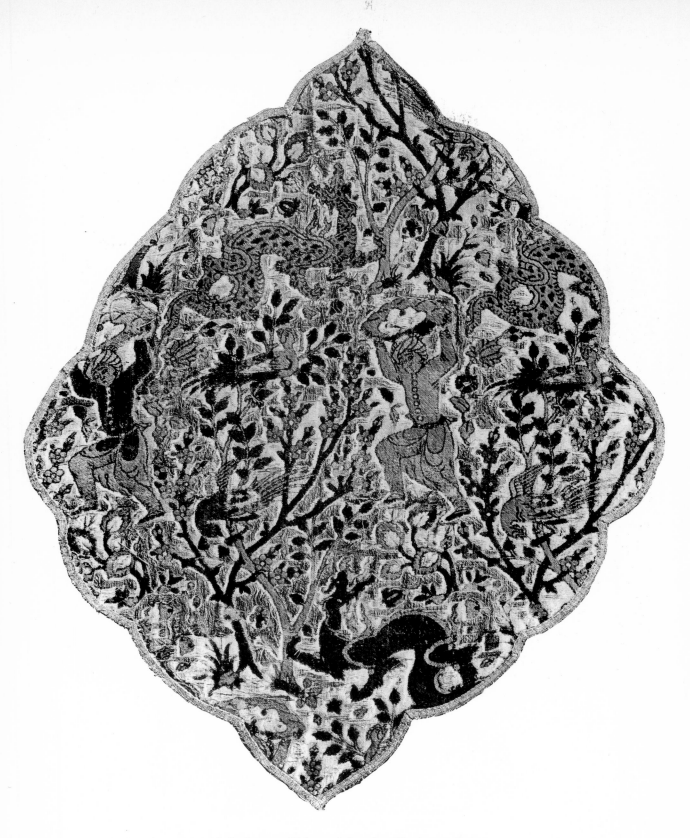

134. Polychrome Velvet. Iskander Slaying a Dragon
PERSIA, SAFAVID, 16TH CENTURY
New York City, The Metropolitan Museum of Art

135. Polychrome Velvet. Floral Design
PERSIA, SAFAVID, 16TH CENTURY
Washington, D. C., Textile Museum

136. Polychrome Velvet. The Falconer

PERSIA, SAFAVID, 16TH CENTURY

The Cleveland Museum of Art

137. Polychrome Velvet, Style of Riza-I-Abbasi

PERSIA, SAFAVID, EARLY 17TH CENTURY

The Cleveland Museum of Art

138. Compound Cloth, Brocaded, Style of Riza-I-Abbasi
PERSIA, SAFAVID, EARLY 17TH CENTURY
The Detroit Institute of Arts

139. Double Cloth. Signed: *Abd Allah*

PERSIA, SAFAVID, 17TH CENTURY

Washington, D. C., Textile Museum

140. Cut Solid Polychrome Velvet

PERSIA, KASHAN, SAFAVID, EARLY 17TH CENTURY

San Francisco, M. H. de Young Memorial Museum

141. Cut Solid Polychrome Velvet
PERSIA, KASHAN, SAFAVID, EARLY 17TH CENTURY
The Detroit Institute of Arts

142. Cut Voided Twill Velvet, Brocaded

INDIA, 17TH CENTURY

New Haven, Yale University Art Gallery,
The Hobart Moore Memorial Collection

143. Compound Twill, Brocaded

INDIA, 17TH CENTURY

The Detroit Institute of Arts

144. Twill Tapestry. Kashmir Shawl
INDIA, 17TH CENTURY
Boston, Museum of Fine Arts

145. Twill Tapestry. Kashmir Panel
INDIA, 18TH CENTURY
The Detroit Institute of Arts

146. Border of a Sari
INDIA, 18TH CENTURY
The Detroit Institute of Arts

147. Five-Color Velvet

SYRIA OR ASIA MINOR, SECOND HALF OF 15TH CENTURY

The Cleveland Museum of Art

148. Three-Color Velvet, Brocaded

TURKEY, BRUSA, EARLY 16TH CENTURY

The Detroit Institute of Arts

149. Five-Color Velvet

SYRIA OR ASIA MINOR, LATE 15TH CENTURY

The Cleveland Museum of Art

150. Cut Voided Velvet, Brocaded
TURKEY, 16TH CENTURY
Boston, Museum of Fine Arts

151. Cut Voided Velvet, Brocaded
TURKEY, 16TH CENTURY

Boston, Museum of Fine Arts

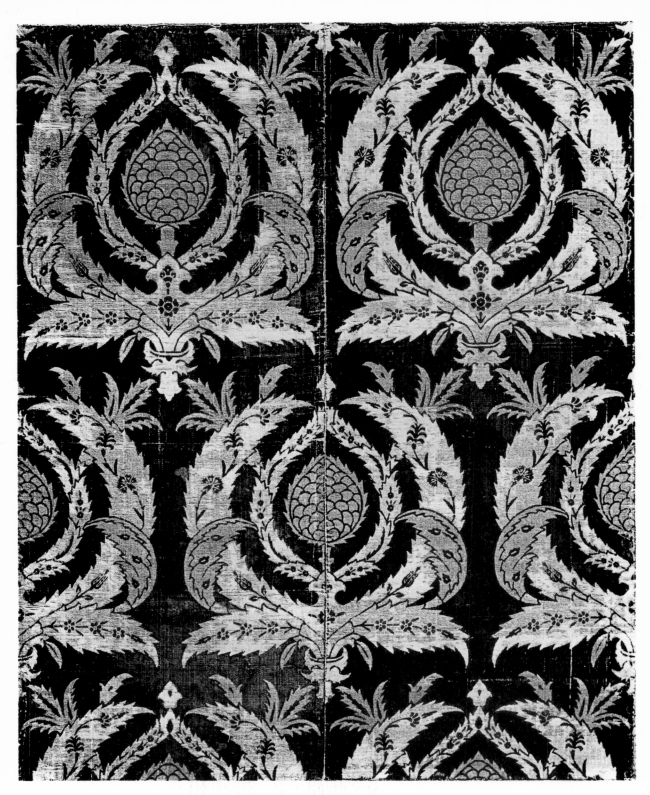

152. Cut Voided Velvet, Brocaded
TURKEY, 16TH CENTURY
New York City, The Metropolitan Museum of Art

153. Two-Color Velvet, Brocaded

TURKEY, DAMASCUS (?), 16TH CENTURY

The Detroit Institute of Arts

154. Two-Color Velvet, Brocaded
TURKEY, EARLY 17TH CENTURY
New York City, The Metropolitan Museum of Art

155. Compound Twill, Brocaded

156. Tablet-Woven Gold Border, Brocaded
SICILY, PALERMO, 12TH CENTURY
The Cleveland Museum of Art

157. Tablet-Woven Gold Border
SICILY, PALERMO, 11TH–12TH CENTURY
The Cleveland Museum of Art

158. Gold-Brocaded Orphrey

SICILY, PALERMO, 12TH CENTURY

Boston, Museum of Fine Arts

159. Satin, Brocaded. Griffins and Bears

SICILY, PALERMO, LATE 12TH CENTURY

The Cleveland Museum of Art

**160. Fragment of the Shroud
of Guy de Lusignan**
SICILY, PALERMO, 12TH CENTURY
Boston, Museum of Fine Arts

**161. Compound Twill.
Parrots and Trees**
SICILY, PALERMO, 12TH CENTURY
Boston, Museum of Fine Arts

162. Compound Twill. Double-Headed Eagles
SICILIAN OR HISPANO–MORESQUE, 11TH–12TH CENTURY
New York City, Cooper Union Museum

163. Compound Twill.
Heraldic Eagles
ITALY, 13TH CENTURY
Hartford, Wadsworth Atheneum

164. Compound Twill, Reversible. Eagles
SOUTHERN ITALY, 13TH CENTURY
Boston, Museum of Fine Arts

165. Compound Twill. Heraldic Eagles
ITALY, 12TH–13TH CENTURY
New York City, Cooper Union Museum

166. Fancy Compound Satin, Brocaded
ITALY, 13TH CENTURY
*Washington, D. C., Dumbarton Oaks Research Library
and Collection, Harvard University*

167. Compound Satin. Heraldic Animals
ITALY, 13TH CENTURY
New York City, Cooper Union Museum

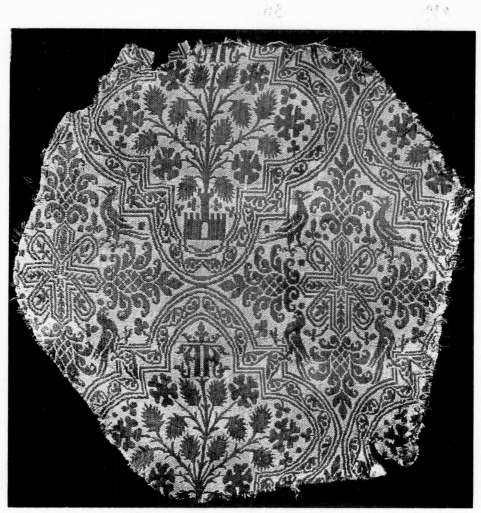

168. Fancy Twill. Crowned Monogram
ITALY, 13TH CENTURY
Boston, Museum of Fine Arts

169. Silk Damask. Lotus Flowers
ITALY, 14TH CENTURY
Boston, Museum of Fine Arts

170. Compound Cloth, Brocaded.
Parrots and Gazelles
SICILY, PALERMO, 12TH CENTURY
The Cleveland Museum of Art

171. Compound Cloth, Brocaded.
Parrots in Roundels
ITALY, 13TH CENTURY
New York City, The Metropolitan Museum of Art

172. Compound Cloth, Brocaded. Parrots and Dragons

ITALY, 13TH–14TH CENTURY

New York City, The Metropolitan Museum of Art

173. Damask. Heraldic Design
ITALY, 14TH–15TH CENTURY
Providence, Museum of Art

174. Plain Compound Satin. Grasshoppers
ITALY, 14TH–15TH CENTURY
Boston, Museum of Fine Arts

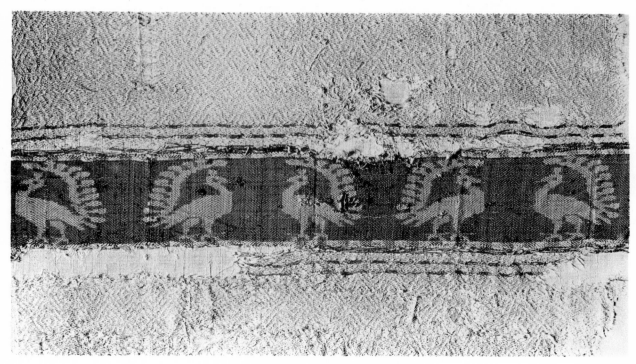

175. Silk Fancy Twill, Reversible
ITALY, UMBRIA (?), 13TH–14TH CENTURY
Boston, Museum of Fine Arts

176. Linen and Cotton Twill. Part of a Towel
ITALY, PERUGIA, 15TH CENTURY
Bloomfield Hills, Michigan, Cranbrook Academy of Art Museum

177. Linen and Cotton Twill.
Borders of a Towel
ITALY, PERUGIA, 15TH CENTURY
Bloomfield Hills, Michigan,
Cranbrook Academy of Art Museum

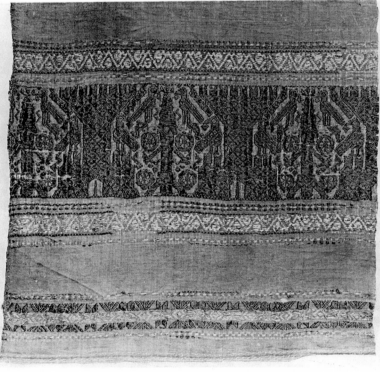

178. Linen, Silk, and Gold Twill. Runner
ITALY, UMBRIA, 15TH CENTURY
Providence, Museum of Art

179. Plain Compound Satin. Phoenixes

ITALY, 14TH CENTURY

New York City, Cooper Union Museum

180. Plain Compound Satin. Rampant Hares

ITALY, 14TH CENTURY

The Cleveland Museum of Art

181. Plain Compound Satin.
Griffins at Fountains
ITALY, 14TH CENTURY
New York City, Cooper Union Museum

182. Plain Compound Satin. Dragons at Fountains
ITALY, 14TH CENTURY
New York City, Cooper Union Museum

183. Silk and Gold
Tapestry. Part of a
Reliquary Bag
FRANCE, PARIS (?),
LATE 13TH CENTURY
The Cleveland Museum of Art

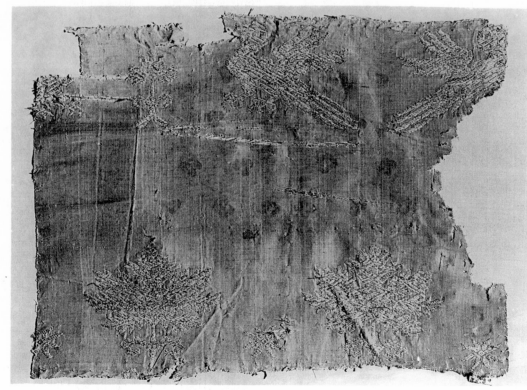

184. Silk Rep, Brocaded. Parrots and Trees
FRANCE, PARIS, LATE 13TH CENTURY
Boston, Museum of Fine Arts

185. Silk Rep, Brocaded. Griffins and Lilies

FRANCE, PARIS, LATE 13TH CENTURY

Boston, Museum of Fine Arts

187. Horizontal Border
GERMANY, COLOGNE, 14TH–15TH CENTURY
The Cleveland Museum of Art

**186. Tablet Weaving,
Brocaded**
GERMANY, RHINELAND (?),
12TH–13TH CENTURY
The Detroit Institute of Arts

188a. Reconstruction of the Regensburg Lions
FROM LESSING, PLATE 101

188. Silk and Linen, Brocaded. Lions
GERMANY, REGENSBURG, 13TH CENTURY
The Art Institute of Chicago

189. A Fragment of the Biura Cope
GERMANY, REGENSBURG, 13TH CENTURY
The Detroit Institute of Arts

190. Compound Satin. Grapevines and Masks
SOUTHERN ITALY, LATE 13TH CENTURY
The Cleveland Museum of Art

191. Satin, Brocaded. Grapevine Tendrils
ITALY, LUCCA, MID-14TH CENTURY
The Cleveland Museum of Art

192. Satin, Brocaded. Flying Phoenixes
ITALY, LUCCA, EARLY 14TH CENTURY
The Detroit Institute of Arts

193. Satin, Brocaded. Eagles, Dogs, and Gazelles

ITALY, LUCCA, MID-14TH CENTURY

The Cleveland Museum of Art

194. Satin, Brocaded. Lotus Palmettes and Animals
ITALY, LUCCA, SECOND HALF OF 14TH CENTURY
The Cleveland Museum of Art

194a. The Complete Design
MANNOWSKI, I, NO. 7

195. Satin, Brocaded. Part of a Chasuble

ITALY, LUCCA, SECOND HALF OF 14TH CENTURY

OPHREY: COLOGNE, 14TH CENTURY

The Cleveland Museum of Art

196. Satin, Brocaded.
Birds and Animals
ITALY, LUCCA, 14TH CENTURY
Boston, Museum of Fine Arts

197. Satin, Brocaded.
Falcons with Prey
ITALY, LUCCA, 14TH CENTURY
Boston, Museum of Fine Arts

198. Satin, Brocaded. Lions in Sunbursts
ITALY, LUCCA, SECOND HALF OF 14TH CENTURY
New York City, Cooper Union Museum

199. Double Twill, Brocaded. Castles and Khilins
ITALY, LUCCA, 14TH CENTURY
Boston, Museum of Fine Arts

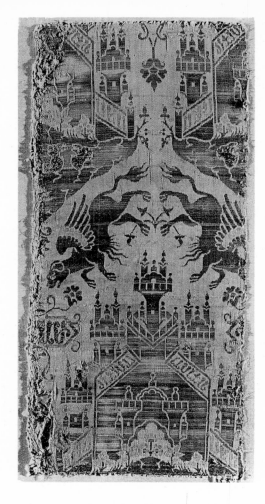

200. Satin, Brocaded. Castles and Basilisks
ITALY, LUCCA, SECOND HALF OF 14TH CENTURY
The Detroit Institute of Arts

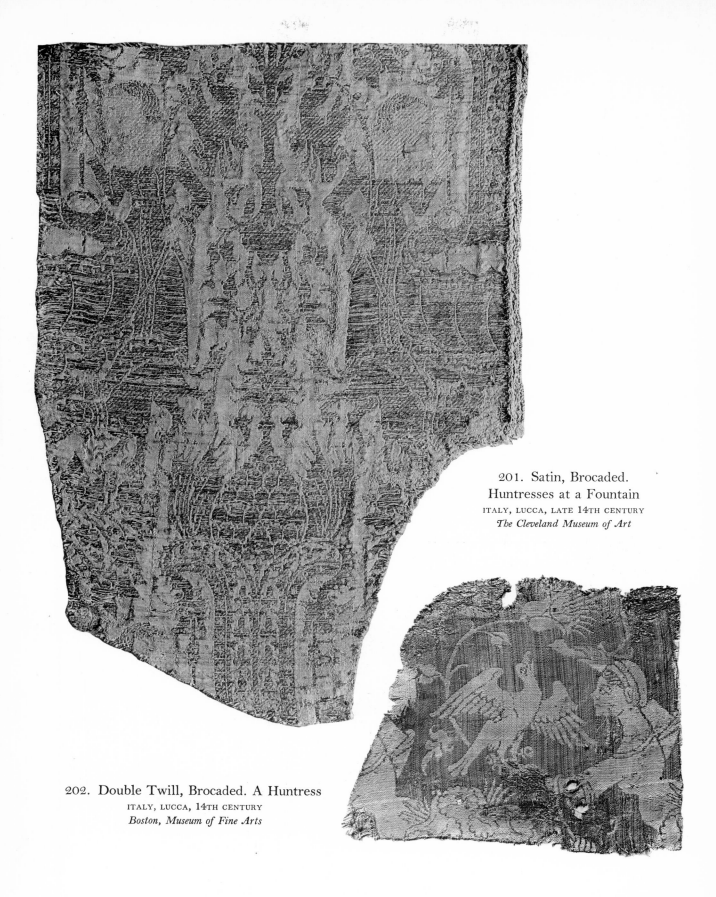

201. Satin, Brocaded.
Huntresses at a Fountain
ITALY, LUCCA, LATE 14TH CENTURY
The Cleveland Museum of Art

202. Double Twill, Brocaded. A Huntress
ITALY, LUCCA, 14TH CENTURY
Boston, Museum of Fine Arts

203. Plain Compound Twill. Cherubs
ITALY, SIENA, FIRST HALF OF 15TH CENTURY
New York City, The Metropolitan Museum of Art

204. Plain Compound Twill. Christ Blessing
ARMENIA, 16TH CENTURY
The Art Institute of Chicago

205. Satin, Brocaded. Noli Me Tangere

ITALY, LUCCA OR FLORENCE, 14TH CENTURY

Boston, Museum of Fine Arts

206. Satin, Brocaded. The Annunciation

ITALY, LUCCA OR FLORENCE, LATE 14TH CENTURY

The Cleveland Museum of Art

207. Satin, Brocaded.
The Nativity
ITALY, SIENA OR FLORENCE, SECOND HALF
OF 15TH CENTURY
New York City, The Metropolitan Museum
of Art

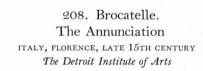

208. Brocatelle.
The Annunciation
ITALY, FLORENCE, LATE 15TH CENTURY
The Detroit Institute of Arts

209. Brocatelle. The Assumption
ITALY, FLORENCE, LATE 15TH CENTURY
The Detroit Institute of Arts

210. Satin, Brocaded. Falcons

ITALY, LUCCA OR VENICE, LATE 14TH CENTURY

The Cleveland Museum of Art

211. Compound Twill, Brocaded.
Burgundian Hats
ITALY, VENICE, EARLY 15TH CENTURY
The Cleveland Museum of Art

212. Satin, Brocaded. Heraldic Motif
ITALY, VENICE, 14TH–15TH CENTURY
New York City, Cooper Union Museum

213. Satin, Brocaded. The Gondola
ITALY, VENICE, LATE 14TH CENTURY
Germany, Danzig

214. Satin, Brocaded. Lions, Dogs, and Birds
ITALY, VENICE, EARLY 15TH CENTURY
The Cleveland Museum of Art

215. Silk Damask. Falcon and Dog
ITALY, VENICE, EARLY 15TH CENTURY
The Cleveland Museum of Art

216. Satin, Brocaded. Falcons and Lions
ITALY, VENICE, MID-15TH CENTURY
Boston, Museum of Fine Arts

217. Satin, Brocaded. After Jacopo Bellini
ITALY, VENICE, MID-15TH CENTURY
The Detroit Institute of Arts

218. Compound Twill. Phoenixes
ITALY, VENICE, MID-15TH CENTURY
Boston, Museum of Fine Arts

219. Plain Compound Twill. Sails and Animals
ITALY, VENICE, MID-15TH CENTURY
New York City, The Metropolitan Museum of Art

220. Voided Satin Velvet. Deer and Lions
ITALY, VENICE, SECOND HALF OF 14TH CENTURY
Providence, Museum of Art

221. Polychrome Velvet. An Impresa
ITALY, EARLY 15TH CENTURY
The Cleveland Museum of Art

222. Five-Color Velvet. Part of a Chasuble
ITALY, VENICE, FIRST HALF OF 15TH CENTURY
The Cleveland Museum of Art

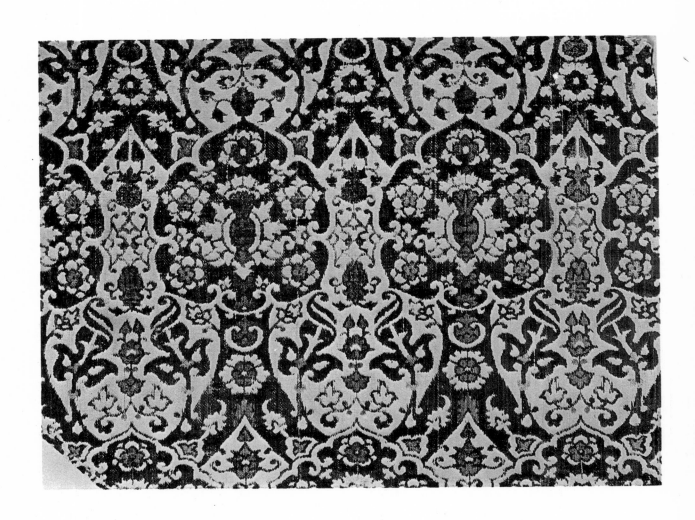

223. Five-Color Voided Velvet

ITALY, VENICE, MID-15TH CENTURY

The Cleveland Museum of Art

224. Five-Color Voided Velvet
ITALY, VENICE, MID-15TH CENTURY
The Cleveland Museum of Art

**225. Five-Color Voided
Velvet, Brocaded**
ITALY, VENICE, LAST QUARTER
OF 15TH CENTURY
The Cleveland Museum of Art

226. Cut Voided Velvet. Ferronnerie
ITALY, MID-15TH CENTURY
The Cleveland Museum of Art

228. Detail of Cope No. 227
The Detroit Institute of Arts

227. Complete Cope
VELVET: ITALY, MID-15TH CENTURY
ORPHREY: GERMANY, COLOGNE, 15TH CENTURY
The Detroit Institute of Arts

229. Pile-on-Pile Sumptuary Velvet
ITALY, VENICE, ABOUT 1500
The Art Institute of Chicago

230. Cut Voided Satin Velvet, Brocaded
ITALY, VENICE, MID-15TH CENTURY
Boston, Museum of Fine Arts

231. Pile-on-Pile Velvet, Brocaded
ITALY, VENICE, SECOND HALF OF 15TH CENTURY
The Cleveland Museum of Art

232. Cut Voided Satin Velvet, Brocaded
ITALY, VENICE, SECOND HALF OF 15TH CENTURY
New York City, The Metropolitan Museum of Art

233. Cut Voided Velvet, Brocaded
ITALY, VENICE OR FLORENCE, LATE 15TH CENTURY
New York City, The Metropolitan Museum of Art

234. Cut Voided Velvet, Brocaded
ITALY, VENICE OR FLORENCE, LATE 15TH CENTURY
Kansas City, William Rockhill Nelson Gallery of Art

**235. Cut Voided Velvet, Brocaded.
Armorial Design**
ITALY, VENICE OR FLORENCE,
SECOND HALF OF 15TH CENTURY
New York City, The Metropolitan Museum of Art

236. Cut Solid Polychrome Velvet, Pile-on-Pile

ITALY, PROBABLY FLORENCE, LATE 15TH CENTURY

The Art Institute of Chicago

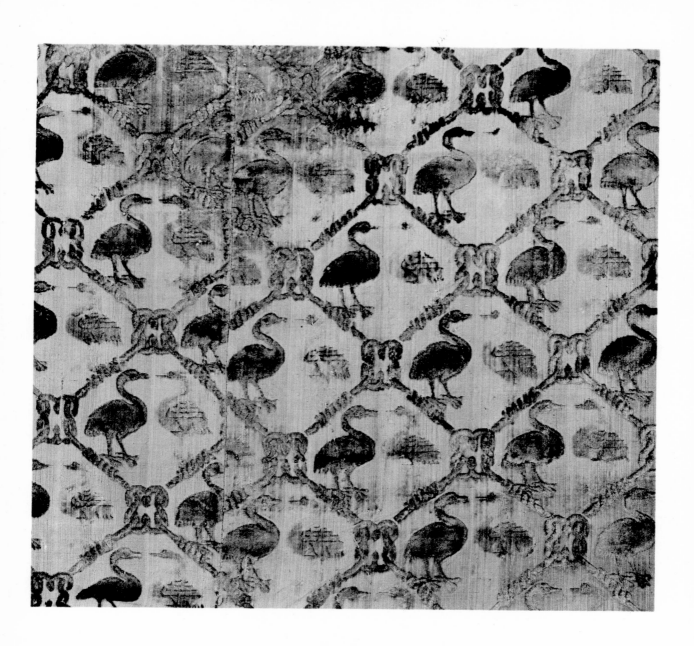

237. Cut Solid Polychrome Velvet, Pile-on-Pile

ITALY, VENICE, LATE 15TH–EARLY 16TH CENTURY

New York City, The Metropolitan Museum of Art

238. Cut Voided Satin Velvet. Heraldic Design

ITALY, FLORENCE, EARLY 17TH CENTURY

The Detroit Institute of Arts

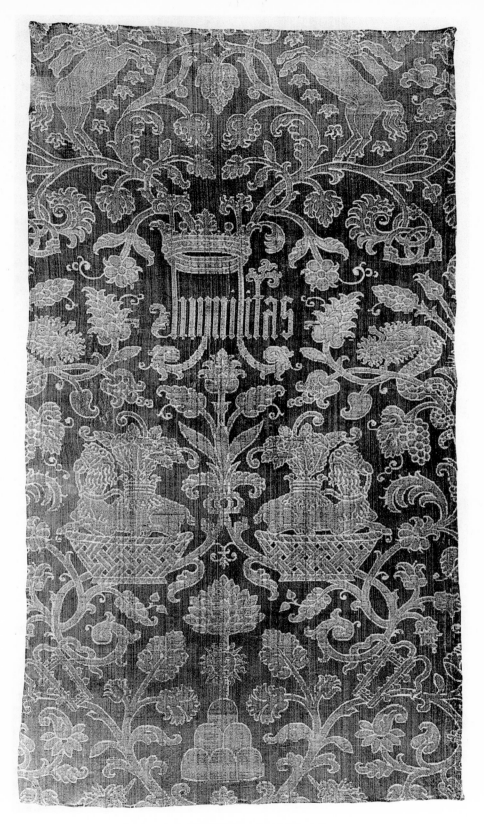

239. Compound Satin. Heraldic Design
ITALY, 16TH CENTURY
Boston, Museum of Fine Arts

240. Fancy Satin, Brocaded. Flowers and Birds

ITALY, VENICE, LATE 15TH CENTURY—EARLY 16TH CENTURY

New York City, The Metropolitan Museum of Art

241. Fancy Satin Reversible. Damask
ITALY OR SPAIN, FIRST HALF OF 16TH CENTURY
New York City, The Metropolitan Museum of Art

242. Silk Damask, Embroidered
ITALY, LATE 16TH CENTURY
Providence, Museum of Art

243. Plain Compound Cloth, Linen. Border
ITALY, 16TH CENTURY
New York City, The Metropolitan Museum of Art

244. Fancy Compound Cloth, Wool and Cotton

ITALY, LAST QUARTER OF 16TH CENTURY

Providence, Museum of Art

245. Plain Compound Cloth, Silk and Cotton. Border

ITALY, 16TH CENTURY

New York City, The Metropolitan Museum of Art

246. Ciselé Voided Velvet
ITALY, GENOA (?), EARLY 17TH CENTURY
Providence, Museum of Art

247. Ciselé Voided Velvet
ITALY, EARLY 17TH CENTURY
Providence, Museum of Art

248. Slashed Silk Rep, Brocaded

ITALY, SICILY (?), EARLY 17TH CENTURY

Providence, Museum of Art

249. Ciselé Voided Velvet

ITALY, GENOA (?), FIRST HALF OF 17TH CENTURY

Providence, Museum of Art

250. Ciselé Voided Velvet
ITALY, GENOA (?), FIRST HALF OF 17TH CENTURY
Providence, Museum of Art

251. Brocatelle
ITALY OR SPAIN, LATE 16TH–EARLY 17TH CENTURY
The Detroit Institute of Arts

252. Brocatelle
ITALY OR SPAIN, 17TH CENTURY
Providence, Museum of Art

253. Ciselé Velvet on Gold-Shot Ground
ITALY, GENOA, LATE 17TH CENTURY
The Detroit Institute of Arts

254. Cut Velvet on Gold-Shot Ground
ITALY, VENICE, FIRST QUARTER OF 18TH CENTURY
The Detroit Institute of Arts

255. Satin, Brocaded. Fantastic Flowers
ITALY, VENICE, EARLY 18TH CENTURY
The Detroit Institute of Arts

256. Satin, Brocaded
ITALY, VENICE, EARLY 18TH CENTURY
Boston, Museum of Fine Arts

257. Fancy Satin, Brocaded
ITALY, VENICE, MID-18TH CENTURY
The Detroit Institute of Arts

258. Fancy Satin, Brocaded. Waistcoat
ITALY, VENICE, MID-18TH CENTURY
The Detroit Institute of Arts

259. Satin, Brocaded. Ships at Sea

ITALY, VENICE, MID–18TH CENTURY

The Detroit Institute of Arts

260a. Fancy Satin, Brocaded.
The Drummer Boy, Detail
ITALY, VENICE, MID-18th CENTURY
The Detroit Institute of Arts

260. Fancy Satin, Brocaded. The Drummer Boy

ITALY, VENICE, MID-18TH CENTURY

The Detroit Institute of Arts

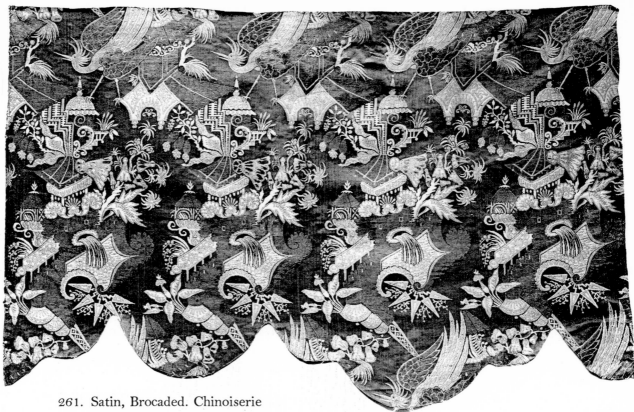

261. Satin, Brocaded. Chinoiserie
ITALY, VENICE, MID-18TH CENTURY
Boston, Museum of Fine Arts

262. Damask. Chinoiserie
ITALY, TURIN, MID-18TH CENTURY
The Detroit Institute of Arts

263. Brocatelle
ITALY, 16TH CENTURY
New York City, The Metropolitan Museum of Art

264. Brocatelle
SPAIN, TOLEDO, 16TH CENTURY
The Detroit Institute of Arts

265. Armorial Brocade
SPAIN, 16TH CENTURY
The Detroit Institute of Arts

266. Armorial Damask
SPAIN, 16TH CENTURY
The Detroit Institute of Arts

267. Linen Damask
SPAIN, 16TH CENTURY
The Detroit Institute of Arts

268. Silk and Cotton Damask
PORTUGAL OR SPAIN, 17TH CENTURY
Providence, Museum of Art

269. Double Cloth, Silk, Wool, and Linen. Obverse and Reverse
SPAIN, 16TH–17TH CENTURY
New York City, Cooper Union Museum

270. Damask, Wool and Linen
ITALY OR SPAIN, EARLY 17TH CENTURY
Providence, Museum of Art

271. Compound Cloth, Linen
SPAIN, 16TH CENTURY
The Detroit Institute of Arts

272. Chenille Brocade. The Pagan Paradise

PORTUGAL OR ANDALUSIA, C. 1700

The Detroit Institute of Arts

273. Chenille Brocade. The Smoker
PORTUGAL OR ANDALUSIA, C. 1700
The Detroit Institute of Arts

274. Chenille Brocade. Mythological Scenes

PORTUGAL OR ANDALUSIA, C. 1700

Boston, Museum of Fine Arts

275. Metallic Twill, Brocaded. Selene and Endymion

PORTUGAL OR ANDALUSIA, LATE 17TH CENTURY

The Cleveland Museum of Art

276. Metallic Twill, Brocaded. Samson and Delilah

PORTUGAL OR ANDALUSIA, LATE 17TH CENTURY

The Cleveland Museum of Art

277. Fancy Satin, Silver-Brocaded

SPAIN, 17TH CENTURY

The Detroit Institute of Arts

278. Cloth of Silver, Brocaded

SPAIN OR ITALY (NAPLES), LAST QUARTER OF 18TH CENTURY

Providence, Museum of Art

279. Compound Satin, Polychrome
PORTUGAL OR ANDALUSIA, C. 1800
Providence, Museum of Art

280. Cut and Uncut Voided Satin Velvet
SPAIN, LATE 18TH OR EARLY 19TH CENTURY
Providence, Museum of Art

281. Blue and White Linen Damask
DUTCH, LATE 17TH CENTURY
Providence, Museum of Art

282. Linen Damask Napkin

FLEMISH, THIRD QUARTER OF 17TH CENTURY

The Detroit Institute of Arts

283. Satin, Brocaded
ENGLAND, SPITALFIELDS, SECOND QUARTER OF 18TH CENTURY
Boston, Museum of Fine Arts

284. Satin, Polychrome, Gold-Brocaded
ENGLAND, SPITALFIELDS, SECOND QUARTER OF 18TH CENTURY
Boston, Museum of Fine Arts

285. Satin, Brocaded
ENGLAND, SPITALFIELDS, MID-18TH CENTURY
Boston, Museum of Fine Arts

286. Ribbed Silk, Brocaded

ENGLAND, SPITALFIELDS, MID-18TH CENTURY

Boston, Museum of Fine Arts

287. Satin, Brocaded

ENGLAND, SPITALFIELDS, MID-18TH CENTURY

Boston, Museum of Fine Arts

288. Faille Silk, Brocaded

ENGLAND, SPITALFIELDS, THIRD QUARTER OF 18TH CENTURY

The Detroit Institute of Arts

289. Compound Satin

FRANCE, LYONS, FIRST QUARTER OF 18TH CENTURY

Providence, Museum of Art

290. Compound Satin

FRANCE, LYONS, FIRST QUARTER OF 18TH CENTURY

Providence, Museum of Art

291. Satin, Brocaded

FRANCE, LYONS, SECOND QUARTER OF 18TH CENTURY
Providence, Museum of Art

292. Satin, Brocaded

FRANCE, LYONS, FIRST QUARTER OF 18TH CENTURY

Boston, Museum of Fine Arts

293. Taffeta, Brocaded

FRANCE, LYONS, SECOND QUARTER OF 18TH CENTURY

Providence, Museum of Art

294. Taffeta, Metal-Brocaded
FRANCE, LYONS, MID-18TH CENTURY
The Detroit Institute of Arts

295. Fancy Satin, Brocaded
FRANCE, LYONS, MID-18TH CENTURY
Providence, Museum of Art

296. Satin, Brocaded

FRANCE, LYONS, MID-18TH CENTURY
The Detroit Institute of Arts

297. Satin, Brocaded. Furs and Flowers

FRANCE, LYONS, MID-18TH CENTURY

New York City, The Metropolitan Museum of Art

298. Faille, Brocaded

FRANCE, LYONS, MID-18TH CENTURY

The Detroit Institute of Arts

299. Satin, Brocaded. The Cockatoos

FRANCE, LYONS, MID-18TH CENTURY

The Detroit Institute of Arts

300. Fancy Taffeta, Brocaded. Chinoiserie

FRANCE, LYONS, MID-18TH CENTURY

Providence, Museum of Art

301. Taffeta, Brocaded. Chinoiserie

FRANCE, LYONS, MID-18TH CENTURY

The Cleveland Museum of Art

302. Faille, Brocaded. Chinoiserie
FRANCE, LYONS, MID–18TH CENTURY
The Cleveland Museum of Art

303. Satin, Brocaded. Chinoiserie

FRANCE, LYONS, MID-18TH CENTURY

New York City, The Metropolitan Museum of Art

304. Taffeta, Brocaded

FRANCE, LYONS, THIRD QUARTER OF 18TH CENTURY

Providence, Museum of Art

305. Corded Silk and Metal Thread, Brocaded

FRANCE, LYONS, THIRD QUARTER OF 18TH CENTURY

The Cleveland Museum of Art

306. Taffeta, Silver-Brocaded
FRANCE, LYONS, THIRD QUARTER OF 18TH CENTURY
The Cleveland Museum of Art

307. Taffeta, Brocaded
FRANCE, LYONS, LAST QUARTER OF 18TH CENTURY
The Cleveland Museum of Art

308. Silk Rep, Brocaded

FRANCE, LYONS, LAST QUARTER OF 18TH CENTURY

Providence, Museum of Art

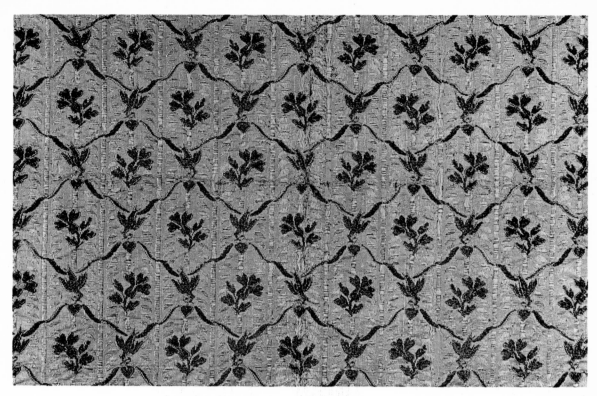

309. Chenille and Metal Brocade
FRANCE, LYONS, SECOND HALF OF 18TH CENTURY
The Cleveland Museum of Art

310. Cut Voided Velvet
FRANCE OR ITALY, LATE 18TH CENTURY
Providence, Museum of Art

311. Cut Voided Twill Velvet
FRANCE, LYONS, LATE 18TH CENTURY
Providence, Museum of Art

312. Plain Compound Satin. Parts of a Waistcoat
FRANCE, ALSACE (?), SECOND HALF OF 18TH CENTURY
New Haven, Yale University Art Gallery

313. Plain Compound Satin. Parts of a Waistcoat

FRANCE, ALSACE (?), SECOND HALF OF 18TH CENTURY

The Detroit Institute of Arts

314. "Le Panier Fleuri," By Philippe De Lassalle

FRANCE, LYONS, C. 1770

The Detroit Institute of Arts

315. Chair Back, By Philippe De Lassalle

FRANCE, LYONS, CAMILLE PERNON ET CIE, C. 1770

New York City, The Metropolitan Museum of Art

316. A Still Life, By Philippe De Lassalle

FRANCE, LYONS, CAMILLE PERNON ET CIE, C. 1770

New York City, The Metropolitan Museum of Art

317. The Bagpipe Player, By Philippe De Lassalle

FRANCE, LYONS, CAMILLE PERNON ET CIE, C. 1770

New York City, The Metropolitan Museum of Art

318. "Les Perdrix," By Philippe De Lassalle

FRANCE, LYONS, CAMILLE PERNON ET CIE, C. 1780
New York City, The Metropolitan Museum of Art

319. "Les Perdrix," By Philippe De Lassalle. Detail

FRANCE, LYONS, C. 1780

The Detroit Institute of Arts

320. Satin, Brocaded. The Pet Lamb

FRANCE, LYONS, C. 1780

The Cleveland Museum of Art

321. Catherine the Great, By Philippe De Lassalle

FRANCE, LYONS, CAMILLE PERNON ET CIE, 1777

New York City, The Metropolitan Museum of Art

322. Lampas

FRANCE, LYONS, LAST QUARTER OF 18TH CENTURY
The Detroit Institute of Arts

323. Lampas
FRANCE, LYONS, LAST QUARTER OF 18TH CENTURY
The Detroit Institute of Arts

324. Lampas
FRANCE, LYONS, FIRST QUARTER OF 19TH CENTURY
Providence, Museum of Art

325. Satin, Brocaded.
The Pheasants,
By J. D. Dugourc

FRANCE, LYONS, CAMILLE PERNON
ET CIE, EARLY 19TH CENTURY
Providence, Museum of Art

325a. The Pheasants, By J. D. Dugourc. Detail
The Cleveland Museum of Art

326. Plain Compound Satin, Brocaded

FRANCE, LYONS, SÉGUIN ET CIE, 1805-1815
New York City, The Metropolitan Museum of Art

327. Plain Compound Cloth, Brocaded

FRANCE, LYONS, SÉGUIN ET CIE, 1811

New York City, The Metropolitan Museum of Art

328. Cut Solid Velvet, Chiné. A Decorative Band,
By Gaspard Grégoire

FRANCE, AIX-EN-PROVENCE, EARLY 19TH CENTURY

New York City, Cooper Union Museum

329. Cut Solid Velvet, Chiné. Portrait of Napoleon I,
By Gaspard Grégoire
FRANCE, AIX-EN-PROVENCE, EARLY 19TH CENTURY
New York City, The Metropolitan Museum of Art

330. Cut Solid Velvet, Chiné. Portrait of Louis XVIII,
By Gaspard Grégoire

FRANCE, AIX-EN-PROVENCE, EARLY 19TH CENTURY
New York City, The Metropolitan Museum of Art

331. Fancy Compound Cloth. Portrait of George Washington

FRANCE, LYONS, MATHEVON ET BOUVARD, 19TH CENTURY
Boston, Museum of Fine Arts